Brains, Buddhas, and Believing

Dan Arnold

Brains, Buddhas, and Believing

•

THE PROBLEM OF INTENTIONALITY IN CLASSICAL BUDDHIST AND COGNITIVE-SCIENTIFIC PHILOSOPHY OF MIND

•

MOTILAL BANARSIDASS PUBLISHERS
PRIVATE LIMITED • DELHI

First Indian Edition : Delhi, 2015

ISBN: 978-81-208-4073-7

Also available at:

MOTILAL BANARSIDASS

41 U.A., Bungalow Road, Jawahar Nagar, Delhi 110 007
8 Mahalaxmi Chamber, 22 Bhulabhai Desai Road, Mumbai 400 026
203 Royapettah High Road, Mylapore, Chennai 600 004
236, 9th Main III Block, Jayanagar, Bangalore 560 011
8 Camac Street, Kolkata 700 017
Ashok Rajpath, Patna 800 004
Chowk, Varanasi 221 001

Library of Congress Cataloging-in-Publication Data
Arnold, Daniel Anderson, 1965-
Brains, Buddhas, and Believing : *The problem of intentionality in classical Buddhist and cognitive-scientific philosophy of mind*/Dan Arnold.
p. cm.
Includes bibliographical references and index.
ISBN : 978-81-208-4073-7
1. Intentionality (Philosophy) 2. Buddhist philosophy,
3. Philosophy of mind. 4. Philosophy, comparative. I. Title
B105.156A76 012
128'.2—dc22 2011015742

Published by
Motilal Banarsidass Publishers Private Limited
www.mlbd.com • mlbd@mlbd.com
Printed by Anupam Art Printers

kuto vā nūtanaṃ vastu vayam utprekṣituṃ kṣamāḥ /
vācovinyāsavaicitryamātram atra vicāryatām //

("How could we discern anything new? Only the variety in the composition should be considered here.")

—Jayanta Bhaṭṭa

I don't know about you guys, but when friends in other lines of work ask me what philosophers are into these days, and I tell them that these days philosophers are into claiming that really, deep down—in a first-class conceptual system, you know?—*it's not true* that "cat" means *cat* . . . they laugh at me. I do find that embarrassing.

—Jerry Fodor

The moment we try to give a precise analysis of anything we cannot doubt, we find we can doubt whether we have given the right analysis.

—Charles Hartshorne

Contents

Acknowledgments

FLEDGLING THOUGHTS in the direction of this book were sketched in my book *Buddhists, Brahmins, and Belief*; following Vincent Descombes, I there (2005, 38–48) briefly characterized some philosophical problems for Dharmakīrti's projects in terms of *intentionality*, in the philosophically technical sense of that word. The present book grew out of that initial attempt at understanding Dharmakīrti in terms suggested by a concept central both in European phenomenological and Anglo-American analytic philosophy of mind. Particularly as understood and deployed in the works of philosophers such as Wilfrid Sellars and John McDowell, *intentionality* affords critical purchase on the complex and elusive thought of one of the most influential thinkers in the history of Indian philosophy—critical purchase that makes sense, moreover, of some of the problems and issues that underlie the burgeoning literature on Buddhism vis-à-vis cognitive-scientific research.

Given the vastness of the philosophical literature pertaining to intentionality (not to mention the particular difficulties that attend attempts at understanding first-millennium Indian philosophers like Dharmakīrti), any project such as the one attempted here is necessarily selective; the particular angles I've developed surely reflect the philosophical conversations I've been part of (here at the University of Chicago and further afield) and all that I've learned therein from my students, colleagues, and critics. While my perhaps eccentric development of this book's various ideas should not, of course, be held against any of them, there are some among these many interlocutors whom it's my pleasure to thank for their special roles in furthering my work.

Much of what shows up in the following pages was first presented at various conferences and symposia; I especially benefited from such opportunities as were made available to me by Piotr Balcerowicz, David Eckel, Jay Garfield, Birgit Kellner, and Tom Tillemans, all of whom I thank both for their invitations and their feedback. (Birgit Kellner was especially indulgent in this regard, allowing for my work toward chapter 5 to include the writing of a "response" paper that really was quite excessively long; Jay Garfield has generously given feedback on more of my work than probably anyone.) I've also greatly benefited from conversations with and suggestions from Akeel Bilgrami, Jason Bridges, Yigal Bronner, Arindam Chakrabarti, Christian Coseru, Whitney Cox, Ryan Coyne, Mario D'Amato, Wendy Doniger, Georges Dreyfus, John Dunne, Jonathan Gold, Richard Hayes, Kevin Hector, Matthew Kapstein, Sara McClintock, Larry McCrea, Rick Nance, Parimal Patil, Graham Priest, Rajam Raghunathan, Rick Rosengarten, Mark Siderits, John Taber, Alex Watson, and Christian Wedemeyer.

Thanks, too, to Tupac Cruz, Eric Huntington, and Sonam Kachru, for the various kinds of help they provided in my researching the stuff considered here (which in Eric's case includes preparation of the index). At a point where the manuscript of this book was excessively sprawling and diffuse, Spencer Dew's skillful editorial interventions were invaluable. That editorial work, as well as a generous subvention for the book's publication, were provided by the Divinity School, and I thank then-Dean Rick Rosengarten for this form of assistance (as well as for all the other kinds he's provided over the years). Closer to completion, Rob Fellman's editorial work was also much appreciated.

A good deal of the material included in this book has appeared in print before. Much of chapter 4 was published in the *Journal of Indian Philosophy* (see Arnold 2006), as was much of chapter 5 (Arnold 2010a); material for chapter 5 also appeared in *Sophia* (Arnold 2008). All of the material here reused from those publications is used with kind permission from Springer Science+Business Media. Much of chapter 1 first appeared in *Philosophy Compass* (as "Dharmakīrti's Dualism: Critical Reflections on a Buddhist Proof of Rebirth," in vol. 3/5 [2008]: 1079–1096); thanks to John Wiley and Sons for permission to reuse that material here.

Thanks, in particular, to Wendy Lochner and Christine Mortlock, with whom it's been a real pleasure to work (and to share musical suggestions) for many years now.

Most deserving of thanks are Deborah, Benjamin, and Katy; while they are, of all the people named here, surely the least likely to care much about the arguments of this book, their care for more important things has been for me the most sustaining support of all. If there's any merit in this book, I'd like to dedicate it to their flourishing and (why not?) to the flourishing of all sentient beings.

Introduction

"NEURAL BUDDHISM": COGNITIVE SCIENCE AND THE PHILOSOPHY OF DHARMAKĪRTI

The *New York Times* columnist David Brooks has ventured, notwithstanding the current popularity of books like Richard Dawkins's *The God Delusion*, that a new wave of cognitive-scientific research on religion may lead not to rampant atheism but to "what you might call neural Buddhism."[1] Brooks's point was that "the real challenge" for theists was likely to come not so much from the avowedly atheistic works of Dawkins and the like as "from scientists whose beliefs overlap a bit with Buddhism." He seems to have meant that cognitive-scientific research supports such characteristically Buddhist beliefs as that (Brooks says) "the self is not a fixed entity but a dynamic process of relationships," and he worries that such research thus encourages "new movements that emphasize self-transcendence but put little stock in divine law or revelation."

Brooks's column occasioned much reflection on the religious studies blog "The Immanent Frame," where scholars noted (among other things) that the assimilation of Buddhism to science represents a century-old apologetic strategy characteristic of modern Buddhism[2] and that the revolutionary character of cognitive-scientific explanation has perhaps been overstated.[3] Both points are important, but this book will focus on variations on the second one. Here, I want to look at what was arguably the dominant trajectory of Indian Buddhist philosophy—that stemming from Dharmakīrti (c. 600–660 C.E.)—through the lens of central issues in contemporary philosophy of mind. I want to suggest that there are indeed important respects in which Dharmakīrti's project is akin to those of contemporary cognitive-scientific philosophers—and that this is so much the worse for Dharmakīrti. My thought is that we can learn much, both about Dharmakīrti and about contemporary philosophy of mind, by appreciating that (and how) some of Dharmakīrti's central positions are vulnerable to arguments that also have been pressed against the kind of physicalist philosophy of mind recently informed by work in the cognitive sciences.

It should be emphasized up front that Dharmakīrti is a particularly difficult thinker; he takes on intrinsically complex and elusive philosophical topics, and his works are, to an even greater extent than is typical of first-millennium Sanskritic philosophers, at once dense and opaquely elliptical, and thus it is unusually difficult to feel confident that one has definitively understood his thoughts on any subject. Dharmakīrti surely admits of various readings, and it would be foolhardy to claim that, by suggesting some respects in which he may be vulnerable to certain arguments, his philosophical project has been exhaustively considered. The present engagement with his thought, however, is animated not only by my sense that we can get some traction on his project by characterizing it as susceptible to certain modern arguments but also by my desire to make the arguments of some of his classical Indian critics seem more interesting than is sometimes appreciated.

In reading Dharmakīrti as I do, then, I am motivated partly by my sense that there are profound philosophical intuitions to be elaborated along lines suggested by some of his Indian critics—and particularly by some proponents of the Brahmanical Pūrva Mīmāṃsā and the Buddhist Madhyamaka schools of thought. I thus hope to reconstruct the arguments of these other Indian philosophers, too, in terms suggested by modern and contemporary philosophical debate. My aims will have been largely fulfilled if we gain some clarity on what may have been at issue among these thinkers—something I hope to achieve in part by showing that the seemingly arcane points at stake for these first-millennium Indian philosophers turn out still to be debated among contemporary philosophers.

I can introduce some of the issues that will come into play with reference to another item from the *New York Times*: a 2005 story concerning a talk by the Dalai Lama at an annual meeting of the Society for Neuroscience. Some five hundred brain researchers, it seems, had signed a petition calling for the talk's cancellation, saying it would "highlight a subject with largely unsubstantiated claims," and that it "compromised scientific rigor and objectivity."[4] The *Times* article centered on debates internal to the scientific community—debates, for example, about whether scientific objectivity is compromised by the fact that some scholars engaged in this research are themselves practitioners of Buddhist meditation, and about what kinds of phenomena will admit of properly scientific study. Regarding the latter point, petition signatory Zvani Rossetti is reported to have said that "neuroscience more than other disciplines is the science at the interface between modern philosophy and science."

While Rossetti may be right, it is tendentious to conclude from this that (as he added in questioning the Dalai Lama's talk) "no opportunity should be given to anybody to use neuroscience for supporting transcendent views of the world." Depending, perhaps, on just what "transcendent views of the world" means, this arguably begs one of the most basic questions in contemporary philosophy of mind—the question whether fundamental issues in philosophy of mind are finally *empirical*, or whether instead they are (and there's a range of options here) metaphysical, transcendental, logical, or conceptual.[5] Impressed by the recently enormous advances in the scientific understanding of the brain (particularly those advances informed by research in computer science and AI), philosophers such as Jerry Fodor and Daniel Dennett take the questions at issue to be finally empirical and thus take it that the findings of empirical research in the cognitive sciences might answer the basic questions of philosophy of mind, which, we will see, chiefly center for these philosophers on the question of mental causation. What cognitive-scientific research provides, on this view, *just is* an account of mind. Against this, philosophers such as John McDowell take the basic issues in philosophy of mind to be (in a sense we shall consider) transcendental; for McDowell, someone like Dennett offers "what may be an enabling explanation of consciousness, but not a constitutive one. . . . We lack an account of what [consciousness] is, even if we have an account of what enables it to be present" (1998a, 357).[6] An account of some of the enabling conditions of the mental, in other words, is not to be confused with an account of what the mental *is*—though it's a fair question whether anything *could* count as an instance of the latter.

In light of this divide among contemporary philosophers of mind, it's revealing that Buddhist thought should have come to figure so prominently in cognitive-scientific discourse; David Brooks is far from alone in taking

Buddhist thinkers and cognitive-scientifically inclined philosophers as philosophical fellow travelers.[7] This makes sense insofar as Buddhist thinkers are virtually defined as such by their upholding the "without self" (*anātma*) doctrine; surely nothing could be more anti-Cartesian than to urge (as Buddhists do in elaborating this idea) that every moment of experience can be shown to depend upon a host of causal factors, none of which is what we "really" are. Many Buddhist philosophers thus urged a broadly *reductionist* account of persons, according to which we are not entitled to infer that our episodic cognitions and experiences must be the states of an enduring "self"; rather, only the particular and momentary causes themselves are to be judged finally real. Elaborating what he took to be the entailments of this idea, Dharmakīrti influentially said that "whatever has the capacity for causal efficacy is ultimately existent (*paramārthasat*); everything else is just conventionally existent."[8] Surely, a reductionist account that thus privileges causal explanation could be taken to complement a characteristically cognitive-scientific project in philosophy of mind.

Pursuing this thought, Mark Siderits asks (in the subtitle of a recent article): "Is the Eightfold Path a Program?" (2001). That is, can characteristically Buddhist accounts of the person be harmonized particularly with those cognitive-scientific projects that, informed by the availability of the computer model, take thought to be somehow "computational"? Among other things, this amounts to the question whether the basic Buddhist commitment to selflessness might be compatible with *physicalism*.[9] For, as we will see in chapter 2, what computational accounts of thought may most significantly advance is broadly *physicalist* explanations of the mental—explanations, that is, according to which everything about the mental can be finally explained in terms of particular goings-on in the brain. Whether Buddhist thought is compatible with such an account (which Siderits calls "technophysicalism") is a pressing question insofar as contemporary technophysicalist accounts are, Siderits holds, "more difficult to resist" than earlier versions of physicalism (2001, 307). Siderits proposes that the basic Buddhist project *is* finally reconcilable with cognitive-scientific physicalism.

There is surely reason to suppose that Buddhist thought, particularly insofar as it centrally involves causal explanation, might thus be compatible with cognitive-scientific accounts. There remains, however, a significant obstacle to the view that Buddhist thinkers elaborated a position that is uniquely compatible with scientific understanding: while cognitive-scientific accounts of the mind are generally physicalist in character, *Buddhist philosophers are emphatically not physicalists.*[10] Indeed, it is important to understand that exemplars of the Buddhist philosophical tradition—including, in Dharmakīrti, one of the most influential of all Indian philosophers—elaborated an eminently dualist account of the person. If, moreover, that account finally gives way to any sort of monism (as it arguably does, we will see in chapter 5, when Dharmakīrti lays his Yogācāra cards on the table), it is surely of the idealist sort.

The Buddhist emphasis on the dynamic and causally describable character of subjectivity is not, then, incompatible with the view that among the causes of this are constitutively *mental* existents that cannot be reduced to physical existents. What is denied by Buddhists, in other words, is only that "the mind" denotes (as the definite article perhaps suggests to speakers of English) an enduring substance; to argue, as Buddhists do, that our experience is better explained by an *event*-based ontology than by a *substance*-based one is not by itself to say anything about whether there could be essentially different *kinds* of events. Indian Buddhist philosophers could (and did) coherently maintain both that "persons" consist simply in causally continuous series of events and that the series of mental events, insofar as it continues after the death of the body, has indefinite temporal extension. It is, indeed, just the postmortem continuity of any series of mental events that is called "rebirth."[11]

It is perhaps especially the significance of rebirth for the Buddhist soteriological project that gave philosophers in this tradition a strong stake in refuting any version of physicalism. Indeed, the traditionally transmitted utterances of the Buddha include passages to the effect that physicalism is finally a more pernicious error even than self-grasping (which is saying a lot, since the latter is taken by Buddhists as the primary cause of our suffering). This is, Richard Hayes explains, because "if there is no rebirth, then the very goal of attaining nirvāṇa, understood as the cessation of rebirth, becomes almost perfectly meaningless. Or rather, nirvāṇa comes automatically to every being that dies, regardless of how that being has lived" (1993, 128). Indian Buddhist thinkers thus held that physicalism was tantamount to the extreme of nihilism, or (as Buddhists say) *ucchedavāda*—an extreme not misleadingly translated (to invoke a position in philosophy of mind) as *eliminativism*. This names views according to which everything of moral significance can finally be "eliminated" or explained away in terms of the preferred explanation—and the characteristically Buddhist conviction is that physicalism would be tantamount to such an "elimination" of the morally significant description of events, since on such a view suffering would be eliminated not by Buddhist practice but simply by dying.

Perhaps insofar as physicalism was not a widely entertained option on the Indian philosophical scene, there were few sustained attempts by Buddhist thinkers to refute such a position. There is, though, one revealing attempt to take on the challenge of physicalism; fittingly, this is to be found in the work that most influentially advanced a trajectory of thought that subsequent Indian philosophers took as practically coextensive with the "Buddhist" position in matters philosophical: Dharmakīrti's *Pramāṇavārttika*, or (we might translate) "Critical Commentary on Epistemic Criteria."[12] As we will see in chapter 1, Dharmakīrti's magnum opus comprises a lengthy refutation of a physicalist interlocutor who denies the possibility of the Buddha's having cultivated his compassion over innumerable lifetimes; against the objections of this interlocutor, Dharmakīrti argues that mental events cannot be thought to depend on the body.

Insofar as Dharmakīrti's critique of physicalism is judged central to his approach, Siderits may be wrong to claim that the characteristically Buddhist form of dualism is not really integral to the Buddhist project; the significance of rebirth for that project is surely among several considerations that can be thought to commit Buddhists to refuting physicalism. It seems to me that Paul Griffiths is right, in this regard, to stress "just how radical a dualism" was advanced particularly by the Abhidharma and Yogācāra trajectories of Buddhist thought; physicalism "in any form (identity theory, epiphenomenalism and so forth) is not an option" for this tradition of Buddhist thought (1986, 112). As Richard Hayes more emphatically says, there is "no other philosophical view that is more radically opposed to the tenets of Buddhism than materialism" (1993, 128)—even if Dharmakīrti's refutation is exceptional in explicitly engaging that.

INTENTIONALITY, THE STATUS OF UNIVERSALS, AND THE PROBLEMS WITH COGNITIVISM

That some Indian Buddhists strenuously rejected physicalism is not, however, the point I am developing in this book. While Dharmakīrti himself pressed the Buddhist tradition's most notable case against physicalism, we can appreciate some central features of his thought by recognizing that his own account of the mental nevertheless turns out to be vulnerable to a cogent line of critique that modern philosophers have leveled against varieties of physicalism. The central premise of this book, then, is that we can learn some important things about the conceptual "deep structure" of what is arguably the dominant trajectory of Indian Buddhist thought—and, as well, about some contemporary cognitive-scientific philosophies of mind—by understanding these significantly divergent traditions of thought as facing some of the same philosophical problems.

In particular, Dharmakīrti shares with cognitive-scientific philosophers of mind a guiding commitment to finally *causal* explanations of the mental, as well as (what arguably follows from this) the view that everything about the mental must be explicable with reference only to things somehow internal to the subject. I follow Vincent Descombes (among others) in characterizing this "solipsistic and causalist position in the philosophy of mind" as *cognitivist* (2001, xvi).[13] Notwithstanding the considerations that (it will be allowed) can be taken to recommend cognitivist accounts in philosophy of mind, we will see that there are significant problems for any such attempt to explain all aspects of the mental in terms of causal relations among local particulars.

These problems, as they commonly arise for Dharmakīrti and for contemporary physicalists, can usefully be framed in terms of the concept of *intentionality*. The various uses of this philosophical term of art—familiar alike to students of continental phenomenology and Anglo-American philosophy of mind—commonly involve the idea of "aboutness"; that is, intentionality picks out the fact that mental events (like *thinking* or *believing*) perhaps uniquely exemplify the fact of being *about* their objects. Mental events, on another way of putting the point, constitutively have *content*; as Franz Brentano puts this in a canonical passage on the subject, "in presentation something is presented, in judgement something is affirmed or denied, in love loved, in hate hated, in desire desired and so on" (1973, 88). Among the ideas here is that whatever we might reasonably say about the relations of (say) a table to its surrounding environment, we would not say that it is *about* anything; the relation that characterizes a thought's being about its content, many have supposed, is peculiarly distinctive of the mental.

There is (we will see especially in chapter 3) much to be said about the history and the varying uses of this idea, but in one form or another, a main question in the philosophy of mind has thus been (in Lynne Rudder Baker's words) "to understand how one thing (some mental item) *can mean or represent or be about* some other thing (for example, some state of affairs)—to understand how anything can have content" (1987, 9; emphasis added). Here, it's relevant to note that for Baker's "some mental item" we might also substitute *some linguistic item*; surely linguistic items (sentences, stories, claims) are also rightly taken to "mean or represent or be about" states of affairs. In fact, there turns out to be a close relationship between the intentionality of the mental and certain features of language; indeed, linguistic items may represent the one case of something other than mental events that exemplifies intentionality.

While there are many ways one might tell the story of this relationship, this fact surely explains why so much contemporary philosophy of mind looks a lot like philosophy of language—a fact humorously noted by Jerry Fodor, who once characterized his own work as exemplifying "the philosophy of mind (or the philosophy of language, or whatever this stuff is)" (1990, 131). Thus, a great many contemporary discussions in philosophy of mind often center on considerations in *semantics*—considerations, for example, having to do with such things as the truth conditions and referentiality of propositions.[14] How we are to understand the relation between (as it were) "linguistic" and "mental" intentionality has, in fact, been chief among the points at issue in twentieth-century philosophy of mind. The contemporary debate can be framed by Roderick Chisholm, who said of Wilfrid Sellars's influential 1956 essay "Empiricism and the Philosophy of Mind" that the main question over which they diverged was this: "Can we explicate the intentional character of believing and of other psychological attitudes by reference to certain features of language; or must we explicate the intentional characteristics of language by reference to believing and to other psychological attitudes?" (Chisholm and Sellars 1957, 215).

Sellars held the first of these positions, arguing in his famous 1956 essay that "the categories of intentionality are, at bottom, semantical categories pertaining to overt verbal performances" (1956, 94). Whatever one thinks is the right direction of explanation here (and in chapter 3, I will make a case for Sellars's view), it is perhaps especially the closeness of the relation between linguistic and mental "aboutness" that makes it so difficult to give (what many would take to define a scientific approach to any matter) a thoroughly *causal* account of the mental; for the way that things like sentences relate to what they are about does not (to say the least) readily admit of causal explanation. Insofar, then, as mental events are like linguistic items in this respect, a mental event's "being about" its content arguably involves something constitutively other than causal relations. The extent to which the intentionality of the mental thus resists causal explanation is, then, commonly problematic for Dharmakīrti and contemporary physicalists just insofar as they are alike committed to the view that only things that can enter into *causal* relations are finally real.

The issues here in play might also be put in terms of the category of "belief," which, despite its occurrence in the title of my first book (Arnold 2005), was not theorized there. In discussions of intentionality, belief represents the paradigm case of what philosophers since Bertrand Russell have called the "propositional attitudes." If mental events are characterized by their having content, propositional attitudes represent the various ways of "being about" any instance of such content; one can, for example, *affirm*, *doubt*, *hope*, or *think* that such-and-such is the case. Of the propositional attitudes, *believing* is arguably the most conceptually basic, since taking any other such attitude toward some state of affairs presupposes one's believing something to obtain; "it's impressive," Paul Boghossian notes, "how many concepts of the propositional attitudes depend asymmetrically on the concept of belief" (2003, 43).[15]

Among the questions raised by this way of talking about intentionality is what sort of thing, exactly, the *content* of any belief is; while particular *acts of believing* are specific to individuals, what these are *about* may be common to many such acts. There is thus a case to be made for thinking that beliefs essentially concern things like *claims* or *states of affairs*—the kinds of things, many philosophers have noted, that can be individuated by *that*-clauses. When one says, for example, "she believes *that* it's raining" or "I believe *that Trout Mask Replica* is a great album," the content of the *that*-clause is a complex state of affairs under some description; these clauses embrace entire sets of facts, something of the world as *taken* from some perspective. To think of any instance of awareness (at least of the believing sort) as *contentful*, on such a view—to think of it as *about* anything—is thus to suppose that individuating or understanding the belief requires reference to some kind of abstraction. This is because "states of affairs" are not unique particulars; unlike, say, fleetingly occurrent mental representations, they are the kinds of things that can simultaneously be the object of many people's beliefs.

Buddhists and other Indian philosophers would recognize that what has thus been brought into play by the foregoing introduction of intentionality and propositional attitudes, then, is the question of the ontological status of universals and the relation of these to cognition.[16] Another form of the question of intentionality, then, is whether it is possible to give a complete account of the mental (more precisely, of mental *content*) in terms of an ontology comprising only unique particulars—or whether, instead, such an account inevitably requires reference to some kind of abstractions or universals, whether those be understood as concepts, propositions, truth conditions, or whatever. Part of what I want to show, then, is the extent to which characteristically Indian philosophical debates about the status particularly of linguistic universals—debates, for example, between basically nominalist thinkers like Dharmakīrti and archrealists like the proponents of Mīmāṃsā—can also be understood to concern eminently contemporary questions about how we should understand our mental lives.

Thus, as we will see in chapter 4, Dharmakīrti (like Jerry Fodor) is centrally concerned somehow to explain linguistic universals with reference only to particulars; this is the point of his famously elusive *apoha* ("exclusion") doctrine. This doctrine elaborates the idea that concepts are more precise or determinate (more *contentful*) just to the extent that they exclude more from their purview; the scope of *cat* is narrower than that of *mammal* just insofar as the former additionally excludes from its range all mammals in the world that are not cats. Typically represented as the signal Buddhist contribution to Indian philosophy of language, this doctrine can also be understood more generally as an account of *the content of beliefs.* According to Dharmakīrti's elaboration of it, this complex doctrine emphasizes that conceptual content can finally be explained just in terms of particular mental representations; particular occurrences of perceiving or sensing, that is, provide the bases for the "exclusions" that finally explain the universals in play whenever we entertain discursive thoughts.

It's important that Dharmakīrti thus be able to explain universals with reference only to particulars since, for him, only particular things—only *this* sensation of a pot, and *this* one, etc.—are finally real; as ultimately unreal, abstractions (like the property *being a pot*) cannot finally explain any belief's having explanatory significance. When we get to Dharmakīrti's arguments for this, we will have seen (in chapter 2) that Jerry Fodor affords us good resources for thinking about what Dharmakīrti is up to in this regard; indeed, Fodor could be talking about Dharmakīrti's *apoha* doctrine when he says of his own representational theory of mind (RTM) that it purports to explain "how there *could* be states that have the semantical and causal properties that propositional attitudes are commonsensically supposed to have. In effect, RTM proposes an account of what the propositional attitudes *are*" (1985, 78).

We will see in chapter 2 that on Fodor's physicalist version of such an account, the particular "mental representations" that explain semantic content can be described in terms of correlated brain events—an idea that the antiphysicalist Dharmakīrti would strongly reject. What commonly characterizes Fodor's and Dharmakīrti's accounts, though, is the essentially cognitivist presuppositions that are arguably most significant for their views. Both accounts are driven by the idea that only causal relations among particulars can be thought finally "real," finally to *explain* anything. These thinkers share, moreover, the idea that the only such particulars that indubitably occur are those that are somehow—Dharmakīrti and Fodor diverge most sharply, of course, with regard to how[17]—internal to a subject. For Fodor, the problem of mental causation thus recommends the adoption of a "methodological solipsism." On this view, anything that is called on to explain the causal efficacy of the mind must be intelligible without reference to the *semantic* properties of mental events—without reference (Fodor says) to "the property of being true, of having referents, or, indeed, the property of being representations *of the environment*" (1980, 283). Instead, the explaining is finally to be done by brain events that can be exhaustively described simply in terms of their intrinsic properties.

We will see in chapter 5 that Dharmakīrti can be understood as similarly grounding his whole account of semantic content (the one elaborated in the form of the *apoha* doctrine) in what is, for Dharmakīrti, arguably the only really indubitable "epistemic criterion" (*pramāṇa*): *svasaṃvitti*, or "self-awareness." It is in the parts of his corpus where he elaborates this doctrine that Dharmakīrti has traditionally been taken most clearly to affirm the characteristically "Yogācāra" doctrine of Buddhist idealism. Whether or not that doctrine can be understood as metaphysical idealism, it is clear that Dharmakīrti's arguments for *svasaṃvitti* represent a case at least for *epistemic* idealism—for the view, that is, that what we are immediately aware of (which, note well, is logically independent of the ontological question of *what there is*) is simply the occurrence and contents of our own mental events. On my reading, the salient point of this epistemological claim is that mental content is autonomously intelligible; this is the idea, in other words, that we can know *how things seem to us* quite apart from any reference to *how things really are*—quite apart (with Fodor) from whether mental representations might have properties like *being true*.

Fodor and Dharmakīrti would, then, commonly have us explain conceptual mental content finally in terms of what irrefragably *seems to a subject* to be the case; anything's seeming so, moreover, is finally to be explained, for both thinkers, in causal terms. Among other things, the kind of cognitivist approach we will thus develop with reference to Fodor and Dharmakīrti can be said to aim at providing a finally *nonintentional* account of intentionality—to aim, that is, at explaining intentionality (at explaining how anything can mean or represent or be about some other thing) in terms of existents that do not themselves intrinsically "mean" anything. Expressing this point, Fodor quips that "if aboutness is real, it must really be something else" (1987, 97). Arguments to this effect represent, in one contemporary idiom, the project of *naturalizing* intentionality.[18]

We will see that there are considerations that recommend such views, which can, it seems to me, be taken to have just the intuitive plausibility that empiricism more generally has. Indeed, the projects of Fodor and Dharmakīrti commonly fall on the side of the broadly empiricist divide in philosophy of mind; on the views of both of these thinkers, the answer to a question such as what it is to *mean* anything takes the form of a psychological account of causally describable processes involving particular states or events. Chief among the problems with such an approach, though, is that it may very well presuppose precisely the kinds of things it aims to explain. This is surely as Dharmakīrti's principally Brahmanical interlocutors argued with respect to his *apoha* doctrine: the very process of exclusion in terms of which Dharmakīrti explains universals is intelligible, his critics argued, only with reference to universals. I will suggest that the conceptual difficulties here can be more generally understood in terms of Dharmakīrti's own attempt to *explain* intentionality as necessarily exemplifying precisely what could be called an *intentional* level of description.

A basically transcendental argument to this effect—one that stems from Kant (and particularly from the *Critique of Practical Reason*) and that is variously carried forward by Wilfrid Sellars and John McDowell—takes its bearings from the idea that reason itself is the "intentional" phenomenon par excellence. Thus, the discursive realm with regard to which Indian philosophers focus on the problem of universals can also be characterized (as it is by Sellars) as the "logical space of reasons" (1956, 76). This is the level of description at which it makes sense to think of persons in their capacity as responsive to *reasons*—the level, that is, at which we find intelligible somebody's demand that we *justify* any action or decision. The question for those who would "naturalize" intentionality, then, is how to account for the status and content of reasons; more precisely, insofar as reasoning constitutively involves (in John McDowell's phrase) "relations such as one thing's being warranted or correct in the light of another" (1996, xv), anyone who would reduce (or "naturalize") intentionality must, ipso facto, be able to show how such conceptual relations can themselves be explained by (or consist in) finally *causal* relations. The broadly Kantian argument against such a project is that any putative explanation of us in our capacity *as reasoning*—a physicalist's, say, in terms of brain events—inevitably turns out itself to presuppose or exemplify an intentional level of description; reason itself cannot be "explained" by any such account just insofar as it is only by reasoning that one could try to do so.

This is much as some of Dharmakīrti's principal Indian interlocutors variously argued. When Indian Buddhists and their Brahmanical interlocutors debate the status of linguistic universals, there is an important extent to which they can be taken as advancing arguments in philosophy of mind; indeed, this centuries-long debate between Buddhists and Mīmāṃsakas can be characterized as concerning precisely Chisholm's question to Sellars. Thus, Buddhists like Dharmakīrti clearly held that "the intentional characteristics of language" (most generally, its *meaning* anything) are to be explained "by reference to believing and to other psychological attitudes"—more specifically, that what language is about can finally be explained in terms of causally describable mental representations. Against this, Mīmāṃsakas who defended the view that language is eternal can be understood to have held, among other things, that there is something *irreducibly* linguistic about the mental—that language is a condition of the possibility of mind, not a product thereof. Among their most interesting arguments to this effect is one that can be generalized as concerning the ineliminable nature of an intentional level of description.

Similarly, Dharmakīrti's fellow Buddhists the Mādhyamikas, who characteristically urged (in Mark Siderits's apt phrase) that "the ultimate truth is that there is no ultimate truth,"[19] can be understood to have argued that the world must finally be understood as *irreducibly conventional*. The characteristically Mādhyamika deference to "conventional truth" (*saṃvṛtisatya*), I will suggest, can be understood as deference to an *intentional* level of description, and Mādhyamikas can be taken thus to have urged that intentionality is ineliminable in favor of any supposedly privileged level of description. I will, then, be characterizing both Mīmāṃsakas and Mādhyamikas (despite their enormously different overall projects) as having variously advanced something very much like the broadly Kantian line of argument that has been, in my view, most cogently advanced against physicalists. By thus reconstructing some Mīmāṃsaka and Mādhyamika arguments against the likes of Dharmakīrti as having advanced significant insights concerning what Kant called "practical reason," it is to be hoped that we will learn something not only about the various first-millennium Indian philosophers in view, but also about the nature and promise of what some have taken to be a profound argument against physicalism.

Whatever the extent, though, to which arguments such as the foregoing are cogent, it's revealing that they have purchase not only against contemporary physicalists but also against the decidedly antiphysicalist Buddhist philosopher Dharmakīrti. It is to the extent that he exemplifies a basically cognitivist approach that, even though having pressed the Buddhist tradition's most sustained case against physicalism, Dharmakīrti turns out himself to be vulnerable to what I will elaborate (in chapters 3 and 6) as perhaps the most cogent argument against physicalism. Insofar, that is, as he takes the mental to be causally explicable in terms of particular moments of awareness, Dharmakīrti is vulnerable to arguments meant to show intentionality to be irreducible to and ineliminable in favor of such terms. If, as Sellars has it, the "logical space of reasons" is *sui generis*—if reasoning and believing will not admit of the kind of finally causal explanation that Fodor and Dharmakīrti commonly aim for—then significant commitments of Dharmakīrti's are called into question.

That Dharmakīrti, who was a strong critic of physicalism and probably himself an idealist, should thus be vulnerable to the same arguments that cut against contemporary iterations of physicalism is, I think, revealing of what are the most philosophically significant presuppositions in play. Our consideration of the Buddhist Dharmakīrti in light of contemporary debates about intentionality may, then, not only help us characterize some of the most significant issues in the interpretation of Dharmakīrti; it may also help us appreciate that despite recently enormous advances in the empirical sciences of cognition, Vincent Descombes is right that "the cognitivist conception of mind has been derived not from cognitive psychology but . . . from a particular philosophy."[20] To hold that only certain kinds of explanations—e.g., causal explanations in terms of existents with specifiable identity criteria—are finally valid is not simply to follow the manifest deliverances of neutral inquiry; it is to have decided, a priori, for metaphysical commitments that are not themselves the results of such inquiry.

PLAN OF THE BOOK

We will begin our development of the foregoing thoughts with a consideration, in chapter 1, of Dharmakīrti's critique of physicalism in the *Pramāṇavārttika*. This will be prefaced by a more general survey of some central commitments of Dharmakīrti; in particular, I will sketch the basics of his epistemology, focused in terms of the causally describable character of perception. We will then determine what kind of argument against physicalism is available to Dharmakīrti in light of these commitments. His argument, we will see, is finally to the effect that mental items are ontologically distinct from physical items—and that this is compatible with (indeed, that it relates closely to) Dharmakīrti's characteristically Ābhidharmika notions of causation. I will characterize his argument as basically empiricist in character, in a sense to be elaborated.

In chapter 2, we will begin a two-chapter excursus on some contemporary philosophical discussions of intentionality, developed with an eye toward giving us some conceptual tools for the interpretation of Dharmakīrti. This chapter will consider the "computational" models of cognitive-scientific physicalism developed by Daniel Dennett and (especially) Jerry Fodor, particularly insofar as these philosophers aim to account for intentionality. We will see that it is particularly the problem of "mental causation" that can be taken to motivate these projects. While Dennett and Fodor both claim to provide accounts that allow us to think of intentional attitudes (like believing and judging) as somehow real, it turns out to be at the scientific level of description that all of the explanatory work is done; this is as it must be, given their sense (comparable to Dharmakīrti's) that only things capable of involving a certain kind of causal efficacy can finally be thought *real*. It is, for these thinkers, only as alternatively described (in terms, e.g., of brain events) that things like "reasons" can be thought to *do* anything.

Aiming to clarify what is most interestingly problematic about the accounts of Dennett and Fodor, I will, in chapter 3, venture a basically Kantian story of intentionality, motivating an account of why concerns having to do with language should figure so prominently in philosophy of mind—an account of why it is reasonable to hold, with Sellars, that "the categories of intentionality are, at bottom, semantical categories pertaining to overt verbal performances." Kant's appeal to the transcendental unity of apperception figures centrally in his development of what Sellars called the "logical space of reasons"—the conceptual order in terms of which it makes sense to think of persons as responsive to reasons as such. Kant characterized this conceptual order as exercising a faculty of "spontaneity," thus emphasizing the extent to which this level of description constitutively resists causal explanation. Chief among the Kantian arguments to be elaborated following Sellars and McDowell is one to the effect that the intentionality of awareness constitutively involves this conceptual space, and that we must, to that extent, suppose that intentionality cannot be exhaustively explained in causal terms. The argument is completed by pressing the point that the foregoing conclusion cannot be denied insofar as it is only by reasoning that one could do so; the cognitivist project of "naturalizing" intentionality cannot go through, then, just insofar as we can make sense of anyone's being *persuaded* of any view on the matter.

With chapter 4, we resume our engagement with Dharmakīrti, considering, in particular, the *apoha* doctrine. Dharmakīrti's peculiarly causal elaboration of this approach to explaining conceptual mental content—the distinctiveness of which will be brought out by comparing his version of the doctrine with that first promulgated by his predecessor, Dignāga (c. 480–540 C.E.)—has striking affinities with the "psychosemantic" account developed by Fodor. Thus, what is excluded from coming under any concept is, for Dharmakīrti, everything that does not produce the same kinds of effects—where, significantly, the "effects" in question consist finally in the cognitive "images" or "representations" produced by sensory contact with objects. I argue that this is an account according to which the intentionality of the mental (of what thought is *about*) is to be explained finally in terms of the proximate causes of particular episodes of awareness—and that despite the considerations that may be taken to recommend such a psychologistic approach, this move brings out the truth in Donald Davidson's observation that empiricism is, problematically, finally "the view that the subjective ('experience') is the foundation of objective empirical knowledge" (1988, 46).

We will complete this thought in chapter 5, which will find us confronting the challenge of understanding Dharmakīrti's arguably foundational doctrine of *svasaṃvitti*, or "self-awareness." This is reckoned by Dharmakīrti as a variety of perception, which is most significantly to say that it is constitutively nonconceptual. Among the arguments for the doctrine of *svasaṃvitti* are some meant to show that what we are immediately aware of (which is logically distinct from the ontological question of *what there is*) is only things—sense data, say, or mental representations—somehow intrinsic to awareness. We will also try to make sense of the stronger claim (arguably advanced by both Dignāga and Dharmakīrti) that *svasaṃvitti* is, in the final analysis, really the only indubitable epistemic criterion (the only real *pramāṇa*)—a view that may amount to a statement of characteristically Yogācāra idealism. It will be clear, in any case, that this doctrine develops the quintessentially cognitivist view that awareness is autonomously intelligible—that, on one way of putting this point, the phenomenological fact of anything's *seeming* blue is logically prior to (and intelligible apart from) our having the idea of anything's *being* blue. An understanding of the foundational role of this idea for Dharmakīrti's project will help us appreciate why Dharmakīrti is committed to explaining mental content as he does in developing the *apoha* doctrine—why Dharmakīrti must, that is, think that contentful thoughts are finally *about* nothing more than subjectively occurrent mental events.

In chapter 6, we will complete the case for thinking that the foregoing project of Dharmakīrti is vulnerable to the same kinds of arguments, first developed in chapter 3, that have been leveled against the physicalist cognitivism of thinkers like Dennett and Fodor. Here, we approach this point by developing arguments from some first-millennium Indian interlocutors of Dharmakīrti and his school. With regard to the *apoha* doctrine, it is surely the Brahmanical school of Pūrva Mīmāṃsā that had the strongest stake in refuting Dharmakīrti; Mīmāṃsakas were archrealists about linguistic universals, and the critiques of *apoha* advanced by the Mīmāṃsaka Kumārila Bhaṭṭa (c. 620–680 C.E.) figured importantly in post-Dharmakīrti revisions of the doctrine. Rather than focus, however, on the arguments explicitly leveled at *apoha*, we will instead consider one of the principal arguments for the characteristically Mīmāṃsaka view that language is eternal—an argument that will be generalized as concerning the ineliminability of an intentional level of description. So, too, some characteristically Mādhyamika arguments concerning the irreducibly "conventional" (*saṃvṛtisat*) nature of existents will be considered through the lens of our issues in philosophy of mind. It will be noted, in this regard, that Mādhyamika arguments to this effect particularly center on questions of *causation*; it is, in other words, the supposedly privileged character of causal explanations that Mādhyamikas particularly have in their sights. It will be suggested that the "conventional truth" (*saṃvṛtisatya*) or "ordinary discourse" (*vyavahāra*) that Mādhyamikas show to be ineliminable in favor of such causal terms can, in keeping with the concerns of this book, be understood as most basically picking out an *intentional* level of description; among the things, then, that are ineliminable from any account of persons on the Mādhyamika view is reference, in one idiom, to their responsiveness to reasons as such.

Throughout the book, my goal is twofold: I want to advance the *interpretive* task of understanding the arguments and commitments of first-millennium Indian philosophers centering on Dharmakīrti, as well as the *philosophical* task of characterizing and advancing some arguments that classical Indian and contemporary philosophers alike would recognize as touching on central issues in (with Fodor) "the philosophy of mind (or the philosophy of language, or whatever this stuff is)." The interpretive, Indological task can be advanced whether or not the arguments here developed against physicalism are finally judged cogent; the exercise is valuable as a way to understand the classical Indian arguments as long as the characterization of the various philosophical interlocutors here invoked helps us to clarify issues of central concern to Dharmakīrti and his Buddhist and Brahmanical interlocutors. It is my hope, though, that the enlistment of some Indian interlocutors can help in the mounting of a cogent case for a philosophical account of contemporary relevance; perhaps, that is, some first-millennium Indian philosophers can help us understand the nature and limits of some eminently twenty-first-century developments in philosophy of mind.

1

Dharmakīrti's Proof of Rebirth

A DUALIST ACCOUNT OF THE CAUSES OF COGNITION

> *There are only two kinds of things, perceptible and imperceptible. With regard to these, that is perceptible which causes the content of awareness to track its own presence and absence.*
>
> —Dharmakīrti

INTRODUCTION: DHARMAKĪRTI AS EMPIRICIST

Elaborating what he represented as the basic purport of his predecessor Dignāga, the Indian Buddhist philosopher Dharmakīrti all but eclipsed the earlier thinker's work; indeed, Dharmakīrti's work would subsequently be taken by nearly all Indian philosophers as practically coextensive with the "Buddhist" position in matters philosophical, and his magnum opus figures, to this day, in the basic curriculum of many Tibetan Buddhist traditions of learning.[1] It is fitting, then, that it should be in the work that has virtually defined Buddhist philosophy—Dharmakīrti's *Pramāṇavārttika*, or "Critical Commentary on Epistemic Criteria"[2]—that we find one of the Indian Buddhist tradition's most sustained critiques of physicalist accounts of the mental.

Despite the unusually extensive character of his argument against physicalism, Dharmakīrti's critique displays some of the characteristically *cognitivist* presuppositions that finally make Dharmakīrti himself vulnerable to some modern arguments against physicalism. Thus, in making his case for rebirth, as John Taber says, "Dharmakīrti considers chiefly the problem: what *causes* a cognition . . . ?" (2003, 490).[3] This picks out one of the most significant aspects of Dharmakīrti's critique of physicalism, which exemplifies the kind of broadly "solipsistic and causalist position in the philosophy of mind" that, with Vincent Descombes,[4] I take to characterize contemporary physicalism. Insofar as he thus frames the issues chiefly in causal terms, Dharmakīrti not only deprives himself of what I will show to be a cogent line of argument against physicalism but elaborates a position that is itself susceptible to that argument.

That he should thus frame the issues is not, however, incidental to Dharmakīrti's position, and there are some eminently plausible intuitions, of a broadly empiricist sort, that can be taken to recommend his so proceeding. We can begin to appreciate this by noting that the context for Dharmakīrti's elaborating his critique of physicalism is (to give the title of what most modern interpreters reckon to be the second chapter of the *Pramāṇavārttika*) *pramāṇasiddhi*—a "proof," that is, "of *pramāṇa*."[5] More precisely, Dharmakīrti's commentators take him here to demonstrate that the Buddha himself was the paradigm case of *pramāṇa*—that he was, as Dignāga had said, *pramāṇabhūta*, or (we might translate) "*pramāṇa*, incarnate."[6]

This characterization of the Buddha reflects the titular concern of Dharmakīrti's *Pramāṇavārttika*, which focuses on the category of *pramāṇa*, that is, "reliable warrant" or "epistemic criterion." Indian philosophers of Dharmakīrti's day were preoccupied with which ways of arriving at beliefs—perception, inference, testimony, comparison, etc.—should be reckoned as basic criteria (as *pramāṇas*) and with characterizing the criteria so identified. While it's perhaps debatable just what is entailed by Dignāga's taking the person of the Buddha to embody, as it were, "epistemic criteria," it's clear enough that what is at stake is the authoritative status of the Buddhist tradition's claim on our belief; elaborating on this, Dharmakīrti tries to show why we should have confidence in the truth of what the Buddha taught. The question of whether or why we are entitled to credit what the Buddha taught is, among other things, an epistemological one. While we will see shortly why Dharmakīrti's discussion of the Buddha's "being a *pramāṇa*" occasions the need for a proof of rebirth, let us, then, first survey some of the basics of Dharmakīrti's epistemology, with an eye toward appreciating what kinds of arguments are available to him in making a case for rebirth.

Dharmakīrti influentially argued—with his predecessor Dignāga, and as would commonly be held by Buddhists writing subsequently—that only perception (*pratyakṣa*) and inference (*anumāna*) have the status of *pramāṇa*; all other ways of arriving at knowledge are reducible to one of these criteria. These two kinds of cognition have as their respective objects the only two *kinds* of things (on one way of dividing up the world) that exist: unique particulars (*svalakṣaṇas*) and such abstractions or universals (*sāmānyalakṣaṇa*) as concepts and complex wholes. Since the kinds of things that figure in conceptual content are not particulars, to say that perception apprehends only unique particulars is thus to be committed (as in fact Dignāga and Dharmakīrti commonly were) to the view that perception is constitutively nonconceptual; as these thinkers put the point, perception is *kalpanāpoḍha*, "devoid of conception."[7]

Among the salient points here is that any conceptual or discursive thought[8]—any taking of an object of cognition *as* something or another—can be thought necessarily to involve reference to some sort of universals, where these just are the kinds of things (concepts, linguistic referents, propositions) that figure in *judgments*. Thus, to take things under some description—to take oneself, say, as perceiving (not undifferentiated sense data but) *a tree*—arguably requires having such concepts as "being a tree" or "the class of all trees." Among the problems with Dharmakīrti's holding, then, that perception is constitutively nonconceptual is that this is arguably to say that perceptual awareness does not (perhaps *can*not) have the kind of content that affords *reasons* for acting one way or another—the kind of content that figures in what Wilfrid Sellars calls the "logical space of reasons."

While we will see that such a view is not without problems, there are nevertheless considerations that can be taken to recommend it; it can, indeed, be taken to have the kind of intuitive plausibility that generally attaches to empiricism.[9] The characterization of this as a broadly "empiricist" trend of thought fits particularly well, I think, with the emphasis on causal explanation that Dharmakīrti adds to the philosophical project he carries on from Dignāga.[10] Among the points I mean to suggest in saying this is that "empiricism" may not represent only an *epistemological* position; characteristically empiricist intuitions, rather, are also apt to involve ontological commitments centering on causal explanation. This is because empiricists are apt to privilege sense perception among ways of knowing, and Dharmakīrti discloses the extent to which this can be thought warranted particularly by the causally describable character of perception.

Thus, for Dharmakīrti, to be "ultimately existent" (*paramārthasat*)—to be the kind of thing that belongs in a final ontology and that can be called upon to explain whatever facts seem to obtain at the reducible level of description that Dharmakīrti characterizes as "conventionally existent" (*saṃvṛtisat*)—just is to be capable of causally interacting with other particulars. As he famously said in this regard: "Whatever has the capacity for causal efficacy (*arthakriyāsamartham yat*) is ultimately existent (*paramārthasat*); everything else is conventionally existent. These [two kinds of things consist, respectively, in] unique particulars and abstractions."[11] This means, however, that only the objects of *perception* count as "ultimately existent," just insofar as only these can *do* anything; whenever, in contrast, one has a discursive thought (a thought involving concepts), one's awareness involves reference to things that are not actually present in anything at all like the same way. Perception is privileged on this account, then, just insofar as the causal efficacy that figures therein is the criterion of the real.

Dharmakīrti alternatively makes the same point in stating what is widely referred to as the "*sattvānumāna*" (the "inference from being existent") argument for momentariness—an argument meant to show that existents must change from moment to moment *simply insofar as they can be thought to exist.* Thus, "Whatever is existent is only momentary, because there is a contradiction with causal efficacy if something is nonmomentary—and being a real thing (*vastutvam*), which is characterized by causal efficacy, is given up in that case."[12] Dharmakīrti here succinctly expresses a thought that animates many Buddhist arguments against putatively enduring wholes, whose relations to manifestly temporal existents are shown by these arguments to be problematic. Against theism, for example, Dharmakīrti and other Buddhists typically argue that insofar as the causation of events in the world has a constitutively temporal unfolding, no putatively unchanging entity can coherently be in any way related to such causation.[13] To be causally efficacious, therefore, is ipso facto to be momentary—*and being so,* on this account, is clearly the criterion of *being existent.* (Among the difficulties with such a criterion is that it is hard to see how the claim setting this forth *as* the criterion could itself be verified in the terms it states.)

Dharmakīrti could take this characterization of the possible objects of awareness in terms of their causal efficacy (or lack thereof) as recommended by its strong Buddhist pedigree; the epistemological intuitions in play here have the advantage that they are reasonably thought to support the cardinal Buddhist doctrine of *selflessness* (*anātmavāda*)—the view that persons are not enduring substances but instead consist in causally continuous series of momentary events. Thus, Dharmakīrti's criterion can plausibly be taken as recommending the conclusion that only our episodic sensations are real, without also warranting the (inferential) belief that these must be the states of an underlying self; the *self* is thus the originating example of the kind of "whole" or abstraction whose reality Buddhists like Dharmakīrti chiefly aim to refute. Just, then, as one can (for example) get milk from some particular bovine critter but not from the abstract property of "being a cow" (*gotva*), so, too, the "self" should be recognized as an explanatorily idle concept; all that is really occurrent (where that just means *causally efficacious*) is the particular sensations that alone are discoverable upon introspection.

The framing of these issues in specifically causal terms is surely as old as "selflessness" itself. Indeed, the flipside of the doctrine of selflessness is the equally cardinal doctrine of *pratītyasamutpāda*, or "dependent origination"; the reason we are not "selves" is that every moment of experience can be shown to be causally dependent upon a host of factors, themselves impersonal, none of which can be taken to be what we "really" are. Thus, the founding insight of the Buddhist tradition encourages the analysis of subjective experience into its constituent causes. The centrality of this idea is reflected in the widely attested use of the "verse of dependent origination" as a *mantra*: "The Tathāgata explained the cause of those existents whose origination is due to causes, as well as that which is their cessation—the great renunciant is one whose doctrine is thus."[14] There are, then, eminently Buddhist reasons for favoring causal analyses.

I said, though, that Dharmakīrti's particular focus on causal analyses can also be understood as reflecting a generally *empiricist* sort of approach; for it follows from Dharmakīrti's elaboration of the foregoing commitments that perception, in particular, represents the unique point in our cognitive relation to the world at which cognition itself is constrained *by the world*. This is because perceptual cognitions, it seems, can be exhaustively described as resulting from causally efficacious "impingements by the world on a possessor of sensory capacities," in John McDowell's felicitous phrase (1996, xv). Dharmakīrti's characteristically empiricist confidence in the foundational character of perception stems, then, from the fact that this kind of cognition, alone among *pramāṇas*, can be described as in contact with (as *caused by*) real existents. Such a view emphasizes, among other things, the phenomenological intuition that we do not have any agency with regard to how perceptually experienced things seem to us; rather, an object of perception is just "given" to us as *this particular thing*, seen on some particular occasion under whatever conditions happen to obtain.

It can reasonably be thought, to that extent, that attending to perceptual cognitions represents the best way to account for the objectivity of our knowledge; what could be more objectively real than the kinds of things that thus impinge upon our bodies? Dharmakīrti advances just such a view in affirming that only causally efficacious particulars should be reckoned as ultimately existent and that such abstract objects as concepts—the things that are the currency of Sellars's "logical space of reasons"—do not have this status. Objective reality is thus to be attributed only to those things that we can, as it were, "come up against," things with *identity criteria*. There is, in contrast, no place or time where concepts can be said to exist—that is, indeed, just what it means to call them "universals." Rather, these have what the Brahmanical thinker Bhartṛhari (himself a realist about linguistic universals) allowed was a kind of "figurative" or "secondary existence" (*upacārasattā*).[15] Dharmakīrti's generally empiricist intuition about the kinds of platonic entities that populate the discursive realm is that their utility must finally be explicable in terms of the kinds of things encountered in perception, and this for the simple reason that only things capable of entering into causal relations, only things with identity criteria, are finally real.

CAUSATION AND SUBJECTIVITY: DHARMAKĪRTI'S REPRESENTATIONALISM

A note of caution should be sounded here, since the seemingly empiricist perspective reflected in a great many of his arguments may, in the end, be only provisionally entertained by Dharmakīrti; on the idealist Yogācāra position Dharmakīrti finally holds, his account of the causal constraints on perceptual awareness will surely look quite different. Dharmakīrti is, in this regard, traditionally read as alternating between arguments for two kinds of views: the generally empiricist approach we have so far been scouting (characterized by most commentators as "Sautrāntika") and the "Yogācāra" perspective that is typically understood in terms of idealism.[16] It is this alternation in perspective that some modern interpreters have proposed we understand in terms of a "sliding scale of analysis"—in terms, that is, of a hermeneutical perspective informed by sensitivity to the fact that it is often difficult to determine, with respect to any particular topic, what Dharmakīrti's definitive position finally is. On John Dunne's elaboration of this idea, what most commentators call the "Sautrāntika" perspective is to be understood as "External Realism"; in contrast, the Yogācāra perspective is to be understood as what Dunne calls "Epistemic Idealism," which is the view (Dunne says) that "All Entities are Mental."[17]

Yet these positions may not be as clearly distinct as supposed; indeed, as we will see with chapter 5's consideration of Dharmakīrti's arguments for the doctrine of *svasaṃvitti*, the epistemology is the same on either account. Thus, Dunne's characterization of Dharmakīrti's Yogācāra as "epistemic idealism" may not, after all, distinguish this perspective from Sautrāntika; indeed, *epistemic* idealism can be understood as just the view these positions share. That is, the difference between Sautrāntika and Yogācāra may not lie in their epistemologies, insofar as the Sautrāntika, too, holds that we are *immediately* acquainted only with the contents of our own awareness; rather, the difference lies in the metaphysical arguments that (the idealist takes it) additionally show that only such mental things as sense data *could* be real.[18] What distinguishes the "Yogācāra" parts of Dharmakīrti's corpus, then, is simply his making explicit that epistemological commitments the Sautrāntika does (or at least coherently can) hold are already compatible with idealism. Among the things that will clearly emerge from our consideration of *svasaṃvitti*, then, is an appreciation of why it makes philosophical sense that, as on traditionally Buddhist doxographical accounts, Dharmakīrti's "Sautrāntika" perspective should give way to Yogācāra.

Notwithstanding the bafflingly elusive thought of a finally idealist position that yet privileges causal description (how are we to understand causal relations among strictly mental events?), it is enough for us now to get a sense of what Dharmakīrti's commitments look like when he argues for them from the more intuitively plausible empiricist perspective that it is strategically advantageous for him generally to adopt.[19] The point to notice here is how Dharmakīrti's elaboration of the causally describable character of perception supports the case for a fundamentally *dualist* account of the mind-body relation; we will shortly see that Dharmakīrti's defense of rebirth is not so much a positive case for the particulars of the "rebirth" process as it is a case for the irreducibility of *mental* events to *physical* events. Of particular interest to us in scouting his epistemology, then, are the mental "appearances" or "representations" (as we can render Dharmakīrti's *ākāra* and *pratibhāsa*) that centrally figure in his understanding of perceptual awareness. It's as involving a fundamentally phenomenalist or *representationalist* epistemology—as involving, that is, mediating mental events that are themselves the direct objects of awareness—that Dharmakīrti's causal account of perception can be thought to fit particularly well with the idea of mind-body dualism.

Dharmakīrti's elaboration of the causally describable character of perception, then, prominently involves reference to mental representations. The beginning of his *Pramāṇaviniścaya*, for example, thus characterizes perceptible (*pratyakṣa*)[20] objects as contra the constitutively imperceptible (*parokṣa*) objects that are knowable only through inference:

> There are only two kinds of things, perceptible and imperceptible. With regard to these, that is perceptible which causes the content of awareness (*jñānapratibhāsam*) to track its own presence and absence.[21] That—

> unique, having the nature of a thing—is a unique particular (*svalakṣaṇa*). But the other, [imperceptible kind of thing], lacking the capacity for projecting its nature directly into thought, just is something acquaintance (*pratipatti*) with which is impossible.[22]

A unique particular's capacity thus to *cause* the content of awareness is contrasted, then, with everything that lacks this capacity thus to "project" (*upadhāna*) its own form "directly into thought" (*buddhau sākṣāt*). An object having specific identity criteria—some particular ruminant, say, located at an appropriate distance from an observer—can actually impinge upon a possessor of sensory capacities in such a way as to produce a cognitive representation whose content varies as a function of the object itself; an abstract item like the concept *being a cow*, in contrast, does not directly "produce" representations in anything at all like the same way.

To similar effect, Dharmakīrti says in the *Pramāṇavārttika* that "there is nothing at all worth the name 'being apprehendable' apart from being a cause."[23] Here, Dharmakīrti anticipates the objection that the sense faculties themselves should also be reckoned as causes of awareness—despite which, we do not speak of the *senses* as what is apprehended in awareness, only the objects disclosed by them.[24] How, then, can we distinguish those causes that are at the same time the *content* of awareness from whatever other causes are rightly thought to figure in the production of cognition? Dharmakīrti answers that it's particularly that cause *whose image* the awareness bears that should be reckoned as what is cognitively apprehended: "With regard to these [various causes of awareness], it's the one in whose image (*yadākārā*) thought arises that is said to be apprehended by that [thought]."[25] We are thus to identify the really existent objects of perception not only in terms of their causally constraining our awareness but also in terms of the phenomenal content that thus tracks these causes.

Insofar as it turns out to be a difficult question whether anything is really identifiable at once as the *content* of cognition and as a *cause* thereof, Dharmakīrti's apparent confidence that we know how to specify that cause "in whose image thought arises" may not be warranted. Indeed, particularly insofar as reference to the causes of cognition brings into play all manner of "sub-" or "impersonal" things (various neurological goings-on, on a contemporary reckoning), it's hard to know how we can be sure we are even talking about the same *kinds* of things at all when we say of any phenomenal object of awareness that it is also among the causes thereof. This problem was incisively scouted by Dharmakīrti's predecessor Dignāga, whose brief

Ālambanaparīkṣā ("Examination of *ālambana*") interestingly problematizes the Ābhidharmika concept on which these issues converge—that of the *ālambana-pratyaya*, which, among the various "causal conditions" (*pratyaya*) of any cognition, is the one that is at the same time the object *of* awareness (its *ālambana*).[26]

The problem, Dignāga argues, is that there seem to be good reasons for thinking that the kinds of things we typically take awareness to be of *could not be* among the causes of cognition; for while we can attribute causal efficacy only to the kinds of atomic particulars that are, for Buddhists, finally admitted as real, such things do not figure at all in the phenomenal content of awareness, which instead typically involves medium-sized dry goods. Thus, the kinds of things that can meet the causal condition do not meet the content condition, while the things that meet the content condition are not reckoned by Buddhists as having causal efficacy. Dignāga takes these considerations to recommend the conclusion that it can therefore only be something *intrinsic to awareness* that finally counts as the *ālambana-pratyaya*: "It is something whose form is knowable internally—appearing as though external—which is the object of awareness, because of its being the form of awareness, and because of its also being a causal condition thereof."[27] Only, then, something *intrinsic to awareness* could meet both of the relevant conditions.

Dignāga has to suggest, though, two ways to make sense of this claim, which we might characterize as alternately reflecting third-personal and first-personal takes on the question. Third-personally speaking—without reference, that is, to what the subject of a cognition herself takes its content to be—the internal cause of cognition is (as *causes* are typically taken to be) something temporally prior: in particular, a "seed" (*bīja*) or "latent disposition" (*vāsanā*), which, though "internal" to the mental continuum, is not itself phenomenologically accessible.[28] First-personally speaking, however—with reference to what *is* phenomenologically accessible to the subject of cognition—Dignāga's "internally knowable form" counts as meeting the causal condition *only on a different understanding of what "being a cause" consists in*. For insofar as the phenomenal content of cognition would also seem to be a *part* thereof, and thus incapable of being at the same time its cause, first-personally accessible content can satisfy the causal condition only insofar as "cause" denotes anything invariably concomitant with the occurrence of what it relates to—in the way, for example, that anything's *defining characteristic* is, ipso facto, present whenever the thing in question is.[29]

That Dignāga, even on the idealist view he takes to be recommended by the foregoing considerations, thus has to invoke a couple of senses of "being a cause" to explain how something mental can satisfy both the *causal* condition and the *content* condition is surely evidence of the difficulty of the problem here. Dharmakīrti, for his part, qualifies Dignāga's arguments on this score; though also holding a finally idealist view of the matter, Dharmakīrti accommodates his intuitions concerning the essentially causal description of perception by allowing (contra Dignāga) that, in fact, *aggregated* atoms *could* at once be "causally efficacious and correspond to the image in cognition."[30] Even so, the fact that phenomenal content thus varies as a function of really constraining causes is finally to be known, for Dharmakīrti, based on phenomenological considerations—which means it remains something *intrinsic* to awareness that represents the basis for Dharmakīrti's claims in this regard. In particular, a cognition's being genuinely caused by its object is finally evident from its phenomenal clarity and vividness—its *sphuṭatva*, or "being distinct," as the commentator Dharmottara (c. 740–800 C.E.) recurrently puts this point.

Dharmottara succinctly says, in commenting on one discussion in Dharmakīrti's *Nyāyabindu*, that cognition is nonconceptual "just insofar as its content is distinct" (*sphuṭābhatvād eva ca nirvikalpakam*); in contrast, a conceptual cognition is characterized by its being "one whose content is indistinct" (*asphuṭābham vikalpakam*).[31] Dharmakīrti himself concisely puts the point just a bit further on, at *Nyāyabindu* 1.13, where he defines really existent particulars themselves in terms of the phenomenal content they cause: "A unique particular (*svalakṣaṇa*) is that object because of proximity or nonproximity to which there is a difference in the phenomenal content of cognition."[32] Elaborating, Dharmottara strikingly relates the *ultimately existent* status of particulars to this fact: "Only that object which, depending on its proximity or nonproximity, produces (respectively) a distinct or indistinct phenomenological content is ultimately existent."[33]

The extent to which Dharmakīrti here takes his bearings from phenomenological consideration of mental content is revealing. Indeed, it is reference to phenomenal content that is finally most important for Dharmakīrti; when he lays his idealist cards on the table (as he is traditionally taken to do with his arguments for *svasaṃvitti*), Dharmakīrti will finally jettison the idea that the causes of perceptual awareness are external objects. A causal analysis can be given, he thinks, without any reference to things other than the intrinsic properties of awareness—it is, he will say in arguing for *svasaṃvitti*, just an *intrinsic* property of causally unfolding cognitions that they seem to be *of* something. To the extent, however, that it is essentially phenomenological considerations that are thus enlisted to account for perceptual cognition's being caused by real existents, the case for a causal account of perception may not be advanced; for to appeal to something *intrinsic* to awareness as evidence of external constraints thereon is to beg precisely the question at issue. Of course, it will finally be just Dharmakīrti's point (we will see in chapter 5) that insofar as it thus remains dubitable whether the phenomenologically distinctive character of perception is explicable in terms of external objects, we ought therefore to conclude that cognition is, ultimately, autonomously intelligible; for the present, however, suffice it to say again that it turns out to be difficult to get *causal* accounts together with accounts of phenomenal *content*.

We clearly have here, in any event, an elaboration of the intuitively plausible idea that perceptual cognition is distinguished by its being among the *effects* produced by causally efficacious particulars—this, finally, is why it's so important that Dharmakīrti thinks both that only causally efficacious particulars are real and that these are uniquely the objects of perception—together with the idea that *what* is thus caused by perceptible particulars is some kind of mental item that is itself the direct object of awareness: phenomenal "images" or "appearances" (*ākāra*, *pratibhāsa*). To that extent, we can say that what is on offer here is something like a sense-datum theory—an account according to which it is really some kind of subjectively occurrent representations that are the direct objects of awareness. Such a picture is perhaps most clearly stated by Dharmakīrti when he addresses the "time-lag" problem that is particularly pressing for those Buddhists who, like Dharmakīrti, uphold the doctrine of momentariness. This is the problem that perception's being an *effect* entails that there is a temporal succession involved in the production of perceptual awareness—and during that time, the perceived object changes, such that it is no longer the same thing at the moment when it becomes present to awareness. In this regard, Dharmakīrti says: "If it's asked how something is apprehendable given its having occurred at a different time, [we reply that] those who understand reasoning know [that being apprehendable] is just *being a cause* (*hetutvam eva*) that's capable of projecting an appearance (*ākāra*) into awareness."[34]

Although Dharmakīrti is guided, then, by the intuitively plausible thought that perception is uniquely constrained by real existents, to conclude that perception is therefore foundational for the objectivity of knowledge is to introduce a surprisingly strong dependence on the subjective; for what is finally caused by the world's impingements upon our sensory capacities is mental representations. This, then, is why Donald Davidson can—counterintuitively, it may seem to those who are impressed by the considerations that recommend typically empiricist accounts of the objectivity of knowledge—reasonably characterize empiricism as precisely "the view that the subjective ('experience') is the foundation of objective empirical knowledge" (1988, 46). Something like Davidson's point is advanced by some of the standard Indian doxographical characterizations of Dharmakīrti's Sautrāntika perspective, which was (like the Yogācāra perspective he finally held) taken by subsequent Indian philosophers as a paradigm case of *sākāravāda*. This names the doctrine that cognition represents the world "with appearances" (particularly as opposed to the *nirākāravāda* position that could be characterized as direct realism);[35] it would not be misleading, then, to characterize *sākāravāda* as referring to epistemological *representationalism*. In the same vein, Dharmakīrti's "Sautrāntika" perspective was often characterized (as, e.g., in the *Sarvadarśanasaṃgraha* of Mādhava, c. fourteenth century) as the view that the reality of external objects can only be inferred (*bāhyārthānumeyavāda*); Dharmakīrti's is, on this way of representing his project, a view of external reality's "being inferable from appearance" (*ākāreṇa tasyârthasyânumeyatā*).[36]

In this as in many respects, Dharmakīrti's account is strikingly similar to the empiricism of John Locke, who also took our knowledge of the external character of the constraints on knowledge to be finally inferential. For Locke, "there can be nothing more certain, than that the *Idea* we receive from an external Object is in our Minds"—despite which, he said, we are entitled to claim knowledge "of the existence of particular external Objects, by that perception and Consciousness we have of the actual entrance of Ideas from them" (1689, 537–538). What warrants this, for Locke as for Dharmakīrti, is an inference to the effect that these "Ideas" must be *caused* by something; " 'Tis therefore the actual receiving of Ideas from without, that gives us notice of the Existence of other Things, and makes us know, that something doth exist at that time without us, which causes that Idea in us" (630).

In addition to its thus dovetailing with some classically empiricist intuitions, though, Dharmakīrti's account can also be seen as recommended by some specifically Buddhist considerations. For just as an emphasis on causal descriptions of experience can be thought particularly to advance the case for selflessness, so, too, the idea that it is specifically *subjective* things that can be so described fits well with central Buddhist commitments. These can be taken to center on the role of *karma* in the Buddhist worldview. For Buddhists, it is the *karma* ("action") of sentient beings that finally explains everything about our situation—that explains, indeed, everything that a theist typically means to explain by invoking God as creator of the world. As Vasubandhu's *Abhidharmakośa* puts this point, "the manifoldness of the world is produced by the *karma* of sentient beings." The same text then immediately proceeds to say that *karma* essentially consists in *cetanā*—a word often rendered as "intention" but perhaps better rendered as *thought* (it denotes, at any rate, something constitutively mental).[37] The intuitively plausible point here is that action, at least insofar as it is ethically significant, is *intentional*—what can, that is, be cultivated by Buddhist practice is finally the *mental* dispositions that inform sentient activity. Insofar, then, as *karma* is thus enlisted to explain the constitution of our experience of the world (and, indeed, that *of the world itself*),[38] what is invoked is above all something mental.[39] The connection, then, between causal description and the subjective is part of the deep grammar of the Buddhist tradition; it is, at the end of the day, particularly *mental* events that Buddhist philosophers like Dharmakīrti would have us understand in causal terms.

While the broadly empiricist intuitions that would equate objectivity with causal constraint should not, to be sure, be taken to *entail* a dualist account of the person, we have seen that Dharmakīrti's intuitively plausible idea of perception as a privileged point of contact with the world—as, indeed, the point at which our cognitive relation to the world is causally constrained *by the world*—can be elaborated in ways that are surely congenial to the view that there is something irreducibly mental in play in cognition. Thus, this kind of account can reasonably be thought to require reference to such constitutively mental items as "representations" or "phenomenal content" (*ākāra, pratibhāsa*), which are themselves the immediate effects of our causally describable encounters with what there is. Let us now see what it looks like when Dharmakīrti argues that whatever finally causes such mental items, they cannot be thought reducible to the body.

"COMPASSION IS THE PROOF": DHARMAKĪRTI'S ARGUMENTS FOR DUALISM

As noted above, the context for Dharmakīrti's arguments for rebirth involves a case for characterizing the Buddha as *pramāṇabhūta*—a case for the view that the Buddha is somehow paradigmatically authoritative and that we are therefore entitled to the beliefs that go with commitment to the Buddhist path. The basis for Dharmakīrti's case is the thought that the Buddha exemplified a fathomlessly profound degree of compassion; as Dharmakīrti says in verse 34 of the *pramāṇasiddhi* chapter (which verse begins his case for rebirth), "the proof (*sādhanam*) is compassion."[40] In other words, the Buddha evinced such remarkable compassion that this can be taken as the basis for an inference to the Buddha's uniquely comprehensive insight.[41] That this thought should occasion the elaboration, in the remainder of the chapter, of a comprehensive defense of a Buddhist worldview nicely exemplifies, I think, what it is to do philosophy. What Dharmakīrti effectively does, in the remainder of the chapter, is systematically consider *what else must be true* for this thought to make sense—and to think philosophically about one's commitments just is to reflect carefully on what else one is committed to in virtue of believing anything. This characterization of philosophy makes sense of the thought (familiar from philosophers of hermeneutics) that there is in all meaningful statements a "surplus of meaning"; for the purport of any thought is always vastly exceeded by the innumerable states of affairs that would be entailed by its truth.

What else, then, must be the case for it to be true that the Buddha exemplified such an astonishing degree of compassion? For Dharmakīrti, the first point to be made here is that thought (*buddhi*) *cannot depend upon the body*. Thus, in the same verse in which he asserts that the Buddha's compassion warrants an inference to the Buddha's authority, Dharmakīrti avers that this compassion is based on disciplined "repetition" (*abhyāsa*) of spiritual practice—repetition, that is, over the course of innumerable lifetimes. This occasions the objection—generally attributed to a physicalist of the "Cārvāka" school,[42] and anticipated in the same verse—that this supposition is unwarranted "because of thought's dependence upon the body." The objection is that the death of the body terminates (insofar as the body is a necessary and sufficient condition of) the mental events that alone can be thought to motivate the alleged "repetition." Dharmakīrti completes this verse (and introduces the ensuing critique of physicalism) by saying that this objection to his demonstration of the Buddha's authority can be put aside "based on a refutation of [thought's] dependence [on the body]."[43]

While the ensuing refutation of physicalism is elaborated over the course of many tens of verses, most of what is significant about Dharmakīrti's characteristic position is actually stated in the next verse-and-a-quarter. Here, Dharmakīrti says: "It is not the case that inhalation, exhalation, sensation, and thought arise, independently of [causes] of the same kind, from the body alone, since there are absurd consequences given the assumption of such arising."[44] A great deal of the argument that follows consists in elaborating the various unwanted consequences of taking sentient phenomena to arise only in dependence upon the body; most of what we need to know in this regard is expressed here in the reference to causes "of the same kind" (*sajāti*).[45] His main point will be that sentient phenomena must have among their causes events that are themselves *sentient*; events, more generally, must have ontologically homogeneous causes. The straightforward claim is thus that the events constituting the physical body are ontologically distinct from those that cause mental events.

In play in Dharmakīrti's assertion here is, among other things, a standard-issue Buddhist analysis of the causal conditions of any moment of awareness. The idea, commonly elaborated in the Abhidharma literature, is that among the causes of any cognition is an immediately preceding moment of awareness—a *samanantarapratyaya*, as this is called. On a standard Ābhidharmika list of the conditions producing any moment of awareness, this "immediately preceding moment" of the same kind is one among four causal conditions. Thus, the causes of (say) a moment of ocular awareness include (1) a properly functioning visual sense faculty (this represents the "predominant condition," or *adhipatipratyaya*); (2) the object seen, reckoned as itself a *cause* of the awareness (the "condition which is an intentional object," or *ālambanapratyaya*, whose problematic status was discussed above); (3) the *samanantarapratyaya*, or immediately preceding moment of the same kind of awareness; and (4) the *hetupratyaya*, which is something of a catch-all category, comprising a collection of other relevant causal conditions.[46]

There is much to be said about the characteristically Buddhist commitments that motivate this picture and about what might be taken to recommend the view that a preceding moment of the same type must thus be among the causes of any moment of awareness; surely it could be said, at least, that this is among the categories posited by Buddhists to try to account for *continuity* in the context of what is basically a causal-reductionist project.[47] In his *Nyāyabindu*, Dharmakīrti invokes (and effectively defines) the *samanantarapratyaya* in connection with an interesting discussion of the vexed category of "mental perception" (*mānasapratyakṣa*), which is one of four kinds of supposedly immediate and nonconceptual awareness standardly counted by Dharmakīrti and his followers as examples of "perception" (*pratyakṣa*).[48] While the particulars of that debate need not detain us here, it's interesting to note that the verse in which Dharmakīrti is thus taken to define *mānasapratyakṣa* does not, in fact, use the latter word at all; rather, he here speaks instead of *manovijñāna*, or "mental awareness"—this as contra *indriyavijñāna*, or "sensory awareness." This notion is of sufficient importance that it's worth lingering for a moment on it.

Indian Buddhists shared with many other Indian philosophers the view that the sense faculties should actually be reckoned as *six*: the five familiar senses plus the "mental" (*manas*) sense faculty. The five familiar sense faculties, understood as based in material sense organs—they are typically distinguished by Buddhists as the *rūpīndriya*, "form-possessing" senses—have as their respective objects the same things we would expect: the ocular sense faculty apprehends color and shape, the auditory faculty apprehends sound, etc. The object of the "mental" sense faculty is *the outputs of the other five*. Thus, the five sense faculties whose respective organs are physical are understood, on this model, as something like simple transducers; contact between any of these and its proper objects generates a "signal" that can then be the direct object of a "mental awareness" (*manovijñāna*), which represents the cognitively contentful part of the process.

The details of this picture are, I think, somewhat obscured by the fact that the "signals" produced by each of the five bodily senses are themselves styled *vijñāna*, "awareness" or "cognition." The point in talking of fully six kinds of *vijñāna*, though, seems to be simply that what each of the material sense faculties generates is something ontologically of the kind that could itself be the *content* that is internally related to (as the direct object of) cognition, as such; but it is only when there is further produced an instance of *manovijñāna* ("*mental* awareness") that any "cognition" worth the name can really be said to have occurred. The role of the mental as a discrete faculty that thus synthesizes the outputs of the senses already stands in contrast to the views of contemporary physicalists; the "mental sense faculty" here envisioned seems, for example, rather like the idea that Daniel Dennett has disparaged as that of a "Cartesian theater"—the idea, that is, of a central spectator that takes in all of the various goings-on that underlie consciousness (and that only when this happens is there any *consciousness*).[49] To be sure, the Buddhist *manovijñāna* is imagined as a series of momentary events and not (as reference to a Cartesian metaphor might be taken to suggest) as a substance; nevertheless, this is clearly the idea that there is one kind of mental event whose function is somehow to be "about" the contributions made by all the other factors.

Here, in any case, is how Dharmakīrti (at *Nyāyabindu* 1.9) deploys the concept of *manovijñāna* together with that of *samanantarapratyaya*: "That is mental cognition (*manovijñāna)* which is produced by the immediately preceding causal condition (*samanantarapratyaya*), which in turn is a sensory cognition (*indriyajñāna)* whose support is the immediately antecedent object which is *its* proper object."[50] Dharmakīrti thus says that a "mental cognition" has as *its* object a "sensory cognition" (*indriyajñāna*); the latter in turn represents some instance of whatever kind of object is proper to the sense capacity in question. The "object" of the sensory capacity is finally *known*, then, only by the mental cognition (*manovijñāna*) and only as represented by the "signal" generated by the material sensory capacity, which is what presents itself to the mental cognition. On this account, then, there can only be said to be any cognitive *content* to the extent to that there occurs a moment of *manovijñāna*.

The commentator Dharmottara thus unpacks the lengthy compound that figures in Dharmakīrti's concise statement:

> The proper (*sva-*) object of sensory cognition, i.e., its own; the immediate successor (*anantara*) of that, i.e., [a successor that] doesn't have any interval. "*Antaram*" is said [to mean both] interval (*vyavadhāna*) and distinction (*viśeṣa*); and because of that, when "*antara*" is negated,[51] it is understood that the object of a sensory cognition has an appropriated moment, of the same type, which is arisen from a second moment. And that being the case, the moment that is subsequent to the moment of the object of the sensory cognition is grasped as included within a single continuum (*santāna*). That sensory cognition whose cooperating condition is that [i.e., this second moment of the same type] is so called.[52]

Among the conceptually significant points in this rather prolix gloss is that the categories here in play are meant to explain how it is that the various outputs of the sensory "transducers" (as I have characterized them) are "grasped as included within a single continuum" (*ekasantānāntarbhūto gṛhītaḥ*); that is, only to the extent that the various sensory output "signals" are, as it were, *received* by the mental sense can there seem to be a single stream of consciousness.

Returning, finally, to the *pramāṇasiddhi* chapter's case for rebirth: Dharmakīrti's point that the various phenomena of sentience can only arise from causes "of the same kind" (*sajāti*) dovetails with the foregoing picture, according to which it is by "mental awareness" (*manovijñāna*) that the outputs of the senses are finally cognized; awareness, then, is preceded by moments ontologically of the same kind at least insofar as the direct objects of *manovijñāna* are themselves *other events of the type* "*vijñāna*." Dharmakīrti can deploy this account to argue that awareness of sensory information is dependent upon *thought*—upon, that is, the *manovijñāna*—and not the other way around. Thus, he says in verse 39 of the *pramāṇasiddhi* chapter: "Even when there is damage of each of the sense faculties, there is not of mental cognition; but when there is destruction of the latter, destruction of the sense faculties is observed."[53] Manorathanandin concludes, in commenting on this, that "thought (*buddhi*) therefore is not dependent on those."[54] Dharmakīrti's point, it seems, is that one can have occurrent cognitions in the absence of any (or even all) of the five bodily sense faculties but not in the absence of the mental sense faculty. It is, in other words, intelligible that there be mental content without sensory input; the "unreceived" transmission of physical-sensory signals, in contrast, would not by itself constitute any awareness at all. To the extent that this asymmetry obtains, then, it is the *mental* that should be understood as conceptually basic.[55] (It has been noted with regard to the foregoing argument that Dharmakīrti, like other premodern thinkers, did not have available to him the idea that something physical other than the apparatus of the five senses—viz., *the brain*—might be invariably concomitant with awareness.)[56]

A few verses later, Dharmakīrti considers one of the problems that can be thought to arise for a proponent of the foregoing picture: if the mental faculty is thus independent of the various faculties of the body (of "material" senses), then why is cognition an invariably *embodied* phenomenon? How can it be denied that cognition depends on the body yet explained that we only see cognition exemplified in embodied beings? This is a familiar problem for dualists: to the extent that one insists on there being two irreducibly distinct *kinds* of things, it becomes difficult to explain how they can interact. Dharmakīrti's answer: "These occur together because there is no difference in their cause"—in the same way, he rather obscurely explains, that the various sense faculties of a single person are independent of one another, respectively yielding knowledge of properties of objects (color, taste, etc.) that too are independent of one another.[57] The point of the example, Eli Franco explains, is that the "sight and hearing of the same person or color and flavour of the same object always subsist together without being each other's cause" (1997, 119).[58] There must, then, be something else that should be reckoned as causing all of these things.

Franco adds that while "Dharmakīrti leaves the cause unspecified . . . all the commentaries identify it as *karman*" (1997, 119).[59] So, for example, Manorathanandin: "But if the body is not the basis [of thought], how is it they occur together? Dharmakīrti says, 'Because of the nondifference of their cause,' which [cause] is known as *karma*."[60] The *karma* of sentient beings, that is, creates (their experience of)[61] a world in which thought interacts with bodies. But *karma*, we have seen, is itself finally something mental (viz., *cetanā*); indeed, the commentator Prajñākaragupta explicitly invokes the traditional equivalence we noted from Vasubandhu, saying (in connection with verse 37 of our text) that "it is only *karma*, defined as thought (*cetanā*), which remains pre-eminent [as explaining the diversity of life]."[62] Dharmakīrti's answer to the dualist's problem of mind-body interaction—at least as that answer is unanimously understood by his commentators—again has the effect of making the mental explanatorily basic.

Much of the balance of Dharmakīrti's case for rebirth then centers on developing the absurd consequences that, on his reading, would follow from holding, contrariwise, that thought *does* depend on the body. These generally boil down to a problem that the commentators note right at the beginning, in regard to Dharmakīrti's opening contention that "there are absurd consequences" given the assumption that thought arises from the body. Thus, with regard to Dharmakīrti's initial statement (in verse 36a) to this effect, the commentator Manorathanandin anticipates a line of thought that recurs throughout the ensuing discussion: "If one assumes that respiration and so forth arise only from the material elements, then these [sentient phenomena] could arise from anything; hence, the whole world would consist of sentient beings—and that isn't the case. Therefore, there is the arising of the senses and so forth from the body only insofar as those are dependent upon previous [causes] of the same kind."[63] If, in other words, it were held that material elements could produce thought, then there would be no principled way to explain why only some arrangements of the elements do so; one would have to suppose that anything at all could give rise to awareness.

It is fitting, given the recurrence of conceptually similar arguments, that Manorathanandin's comment on the initial statement of this argument represents it as effectively completing Dharmakīrti's case for the possibility of rebirth; "hence," he says, "there is proof of connection with previous births" (*iti pūrvajanmapratibandhasiddhiḥ*).[64] The same idea—that there would be no principled way to distinguish any other arrangement of material elements from a living being if sentience depended upon the body—is in play when Dharmakīrti argues (at verse 51) that death itself would not make sense given the body's being a necessary and sufficient cause of life. As Dharmakīrti here says, "There is the unwanted consequence of thought's noncessation while the body, [even though dead, yet] abides." Manorathanandin explains that this is "because of the impossibility of the failure of an intact (*avikala*) cause, i.e., of that whose cause is the body alone, independent of [causes] of its own kind; because of that, as long as the cause obtains"—as long, that is, as a body is present—"there would be no death."[65] It cannot, that is, be the body itself that produces awareness, since the material elements do not by themselves suffice to distinguish a live body from a dead one; a material body is, after all, still present after death. This fact—that, in one contemporary philosopher's words, "the stuff out of which we're made survives us even though it seems identical to us while we're alive"[66]—remains, some still hold, a powerful objection to some accounts of what we are.

Among the things that do distinguish live from dead bodies is the occurrence of respiration; hence, the foregoing point gives rise to the question of whether respiration, like the senses, depends on thought, or vice versa. Against the interlocutor's comment that respiration continues during sleep (when, presumably, consciousness is not present), Dharmakīrti ventures the (not very promising) argument that respiration must result from conscious effort; otherwise, he suggests, awareness would wax and wane as the rate of respiration does: "How could there be exhalation and inhalation of air without effort?" (Manorathanandin explains that "effort" here is *buddhilakṣaṇa*, "characterized by thought.") "There would," Dharmakīrti continues, "obtain a decrease and increase [of cognition] because of the decrease and increase of these two."[67] This is, Manorathanandin explains, because the characteristics of an *effect* tend to correspond to the characteristics of its *cause* (*kāraṇaviśeṣānukāritvāt kāryaviśeṣasya*); thought that depended on respiration (rather than conversely) would thus have the same characteristics (viz., rising and falling) that obtain with respect to respiration.

It is perhaps tempting here to join Richard Hayes in regarding this argument as an example of Dharmakīrti's "philosophical playfulness" (1993, 121–122). I think, however, that Eli Franco is probably right to suggest that "the same argument is repeated too often to be a joke, and it is, in fact, one of the cornerstones in Dharmakīrti's doctrine of determination of a causal relationship" (1997, 237). To the extent that is right, perhaps the main thing the argument shows is the limits of the kind of causal argument Dharmakīrti is most concerned to advance. Be that as it may, Dharmakīrti clearly presses the point; thus, the foregoing argument makes it necessary for Dharmakīrti to explain what causes respiration during the kind of deep sleep in which conscious effort is clearly not in play—and, as well, why the first moment of cognition upon waking from deep sleep should not be taken as an example of a cognition caused by the bodily factors (such as respiration) that continue during sleep. While the argument here is, again, not very promising as an account of the supposedly deliberate character of respiration, it usefully illustrates what is perhaps the most difficult problem for the whole approach that takes moments of cognition invariably to have *previous moments of cognition* among their causes.

It seems, then, that some key Buddhist commitments must here be salvaged by an appeal to something like remote causation—to, that is, a remotely preceding cognition as causing the first moment of waking cognition. Here is how the commentator Prajñākaragupta (explicating verses 56 and 57) puts the point: "Neither the body nor inhaling, etc., are the cause of cognition [after dreamless sleep]; only the cognition previous [to dreamless sleep] is the cause (*pūrvakam eva vijñānaṃ kāraṇaṃ*)." This move is defensible, he argues, insofar as there would otherwise obtain the same kinds of absurd consequences, noted in regard to the case of death, that were taken to follow from supposing material factors could account for sentience; thus, Prajñākaragupta immediately adds that "if that [previous cognition] had arisen from the body, then the inadmissible consequence would follow that [the cognition] would not cease [as long as the body lasts]."[68] The appeal to a temporally remote cognition as the cause of cognition-upon-waking can thus be motivated, then, by a desire again to foreclose the unwanted conclusion that, as Manorathanandin said at the outset, sentience "could arise from anything." Expressing the same line of thought in commenting on a later verse, Prajñākaragupta says: "The cognition [after awakening], depending upon a previous trace (*saṃskāra*), arises from a [preceding] cognition, even though separated [from it in time] (*vyavahita*). There is no interruption [of the causal efficacy] of this [preceding cognition] by the [intervening] sleep."[69]

In order to salvage the idea that cognitions must always have previous cognitions among their causes, Dharmakīrti must thus hold that any cognition that is immediately preceded by an absence of consciousness is somehow caused by *the last cognition to precede the loss of consciousness.*[70] It could reasonably be objected, I think, that this compromises precisely the intuition behind the Buddhist appeal (noted at the beginning of our survey of Dharmakīrti's arguments) to the "immediately preceding moment of awareness" (*samanantarapratyaya*)—that this shows, in other words, how difficult it is to defend a reductionist account that (as Dharmakīrti arguably does) takes mental events to be explicable entirely in terms of efficient, local causation. Once it is granted, however, that the apparent interruption of awareness by sleep is not an impediment to the view that cognitions always result *from preceding cognitions*, the way is cleared for the point Dharmakīrti has all along been trying to make here.

Whatever problems there are for an account that thus invokes the possibility of remote causation, then, are not incidental to Dharmakīrti's position here; for the discussion of the case of deep sleep crucially advances the case for rebirth, which is what Dharmakīrti has all along been aiming for. "Indeed," Prajñākaragupta thus continues the foregoing passage by adding, "sleep is not able to impede the causing of awareness; since we see the arising [of cognition] even from a cognition that has been interrupted [by sleep], there is no ascertainment of a distinction, with regard to interruption, between death and sleep."[71] If, that is, unconsciousness during sleep cannot be thought to prevent the continued causal efficacy of conscious events, neither can a body's loss of consciousness at death. Thus, the conclusion: "At the beginning of birth and when awakening [from dreamless sleep], cognition is experienced only as following a previous trace."[72]

The arguments canvassed here are finally meant to show, then, that what we take to be the first moment of a newborn baby's awareness is really like the initial awareness one has upon waking from deep sleep; just as the cognitive emergence from sleep is caused by a preceding cognition (albeit, one that itself precedes an intervening period without consciousness), so, too, the "first" awareness of a baby is really not primary at all—rather, it must, for just the reasons considered here, have among its causes the last moment of awareness in what is conventionally called a "previous life." This, finally, is why it's reasonable to think the Buddha's compassion could have been cultivated over the course of innumerable lifetimes.

WHAT KIND OF ARGUMENT IS THIS? ON THE CAUSES OF COGNITION, AND THE REST OF THIS BOOK

Dharmakīrti's case for the status of the Buddha as "*pramāṇabhūta*"—a status that presupposes, on his account, the possibility of rebirth—thus comprises a series of arguments meant to show that mental events cannot be thought to depend on physical events. While Dharmakīrti will eventually make clear that it is really a case for idealism that he is finally most concerned to advance, he obviously means here at least to argue for the irreducibly *mental* character of certain events. It must be appreciated, then, that a distinctly dualist account of the mind-body relation is not incompatible with the broadly reductionist account of the person that Dharmakīrti, as a Buddhist proponent of the cardinal doctrine of "selflessness" (*anātmavāda*), is chiefly concerned to defend; one can, that is, argue that "persons" are individuated only by causal continuity (and not by anything like enduring substances), even while arguing that mental events are of an ontologically different *kind* than physical events. Thus, Dharmakīrti clearly argues for an epistemology that privileges perception especially insofar as it is causally describable (an epistemology that recommends the conclusion that only our episodic cognitions are real and that they do not inhere in anything inferable as over and above these)—while yet arguing that the causes of specifically *mental* events must themselves be ontologically of the same, distinctive kind. The Buddhist doctrine of selflessness is not, we can therefore say, incompatible with the kind of *vitalism* that Dharmakīrti has effectively developed in arguing for rebirth.[73]

If this combination of commitments raises questions about what could finally cause those mental items (*ākāras*, *pratibhāsas*) that figure in Dharmakīrti's representationalist account of perception, surely that is because these are just the kinds of questions Dharmakīrti finally means to press. When we consider (in chapter 5) his arguments to the effect that the foundational kind of perception is finally *svasaṃvitti*, or "self-awareness," we will appreciate why it is useful for him to have exploited the broadly empiricist intuitions according to which it is both the case that only particulars are real, and (with Donald Davidson) that "the subjective ('experience') is the foundation of objective empirical knowledge." For now, though, I want to conclude our present engagement with Dharmakīrti's thought by trying to characterize the kind of arguments against physicalism that he has made here—and by appreciating, as well, what our characterization may tell us about the kinds of arguments he does *not* make.

Recently elaborated arguments against physicalism have typically centered on one or both of two approaches: one (such as will be developed in chapter 3) based on the irreducibility of intentionality and propositional attitudes, the other based on the ineliminable character of phenomenal "qualia." The former approach, we will see, emphasizes *reasoning itself* as the "intentional" phenomenon par excellence and presses the points that reasoning can neither be reduced to causal terms, nor (as some would conclude from that fact) finally eliminated from an account of what we are like. The appeal to phenomenal "qualia," in contrast, takes it that the constitutively subjective character of any experience—*what it is like*, for the subject, to have that experience—is invariably *additional to* any of the objectively describable factors that might be adduced, from a third-person perspective, as explaining that; simply in virtue of being the subject of an experience, one "knows" something about it (namely, what it is phenomenally like) that is necessarily additional to anything that can be said about it objectively.

It seems clear that if either of these is the kind of approach exemplified by Dharmakīrti's case for rebirth, it would have to be the latter; we have seen, surely, that there is an emphasis, in his account of perception, on phenomenological considerations (such as that perceptual cognitions are characterized by their phenomenally vivid content), and on the constitutively "phenomenal" representations (*ākāras*, *pratibhāsa*) that are caused by perceptual encounters with the world. It does not seem right, though, to say that Dharmakīrti particularly emphasizes—or even that he notes—the peculiarly *subjective* character of these; he is not, I think, finally interested in the idea that such mental items are characterized by their being "had" *from some perspective*. Indeed, we will see that the constitutively perspectival character of experience—its representing, that is, a subjective "point of view" on the world—is arguably chief among the things that Dharmakīrti, in his capacity as a proponent of Yogācāra, finally means to deny. This is (to simplify what is an elusively complex matter at the heart of Buddhist philosophy) because what finally exists, for Dharmakīrti, is events that are somehow at once mental *and impersonal*. To argue that the irreducibly mental character of experience consists in the subjective *what-it-is-like-ness* that proponents of "qualia" identify would be, from this point of view (if we can say as much!), to exploit what Dharmakīrti finally thinks is a merely apparent fact about experience.

It is clear, rather, that Dharmakīrti's arguments for rebirth press a case for a strongly *ontological* sort of dualism—his is not, in other words, simply a "dual-aspect" view such as we might take to be recommended by the broadly Kantian line of argument to be developed in chapter 3. But it is not at all clear that his arguments for such a view reflect any of the strategies typically deployed by contemporary critics of physicalism—which is, of course, just the point of departure for this book; what is perhaps most notable about Dharmakīrti's arguments *against physicalism*, I am proposing, is the extent to which they finally depend on precisely the kinds of presuppositions that most significantly characterize physicalism, too. This is reflected, I said in beginning this chapter, in the aptness of John Taber's characterization of Dharmakīrti's critique of physicalism as centering on the question: "what *causes* a cognition?"

We can appreciate something of the significance of this characterization by attending to two more passages from the *pramāṇasiddhi* chapter's case for rebirth—passages that are revealing with regard both to the nature and the limitations of Dharmakīrti's characteristic approach. Let us start with verse 36, *pādas* b–d. It was noted above that verses 34–36a effectively encapsulate Dharmakīrti's whole argument for rebirth and that the commentator Manorathanandin accordingly concluded that "hence, there is proof of connection with previous births" (*iti pūrvajanmapratibandhasiddhiḥ*).[74] It is not insignificant that Manorathanandin thus represents the argument up to that point as demonstrating the reality only of *previous* lives; according to Eli Franco, Dharmakīrti's commentators are unanimous in then taking the remainder of verse 36 as instead concerned to establish the reality, as well, of *future* lives.[75] I must confess that it's not altogether clear to me how this and the next verse can be taken to effect this shift in a prospective direction; I take some comfort, though, in the fact that it seems not to have been entirely clear to Dharmakīrti's commentators either. Indeed, the lack of clarity here may be a testament to the difficulty of this particular case, given Dharmakīrti's characteristic commitments.[76] For our purposes, it will be enough to appreciate why this is a problem for Dharmakīrti.

Eli Franco rightly notes, in this regard, that "the inference of future life cannot be based on a *kāryahetu* and, therefore, must rely on a *svabhāvahetu*" (1997, 109). Franco thus invokes the two main kinds of inferential reasons standardly admitted by Dharmakīrti and his philosophical fellow travelers—these corresponding, for Dharmakīrti, to the only two kinds of relations that can be thought to obtain between any two things. Thus, two things—smoke and fire are a standard example—can stand in a *causal* relation (the relation of *tadutpatti*, or "arising from that") or in the kind of *conceptual* relation that obtains, on a standard example, between *being an oak* and *being a tree*, which Dharmakīrti characterizes as an "identity" (*tādātmya*) relation. Accordingly, one can perform an inference whose reason is an *effect* (such an inference is thus said to involve a *kāryahetu*, "a reason which is an effect"), from which one infers the presence of an unseen cause—as when one infers from the sight of smoke that there must be a fire; or one can perform an inference whose reason is the *nature* of the things involved (such an inference is said to involve a *svabhāvahetu*), as when one infers that something must be a *tree* insofar as it is an *oak*.

There is much to be said particularly about the latter case, which raises such questions as whether Dharmakīrti can reasonably think of it as involving a relation of *identity*, even though there is an asymmetry that makes the inference work in one direction but not in the other (for not all trees are oaks).[77] It is clear, in any case, that the inferences in Dharmakīrti's arguments for rebirth generally involve reasons that are *effects*; he would have us infer, that is, that simply insofar as any present moment of awareness obtains, there must always already have been a preceding such moment as its *cause*, on pain of accepting the problematic consequences that he thinks are entailed by assuming otherwise. The point to be made for the time being is just that, whether or not the arguments here considered are promising, it's hard to see how Dharmakīrti can, in light of his commitments, offer any other kind of argument.

This is because conceptual relations, by his own account, cannot give us knowledge of *existential* facts; whatever we might say about the kind of "nature" (*svabhāva*) that is involved, for Dharmakīrti, in the "identity" relation—and we will see in chapter 4 that he finally gives a basically causal account even of this relation—facts about concepts remain essentially *nominal* for Dharmakīrti and therefore cannot warrant any conclusions about anything to do with *what is really existent* (about what is, in Dharmakīrti's Buddhist idiom, *paramārthasat*). This is, among other things, to say that Dharmakīrti does not have available to him anything like *metaphysical* arguments. While there are many philosophers who would conclude that that is so much the better for Dharmakīrti, it means at least that he can, despite the evident desire of his commentators to see something more in verses 36–37, only reason inductively about the reality of rebirth. To the extent, however, that some of the centrally contested questions in philosophy of mind have to do (as I said in the introduction) with whether basic issues in philosophy of mind are finally *empirical* or whether instead they are somehow metaphysical or transcendental, the difficulty of Dharmakīrti's making the case the commentators want to see him making in verses 36–37 may reflect a significant blind spot.

The other passage that I find instructive regarding the nature and limits of Dharmakīrti's characteristic mode of argument comes when he clarifies that talk of thought's *dependence* on this or that—as he puts it in verse 34, thought's *āśraya*[78]—is really talk of the *causes* of thought. Trying to explain, then, that thought's always occurring with a body cannot be taken to show that the latter is a *cause* of thought, Dharmakīrti says in verse 49: "That is a cause whose presence (*sattā*) assists [in realizing the effect in question], due to its always being connected to that effect." Of the remainder of this verse, Eli Franco comments: "In a rather abrupt manner Dharmakīrti adds that it was with this kind of cause in mind that the Buddha used the locative and the ablative cases in the two formulations of *pratītyasamutpāda* (i.e., *asmin sati, idaṃ bhavati* and *asyotpādād idam utpadyate*)."[79] Franco thus follows Dharmakīrti's commentators in seeing a reference by Dharmakīrti to two canonical formulations of the standard Buddhist claim that things—preeminently, of course, moments of experience—arise only in dependence upon other things. One such formulation involves a locative absolute construction: "when this exists (*asmin sati*), that arises (*idaṃ bhavati*)"; the other involves a use of the ablative case: "because of the arising (*utpādāt*) of this, that is arisen."

Manorathanandin takes Dharmakīrti's point to be that only when something like either of these expressions can properly be used can we be confident in having identified a thing's *cause*; thus, "it's not just the 'auxiliary factors' (*upakāraka*) that [can be said to be the] *āśraya* [of anything]; rather, it is the producer (*nirvartaka*). So, [Dharmakīrti] says, 'That whose existence assists the thing to be produced—that is a cause, only that (*sa eva*) is the *āśraya.*'"[80] These canonically Buddhist conditions for the identification of anything as a cause amount, in effect, to the same conditions that are referred to, in various contexts within the Sanskritic world of discourse, as *anvaya* and *vyatireka*. In the context of Indian logic, for example, these are often translated as something like (respectively) "positive and negative concomitance." In that context, these terms pick out (again, respectively) the facts that, (a), every instance of some inferential reason is known to occur with the thing inferred therefrom—wherever, e.g., there's smoke, there's fire; and, (b), that there is no known case of the reason's occurring where the thing to be inferred is not also present.[81] Similarly, in the context of discussions among Indian grammarians, *anvaya* and *vyatireka* pick out the conditions for learning the proper use of a word: one first learns what, say, "cow" refers to by hearing the word uttered in the presence of some particular ruminants (*anvaya*) and not when such things are not somehow present (*vyatireka*).[82]

So, too, Dharmakīrti, with his invocation of two standard Buddhist formulations of *pratītyasamutpāda*, now says nothing more than that something counts as a *cause* of X just in case, (a), it is invariably present prior to the emergence of X, and, (b), its absence corresponds to the failure of X to occur. Indeed, Dharmakīrti explicitly invokes the *anvaya* and *vyatireka* conditions in the passage from the *Pramāṇaviniścaya* with which we began our consideration, in the first section of this chapter, of Dharmakīrti's causal account of perception. There, I translated him as saying that "that is perceptible which causes the content of awareness to track its own *presence and absence*"—thus rendering "*anvaya-vyatirekāv ātmano 'nukārayati.*"[83] That a perceptible object, then, *causes* the perceptual cognition thereof is finally clear, for Dharmakīrti, simply from the fact that a phenomenologically vivid cognition occurs when such an object is present and does not occur when such an object is absent.[84]

There are many things that might be asked with regard to this idea—whether, for example, it is begging the question thus to invoke the actual presence or absence of a causally efficacious particular based only on the *phenomenological* character of the cognition thereof. The main point I want to note for now, though, is that Dharmakīrti's understanding here amounts to what G. F. Schueler—in the context of considering (what will much concern us in this book) whether *reasons* should really be understood as *causes*—has characterized as a "promissory note" understanding of causation.[85] That is, the *anvaya* and *vyatireka* conditions for the identification of anything as a cause do not tell us anything at all about what *kind* of relation "causation" finally is; to discover that these conditions obtain is not, ipso facto, to discover the *causing* that is itself supposed to be picked out by these.[86] To say as much, of course, is in effect to make a characteristically Humean point about causation; as Hume said in this regard, "When I cast my eye on the *known qualities* of objects, I immediately discover that the relation of cause and effect depends not in the least on *them*. When I consider their *relations*, I can find none but those of contiguity and succession" (1739, 77).

This familiar critique does not, to be sure, spell doom for all projects that invoke causation; Hume, for one, certainly did not conclude from his observation that we should therefore jettison the category. To the extent, however, that causal explanation is taken (as by Dharmakīrti) to have a peculiarly privileged status—for Dharmakīrti, recall, only causal relations among causally efficacious particulars are finally *real*—it is reasonable to think we are owed something more of an account than is on offer in the standard Buddhist formulations of *pratītyasamutpāda* to which we have now seen Dharmakīrti allude. I think, then, that there is a real question whether Dharmakīrti's conception of causal relations can finally bear the weight these are asked to carry in his philosophical project. We will see in chapter 6 that Dharmakīrti himself was not unmindful of the limits of appeals to causation—but we will also have seen, by then, that such appeals are doing enough work for him that his acknowledgment may be hollow. In particular, I will argue in this regard that much of what Dharmakīrti says, perhaps especially in elaborating the *apoha* doctrine—which, on my reading, amounts to a peculiarly causal account of conceptual mental content—depends on his supposing specifically that only *efficient* causation is finally real; this is, indeed, why it makes sense that his *apoha* doctrine should be finally grounded (as we will see in chapter 5) in his account of *svasaṃvitti*, or "self-awareness."

In the next chapter, we will see that some contemporary physicalists, too, have supposed that everything about the mental must similarly be explicable in terms of the kinds of efficient-causal relations that, on Jerry Fodor's account, recommend our adopting a position of "methodological solipsism."

Before turning to that, however, let us briefly consolidate our findings here. We have seen something of Dharmakīrti's characteristic epistemological intuitions, which I have characterized as generally empiricist; in particular, we have seen something of his characteristically causal account of perceptual cognition. We have seen as well that such an account involves, for Dharmakīrti, significant reference to the phenomenological vividness of perceptual awareness as well as to the constitutively *mental* representations (*ākāras, pratibhāsas*) that he takes to be produced by our causally describable encounters with the world. And we have seen, finally, a striking defense of a clearly dualist account of the mind-body relation (or at least, an account of the irreducibility of mental events to physical events)—one, it seems, according to which precisely such events as Dharmakīrti's mental representations cannot, in the end, be thought reducible to the physical events that constitute the body.

It is unmistakably clear from this defense of the possibility of rebirth that Dharmakīrti is emphatically not a physicalist; it seems, to that extent, that he would likely have no truck with those cognitive-scientific philosophers of mind for whom questions of the *mental* are finally to be understood as questions about the *brain*. But I have tried to suggest, as well, that Dharmakīrti's defense of rebirth is as striking for the kinds of arguments that are not available to him as it is for the arguments he does make. In particular, Dharmakīrti's overriding concern to argue entirely from consideration of the *causes* of cognition means he not only cannot make arguments that press the case for the mental's involving something other than causal relations, but also that he may be vulnerable to such arguments himself. To that extent—and notwithstanding his unmistakably strong critique of physicalism—Dharmakīrti's philosophical project may in the end share precisely the presuppositions that most significantly and problematically characterize physicalism. Like contemporary physicalist philosophers of mind, Dharmakīrti can be understood as finally concerned to "naturalize" the intentionality of the mental; arguments to the effect that that is a problematic undertaking will cut, then, as much against him as against physicalists.

2

The Cognitive-Scientific Revolution

COMPUTATIONALISM AND THE PROBLEM OF MENTAL CAUSATION

[The computer metaphor is] the only respect in which contemporary Cognitive Science represents a major advance over the versions of [representational theories of mind] that were its eighteenth- and nineteenth-century predecessors.

—Jerry Fodor

THE "AMAZINGLY HARD PROBLEM": MENTAL CAUSATION AND PHILOSOPHY OF MIND

In an article surveying the state of a widely entertained philosophical discussion, Paul Boghossian ventures the conclusion that "meaning properties appear to be neither eliminable, nor reducible. Perhaps it is time that we learned to live with that fact" (1989, 548). Boghossian's conclusion follows from his survey of "the rule-following considerations"—from a line of argument, that is, framed by Saul Kripke's (1982) influential reading of Wittgenstein's famous but elusive arguments concerning the impossibility of a private language. On Boghossian's account, these arguments most fundamentally disclose the *normativity* of conceptual content—the fact, on one way of putting the point, that the content of any belief may not be identifiable apart from considerations having to do with how or whether it might be true. As Boghossian says, "if I mean something by an expression, then the potential infinity of truths that are generated as a result are *normative* truths: they are truths about how I *ought* to apply the expressions, if I am to apply it in accord with its meaning, not truths about how I *will* apply it" (1989, 509). Boghossian takes it that the rule-following considerations suggest that our understanding any thought or expression *as meaning* what it's about cannot be explained by reference only (for example) to behavioristic dispositions; the normativity that constitutively characterizes mental content cannot be accounted for in terms that are not themselves normative or semantic.

I'll explore "normativity" more in chapter 3; for now, I want to focus our concerns by considering what Boghossian thinks is the most difficult problem occasioned by his argument for the ineliminability of *meaning* from our understanding of mental content. What makes this conclusion hard to accept, he says, is "the question of mental causation: how are we to reconcile an anti-reductionism about meaning properties with a satisfying conception of their causal or explanatory efficacy?" More starkly, "how is an anti-reductionist about content properties to accord them a genuine causal role without committing himself, implausibly, to the essential incompleteness of physics? This is, I believe, the single greatest difficulty for an anti-reductionist conception of content" (1989, 548–549).[1]

The problem thus introduced by Boghossian is basically the converse of the problem we saw Dharmakīrti address in the last chapter. While Dharmakīrti was concerned with how or whether physical events might give rise to moments of mind, the problem raised by Boghossian is how or whether mental content can cause physical events in the body. After all, human bodies are manifestly material objects and so, presumably, subject to whatever laws of physics we take to describe the actions of other such objects. Is there a way, then, to understand the content of mental events to be causally efficacious with respect to the physically described actions of our bodies, so that intentional phenomena—phenomena like *believing* something or *having a reason*—can be thought to play some explanatory role in our behavior? While the conscious character of the mental has been characterized by some philosophers as "the hard problem," the question now before us has been characterized as *the amazingly hard problem.*[2]

The difficulty is that it's hard to see how the semantic content of reasons and beliefs could *cause* anything, insofar as such content constitutively involves the kinds of abstractions (concepts, states of affairs, linguistic universals) that, as Dharmakīrti emphasizes, do not have causal efficacy. Many have supposed that things like *having a reason* must therefore admit of description otherwise than in terms of their semantic content—that reasons and beliefs really *do* whatever they do only under some description (as, say, "instantiated in neurophysiological event *x*") that may not make reference to what their subjects take them to be about. Whether it makes sense to think this is right is among the central issues of Kant's *Critique of Practical Reason*, which centers on the question "whether pure reason of itself alone suffices to determine the will or whether it can be a determining ground of the will only as empirically conditioned" (1788, 12). This is the question whether propositional attitudes are finally significant *in virtue of their semantic content*—whether, in a different idiom, persons are *responsive to reasons as such*—or whether, instead, these are explanatorily significant only insofar as they can also be described as particular states or events (brain events, for example) with specific identity criteria. The problem of mental causation particularly motivates the latter conclusion; insofar as things like *the truth of a claim* cannot cause such physical events as muscle contractions, it must therefore be, as G. F. Schueler says in sketching the guiding intuition here, "the *things* ('mental states') that *have* these true or false contents that do the explaining" (2003, 58).

Elaborating on the difficulties thus raised by his arguments for the ineliminability of meaning, Boghossian invokes Donald Davidson, who is widely taken to have shown that "if propositional attitude explanations are to rationalize behaviour at all, then they must do so by causing it" (Boghossian 1989, 549). Davidson's essay "Actions, Reasons, and Causes" (1963) is indeed a *locus classicus* for the issues here at stake, and we can usefully sharpen some of the questions about mental causation by briefly considering it. Against the many philosophers who have held that "the concept of cause that applies elsewhere cannot apply to the relation between reasons and actions"—that, more particularly, "nonteleological causal explanations do not display the element of justification provided by reasons" (1963, 9)—Davidson argued that "the justifying role of a reason . . . depends upon the explanatory role, but the converse does not hold. Your stepping on my toes neither explains nor justifies my stepping on your toes unless I believe you stepped on my toes, but *the belief alone, true or false, explains my action*" (1963, 8; emphasis added).

This amounts to a "nonteleological" sort of explanation in the sense that it brackets (what is arguably integral to the content of a belief) the possible *truth* of the belief from the subject's perspective. Insofar as one acts *for a reason*, one might be said to act in order to realize a not-yet-obtaining state of affairs, where the possible realization relates closely to questions of truth. This represents the *telos* in virtue of which the action is judged *intentional*—a point Kant expressed by characterizing the problem of mental causation as that of "how the *ought*, which has never yet happened, can determine the activity of this being and can be the cause of actions whose effect is an appearance in the sensible world" (1788, 96).[3] The point is that what is needed for a solution to the problem of mental causation is an account that makes reference particularly to *efficient* causes. This is because the events we want to understand in this case are epitomized by bodily movements; insofar as those clearly originate in the central nervous system, and insofar as physical causation is local, any entertainings-of-reasons that can be causally efficacious must therefore finally be similarly "in" specifiable mental states or brain states. So, what is really at issue is (in Schueler's words) "whether reasons explanations, which *on their face* always involve goals or purposes . . . are completely analyzable in terms of *efficient* causes which make no essential reference to any goals or purposes" (2003, 18).[4]

Now, whatever Davidson's arguments show, we can reasonably ask whether they vindicate the idea that reasons are causes *in the strong sense thus demanded by the problem of mental causation.* Davidson's argument turns on his analysis of the word "because": "Central to the relation between a reason and an action it explains is the idea that the agent performed the action *because* he had the reason" (1963, 9). It won't do, Davidson urges, to suppose that this relation is satisfactorily accounted for simply by the use of such an expression in the context of justifying an action—what is wanted is an *explanation* of the justificatory use; "the notion of justification becomes as dark as the notion of reason until we can account for the force of that 'because' " (1963, 9). Davidson argues that what is explanatorily basic must be a description under which the reason *causes the agent's actions*; the *justificatory* use of the word "because" is intelligible, he says, only insofar as "a primary reason for an action is its cause" (1963, 12).[5] Davidson's claim is thus that an action is reasonably judged to have been done for a reason whenever its *cause* is somehow the same as what shows up in expressions like "*He did it because . . .*"

It is, however, only a very minimal sense of causation that is vindicated by this argument; all we are entitled to conclude from this is that a "primary reason" is a cause in the sense of being *somehow* concomitant with an intentional action. This amounts to what Schueler characterizes as a promissory note: "The term 'because' cites *the fact that* there is an explanatory story connecting two things, but by itself actually *tells* none of that story at all" (2003, 14)—an observation, he says, that should have the effect of "demystifying claims about causation such as Davidson's" (2003, 17). Like the point I raised regarding one of Dharmakīrti's formulations of the causal relation,[6] Schueler's is a basically Humean point about the limits of causal explanations; to affirm that one's reason is a cause in Davidson's sense is to affirm little more than that relations of Hume's "contiguity and succession" obtain. But that hardly suffices to separate *final* from *efficient* causation.

Whatever the cogency of Davidson's arguments, then, they do not obviously support the conclusion that reasons (or even *reason-containing mental states*) must finally consist in the kinds of things that can function as the efficient causes of physical events.

However, some of Davidson's formulations do stack the deck in favor of such a view. For example, he expresses one objection to his own position as being to the effect that "primary reasons consist of attitudes and beliefs, *which are states or dispositions*, not events; therefore they cannot be causes" (1963, 12; emphasis added). But the question of our responsiveness to reasons as such is begged by too quickly identifying propositional attitudes with "states or dispositions"; the latter should, rather, be understood as *having* whatever semantic content figures in reasons explanations, and the question just is whether it is *in terms of their content* that reasons might be significant for action.[7] To allow, then, that talk of "attitudes and beliefs" is, ipso facto, talk of "states or dispositions" is already to concede the point that Kant took to be most crucially at issue—already to concede that reason "can be a determining ground of the will only as empirically conditioned," leaving altogether out of account the possibility that "reason of itself alone suffices to determine the will" (1788, 12).[8] If it's really just content-bearing "states or dispositions" that explain the sense in which reasons are explanatorily significant—if it's only under a different description (*as instantiated in mental state* X) that a belief can really be thought to *do* anything—then the semantic content of the reasons "had" by these states may turn out to be epiphenomenal.[9] Insofar as everything we want to understand can on such a view be accounted for without any reference to what beliefs are *about*, it is arguably no longer *beliefs* that we are talking about at all.

ENTER COMPUTATIONALISM

For Jerry Fodor, too, the problem of mental causation is paramount, and the foregoing issues figure centrally in his work. An influential proponent particularly of the "computational" program of cognitive-scientific research, Fodor is perhaps most widely known for his defense of the *language of thought* (or "mentalese") hypothesis, which has its place in a computational account of the mental. The problem of mental causation drives such an account. Computational accounts of the mental, that is, represent a contemporary iteration of the idea that "meaningful" or "contentful" episodes of awareness will also admit of an altogether different description—one in terms of which they can be understood as causally efficacious with respect to the body. Fodor's approach, then, centrally involves "that part of psychology which concerns itself with the mental causation of behavior" (1980, 277). Indeed, Fodor's view is that "a cognitive theory seeks to connect the *intensional* properties of mental states"—the character of mental states, that is, *as* contentful—"with their *causal* properties vis-à-vis behavior. Which is, of course, exactly what a theory of the mind ought to do" (1980, 292). Fodor thus affirms that an account such as his is "required by theories of the mental causation of behavior" (1980, 292).

Fodor embraces a broadly empiricist tradition of thought that includes the likes of Locke, Hume, and Berkeley, whom he takes commonly to have advanced the kind of *representational theory of mind* that he also favors. The salient point of such theories is their aiming to explain "how there *could be* states that have the semantical and causal properties that propositional attitudes are commonsensically supposed to have" (Fodor 1985, 79). These accounts commonly represent an empiricist answer to Kant's question (noted above) whether "reason of itself alone suffices to determine the will, or whether it can be a determining ground of the will only as empirically conditioned." Upholding the latter alternative, representational theories of mind amount to a paradigm case of the view that it is only *as empirically conditioned* that reasons do what they do; for these are theories, on Fodor's account, according to which it is the empirically real *things* ("representations") that *have* content that do the explaining.[10] Such theories most basically involve, then, some kind of reference to particular mental events or states (*representations*) that are at once the "bearers" of mental content and themselves the causes of behavior. (Insofar as they are suitable as *causes*, these representations will also be finally describable as *effects*—the effects, for example, of environmental stimulus of sensory capacities.)

It is particularly with respect to these modern empiricist accounts, Fodor suggests, that we can understand the revolutionary character of computationalism; for the availability of the computer metaphor enables us to abandon the problematic "associationism" of the earlier accounts and thus to address what had always been their principal weakness. Indeed, Fodor says in this regard that the significance of the computer model represents "the *only* respect in which contemporary Cognitive Science represents a major advance over the versions of [representational theories of mind] that were its eighteenth- and nineteenth-century predecessors" (1985, 93). As for the "associationist" accounts that are thus superseded by the appeal to computational processes, Fodor rightly thinks it chief among the failures of predecessor approaches to the problem of mental causation that they "failed to produce a credible theory of the [propositional] attitudes. No wonder everybody gave up and turned into a behaviourist" (1985, 93). Earlier iterations of the representational theory of mind may have managed, among other things, to explain how mental states could be causally efficacious, but only at the cost of making the *content* of such states finally epiphenomenal; "Cognitive Science," Fodor says, "is the art of getting the cat back in" (1985, 93). The possibility, then, of addressing the problem of mental causation *while still saving mental content* represents, at the end of the day, the major promise of the computational version of cognitivism.

Chief among the obstacles to "getting the cat back in," we noted above with reference to Paul Boghossian, is the normativity of mental content. It is difficult to give an account of the mental that makes reference only to things (neuroelectrical events, for example) that can be causally efficacious with respect to the body *and* thereby to explain the kind of cognitive content—that of an act of believing, for example—regarding which one could be judged right or wrong. The difficulty is that the relations involved in *believing something to be true*—relations such as *being warranted or correct in virtue of another belief*—are not obviously reducible to causal relations among particulars. Even, for example, to judge two objects as the same involves, it seems, reference to some additional fact (*their being the same*) that is not itself either of the particular objects, and that is not obviously *seen* in the same way these are. To that extent, however, it turns out to be very hard to say what it is in virtue of which one could be right or wrong in so taking things.

The problems here at issue can be gleaned from John Locke's canonical statement of a representationalist view of the mental:

> Since *the Mind*, in all its Thoughts and Reasonings, hath no other immediate Object but its own *Ideas*, which it alone does or can contemplate, it is evident, that our Knowledge is only conversant about them. *Knowledge* then seems to me to be nothing but *the perception of the connexion and agreement, or disagreement and repugnancy of any of our Ideas*. In this alone it consists. (1689, 525)

The problem we are scouting here is that of explaining this "connexion and agreement" among ideas; what is it in virtue of which one could be judged right or wrong in thinking "connexion and agreement" to obtain? Can one's knowing this be finally explained with reference only to particulars, or are "connexion and agreement" constitutively abstract relations?[11] Locke is ultimately committed to explaining these in terms of particulars; in thrall to the ocular metaphor that Richard Rorty takes to drive Locke's empiricism, Locke can only say you just *see* them.[12] While this is a problematic answer, it is hard to see what other resources the empiricist has for understanding the relations among concepts and thoughts.

Hence, on Fodor's view, the question that was never satisfactorily addressed by predecessor proponents of representational theories of mind is what things like *believing* and *inferring* could be, "such that thinking the premisses of a valid inference leads, so often and so reliably, to thinking its conclusion" (1985, 91). What could these intentional phenomena be, more particularly, if things like *being led to a conclusion* will not readily admit of a causal description? "How," as Vincent Descombes effectively puts the same point, "can a mechanical sequence of mental states also be a chain of reasoning?" (2001, viii–ix). This, finally, is the problem with respect to which computers have been found helpful; computers, as Fodor says, represent "a solution to the problem of mediating between the causal properties of symbols and their semantic properties" (1985, 94). The computer model helps us imagine how the particular states or events that *bear* mental content might really do the causing, but without our having to deny that those states can also be individuated by their content. Thus, computers surely involve causally describable operations involving information-bearing states, but these operations "respect" the semantic character of the states involved—leave intact, that is, the fact of their being *about* something—in the sense, at least, that these computational operations can also be taken to *represent the steps in an argument.*

Consider, in this regard, the operation of a simple calculator.[13] Its execution of an algorithm can be described entirely in causal terms: the completion of each instruction causes the machine to pass into a consequent electrical state, which in turn causes successor states as a function of the algorithm. What is remarkable is that these causally describable electrical events at the same time represent a *calculation*—something, that is, that can also be represented in terms of the steps of an argument. Here, then, is a causally describable sequence of states that seems precisely to *be* a chain of reasoning. What is thus advanced by the computer analogy is a way to imagine that semantically meaningful phenomena—contentful mental events like entertaining reasons or beliefs—can be explained with reference to (as, for example, *really consisting in*) causally efficacious states. Computational processes provide a model for understanding how processes can be described at the same time in *causal* terms (like the conduction of electricity through the circuits of a computer) and in logical or *semantic* terms (the terms, that is, in which the same process can be understood as an *argument*).

Fodor puts the point thus: "I take it that computational processes are both *symbolic* and *formal*. They are symbolic because they are defined over representations, and they are formal because they apply to representations in virtue of (roughly) the *syntax* of the representations" (1980, 279). That is, such processes immediately operate only (I suppose) with respect to electromagnetically represented zeros and ones, which are all the computer need "know" anything about; but despite their thus *doing* all the computing in these "syntactically" describable terms, computers operate regarding states that can also be readily understood, "semantically," as *meaning* something (for the user of a computer, anyway). Of the "syntactic" description of the terms involved in computational processes, Fodor explains:

> What makes syntactic operations a species of formal operations is that being syntactic is a way of *not* being semantic. Formal operations are the ones that are specified without reference to such semantic properties of representations as, for example, truth, reference, and meaning. . . . Formal operations apply in terms of the, as it were, shapes of the objects in their domains. (1980, 279)

More precisely, "the syntax of a symbol is one of its second-order *physical* properties. To a first approximation, we can think of its syntactic structure as an abstract feature of its (geometric or acoustic) shape" (Fodor 1985, 93; emphasis mine).[14]

On Fodor's usage, then, "syntactic" relations can be thought of as those obtaining not just (or not finally) among *words* but between all the *meaningful* parts of utterances—including those aspects of sentences having to do with what linguists mean by "syntax"—and the nonmeaningful *physical* factors that are the enabling conditions of any sentence's being expressed and understood. The gap that is thus meant to be bridged by the appeal to computer models is, in other words, not one between items that are all already understood *as* "meaning" something (since the possibility of that is just what we want to explain); rather, it is the gap between meaningful items (sentences, thoughts, etc.) and the causally describable particulars (acoustic or printed "shapes") that are somehow the *vehicles* of such items.

It is clear, in any case, that Fodor's "formal" and "syntactic" here are most significantly to be understood as meaning *causally describable*. Fodor is speaking to this point when he notes—apropos of how "the representational theory of mind and the computational theory of mind merge here"—that, "on the one hand, it's claimed that psychological states differ in content only if they are relations to type-distinct mental representations" (1980, 292). That is, insofar as any two people experience different cognitive content, it is, on a representational theory of mind, just because they have distinct mental states involving different, subjectively occurrent representations. On the other hand, however, the real point in thus invoking representational states is that only these are the kinds of things that can be thought to enter into causal relations. To that extent, the salient point about representations is that they are events or "states" with spatio-temporal identity criteria (they are *particulars*) such that they can be said to differ from one another in something like the way that, say, marks on a page differ from one another; cognitive processes, Fodor thus holds, "are constituted by causal interactions among mental representations, that is, among semantically evaluable mental particulars" (2006, 135). Computers, then, complement the representational theory of mind by offering a way to imagine how phenomena like *believing* something might really "do" what they do at the level of description that involves particulars, since (Fodor says) "computations just *are* processes in which representations have their causal consequences in virtue of their form" (1980, 292). Significantly, though, it's finally in terms only of such particulars that the real explaining is done; "only formal properties of mental representations contribute to their type individuation for the purposes of theories of mind/body interaction" (1980, 292).

Phenomena like *having a reason*, on this view, can thus be understood as interacting with the body only insofar as they can be individuated in terms of something other than their content. To the extent, in other words, that we would understand them in their capacity as causally efficacious with respect to the body, these representational "states" must be held to differ from one another not only in terms of what they are *about* but also (and primarily) in terms of their "as it were, shapes." "Or, to put it the other way 'round," Fodor concludes, "it's allowed that mental representations affect behavior in virtue of their content, but it's maintained that mental representations are distinct in content only if they are also distinct in form" (1980, 292). The point chiefly advanced by this is thus that being *contentful* is secondary to representations' having whatever *causal* properties they do; when it comes to mental representations, their being distinct in *form* is what does the explaining. While it is thus "allowed" that the content of these representations is significant with respect to behavior, Fodor's view is that their *being* contentful must finally be explicable in the same "formal," "syntactic," or *causal* terms in which we understand them also to be the efficient causes of bodily actions.

NARROW CONTENT AND METHODOLOGICAL SOLIPSISM: FODOR'S BRIEF FOR INTERIORITY

It's in the context of an account like the foregoing that Fodor develops his commitment to the related ideas of "narrow content" and "methodological solipsism." These are parts of a case for thinking there are states of mental representing that are *contentful* (that are somehow *about* something), but not in anything like the abstract way in which linguistic items are about what they mean. What is wanted is thus a kind of "aboutness" that is somehow inextricably related to a mental event's character *as* causally efficacious—a place, as it were, where the *intentional* properties of a mental state (its being contentful) come together with its *causal* properties. Here it is not beside the point to recall Dharmakīrti's consideration of the problem of how to distinguish those causes that are at the same time the *objects* of awareness from whatever other causes figure in the production of cognition.[15] Dharmakīrti's problem, too, was to get the *intentional* and the *causal* descriptions of mental events to come together. (We saw, in this regard, that Dharmakīrti rather question-beggingly answered that it is just that cause *whose image* an awareness bears that should be reckoned as what is cognitively apprehended.) Fodor is similarly after an explanation that comes to rest with mental events that are somehow *about* the same things that will admit of causal description.

Interestingly, we will see that Fodor is after something like the same thing when it comes to his philosophy of language; with regard to linguistic reference, he also advocates an account that is finally grounded in linguistic items—paradigmatically, words on the occasion of their first learning—that are somehow "about" their causes. To the extent that the issues thus dovetail here, we can return again to Boghossian's reflections on the rule-following considerations and say that Fodor's approach resembles what Boghossian characterizes as an "optimality" version of a dispositional theory. The idea behind such an account, on Boghossian's view of the matter, "is that there is a certain set of circumstances—call them 'optimality conditions'—under which subjects are, for one or another reason, incapable of mistaken judgements" (1989, 537).

On one important version of such an account, "optimal conditions are the conditions under which the meaning of the expression was first acquired" (Boghossian 1989, 537). Thus, someone's *meaning* something by any thought or utterance might be thought to be finally fixed by some paradigm instance—one that can be described in terms of the ostension of particulars. Such an account was famously suggested by St. Augustine:

> When they (my elders) named some object, and accordingly moved towards something, I saw this and I grasped that the thing was called by the sound they uttered when they meant to point it out. Their intention was shewn by their bodily movements, as it were the natural language of all peoples. . . . Thus, as I heard words repeatedly used in their proper places in various sentences, I gradually learnt to understand what objects they signified. . . .
>
> (CONFESSIONS 1.8, AS QUOTED AND TRANSLATED IN WITTGENSTEIN 1958, 2)[16]

Insofar as one's *meaning* anything by words so learned can, then, ultimately be understood in terms of memory of some particular occasion, the intelligibility of this does not require reference to universals.

Whatever the specifics of the "optimality conditions" on offer, the upshot is a *dispositional* reconstruction of meaning facts, such that (for example) "for Neil to mean horse by 'horse' is for Neil to be disposed to call only horses 'horse,' when conditions are optimal" (Boghossian 1989, 538). Significantly, these "optimal conditions" must be such that they will admit of a finally causal description; this is, Boghossian says, really the idea that "there is a set of *naturalistically specifiable* conditions under which [a subject] cannot make mistakes in the identification of presented terms" (1989, 538; emphasis added). Not only, then, will this account go through only if the specified conditions really are such as to preclude the possibility of error, but "the conditions must be specified purely naturalistically, without the use of any semantic or intentional materials—otherwise, the theory will have assumed the very properties it was supposed to provide a reconstruction of" (1989, 538). Insofar, that is, as the point of these "dispositional" accounts is to *explain* how we mean things by thoughts and utterances, it will not do for the explanation itself to presuppose that we already understand the idea of *being meaningful*.

Fodor's "narrow content" is meant to fit the same bill; what is picked out by Fodor's notion, too, is "naturalistically specifiable conditions" meant to ground or explain awareness's *being*, in general, contentful.[17] The main point to understand about narrow content, then, is that it's to be understood in such a way that it will admit of description both in terms of its content *and* in terms of its causal properties. The contrastive category of "broad content," on this account, picks out the level at which we entertain discursively elaborated judgments (like "it's sunny outside")—judgments, that is, which are intelligible only with reference to the conditions under which they would be true. This is, we have begun to appreciate, a level of description that involves normativity; the main point to be made about that in the present context is that *what it is in virtue of which* one could be right or wrong about such judgments surely includes a great many things (facts having to do with *its being sunny outside*, facts about conventions for the use of the word "sunny," etc.) that are external to a subject. What Fodor aims to explain, though, is how we can get judgments like "it's sunny outside" out of the kinds of things—photostimulation of retinal nerve endings, for example—that can themselves serve as the efficient causes of behavior. Precisely to the extent, however, that it will thus admit of causal description, this level of contentfulness must be "narrow" in the sense that it is explicable in terms that can be individuated independently of factors external to the subject. "The intrinsic nature of inner states and events," as John McDowell says of this kind of approach, must be "a matter of their position in an internal network of causal potentialities, in principle within the reach of an explanatory theory that would not need to advert to relations between the individual and the external world" (1998, 250).[18]

Chief among the considerations recommending such a view is that the brain states that must (if they are to be the efficient causes of bodily actions) ultimately *have* whatever content we're aware of are themselves *inside the head*. It seems, to that extent, that it must be possible to individuate the content of mental events in terms that will somehow admit of its thus being "in" one's head. But what can be "in" the head does not include, for example, the various factors out there in the world that would have to obtain in order for one's thought to be *true*. While experience may be, at least phenomenologically, contentful in the "broad" sense that consists in its seeming to represent true things about a real world, its thus *being* contentful must, on Fodor's account, finally be explicable in terms of proximal factors. While Fodor says in a related vein that "it's what the agent has in mind that causes his behavior" (1980, 290), it should be clear that the pressure to posit something like "narrow" content really comes from the considerations that recommend thinking of mental content as being finally "in" *a brain*.

Yet Fodor does not take himself to be an eliminative physicalist; his is not, that is, the idea that the commonsense view of the mental may one day be altogether superseded by an impersonal, scientific description.[19] Indeed, he thinks a computational account such as his represents the only way to be a realist about propositional attitudes, the only way to *retain* the idea of thought as constitutively contentful. On Fodor's account, however, one counts as a realist about propositional attitudes only insofar as she holds both that "there are mental states whose occurrences and interactions cause behaviour," *and* that "these same causally efficacious mental states are also semantically evaluable" (Fodor 1985, 78). While the second claim thus affirms (against the eliminativist) that the semantic content of mental states cannot be explained away, the salient point for our purposes is Fodor's affirmation, with the first condition, that a propositional attitude's *causing* any behavior would be the only way to think it "really" in play at all. Fodor's claim here thus reflects, in effect, something very much like Dharmakīrti's idea of causal efficacy as the criterion of the real (though it's especially clear in Fodor's case that it is particularly *efficient*-causal efficacy that makes the difference). To the extent that such a criterion is taken as axiomatic, it seems that one only *could* be a "realist" about propositional attitudes by showing these finally to consist in causally efficacious particulars.

To frame the issue of content, in this way, as centrally concerning the question of its causal efficacy is effectively to advance what has been characterized as a *causal* argument for the necessity of positing narrow content. This can be understood as a transcendental argument of sorts: if one is going to be a realist (of Fodor's kind) about the propositional attitudes, it must be the case that these can be explained in terms of something like "narrow content"; for it is a condition of the possibility of cognition's being both *contentful* and *causally efficacious* that mental content be finally intelligible only in terms internal to a subject, since otherwise there will be no way to think of our mental content as causally efficacious with respect to bodily events.[20] Insofar, that is, as one holds that a reason's *causing* some behavior is the only way to think it "really" in play at all, there is pressure to think that such things must finally be explicable only in terms of narrow content—the kind of "content," that is, that can be *in* a brain.

If, as thus stressed by the causal argument, the kind of content here in view is "narrow" in the sense that it is "in" a brain, it is also meant to be narrow in an *epistemic* sense; narrow content can also be characterized, that is, in terms of *how things seem to a subject*.[21] Here we encounter Fodor's "methodological solipsism," which can be said to figure in an epistemic argument for narrow content. The epistemic implications of Fodor's commitment to narrow content are evident in his contention that "if mental processes are formal, they have access only to the formal properties of such representations of the environment as the senses provide. Hence, they have no access to the *semantic* properties of such representations, including the property of being true, of having referents, or, indeed, the property of being representations *of the environment*" (1980, 283).

The idea that it is only *as narrow* that mental content really "does" anything recommends, in other words, a bracketing of questions of truth and reference; Fodor's stance must be "solipsistic," then, in the sense that attention to narrow content is, ipso facto, attention to something that (unlike the truth conditions of a belief about the environment) is somehow "in" a subject. Hilary Putnam has said in this regard that a "methodological solipsist" is "a non-realist or 'verificationist' who agrees that truth is to be understood as in some way related to rational acceptability, but who holds that all justification is ultimately in terms of experiences that each of us has a *private* knowledge of" (1981, 121–122). That is, an account is methodologically solipsistic if it initially brackets questions of truth, instead taking *what irrefragably seems to a subject* to be the case as foundational for understanding as such; the very idea of any belief's possibly being *true* is finally to be explained, then, based on this "seeming," rather than conversely—a version of the idea (familiar from Locke and others) that while we can coherently doubt whether things in the world are as represented in any cognition, we cannot doubt that *that is how it seems.*

What I want to ask with respect to Fodor's elaboration of a similar idea is whether there is any reason to think that Fodor's "methodological solipsism"—his *epistemic* case for narrow content—yields the same conclusion as the causal argument so far canvassed. Is there any reason to think that facts about *what irrefragably seems to a subject to be the case* put us more immediately in the vicinity of brain events than other things that might figure in the content of a thought? As with Dharmakīrti's answer to the question of how to distinguish the *objects* of awareness from whatever other causes figure in its production, what is needed here is for *both* of these arguments (the causal and the epistemic arguments for narrow content) to pick out *the same thing*. These lines of argument effectively dovetail, then, only insofar as it is presupposed that we are, in virtue of picking out *epistemically* "narrow" content, ipso facto picking out the mental state that *has* that content. I think, however, that there is a real question whether the two different lines of argument succeed in picking out the same things; even if we grant that the causal argument for narrow content is cogent and that the epistemic considerations that recommend Fodor's methodological solipsism are compelling, it may be that these arguments fail to converge on the same "mental states."

In an epistemic key, Fodor's point is that if we are interested in understanding the "mental causation of behavior," it stands to reason that we must attend to what the subject *takes herself to believe* (or desire, intend, etc.)—which of course may be quite independent of whether the thought is true. Fodor's argument in this regard is effectively the same one that Donald Davidson took to recommend the conclusion that the *justifying* role of a reason depends upon the *explanatory* role—that, as Davidson put it, "your stepping on my toes neither explains nor justifies my stepping on your toes unless I believe you stepped on my toes, but the belief alone, true or false, explains my action" (1963, 8). To the extent, that is, that we are interested in what *caused* me to step on your toes, *my belief* that retaliation is called for does the trick, quite independently of whether or not I'm right in so believing. Expressing the same point in terms suggested by Frege, Fodor says that "when we articulate the generalizations in virtue of which behavior is contingent upon mental states, it is typically an opaque construal of the mental state attributions that does the work; for example, it's a construal under which believing that *a is F* is logically independent from believing *b is F*, even in the case where a = b" (1980, 286).

Thus casting his epistemic argument for narrow content in the semantic terms of "referential opacity," Fodor emphasizes that it is "typically under an *opaque* construal that attributions of propositional attitudes to organisms enter into explanations of their behavior" (1980, 286). To attribute beliefs under a referentially "opaque" construal, on this usage, is to describe the contents thereof only in terms accessible to the subject—only, that is, in terms of *the mode of presentation to a subject*, which may of course fail to correspond to how things really are. On a referentially *transparent* construal, in contrast, propositional attitudes are individuated with regard to their *referents*, regardless of whether the subject happens to know anything about that. So, for example, it makes all the difference for our understanding of the tragedy of Oedipus that we attribute to Oedipus the belief "I want to marry Jocasta" under a referentially opaque construal; under a referentially transparent construal, that belief would be recognized as equivalent to "I want to marry my mother," which, tragically, Oedipus was not aware that he thus intended (Fodor 1980, 287).[22]

It is under a referentially transparent construal, then, that we can see that it's really *true* that Oedipus thus wished to marry his mother, but it's the referentially opaque construal that explains (because it *causes*) his actions.

"Ontologically," Fodor thus concludes, "transparent readings are stronger than opaque ones; for example, the former license existential inferences, which the latter do not. But psychologically, opaque readings are stronger than transparent ones; they tell us more about the character of the mental causes of behavior" (1980, 297). Bringing this epistemic argument for narrow content together with the terms that figure in the causal argument, Fodor says that "narrow psychological states are those individuated in light of the formality condition; viz. without reference to such semantic properties as truth and reference" (1980, 297). Not only is "narrow content" what is captured by referentially opaque attributions of belief; it is also, Fodor here further asserts, the same thing captured by the description of a mental state in strictly formal or "syntactic" terms.

As we saw with reference to Davidson, though, there is no reason to think that this line of argument, even if rightly showing a sense in which "reasons" can be "causes," shows us that these are also (under their description, presumably, as content-bearing brain states) the *efficient causes* of things like muscle contractions. In order, however, for Fodor's "methodological solipsism" to recommend his idea of "narrow content," what is picked out by propositional attitudes on referentially opaque construals has to be somehow *the same thing* that is picked out by a description of causally efficacious narrow content; only if the same thing can be described both ways will we have learned that the state or event individuated by a "referentially opaque" construal of mental content is just the state that *causes* behavior, in the strong sense required by Fodor's preoccupation with the problem of mental causation.

Fodor thus exploits the idea of referential opacity—which amounts to the adoption of a first-person epistemic perspective on any subject's beliefs—to recommend the view, *already preferred on grounds having to do with the problem of mental causation*, that only things internal to the subject's head can be causes of behavior. But in fact, we are not entitled to take Fodor's "formally" described mental content as similarly representing a first-person perspective, since however intimately brain events may be involved in our having of experience, surely it is not brain events that our experiences are *of*. It is not obvious, then, that the "methodologically solipsistic" identification of a mental cause—an identification essentially like the one disclosed by Davidson's analysis of the word *because*—necessarily tells us anything whatsoever about the kinds of *efficient* causes (viz., brain events) that Fodor means to pick out with the causal argument for narrow content. Insofar as causation is still individuated by way of an *intentional* level of description—a "referentially opaque" description, to be sure, but *referential* (and therefore semantic) nevertheless—this does not necessarily tell us anything about causes *as those are individuated at a physicalist level of description*. Or rather, whether there is any relation between these is just what we want to know—and exploiting the sense of "causation" that is in play at a *semantic* level of description (the sense in play when one says "I did it because . . . ") does not help us with that.[23]

We are thus entitled to ask whether it makes sense to think that what Fodor really intends by "narrow content" counts as *contentful* at all.[24] The failure of the two foregoing lines of argument to converge on the same causes reflects a fundamental tension in Fodor's approach. As John McDowell says of a similar program, it "generates the appearance that we can find (narrow) content-bearing states in the interior considered by itself. But the idea looks deceptive. If we are not concerned with the point of view of the cognitive system itself (if, indeed, we conceive it in such a way that it has no point of view), there is no justification for regarding the enterprise as any kind of phenomenology at all" (1998, 256n).[25] To the extent, in other words, that Fodor is finally concerned to pick out only such causal or "formal" properties of representations as the senses provide—only such properties as can be individuated without reference even to their being representations *of the environment*—he cannot claim also to be talking about *beliefs*. Even on a referentially opaque construal, beliefs are, phenomenologically, *about* things like "states of affairs"; they are not "about" their own proximate causes.

The divergence of the causal and the epistemic arguments for narrow content thus reflects, on Lynne Rudder Baker's account of the problem, a dilemma: "On the one hand, if we take narrow content to be the product of input analysis, then the wrong things get semantically evaluated." In other words, if we take "narrow content" to consist essentially in, say, the brain states precipitated by environmental stimulus ("the intermediate outputs of perceptual systems," as Baker says), we haven't identified anything at all like what a subject would take to be the content of her belief. "On the other hand," Baker continues, "if we take narrow content to be the product of higher-level processing, then we remove the psychological warrant for construing narrow content in terms of symbols denoting [nothing but] phenomenologically accessible properties" (1986, 67). That is, to bring in such factors as *would* make the content of a belief recognizable to the subject thereof is, ipso facto, already to bring in the world. It thus turns out, as we noted in chapter 1 with reference to Dharmakīrti, to be difficult to distinguish those causes of any cognition that are at the same time what that cognition is *about* from whatever other causes (e.g., properly functioning sensory capacities) are appropriately thought to figure in causing the awareness; the same problem, we now see, figures centrally in Fodor's cognitive-scientific philosophy of mind, as well.

THE "LANGUAGE OF THOUGHT": AN ACCOUNT OF LANGUAGE ITSELF AS CAUSALLY DESCRIBABLE

To ask whether mental states with "narrow content" really count *as contentful* is effectively to ask whether Fodor's way of reconciling the two levels of description (intentional and causal) really counts as *realism* about propositional attitudes. The problem with Fodor's view is that all of the explanatory work is done here by mental representations *only insofar as they are "formally" describable*; it is only in their capacity as having causally efficacious "shapes" that representations really *cause* anything. All the computer metaphor gets us, then, is a way to think of "formally" (syntactically, *causally*) described representations as *also* "meaningful"; it remains the case on this account, however, that it's not in their capacity *as* meaningful that we are to understand them as doing what they do. Despite the promise of the appeal to computationalism, the character of mental events *as* meaning something may after all be epiphenomenal on Fodor's account.

Fodor is not unaware of this objection, which is one to the effect (he says) that "it is the computational roles of mental states, and *not* their content, that are doing all the work in psychological explanation" (1994, 49–50). In that case, he allows, it may be that "the attachment to an *intentional*, as opposed to computational, level of psychological explanation is merely sentimental" (1994, 50). While eliminative physicalists like Paul Churchland are willing to embrace just such a conclusion, Fodor appreciates the "well-known worry about *narrow* content that it tends to be a little suicidal" (1994, 49); to hold, that is, that mental content in general must be explicable with reference to Fodor's causally describable narrow content is arguably to do away with the very level of description in terms of which *one's making this very argument* makes any sense.[26]

In trying to dispel this objection (here anticipated in a work written some time after the earlier works to which we have hitherto referred), Fodor backs away somewhat from his commitment to narrow content—not, to be sure, so far as to disavow the idea, only far enough that he no longer thinks his position can only be defended with reference to that.[27] Instead, he now thinks he can defend his account of mental causation even with reference to the kind of "broad" content that is necessarily involved in thinking one's own position true. While I must confess that I'm not altogether sure how his argument in this regard is meant to meet the epiphenomenalism objection, it is clear, at least, that it's crucial to his answer that we "suppose . . . that some sort of causal account of broad content is correct" (1994, 52); it is, in other words, only insofar as *broad* content, too, will admit of causal explanation that he can concede its significance.

On a causal account of broad content, he says, anyone having propositional attitudes regarding (say) what we would identify as "water," *regardless of the description under which they experience it*, "must have modes of presentation that trace back, in the right way, to interactions with water. My point is that, qua *water*-believers, they needn't have *anything else* in common: Their shared causal connection to water has left its mark on each of them" (1994, 52). This is a view according to which *believing* that *P* can thus be understood in terms of "being in states that are caused by, and hence bear information about, the fact that *P*" (1994, 53). Fodor's project, he thus thinks, is still viable even if mental content is understood as "broad" (in the sense of essentially consisting in representations *of the environment*)—but only insofar as broad content, too, is *causally related to* the environment.

On this alternative development of his position, "content is broad, the metaphysics of content is externalist (e.g., causal/informational)"—*and*, Fodor immediately continues, "modes of presentation are sentences of Mentalese" (1994, 52). In backing away from narrow content and embracing thought's relatedness to the world, then, Fodor here appeals (with his reference to "Mentalese") to the idea of a "language of thought." In his 1975 book of that title, Fodor thus sketches the idea here invoked:

> To have a certain propositional attitude is to be in a certain relation to an internal representation. That is, for each of the (typically infinitely many) propositional attitudes that an organism can entertain, there exist an internal representation and a relation such that being in that relation to that representation is nomologically necessary and sufficient for (or nomologically identical to) having the propositional attitude. The least that an empirically adequate cognitive psychology is therefore required to do is to specify, for each propositional attitude, the internal representation and the relation which, in this sense, correspond [*sic*] to it.
>
> (1975, 198)

In the context, then, of what we can recognize as Fodor's representationalist theory of mind—a theory according to which a phenomenon like *believing something* is to be explained in terms of a subject's relation to an internal representation—the "language of thought" represents something like the system of rules regulating the well-formed "sentences" of such mental relating.[28] Among the salient characteristics of this "language" is that it can be exhaustively described in terms of unique particulars—in terms, e.g., of brain states, the "syntax" of whose relations is here imagined as language-like.[29]

While it's perhaps possible to imagine something like the "syntax" of a language of thought—to imagine, for example, that there are structural regularities in neurophysiological events that impose some constraints on what we can represent or that are isomorphic with what we "think"—the hard thing, just as in Fodor's development of the computer metaphor, is to explain how the regularities so described can mean or represent or be about anything. The problem, once again, is to get a *semantic* level of description into the picture. Fodor appreciates as much, allowing of the representational theory of mind he more generally aims to advance that it "needs *some* semantic story to tell"; *which* semantic story to tell, he says, is "going to be *the* issue in mental representation theory for the foreseeable future" (1985, 96). Indeed, on Fodor's view, this is pretty much the whole shootin' match; "the problem of the intentionality of the mental is largely—perhaps exhaustively—the problem of the semanticity of mental representations. But of the semanticity of mental representations we have, as things now stand, no adequate account" (1985, 99).

Fodor's "language of thought" figures centrally in his attempt to rectify that situation. Here, let's recall Augustine's account of language acquisition as exemplifying the sort of "optimal" conditions invoked by some philosophers to explain what fixes content. Augustine, we saw, said that the first learning of a language consists in watching one's elders naming indicated objects and grasping thereby that "the thing was called by the sound they uttered when they meant to point it out"; their intentions were reflected "by their bodily movements, as it were the natural language of all peoples." Wittgenstein's *Philosophical Investigations* famously begins with a consideration of Augustine's account of this, which so preoccupies Wittgenstein that the lengthy discussion that follows represents one of the most sustained engagements with any thinker explicitly addressed in the *Investigations*. For our purposes, the insight Wittgenstein most compellingly presses against Augustine's picture is this: "Augustine describes the learning of human language as if the child came into a strange country and did not understand the language of the country; that is, as if it already had a language, only not this one. Or again: as if the child could already *think*, only not yet speak. And 'think' would here mean something like 'talk to itself' " (1958, 15–16).

Among Wittgenstein's points, I take it, is that *knowing a language* involves something more—indeed, much more—than knowing (what can at least arguably be taught by ostension) "the names of things." It involves, more basically, the very idea that there could *be* names of things—that by any act of speech or ostension, one could *mean* what one thus refers to. What we really want to understand when we ask for an account of an infant's language acquisition is how the child acquires the very idea of *meaning* something and in what that consists; to that extent, an account like Augustine's begs the question most centrally at issue, presupposing as it does that the idea of meaning something is already intelligible to the language learner and that she therefore requires only to learn *which* sounds "mean" which things.

What, then, are we to say about the relations involved in anything's meaning something else? Insofar as he is preoccupied with the question of mental causation, Fodor is inclined to say that it is only in virtue of *causal* relations that anything can be thought finally real; the relations involved in meaning anything raise, however, what Fodor calls the *disjunction problem*. This is the problem that "it's just not true that Normally [*sic*] caused intentional states ipso facto mean whatever causes them" (1990, 89)—which relates, again, to the problem recurrently noted since we saw Dharmakīrti address it in chapter 1. Thus, on Dharmakīrti's eminently causal account of perception, all manner of things (properly functioning sense capacities, for example) are among the *causes* of any cognition—but these are not among the things that we say are thus perceived.[30] A causal theory of perception thus requires that there be some principled way to explain which of the relevant causes of any perception is at the same time *what is perceived*; "there has to be some way," as Fodor similarly allows in the present case, "of picking out *semantically relevant* causal relations from all the other kinds of causal relations that the tokens of a symbol can enter into" (1990, 91). The problem, then, is again that of getting *causal* and *intentional* descriptions (here, of language) together.

Providing such an account with regard to perception is far from straightforward; the explicitly semantic version of the problem is even more difficult. Here, "what the disjunction problem is really about deep down is the difference between *meaning* and *information*" (1990, 90). The latter, for Fodor, denotes mental content that is, as it were, efficiently precipitated by its causes; "information is tied to etiology in a way that meaning isn't."

Mental content that is, in contrast, *meaningful* is relatively unconstrained; symbols are *meaningful* just insofar as they are somehow about something other (or something *more*) than the particulars that cause them, a fact that Fodor characterizes in terms of the greater "robustness" that characterizes meaning. In contrast to "information," "*the meaning of a symbol is one of the things that all of its tokens have in common, however they may happen to be caused.* All 'cow' tokens mean cow; if they didn't, they wouldn't be 'cow' tokens" (1990, 90). The problem is how to tell a finally causal story about meaning while allowing that what thus distinguishes the "meaning" relation just is its "robustness," or apparent lack of causal constraint.

With regard to this problem, Fodor's proposal is that " 'cow' means *cow* and not *cat* or *cow or cat* because *there being cat-caused 'cow' tokens depends on there being cow-caused 'cow' tokens, but not the other way around.* 'Cow' means *cow* because *but that 'cow' tokens carry information about cows, they wouldn't carry information about anything*" (1990, 90). The account thus concisely stated involves an appeal to *asymmetric dependence*, which is crucial to unpacking this. For example, Fodor says, "you have to invoke the practice of naming to specify the practice of paging. So the practice of paging is parasitic on the practice [of] naming; you couldn't have the former but that you could have the latter. But not, I suppose, vice versa? . . . so I take it to be plausible that paging is *asymmetrically* dependent on naming" (1990, 96–97). This notion is thus invoked with respect to the Wittgensteinian example of bringing slabs in response to the command "bring me a slab" (cf. Wittgenstein 1958, §20): "it's plausible that the cluster of practices that center around bringing things when they're called for is asymmetrically dependent on the cluster of *practices that fix the extensions of our predicates*" (Fodor 1990, 97; emphasis mine). Any particular utterance of "slab," in other words, is intelligible *as the practice it is* only relative to earlier practices fixing the use of the word—and insofar as these earlier practices are causally describable, the later uses, too, are rightly considered to be grounded in a causal description.

The point, then, of Fodor's account of what it is in virtue of which "cow" means what it does is this: "All that's required for 'cow' to mean *cow*, according to the present account, is that some 'cow' tokens should be caused by (more precisely, that they should carry information about) cows, and that noncow-caused 'cow' tokens should depend asymmetrically on these" (1990, 91). The claim is that while not all particular utterances of any word will demonstrably be causally relatable to some token of the type denoted—the fact that they will not is just what is identified in terms of the "disjunction problem"—it will always at least be the case that *some* such tokens are so relatable. Fodor's point is that while the intelligibility of the causally describable tokens does not depend on there being tokens that are not so describable, the intelligibility of the latter *does* depend on there being some instances of the former; in order that there be *any* cases of rightly calling particular bovine critters *cows*, there must be *some* cases of this that will admit of causal description. What is thus claimed is that there is a causal chain linking any use of a term to some first use that itself causally links the term to its referent—and the whole point of the exercise is that "you can say what asymmetric dependence is without resort to intentional or semantic idiom" (1990, 92).[31] Here, then, the project of "naturalizing" intentionality could come to rest.

Now, in order to specify—in nonsemantic terms—what it is upon which all correct uses of a word asymmetrically depend, it becomes necessary to have a nonsemantic account of those "practices" that, Fodor said, initially "fix the extensions of our predicates." What is properly basic on the account thus proposed is the initial *application* of terms: "Some of our linguistic practices presuppose some of our others, and it's plausible that practices of *applying* terms (names to their bearers, predicates to things in their extensions) are at the bottom of the pile" (1990, 97). It's unclear whether we are to understand this initial "application" in terms of someone's first *assigning* a name to anything or (more likely) of someone's first *learning* the name so assigned. (We will see in chapter 4 that there is a similar ambiguity in Dharmakīrti's account and that the problem may be conceptually the same regardless.) Either way, the point is that the process is understood to be causally describable—in terms, indeed, rather like those imagined by Augustine.

Putting the point in terms of the above-described sense of "information," Fodor says "the idea is that, although tokens of 'slab' that request slabs carry no information about slabs (if anything, they carry information about wants; viz., the information that a slab is wanted), still, *some* tokens of 'slab' presumably carry information about slabs (in particular, *the tokens that are used to predicate slabhood of slabs do*)" (1990, 97; emphasis added). The initial "tokens that are used to predicate slabhood of slabs," he thus suggests, will admit of causal description; insofar as all subsequent understandings of the idea of *being a slab* can then be taken asymmetrically to depend on these baptismal tokenings—"but for there being tokens of 'slab' that carry information about slabs, I couldn't get a slab by using 'slab' to call for one"—*meaning* has been grounded in causation. "My 'slab' requests are thus, in a certain sense, *causally dependent on slabs even though there are no slabs in their causal histories*" (1990, 97–98).

This amounts to just the Augustinian idea that so preoccupied Wittgenstein; what is distinctive, that is, about the tokens that initially "predicate slabhood of slabs" is that they can plausibly be described in terms of the ostension of perceptible particulars—in terms (as Augustine said) of "bodily movements" that represent "as it were the natural language of all peoples." Fodor's approach here would seem, then, to be vulnerable to the critique ventured by Wittgenstein; recognizing as much, Fodor precisely identifies the problem that remains in terms that echo Wittgenstein's objection: "as it stands none of this is of any use to a reductionist. For, in these examples, we've been construing robustness by appeal to asymmetric dependences among *linguistic practices*. And linguistic *practices* depend on linguistic *policies*." The problem is that "being in pursuit of a policy is being in an intentional state," so how "could asymmetric dependence among linguistic practices help with the naturalization problem?" (1990, 98). The intelligibility of any of these baptismal tokenings *as* a linguistic act—the understanding of any particular utterance together with ostension as *naming* the thing indicated—already presupposes our knowing what it means to *mean* something; insofar, however, as that is just what we were trying to explain, the question is begged.

It is, finally, Fodor's recognition of this problem that drives his argument for the necessity of positing a "language of thought." Fodor's argument, most basically, is that the point here developed opens an intolerable regress that can only be terminated by positing something, in a sense, that both *is* and is *not* a "language." What is needed is again something that can be described both in terms of its semantic content (this is the sense in which it is like a language) and in terms of causally relatable particulars (this is the sense in which it is not). Here is a succinct statement of the argument:

> Learning a language (including, of course, a first language) involves learning what the predicates of the language mean. Learning what the predicates of a language mean involves learning a determination of the extension of these predicates. Learning a determination of the extension of the predicates involves learning that they fall under certain rules (i.e., truth rules). But one cannot learn that *P* falls under *R* unless one has a language in which *P* and *R* can be represented. So one cannot learn a language unless one has a language. In particular, one cannot learn a first language unless one already has a system capable of representing the predicates in that language *and their extensions*. And, on pain of circularity, that system cannot be the language that is being learned. Bur first

languages *are* learned. Hence, at least some cognitive operations are carried out in languages other than natural languages.

(FODOR 1975, 63–64)[32]

That is, there must be some kind of "language" other than languages like English and Sanskrit and Tibetan, since it could only be "in" some other language that one transacts the business of first learning any one of these. Contra Wittgenstein, then, it must actually be the case that a language-acquiring child *does* "already have a language, only not this one." (We will see in chapter 6 that Mīmāṃsakas pressed a strikingly similar argument to very different ends.)

Fodor thus affirms that Wittgenstein's characterization of Augustine's account is "transparently absurd," urging instead that the argument just sketched "suggests, on the contrary, that Augustine was precisely and demonstrably right and that seeing that he was is prerequisite to any serious attempts to understand how first languages are learned" (1975, 64). Augustine was right, in particular, to think there must be some *naturalistically* specifiable conditions ("as it were the natural language of all peoples") upon which all instances of *meaning*, more generally, are asymmetrically dependent. The idea, then, that Fodor invokes—when, allowing that "broad" content may be compatible with his approach to mental causation, he says (we saw above at p. 67) that "modes of presentation are sentences of Mentalese"—is that a fundamentally *causal* account of thought's relatedness to the world is possible insofar as language itself can be so described. *Sentences of Mentalese*, it thus seems we are to understand, are the language-like neurophysiological precipitates of perceptual encounters with the environment—encounters that can be causally described and upon which all other instances of meaningful thought are asymmetrically dependent. These primitive modes of presentation are like "sentences" in that their well-formedness is a function of "rules" that can be understood on the model of *syntax*—and, as well, in that they are the bearers of "information" regarding what causes them. It is, Fodor has thus argued, only in virtue of there being this kind of causally describable "content"—the kind that can be described in terms of things like photostimulation of retinal nerve endings or in terms of the demonstrative indication of perceptible particulars—that we can have the kind of *meaningful* content reflected in overt judgments.

Fodor's solution to the disjunction problem—and, more generally, to the question of naturalistically specifiable conditions for our *meaning* anything—thus involves the idea that all instances of meaningful thought are asymmetrically dependent upon causally describable episodes that are just *intrinsically* language-like. This can be understood as amounting to a concession that, in effect, *we don't know* how a mental event can mean or represent or be about some other thing—that, in other words, if there seems to be no way to get the semantic character of the mental into a naturalistically described picture, it must just be part of that picture from the beginning. Characterizing the argument we've just rehearsed, Daniel Dennett says to similar effect that "some elegant, *generative*, indefinitely extendable principles of representation must be responsible" for the brain's having "solved the problem of combinatorial explosion," but "we have only one model of such a representation system: a human language. So the argument for a language of thought comes down to this: what else could it be?" (1987, 35). Insofar, that is, as the intentionality of the mental cannot be characterized without reference to certain features of language, the would-be naturalizer of mental content can simply hold that the relevant features of language must therefore *just intrinsically characterize the structure and function of the brain.*

This move, we saw from the beginning of this chapter, is motivated by the problem of mental causation; the foregoing is proposed as an account on which the kinds of things that explain how we can *mean* anything are at the same time the kinds of things—things, like brain events, with spatiotemporal identity criteria—that can cause movements of the body. If Fodor has in more recent years been willing to account for mental content *as* constitutively related to the world, the salient point remains his insistence that it is only as *causally* related that it can "really" be so. Whatever else it's meant to do, Fodor's language of thought thus undergirds an approach according to which a propositional attitude's *causing* behaviors is the only way to think it *real*. To the extent, however, that the "language"-like features of the brain are thus invoked chiefly to explain how mental states that are *about* things can also be the causes of things like muscle contractions, their *being* "about" their contents may remain finally epiphenomenal; it is, once again, only the causal level of description that has explanatory significance here. We still have, to that extent, the problems that go with thinking that reasons are explanatorily significant only insofar as they can be described in terms of something other than their semantic content. Mental content is here finally *explained*, moreover, by a redescription in causal terms of what is supposedly the same thing—but it remains unclear whether we are entitled to think such an alternative description really picks out the same thing we have in view when we talk of reasons and beliefs.

CONCLUSION: DOES DENNETT'S APPROACH REPRESENT AN ALTERNATIVE?

We can usefully conclude our survey of the computational iteration of cognitivism by looking briefly at some proposals from Daniel Dennett, whose project differs from Fodor's in ways that can help us bring more sharply into relief some of the basic problems with characteristically cognitivist approaches. Much influenced by cognitive-scientific research in artificial intelligence and related fields, Dennett is inclined to embrace Fodor's "language of thought" hypothesis but recognizes it as distinct from the position he (Dennett) most wants to defend—a position that can be represented as an alternative way to be a realist about propositional attitudes. Thus, in contrast to the focus on efficient causation that can be said to characterize Fodor's project, Dennett's approach can be taken to allow for something like a teleological level of description; reflecting as much, Dennett says that "while belief is a perfectly objective phenomenon (that apparently makes me a realist), it can be discerned only from the point of view of one who adopts a certain *predictive strategy*" (1987, 15).[33]

The idea here introduced is that intentionality is best understood in terms of what Dennett calls the "intentional stance." Attributing the intentional stance to (*nota bene*) an object consists, he says, in "treating the object whose behavior you want to predict as a rational agent with beliefs and desires and other mental stages exhibiting what Brentano and others call *intentionality*" (1987, 15). That is, we invoke "intentional stance" descriptions whenever we usefully treat some object or creature *as though* it entertained the kinds of discursive thoughts in terms of which its patterned behaviors are reasonably thought of as purposeful. My "as though" locution should not be taken to suggest that Dennett denies the reality of the patterns that come into view by assuming the intentional stance; it is just Dennett's point to stress that "intentional stance description yields an objective, real pattern in the world" (1987, 34). If we imagine, for example, extraterrestrial observers experiencing highly complex rational behaviors—those, for example, constituting the commerce of a stock exchange—as consisting in nothing more than interactions among fathomlessly many subatomic particles, we would be right to judge them as having "failed to see a real pattern in the world they are observing" (1987, 26).

Distinguishing the intentional stance idea from Fodor's language of thought hypothesis, Dennett emphasizes that the latter represents only one possible way (albeit one he thinks probably correct) to explain *how and why intentional stance descriptions work.* Given Fodor's hypothesis, the patterned behaviors of some objects can be successfully predicted by attributing the intentional stance just insofar as those behaviors are "*produced by* another real pattern roughly isomorphic to it within the brains of intelligent creatures" (1987, 34). The language of thought hypothesis thus has it that insofar as there are real behavioral patterns of the sort that would lead us to characterize an object's behavior as purposeful, there must be corresponding patterns in the object's internal states (in, e.g., its brain events). While Dennett thinks this is probably right, he urges that one does not need to accept that view in order to hold the view he chiefly wants to defend, which is that an intentional level of description picks out patterns that only emerge given the adoption of this stance.

Nevertheless, it's chief among Dennett's points to urge that intentional characterizations do not require that we invoke the kinds of universals that arguably figure in accounts of the semantic *content* of intentional states. With respect, for example, to the operations of a computer that is "playing" chess, he says that "doubts about whether the chess-playing computer *really* has beliefs and desires are misplaced; for the definition of intentional systems I have given does not say that intentional systems *really* have beliefs and desires, but that one can explain and predict their behavior by *ascribing* beliefs and desires to them." Precisely how one imagines what is thus ascribed, he says, "makes no difference to the nature of the calculation one makes on the basis of the ascriptions" (1981, 7). Like Fodor, Dennett thus takes his bearings from the eminently computationalist idea that it is the patterned "syntax" that really matters and that beliefs therefore need not be individuated in terms of their semantic *content*. The claim, rather, is that "*all there is* to being a true believer is being a system whose behavior is reliably predictable via the intentional strategy, and hence *all there is* to really and truly believing that *p* (for any proposition *p*) is being an intentional system for which *p* occurs as a belief in the best (most predictive) interpretation" (1987, 29).

Central to this proposal, I think, is the idea that intentionality can thus be described from a third-person perspective; that is the real point in understanding the intentional stance as usefully *attributed* to any of the various objects whose behaviors might usefully be predicted in terms thereof. *Being rational*, Dennett thus says, "is being intentional[,] is being the *object* of a certain stance" (1981, 271; emphasis mine).[34] By thus characterizing intentionality, Dennett aims to avoid invoking anything that will not admit of *explanation*; "whenever we stop in our explanations at the intentional level we have left over an unexplained instance of intelligence or rationality" (1981, 12). Reference, in any account of a person's intentionally describable actions, to *the content of her beliefs* is problematic, then, just insofar as "rationality is being taken for granted, and in this way shows us where a theory is incomplete" (1981, 12). Reference to the content of a subject's beliefs does not, that is, *explain* anything; indeed, this is precisely the point where, for Dennett as for Fodor, explanation is called for. The idea that the explanation must be essentially "third-personal" reflects Dennett's confidence that this is a finally empirical matter, such as will admit of a scientific answer; his idea of "intentional systems" is invoked as "a bridge connecting the intentional domain (which includes our 'common-sense' world of persons and actions, game theory, and the 'neural signals' of the biologist) to the non-intentional domain of the physical sciences" (1981, 22).

Significantly, though, Dennett allows that anything can be an intentional system "only in relation to the strategies *of someone* who is trying to explain and predict its behavior" (1981, 3–4; emphasis mine). It's revealing to ask, in this regard, *for whom* the system in question is thus the "object" of a "stance"; more compellingly, what is the person for whom some system is thus an "object" of the intentional stance *doing* in attributing that stance? The point is that *attributing the intentional stance to anything*—regarding any object as though it were acting *as we act* when we act purposefully—is itself an *intentional* idea par excellence. The intentional stance idea does not, to that extent, explain anything at all about intentionality; for we understand what it means to attribute the "intentional stance" to anything only insofar as we already have a first-personal experience of acting based on reasons. Insofar as it is thus intelligible only with reference to our own experienced intentionality, this idea cannot explain the very thing we supposedly want to understand.

Dennett seems to acknowledge as much when he notes an asymmetry that is crucial to his thought experiment about alternative descriptions of the workings of a stock market: namely, "*the unavoidability of the intentional stance with regard to oneself and one's fellow intelligent beings*" (1987, 27). I do not see, however, that he addresses the significance of this concession. What this unavoidability brings into view is the extent to which intentionality may not, in principle, *be* exhaustively describable with reference only to a third-person perspective. There is, as G. F. Schueler puts the point I'm after, "a 'non-theoretical' element at the heart of reasons explanations, namely the way I understand my own case when I act for a reason" (2003,160). The "furthest down" we can go, that is, in thinking about what is meant by the kind of constitutively intentional action that will admit of demands for justification, is to understand it in terms of *what I am doing when I experience myself as acting for a reason.*[35] This, I think, is effectively the point John Haugeland makes in characterizing "the ultimate limitation" of the intentional stance idea as being that "neither knowledge nor understanding is possible for a system that is itself incapable of adopting a stance" (1993, 67).

This is the problem, finally, with what Dennett allows is his "apparently shallow and instrumentalistic criterion of belief" (1987, 29).[36] However *instrumentally* useful it is to make reference to belief, the intentional level of description is not, on Dennett's account, to be reckoned as picking out anything that is (in Dharmakīrti's idiom) "ultimately real." As Lynne Rudder Baker puts the same point, Dennett is "explicitly committed to . . . the 'stance-dependence' of features attributed from the intentional stance" (1987, 154). That is, an intentional level of description picks out phenomena that are, on Dennett's account, real only insofar as they are conveniently assumed for purposes of attributing the intentional stance; this is in contrast to the ontology of items invoked in the kinds of "physical stance" descriptions that ultimately ground Dennett's explanations. Insofar, however, as the very idea of the intentional stance is intelligible only given our own understanding of what we are doing *in attributing this stance*, it cannot be right to say that its reality depends only upon the predictive strategies *of others*; it must, rather, always already be integral to what we are trying to understand—indeed, integral to *our trying to understand it*.

But it seems, to that extent, that an intentional level of description is not so much instrumental as *constitutive*—in which case, the conceptual work done by the contrast between Dennett's levels of explanation is empty. Insofar as an intentional level of description is necessarily presupposed even by the proponent of an account on which that is only "instrumental," one cannot coherently claim to offer an explanation *of* the intentional level in terms of a putatively privileged level of description.[37] Despite Dennett's differences from Fodor, we thus see here, too, something of how difficult it is to advance a naturalistic (read: *nonintentional*) explanation of intentionality—how difficult it is, in particular, to reconcile any intentional description of the mental (a description of the mental *as contentful*) with causal descriptions thereof. While Dennett's project may, then, be taken to represent an alternative to Fodor's as a way to be realist about the propositional attitudes, both approaches essentially privilege causal explanation; it is finally to this extent that they are similarly problematic.

We have seen, then, that Fodor's appropriation of the computer metaphor is guided by a preoccupation with the problem of mental causation; what the example of computation most compellingly offers is a way to imagine how a sequence of causally related states can at the same time represent the steps in a chain of reasoning. Elaborating this insight, Fodor develops the idea that the "contentful" character of thought is finally explicable in terms of *narrow content*—in terms, that is, of a level of description that can be individuated with reference only to factors somehow internal to a subject. Fodor takes this view to be supported by the same considerations that make the problem of mental causation pressing in the first place—considerations that recommend the conclusion that thought's content must be *inside the head*. He also takes it, though, to be supported by the kinds of considerations that Donald Davidson marshaled to argue that *reasons* explanations should finally be reckoned as *causal* explanations—epistemic considerations, that is, having to do with what a subject believes to be the case, which are logically independent of the objective states of affairs that a subject takes her beliefs to be about. There is, however, a real question whether these two lines of argument (the causal and the epistemic arguments for narrow content) converge on the same conclusion; arguing that they do not, I suggested that, as we initially saw regarding Davidson, there is no reason to think, given the minimal sense in which reasons may be causes, that reasons must therefore consist in the kinds of *efficient* causes that can be thought to impel movements of the body.

Moreover, we have seen that the computational model problematically recommends the view that beliefs can (as Fodor's methodological solipsism is meant to suggest) finally be individuated without any reference to what they are *about*; if Fodor's computational processes involve factors that are both "syntactically" and "semantically" evaluable, it is nevertheless only in terms of the former level of description that any explanatory work is done. To that extent, and despite the very basis of the appeal to computers, reference to *beliefs* arguably remains epiphenomenal on the computational iteration of cognitivism. Noting Fodor's concession that this was a significant concern, we turned to his attempt to ground the contentfulness of thought in what he figuratively calls a "language of thought"—in the "syntax" of thought's relations to internal representations that, though intrinsically related to the environment, are still reckoned to be real only as *causally* related. But even when Fodor tries to allow that "broad content" may figure in the explanation of behavior, he remains committed to the idea that it's only under a causal description that this could be so; we are, to that extent, still faced with the problem that the *content* of beliefs may be epiphenomenal. As long as it's supposed that beliefs do what they do only insofar as they can be described in terms of something other than their semantic content—as long, in Kant's terms, as it's supposed that reason finally figures in accounts of what we are "only as empirically conditioned"—this will be a problem.

Dennett, in contrast to Fodor, advances a basically computationalist approach that nevertheless aims to allow for the reality of the patterns that emerge on something like a teleological level of description. Despite the significance of this gesture of accommodation with regard to semantic content, Dennett's "intentional stance" idea nevertheless relegates reason and belief to merely instrumental status; reference to these is *instrumentally* useful, that is, in predicting the seemingly purposeful behaviors of certain objects, but the whole point of the idea is to circumvent the question whether these "objects" *really* have the beliefs we find it useful to attribute to them. The very idea of intentionality as a possible "stance" is itself intelligible, however, only given our own first-personal acquaintance with what it is to have the kinds of beliefs thus attributed; to that extent, what we are doing *in attributing* the intentional stance to any object is already exhibiting intentionality, which turns out therefore to be presupposed by Dennett's proposed explanation thereof. Dennett's distinction between the instrumentally real and the *really* real parts of his picture thus turns out to be incapable of doing the work it needs to do, and the intentional stance idea finally gives us no traction on the problem of intentionality.

We will see in chapters 4 through 6 that many of the essentials of the foregoing picture apply, *mutatis mutandis*, to Dharmakīrti's project as well. Thus, having already seen in chapter 1 something of the extent to which Dharmakīrti privileges causal explanation, we will see in chapter 4 that Dharmakīrti's *apoha* doctrine represents a full-fledged attempt to explain conceptual mental content in just such terms; we will see in chapter 5 that that account relates closely to his doctrine of *svasaṃvitti*, which can be understood as in important respects similar to Fodor's methodological solipsism; and we will see in chapter 6 that Brahmanical philosophers of the Mīmāṃsā school and Buddhist philosophers of the Madhyamaka school pressed, with regard to these commitments of Dharmakīrti, arguments to the effect that Dharmakīrti cannot make his own case for these without helping himself to precisely the kinds of things he claims to explain thereby. Before returning, however, to the project of Dharmakīrti, we will first try to get a bit more clear, in the next chapter, on just what it is we are talking about when we ask about intentionality, and about why it's reasonably thought that an intentional level of description may *constitutively* be the sort of thing that resists such explanations as Fodor and Dennett have proposed. More particularly, we turn now to the elaboration of a basically Kantian story of why and how *reason itself* can be taken to epitomize what Brentano characterized as "reference to a content, direction toward an object."

3

Responsiveness to Reasons as Such

A KANTIAN ACCOUNT OF INTENTIONALITY

> *Empiricism is a game. Its central rule forbids you to understand what you are talking about.*
>
> —Hugh Kenner

INTRODUCTION: FROM BRENTANO'S "REFERENCE TO A CONTENT" TO PROPOSITIONAL ATTITUDES

We saw in the last chapter that there are important considerations that might recommend the project of "naturalizing" the intentionality of the mental—considerations centering on the problem of mental causation and on commitments, taken as axiomatic, regarding the understanding of causation that must figure in addressing that problem. In this chapter, I want to make a case for thinking that *reason itself* is centrally implicated in the nature of intentionality—and that it's chiefly insofar as *reasoning* will not admit of efficient-causal explanation that intentionality essentially resists explanations such as proposed by Fodor and Dennett and their philosophical fellow travelers.

The avowedly eliminative physicalist Paul Churchland has recognized that in recent debate it has particularly been "the realm of the intentional, the realm of the propositional attitude, that is most commonly held up as being both irreducible to and ineliminable in favor of anything from within a materialist framework." On Churchland's account, this reflects a retreat on the part of critics of the properly scientific sort of program he commends; the "locus of opposition" to physicalism has thus shifted, he says, insofar as arguments appealing to constitutively *subjective* phenomena—

phenomena like emotions, qualia, and "raw feels," formerly taken to represent "the principal stumbling blocks for the materialist program"—have been shown to fail (1981, 67–68).

Churchland takes arguments from intentionality, then, to represent a not very promising last line of defense for critics of physicalism. While there are philosophers on both sides of the debate who may not share Churchland's confidence that proponents of physicalism have finally dispatched the other line of argument,[1] my interest is in showing that the argument from intentionality has rather more going for it than Churchland grants. We can begin to develop a case for this by asking why it makes sense, in the first place, that "the realm of the intentional" can be glossed, with Churchland, as "the realm of the propositional attitude." Why is it reasonable to think that the "aboutness" that characterizes the mental is paradigmatically reflected in the ways—believing, doubting, affirming—in which one might relate to propositions?

I first mentioned the category of intentionality in my introduction, with reference to Franz Brentano, whose recovery of this term of art from medieval scholastics made it an idea of central concern in twentieth-century philosophy (continental and Anglo-American alike).[2] Typically invoked in discussions of intentionality is a canonical passage from Brentano: "Every mental phenomenon is characterized by what the Scholastics of the Middle Ages called the intentional (or mental) inexistence of an object, and what we might call, though not wholly unambiguously, reference to a content, direction toward an object (which is not to be understood here as meaning a thing), or immanent objectivity" (1973, 88). Brentano explains that "inexistence" here means essentially the same thing as "immanent objectivity"—that, in other words, it is characteristic of the mental somehow to *contain* its content, which therefore "exists" *in* thought: "We can . . . define mental phenomena by saying that they are those phenomena which contain an object intentionally within themselves" (1973, 89).

This formulation reflects something of Brentano's basically representationalist epistemology—a point we can appreciate by noticing that in the foregoing, he distinguishes "mental phenomena" not from physical *objects* per se but from "physical *phenomena*." In considering, that is, the distinguishing characteristics of the "mental" and the "physical," Brentano is in both cases considering only (what he thinks is autonomously intelligible) *what appears to us in thought*; "physical phenomena" are on this account *mental representations* of "physical" things, and these representations—as contra the mental acts that are aware *of* these *as* one's representations—

are distinguished from "mental" ones only in that they do not themselves "contain" further objects. (A *tree*-representation appearing in thought is not itself *about* anything further.) While intentionality, on this account, is thus the criterion of mental phenomena, it's important to appreciate that for Brentano, it's really *phenomena* all the way down. Insofar as his account of intentionality thus turns our attention inward, Brentano's account raises all manner of difficult questions about the ontological status of the *objects* of awareness (note Brentano's insistence that "object" here is "not to be understood here as meaning a thing"), and about how we are to understand the intentionality of thoughts whose contents (whose "in-existent objects") are *non*existent objects. (What, for example, is "intentionally contained" in thought when one thinks of unicorns?)[3]

What I here want to emphasize is just that Brentano's introduction of the idea that mental events are constitutively contentful does not obviously entail the idea that, as Wilfrid Sellars argues, "the categories of intentionality are, at bottom, semantical categories pertaining to overt verbal performances" (1956, 94). Nothing about Brentano's canonical formulation obviously suggests that understanding intentionality might involve understanding such things as language and reasoning. How, then, might it come to be thought that Brentano's "reference to a content" involves—perhaps essentially—the peculiar kind of "aboutness" that is exemplified by language? What might it be about thought's representing its contents that essentially involves reasoning?

Roderick Chisholm—himself centrally involved in introducing Brentano's thought (and other themes from European phenomenology) to the mainstream of Anglo-American analytic philosophy[4]—differed from Sellars precisely over the question of whether we are to understand "the intentional character of believing and of other psychological attitudes by reference to certain features of language," or conversely (Chisholm and Sellars 1957, 215).[5] Despite, however, Chisholm's resistance, and despite its not being obvious from Brentano's introduction of the category that intentionality essentially involves semantics, something like Sellars's view is reflected in a use of the word "intentional," common in recent Anglo-American philosophy, to characterize not just contentful mental acts but the level of description at which we speak of anyone's *meaning* something. While there are many ways to tell the story of intentionality and its role in twentieth-century philosophy,[6] I am here aiming for an account that makes sense not only of Brentano's idea of thought as contentful but also of this contemporary use of the qualifier "intentional" to characterize (say) any instance of someone's *saying* something (particularly insofar as that essentially differs from their simply producing acoustic disturbances)—an account, indeed, that shows why it is as we should expect that these ideas should go closely together.

Sellars himself (Robert Brandom reports) said in this regard that "the aim of his work as a whole was to begin moving analytic philosophy from its *humean* phase into a *kantian* one" (Brandom 2000, 32).[7] Concisely suggesting what's involved in thus ushering in a Kantian phase, Sellars said that "Kant insists on the irreducibility of judgmental to non-judgmental content. This, indeed, was the very heart of his insight" (1967, 61). This characterization of Kant's project reflects the idea that Kant took the basic units of experience to be not (as for empiricists) discrete, causally describable sensations, but *judgments* such as are not themselves explicable in terms of the empiricists' sensations. (Sensations by themselves, Sellars said, "are no more epistemic in character than are trees or tables" [1991, 336].) Our task, then, is to see what sense it makes to think about intentionality from the point of view of the characteristically Kantian emphasis on judgment; insofar as this turns out to be a helpful way to think about intentionality, we will see that it's not inappropriate to say that Kant's *transcendental unity of apperception* represents perhaps the most significant forerunner to the contemporary idea that people typically take Brentano to have introduced.

THE "TRANSCENDENTAL UNITY OF APPERCEPTION" AND THE NATURE OF JUDGMENT

The "transcendental unity of apperception"—also referred to by Kant as "pure apperception," "original apperception," and the "synthetic original unity of apperception"—is central to Kant's project.[8] This represents the basis of Kant's "Transcendental Deduction of the Pure Concepts of the Understanding"; it is, indeed, the transcendental unity of apperception *from which* these concepts are deduced. These represent, in turn, the basis of Kant's claim to have developed an account of the objective validity of knowledge. While Kant's "Copernican Revolution" famously turned attention away from objects in the world and toward the knowing subject—emphasizing that we cannot be cognitively acquainted with things-in-themselves, only with things-as-they-appear-to-us—it was because he thought he could show that *how* things appear to us is necessarily structured in certain ways that Kant could nevertheless claim to offer an account of the objectivity of knowledge. His claim is that the conceptual order he deduces represents a condition of the possibility of experience's being *about* a world at all—that our "having the world in view" (as John McDowell says)[9] is possible only insofar as experience is conceptually structured in the ways Kant aimed to show.

The transcendental deduction of the conceptual order begins, then, from what Kant takes as an essentially basic fact about experience: that it consists in the imposition of some perspectival unity on the irreducibly plural data of perception or (Kant's term) "intuition." Experience essentially consists in the ordering or "synthesis" of a sensory "manifold" such as might be characterized (following John McDowell) in terms of causally describable "impingements by the world on a possessor of sensory capacities" (1996, xv). Among the ideas here is that to be the subject of any experience *just is* to have a unifying perspective on the world as seen from some perspective. Despite the centrality of this idea for his project, though, Kant had a hard time expressing clearly just what the transcendental unity of apperception *is*, and the idea is developed rather differently in the first and second editions of the *Critique of Pure Reason*; indeed, this is among the points on which the two editions significantly differ, and we can usefully get a handle on some of the issues in play by scouting the different ways Kant develops it.

In the first edition, Kant develops the idea in response to David Hume, particularly insofar as Hume had argued that there is nothing more to subjectivity than a "bundle or collection of different perceptions, which succeed each other with an inconceivable rapidity, and are in a perpetual flux and movement" (Hume 1739, 252). What is real, Hume had thus urged, is only episodic cognitions, and there is no enduring subject that "has" these fleeting states; insofar, rather, as episodic perceptions exemplify "our notion of diversity, it can only be by mistake we ascribe to [the series] an identity" (1739, 255). Consisting, then, in an always-vanishing subjective "now," awareness represents the paradigm case of something essentially momentary; to that extent, we are misled by the *phenomenological* continuity that characterizes awareness. The phenomenologically continuous character of experience, Hume argued, is explicable in terms of memory and recognition: "as the relation of parts, which leads us into this mistake, is really nothing but a quality, which produces an association of ideas, and an easy transition of the imagination from one to another, *it can only be from the resemblance, which this act of the mind bears to that*, by which we contemplate one continu'd object, that the error arises" (1739, 255; emphasis added). It's only, then, insofar as successive mental states "resemble" one another that they are experienced as states of an enduring subject; in fact, what is real (Hume says in terms that Dharmakīrti would approve) is only existents "such as consist of a succession of related objects" (1739, 255).

Kant first elaborates the idea of the transcendental unity of apperception by way of a compelling rejoinder to this; how, he asks, could we recognize two moments or representations *as similar* without presupposing just the continuity that is supposed to be explained by this recognition? How, in particular, are we to understand the unified perspective *from which* it could alone make sense to say that any two such moments are thus "taken" as similar? "Without consciousness that that which we think is the very same as what we thought a moment before," Kant says, "all reproduction in the series of representations would be in vain." Insofar as mental events are considered as discrete and momentary, he explains, none could ever represent a unified perspective *on* a series thereof; each such event "would be a new representation," and its content could "never constitute a whole"—could never constitute a unified perspective on its predecessors (A103). If, that is, mental events are genuinely discrete, no one of them could so much as *take* its own predecessors as phenomenally similar; to the extent that there is no single "act" somehow comprising others, experience would consist in a series of utterly particular, always unfamiliar cognitive events.

"There must therefore be something," Kant concludes, "that itself makes possible this reproduction of the appearances"—something that grounds "even the possibility of all experience (as that which the reproducibility of the appearances necessarily presupposes)" (A101–102). To characterize the necessary "unity of apperception" as *transcendental* is to say that this perspectival unity cannot itself be encountered in experience; it is, rather, always already in play in any experience that could encounter anything in the first place. Kant thus argues that Hume's appeal to the experienced "relation of parts" that tend to produce "an association of ideas" is itself intelligible only insofar as *being a subject* already consists in having some perspective *on* these "parts"; what it is to have a perspective therefore cannot be explained *by* these parts, since they are always already intelligible to a subject only as the "parts" *of her experience*. Reflecting the transcendental logic that is Kant's defining preoccupation, the point is effectively that Hume's own account (his own denial of the point Kant is after) could itself be intelligible only *given* Kant's point.

Among the questions this raises, though, is what *performs* the synthesis that thus characterizes experience, what the *agent* of this act is. To press this question is effectively to ask for an empirical locus of the action of "synthesis"; but that such a thing could be identified seems to be just what the characterization of this as "transcendental" is meant to rule out. P. F. Strawson notes in this regard that many misgivings about Kant's account thus involve the thought that insofar as we ascribe states to a subject, the latter must be "an intuitable object for which there exist empirically applicable criteria of identity" (1966, 107). If that's right, though, Kant's point would look very much like the Cartesian sort of argument he so unambiguously eschews. The representation "I think" is not, Kant emphasized in this regard, to be understood as anything like the content of a perceptual encounter with one's "self." Indeed, the distinctiveness of Kant's constitutively transcendental approach is clear from his critique of Descartes, against whom he argued that "since the proposition 'I think' (taken problematically) contains the form of each and every judgment of the understanding and accompanies all categories as their vehicle, it is evident that *the inferences from it admit only of a transcendental employment of the understanding*" (A348; emphasis added). The "I think" of transcendental apperception, then, is nothing perceptible; it is, rather, something like the logical or conceptual limit of any conceivable act, even one of inquiring about the empirical self. This point remains obscure, though, as long as Strawson's worry remains in play.

Kant surely aimed to clarify just this point in the second edition of the *Critique*, where his alternative elaboration more clearly emphasizes a strictly *logical* condition of the possibility of experience. Thus, in a passage from which we will take our bearings:

> The **I think** must **be able** to accompany all my representations; for otherwise something would be represented in me that could not be thought at all, which is as much as to say that the representation would either be impossible or else at least would be nothing for me. That representation that can be given prior to all thinking is called **intuition**. Thus all manifold of intuition has a necessary relation to the **I think** in the same subject in which this manifold is to be encountered. But this representation is an act of **spontaneity**, i.e., it cannot be regarded as belonging to sensibility. I call it the **pure apperception**, in order to distinguish it from the **empirical** one, or also the **original apperception**, since it is that self-consciousness which, because it produces the representation **I think**, which must be able to accompany all others and which in all consciousness is one and the same, cannot be accompanied by any further representation. I also call its unity the **transcendental** unity of self-consciousness in order to designate the possibility of *a priori* cognition from it.
>
> (B131–132)

Among other things, Kant here more clearly makes the strictly *formal* point that any experience counts as such only insofar as it is at least *possible* for it to be expressed in terms of the content of some subject's judgment. Note that this is very different from saying (what is surely false) that all experiences *are* expressed as judgments; the point is only that a subject *could* thus attend to her own experience. To emphasize the formal character of this point is, among other things, to say that it does not warrant any inferences about what (if any) kind of existent the referent of this "I" must be; it's not, then, because it gets us anything like a Cartesian "thinking substance" that Kant's argument will provide the basis for a cogent critique of physicalism. (The argument here is not, to that extent, necessarily incompatible with the Buddhist doctrine of selflessness, depending on how that is understood.) The point, rather, is just that "experience" is essentially such that it's only *with reference to a point of view* that we can make sense of anything's *being* an experience; the idea of an experience of, say, *feeling warm* which is such that it's unclear to the subject thereof *whose* experience it is would seem to be unintelligible.

But Kant's passage doesn't make a point only about *being the subject* of experience; it also advances a point (for us the more important one) about being the *content* thereof. The really significant point for us is that it follows from the constitutively synthetic character of experience that the content of experience must be such that it will at least admit of expression *as the content of judgments*; to affirm that the expression " 'I think' must be able to accompany all my representations" is also to say that what is given to any subject in experience must be such that it would at least be possible for her to express its content with a sentence on the model "I think *that* (it's raining, she's late, this is blue, that's too fast, etc.)." The significant upshot of this is that the content of any experience must therefore be the kind of thing that will admit of individuation as the object of a "that"-clause; as John McDowell says in emphasizing the same point, "what one takes in is *that things are thus and so*. *That things are thus and so* is the content of the experience, and it can also be the content of a judgment" (1996, 26).

Among the intuitions here is that only the kind of content that can thus be individuated by "that"-clauses could count as constituting genuinely *objective* knowledge; mental content that's not so describable—the kind of content we would have, for example, given only bare sensings produced by impingements on our senses—would consist simply in *subjectively* known mental representations (would consist in a subject's simply having something appear *to her*). "The difference between truth and dream," Kant says to similar effect in the *Prolegomena*, "is not decided through the quality of the representations that are referred to objects, for they are the same in both, but through their connection according to the rules that determine the connection of representations in the concept of an object" (1783, 42). Any account that grounds our knowledge simply in the images that are causally produced by sensory contact would thus take something eminently subjective as the basis of supposedly objective knowledge; against that, the argument here advances the thought that only *conceptually structured* content could be intersubjectively available.

Among the salient points of the long passage on the transcendental unity of apperception, then, is that only things that are somehow *conceptually structured* can thus be individuated by "that"-clauses; what "that" introduces, in any sentence of the form "I think that *x*," is the *predicate* of a judgment—and "concepts" (Kant says) just are the kinds of things that can serve as "predicates of possible judgments" (A69/B94). In order to enlist Kant's arguments concerning the transcendental unity of apperception for our account of intentionality, the principal point is that the content of experience must be logically of the same kind as what we adduce to justify beliefs or actions; this is finally why it can make sense for Sellars to aver that "the intentional is that which belongs to the conceptual order" (1967, 23). From the fact that (as Kant says following the above passage) "the manifold representations that are given in a certain intuition would not all together be *my* representations if they did not all together belong to a self-consciousness," Kant concludes that "much may be inferred" (B132–133). In particular, what can be inferred just is the "pure concepts of the understanding"—which is to infer that the content of any possible experience must be conceptually structured in something like the same way that *propositions* are logically structured.

Just insofar, then, as experiences are constitutively had from some point of view, they are characterized by the same kind of unity that essentially characterizes propositions—by the fact that the various inputs to experience at any moment are commonly brought together as the unified states of affairs that are picked out by "that"-clauses. The point is that what is individuated by any such thought is complex states of affairs *under some description*, something of the world *as characterized* somehow or another. Insofar as we thus experience things always under some description, it makes sense to suppose that the rules that describe our bringing various inputs (a sensible "manifold") under a unifying perspective are something like the same rules that describe the structure of propositions—that experiential inputs are brought under a point of view (are "synthesized in a consciousness") in something like the same way that the parts of well-formed propositions are related to one another.[10] What any experience is *of*, this is all to say, must be the same kinds of things that also figure in the contentful *sentences* that it's the task of logic and semantics to systematize; "our original idea-contents," as Sellars puts this, "turn out to be the sort of thing which serve as the senses of linguistic expressions" (1967, 66).

We should not here be misled by the fact that Kant's paradigmatic expression involves the verb "think"; his point applies just as well to all of the other propositional attitudes, too. The argument is not, that is, that all experience consists in *thinking*—it is that we can only experience the same kinds of things we can in principle *mean*. The claim is not that all experiences explicitly involve judgments, understood as the conclusions to inferences or arguments; it is, rather, that experience is only contentful, is only meaningfully *about* anything, insofar as it involves the same kinds of things (*conceptually structured* things) that also figure in whatever we *can* say about it.[11]

The transcendental unity of apperception—the idea that experience essentially consists in *some subject's* unifying perspective on the world, which therefore always appears to a subject *under some description*—represents, then, the basis for an account according to which intentionality is a constitutively *semantic* affair. The line of argument here sketched is succinctly expressed by John McDowell: "Experiences in which the world is disclosed," he says, "are apperceptive. Perception discloses the world only to a subject capable of the 'I think' that expresses apperception." That is, there is no perceptual experience that is not *someone's* perceptual experience, no experience that is such that its subject could not attend to it, under any propositional attitude, as *his* experience. And "if an experience is world-disclosing, which implies that it is categorially unified"—which implies, that is, that it is *synthesized* in the way that goes with its being an experience had from a unitary point of view—then "*all* its content is present in a *form* in which . . . it is suitable to constitute contents of conceptual capacities" (2009, 318–319). The extent, that is, to which we can *say* anything about an experience—as, for example, when we adduce it as affording reasons for belief or action—is just the extent to which its content always already occupies Sellars's "logical space of reasons."

ON CONCEPTUAL CAPACITIES AS "SPONTANEOUS"

In a hitherto neglected part of the long passage above, Kant says that the representation "I think" is "an act of **spontaneity**, i.e., it cannot be regarded as belonging to sensibility."[12] He thus contrasts conceptual capacities—those in virtue of which a subject can take it *that* anything is the case—with perceptual "sensibility," which instead involves a faculty of "receptivity." Insofar as our sensory capacities passively "receive" the environment's impingements upon our bodies, we can be said to be "affected" by perceptual objects, where that represents a *causal* relation.[13] The conceptual *synthesis* of the sensory manifold that thus impinges upon us—the bringing of environmental stimuli under the kind of description that can be the content of a "that"-clause—is essentially different from that.

Among the points advanced by Kant's reference to "spontaneity" here is that the unified character of experiential content is not something that could itself be given to us by the irreducibly diverse objects in any sensory field; it's not, for example, determined *by* any particular cluster of vertical objects whether we see them *as trees*, or whether instead we see them as *elms* or as *a forest*.[14] The description under which these are experienced is not itself part of what is *caused* by these objects' "affecting" our senses; this represents, rather, how a subject *takes* them to be. Just insofar as what is thus present to thought is necessarily a complex state of affairs *under some description*, it cannot be thought that the intentionality of the mental will admit of an exhaustively causal description—this is the point Kant means to identify with his characterization of our conceptual capacities as a faculty of spontaneity.

There are, to be sure, problems with this characterization. In the *Prolegomena*, for example, Kant says that "if an appearance is given to us, we are still completely free as to how we want to judge things from it" (1783, 42). But surely it's not right that we are "completely free" in this; we rarely (if ever) *decide* what to make of experienced states of affairs, and a characteristically all-or-nothing notion of freedom—one such as figures, too, in Kant's moral philosophy—here represents an unhelpful characterization of Kantian spontaneity. If, however, Kant is thus "prone to suppose genuine spontaneity would have to be wholly unconstrained" (McDowell 1996, 96), that should not obscure the real insight, which has to do with the very idea of our being held *responsible for* our judgments and beliefs. It is in virtue of the "spontaneity" of the logical space of reasons that it's so much as intelligible to us that we could be *right* or *wrong* in ever thinking as we do and that the activity of justifying our beliefs could thus make sense.

Here, recall (from chapter 2) Boghossian's reflections on the normativity that essentially characterizes the possibility of our *meaning* anything by expressions. The innumerable truths entailed by any utterance, he said, are "truths about how I *ought* to apply the expressions, if I am to apply it in accord with its meaning, not truths about how I *will* apply it" (1989, 509)—a fact that cannot be accounted for by any empirical survey of the dispositions of language-users, since "to be disposed to use a word in a certain way implies at most that one *will*, not that one *should* (one can have dispositions to use words *incorrectly*)" (1989, 513).[15] It is, Boghossian thus argued, the essentially normative character of linguistic understanding that most compellingly resists causal explanation. There is a case to be made for thinking that Kantian "spontaneity" essentially involves the same recognition—the recognition, as McDowell puts this point, that "we need to see intuitions as standing in rational relations to what we *should* think, not just in causal relations to what we *do* think. Otherwise the very idea of what we think goes missing" (1996, 68; emphasis added).

Robert Pippin offers a helpful interpretation along these lines. On Pippin's reading, what is reflected in Kant's discussions of the transcendental unity of apperception is the view that "it is criterial that we must be implicitly aware of our having 'taken' the world to be such and such, and *thereby* of its possibly *not being* such and such" (1987, 462). The argument that the content of any experience must be such as could be expressed by saying "*I think* (hope, believe, doubt . . .) *that* x" advances, then, not only the idea that the content of experience consists in the conceptually shaped states of affairs that can be individuated by "that"-clauses; it also advances the thought that experience essentially involves the subject's awareness *of herself as so taking things*—the awareness of herself, that is, as actively appropriating something that may, to that extent, be mistaken. Pippin thus takes Kant to argue that for any of my experiences to inform an epistemically contentful claim, "*I* must take up the contents of intuition and the mental states that can be said to be produced by such intuitions, and *make* such a claim. *It* cannot both be said simply to occur in a relation of existential dependence on other mental states, and to be 'objective' (possibly true or false) representing of mind, unless I so 'take' it" (1987, 468).

On this reading, it is any subject's awareness of himself as thus *taking* things to be somehow or other that makes intelligible the very idea that we might be asked to justify (by giving reasons for) any of the judgments we so form. It makes sense, that is, that the rightness of any judgment can be challenged only to the extent that it's already integral to the experience of judging that we might *mis*-take things. That we necessarily experience things always under some description means, then, that we are *answerable for* our descriptions. The "spontaneity" of our conceptual capacities reflects, therefore, the essentially normative character of meaning one thing (and not another) by how we take anything to be—the fact, among others, that just *what it is* in virtue of which anyone could be thought right or wrong in describing any state of affairs is not itself something that will finally admit of causal explanation, any more than what it is to *know what a sentence means* will.

This point can be brought into relief by considering the idea of a *causal* account of the very features of experience here characterized. Suppose that it only *seems* to us that our thinking is "spontaneous" in something like the sense here sketched—but that thought's unfolding is *really* more like the sequence of states that constitute the running of a computer program. On Pippin's reading, Kant's idea of spontaneity reflects an insight to the effect that it could never make sense to *know* that such an account of our thinking is true. The very idea of *knowing* oneself really to consist in a causal series is itself intelligible only insofar as the various states in question are "considered as known *to a subject* as caused"—and, Pippin continues, "*this* is only possible by virtue of that subject and its thoughts *not* being considered part of the original causal order" (1987, 466–467). Among the insights reflected in the "spontaneity" idea, in other words, is that it's not intelligible that any moment within a causal series could itself "take" the series as a whole to be some way or another.

What Kant's account can help us see, then, is that for the case of knowing even that *thought consists in a causal sequence*, it is criterial "that I be able to decide whether it is or not, be able to distinguish objective from subjective succession, and this condition could not be satisfied if I were simply *caused* to represent some succession as objective. (That *could* occur, but it would not be *judging*.)" (1987, 467). *Knowing* that thought can be exhaustively described in causal terms would involve the essentially normative idea that one could be right or wrong in thinking so, and that it therefore makes sense that one might be challenged to justify any claim in this regard. On Pippin's reconstruction of Kant's arguments, though, the point just is that we can only have this idea—the idea that how one takes anything to be is itself independent of "knowing whether the truth conditions are satisfied"—if the judging is " 'self-conscious,' not just another in a series of causally produced states" (1987, 467).

This, finally, gets at the point Sellars influentially expressed by saying that "in characterizing an episode or a state as that of *knowing*, we are not giving an empirical description of that episode or state; we are placing it in the logical space of reasons, of justifying and being able to justify what one says" (1956, 76). To characterize someone as *knowing* anything is to characterize her not only as rightly *taking* things as thus-and-so but as *responsible for* her so taking things—and when anyone is called on to justify her so taking things, we understand that what is demanded is not an account of how she happens to have come to believe, but *reasons* for so believing. *Giving reasons*, we have now seen Kant argue, essentially involves "spontaneity," insofar as the constitutively normative dimension of this activity cannot itself be explained in causal terms; this, finally, is why the foregoing arguments are significant for a cogent critique of physicalism.

FIRST PART OF A CASE AGAINST PHYSICALISM: MCDOWELL'S RECONSTRUCTION OF THE "SELLARSIAN TRANSCENDENTAL ARGUMENT"

We now have in place a conception of intentionality as essentially *semantic*, such that thought's being about its contents is appropriately understood on the model of linguistic items as *about* what they mean. This is why it makes sense to say, with many contemporary philosophers, that an "intentional" level of description is exemplified whenever we talk of understanding what somebody *means* by what they say. On Brentano's canonical formulation of intentionality as the hallmark of the mental, we were encouraged to imagine the contentful character of thought on the model of a mental space that *contains* phenomenal representations, which are thus to be understood as having only "immanent objectivity"—and of which it will therefore always be possible to ask whether they can be known to represent anything "outside" of mental space. On my account, in contrast, thoughts have content in something like the same way that sentences expressing judgments do—and whatever we say about a sentence's being about what it means, it's clear at least that this will not admit of efficient-causal explanation.

The question now before us is straightforward: how could this account of intentionality possibly be right? To the extent that, with philosophers like Jerry Fodor, we take the problem of mental causation to be of paramount concern—and to the extent that we take it as axiomatic that only an account involving efficient, local causation could count as addressing that problem—the very fact that the view here proposed will not admit of causal description makes it seem a reductio ad absurdum of the view on offer. Just insofar as our understanding of intentionality is such that it will not admit of a certain kind of scientific explanation, it can reasonably be thought that we must be wrong to suppose either that the conceptual character of experience really is integral to it, or that it really will not admit of causal explanation.

In the remainder of this chapter, I want to develop a case for thinking that *even given the irreconcilability of these levels of description*—even given, that is, the sui generis character of the "logical space of reasons" and the consequent intractability of the question of its relation to what might, following McDowell, be called the "logical space of nature" (1996, xv)—our experience must nevertheless be more or less as Kant describes. Whatever we take to be the upshot of this, there are compelling reasons for thinking that the difficulties entailed by accepting our broadly Kantian account of intentionality are not reasonably taken to count against the rightness of that account—good reasons for thinking, in other words, that if there's a problem here, it must lie elsewhere. These arguments amount, to that extent, to a cogent critique of physicalist (and other exhaustively causal) accounts of the mind; to argue that something like the "spontaneously" conceptual character of intentionality is finally ineliminable from any full understanding of what we are like just is to argue that exhaustively causal accounts of this cannot be right.

I want to develop this line of argument chiefly in conversation with John McDowell, who takes his bearings from Kant (typically by way of Wilfrid Sellars). Among my reasons for so proceeding is that I have for some time been struck by the purchase McDowell's thought affords both with respect to the thought of Dharmakīrti and with respect to contemporary proponents of the project of "naturalizing" intentionality—yet I am frustrated by McDowell's avowedly "therapeutic" stance, which obscures the extent to which his commitments are mutually exclusive of such alternatives. Typically representing his work not as advancing a "constructive" philosophical project but as "exorcizing" certain philosophical "anxieties"—as showing, he says, "how we need not seem obliged to set about *answering* the questions that express the anxieties" (1996, xx)—McDowell urges a "rejection of the traditional predicament, not an attempt to respond to it" (1996, 112). On my reading, though, McDowell consistently advances a straightforward transcendental argument, among the conclusions of which is that physicalist accounts in philosophy of mind (as I here understand those) cannot be right.[16]

Insofar as his account thus precludes particular alternatives, it must be acknowledged, notwithstanding his frequent protests to the contrary, that McDowell's arguments entail essentially metaphysical commitments. In thus trying to make explicit what I take McDowell to be committed to, I am offering a reconstruction, from a large corpus of works that itself reflects a developing perspective (which is another way to say that McDowell can be very hard to pin down), that will not always be consistent with all of the works cited or with McDowell's own stated aims. Not only, though, will this way of developing the argument prove to be helpful when we try, in chapter 6, to characterize Mādhyamika objections to an understanding of the Buddhist project such as Dharmakīrti's, but it also seems to me worth the effort to gain some perspective on the thought of this recently influential philosopher.

Let's begin, as McDowell often does, with reference to Wilfrid Sellars's influential critique of the "myth of the given," as elaborated in Sellars's "Empiricism and the Philosophy of Mind." Sellars here aimed to argue against the kind of "givenness" that consists most basically in the view that "epistemic facts can be analyzed without remainder . . . into non-epistemic facts" (1956, 19)—in the view, that is, that our experience is finally constrained by something (the world as "given" to us in sensory impingements) that is not itself within the logical space of reasons. McDowell characterizes the kind of view against which Sellars thus directs his critique as involving "highest common factor" arguments.[17] Such arguments exploit the fact (if it is one) that an illusory cognition can be phenomenologically indistinguishable from a veridical one of the same thing. That it is possible to have mistaken cognitions that *seem* the same as veridical ones is taken, by proponents of such arguments, to recommend the conclusion that there must therefore be some type-identical kind of *thing*—a mental representation—that is commonly present to both cognitions, a "highest common factor" in virtue of which the illusory and the veridical cognition can commonly seem to be *of* the same thing.[18]

It's clear from this characterization that the kind of view targeted by Sellars dovetails with what we have seen Fodor characterize as a "Representational Theory of Mind"; recalling, then, Fodor's "methodological solipsism," we can understand highest common factor arguments as recommending the view that cognition is autonomously intelligible—that it is *not*, that is, constitutive of cognition for it to have what McDowell typically refers to as "objective purport." The direction of explanation ought therefore to be, on this kind of view, from *seeming* to *being*. Sellars expresses this as the claim that "*looks-F* talk, with which it is possible to form a class of statements about which subjects are incorrigible"—*incorrigible* since one can doubt whether things are as represented in awareness but cannot doubt that *that is how it seems*—"is a foundation of knowledge, and so must be prior in this sense to *is-F* talk, with which it is possible to express only corrigible, inferred beliefs" (1956, 35). That cognition is *of a world* is not, on such a view, among the things we can be certain of; only that it *seems* so is indubitably known. This is, Hilary Putnam says, effectively a line of argument for the view ("almost universally" held) that experience is essentially "something 'inside' us, something in a private mental theater (identified by materialists with the brain, of course)" (2002, 177).

Proponents of empiricist versions of such arguments will take this to represent the best way to secure the certainty of our knowledge about a world; they affirm that reference to causally describable mental representations is a reasonable price to pay for anchoring our knowledge in those *perceptual* encounters in which the world itself, by its impingements upon our senses, actually constrains our thought. Insofar, however, as it ends up being only inferentially, on such views, that one knows one's autonomously intelligible "seemings" to be *of a world*, this approach ends up raising intractable skeptical problems—problems having to do with how (or even whether) the mental representations occupying the "inner space" of our heads can be related to the external world they ostensibly represent. Against, then, "highest common factor" arguments that thus render problematic our epistemic access to anything's really *being* as it seems to a subject to be, Sellars aimed to show that "*being red* is logically prior, is a logically simpler notion, than *looking red*"; it cannot be right, Sellars thus urged, "that *x is red* is analyzable in terms of *x looks red to y*" (1956, 36).

Among Sellars's arguments to this effect is one that invokes the essentially normative character of ordinary linguistic usage regarding such things—a normative character, he argues, that is only intelligible given that "the concept of *looking green*, the ability to recognize that something *looks green*, presupposes the concept of *being green*" (1956, 43). This is evident from the fact that "looks" locutions ("that *looks* green to me") do not concern essentially different content than "is" locutions. Thus, to say that something *seems* thus-and-so is to relate tentatively to some of affairs; to say, instead, that one *sees that* thus-and-so is not to introduce a proposition concerning an altogether different state of affairs—it is to characterize the same one as "making an assertion or claim, and . . . to *endorse* that claim" (1956, 39).[19] The relevant sense of thus *endorsing* a claim is that this involves taking the content thereof to be "in the logical space of reasons, of justifying and being able to justify what one says"—and this just is to take the content of the claim as rationally relatable to all manner of other claims. Sellars can thus conclude this line of thought in a way that echoes Kant's transcendental deduction of the categories: "one can have the concept of green only by having a whole battery of concepts of which it is one element." Indeed, he says, "one has *no* concept pertaining to the observable properties of physical objects in Space and Time unless one has them all" (1956, 44–45).

The argument here, McDowell says, is generally to the effect that "reality is prior, in the order of understanding, to appearance" (1998, 410)—that, inter alia, experience *constitutively* has objective purport; experience is intelligible only *as being of a world*. Advancing this argument, McDowell takes his bearings from a basic disjunction: perceptual appearances, he argues, must be understood *either* as "objective states of affairs making themselves manifest to subjects, or [as] situations in which it is as if an objective state of affairs is making itself manifest to a subject, although that is not how things are" (2009, 231).[20] The relevant disjunction, then, is between views on which cognition is *essentially* of a world, and views according to which it is so much as intelligible that it might not really be so. Chief among the reasons for thinking these disjunctive, McDowell takes Sellars to have shown, is that there is no way to get *from* the second of these to the first; if, that is, it's so much as intelligible that cognition merely *seems* to have objective purport ("although that is not how things are"), the entailed skeptical problems undermine any understanding of the thought that it *does*.

This disjunction represents the basis for the kind of transcendental argument that can be encountered throughout McDowell's works—one to the effect that insofar as there is no sure way *from* things' seeming some way to a subject *to* their really being so, it must be a condition of the possibility of our knowing the latter that cognition is always already *of* a world. Of course, Buddhists such as Dignāga and Dharmakīrti mean (we will see in chapter 5) to challenge precisely the idea that we are right about what McDowell characterizes as the "epistemic position we are manifestly in" (1998a, 344); their Buddhist project is predicated on the thought that awareness is not really *of* what it seems to be of. McDowell might be said, in this regard, to argue only that *if* one would take cognition really to concern a world, it must do so intrinsically—that cognition's *intrinsically* being of a world can only be denied at the cost of denying that it could be of a world *at all*. His point, though, is stronger than this conditional one; he takes Sellars to have shown that we can make sense *even of the phenomenological facts* (even of cognition's so much as *seeming* as it does) only given the rightness of his picture. Thus, the problem with the "highest common factor" conception is that on such a view, "appearances can never yield more, in the way of warrant for belief, than do those appearances in which it merely seems that one, say, sees that things are thus and so"; on McDowell's reading of the "Sellarsian transcendental argument," however, "that thought undermines its own entitlement to the very idea of appearances" (2009, 231). We can, in other words, find it intelligible that experience *has any content at all* only to the extent that it *intrinsically* has objective purport.

McDowell concisely represents the whole line of argument in terms of "Kant's advance over Hume," insofar as Hume takes from his empiricist predecessors "a conception according to which no experience is in its very nature—intrinsically—an encounter with objects" (1998a, 344). Hume was heir, that is, to the Lockean idea that insofar as we can always doubt whether experience is really *of* what it *seems* to be of, we ought therefore to derive our account of knowledge simply from what *seems* to be the case. Hume drew skeptical conclusions from this, arguing that cognition's seeming to be of something could never finally provide assurance that it *is*. On McDowell's reading, Kant credits Hume's argument but builds on it; Kant's advance consists in recognizing that "since there is no rationally satisfactory route from experiences, conceived as, in general, less than encounters with objects—glimpses of objective reality—to the epistemic position we are manifestly in, experiences must be intrinsically encounters with objects" (1998a, 344). Crediting the argument that we could never *know*, of experiences that are intelligible just in terms of how things appear to a subject, that they really afford a perspective on an objective world, Kant effectively reversed the argument; taking the Humean argument as a reductio ad absurdum with regard to the view of knowledge Hume presupposes, Kant concludes that *it cannot be right that experience is intelligible simply in terms of what appears to its subject.*[21] It is, rather, a condition of the possibility of our experience's so much as *seeming* to be of an external world that it already be *intrinsically* so.

All of this, for McDowell, recommends the conclusion that our perceptual awareness can be epistemically contentful only to the extent that our *conceptual* capacities are always already in play therein. An experience, that is, can only be "world-disclosing"—which (recall) "implies that it is categorially unified" such that it is an experience whose content is *that* such and such is the case—to the extent that "*all* its content is present in a *form* in which . . . it is suitable to constitute contents of conceptual capacities" (2009, 319). Just as we should conclude from the impossibility of inferences from *seeming* to *being* that we cannot take the former as foundational, so, too, the fact that there is no way to get *from* essentially nonepistemic facts *to* epistemically contentful experience—from, for example, causally describable impingements upon our sensory apparatus to the kinds of conceptual items that figure in the logical space of reasons—means that it cannot be right to think the latter must be explicable in terms of the former. It must be the case, rather, that we always already experience things (even perceptually) only *as* some way or another, only *under some description* such as could in principle figure (whether as premise or conclusion) in the justification of further belief or action.

Perception can, to that extent, be thought to give us *reasons* for anything only insofar as perceptual content itself is always already essentially incorporated in the logical space of reasons. This, finally, is Sellars's point in concluding (as he chiefly aims to do in "Empiricism and the Philosophy of Mind") that "the categories of intentionality are, at bottom, semantical categories pertaining to overt verbal performances" (1956, 94). We should, that is, understand intentional mental content on the model of the *meanings of utterances*; as Sellars elsewhere says, "the counterpart attributes of conceptual episodes, by virtue of which they, in their own way, stand for their senses, are to be construed on the analogy of whatever it is about linguistic episodes by virtue of which they stand for their senses" (1967, 66). This follows from the Sellarsian argument that *being red* is a more logically basic notion than *looking red*, which amounts to an argument that the "root idea" even of our talk of anything's *seeming* as it does is that of truth. To find intelligible the very idea of characterizing anyone's experience not as a "seeming" but as a *seeing*, in other words, just is to have the idea of applying "the semantical concept of truth to that experience" (1956, 40). And thus to characterize any subject as "applying" to her experiential content the idea of its *being true*—the "semantical concept" par excellence—just is to characterize her as exercising a faculty of spontaneity.

"SECOND NATURE": ON READING MCDOWELL AS A CRITIC OF PHYSICALISM

McDowell has said he takes "transcendental" to characterize "any philosophical thinking whose aim is that there not be a mystery in the very idea of objective purport" (1998c, 365). He thus suggests that the foregoing arguments show that we are mistaken to think there is any *problem* concerning the relation of "mind and world"—or rather, that any account on which this relation *is* problematic is, ipso facto, to be eschewed. Notwithstanding Mc-

Dowell's confidence, the idea that conceptual capacities are necessarily in play even in perception can reasonably be taken as quite mysterious. Considerations centering on the problem of mental causation can be taken to recommend just the view—viz., that "epistemic facts can be analyzed without remainder into non-epistemic facts"—that Sellars targeted as a "radical mistake" (1956, 19). It seems reasonable, that is, to think that epistemic facts *must* admit of analysis in terms of such essentially nonepistemic facts as brain events if we are to address the problem of mental causation. As long as this concern remains in play, it seems to me that, whatever their cogency, the foregoing arguments do not as decisively dispel the mysteriousness of the mental as McDowell typically seems to suppose.

McDowell can be taken to invoke the Aristotelian idea of *second nature* as addressing precisely this worry. Recurrent particularly throughout his *Mind and World*, "second nature" generally represents the idea that "human life, our natural way of being, is already shaped by meaning" (1996, 95)—the idea that it's *just our nature* for humans to "acquire a second nature in part by being initiated into conceptual capacities, whose interrelations belong in the logical space of reasons" (1996, xx), and for our cognitive relation to the world therefore to involve conceptual capacities. If we but remembered this, McDowell suggests, we would see "that operations of nature can include circumstances whose descriptions place them in the logical space of reasons, *sui generis* though that logical space is" (1996, xx). Faced, then, with the kinds of philosophical demands ventured by those who are preoccupied with the problem of mental causation, "We need not connect this natural history to nature as the realm of law any more tightly *than by simply affirming our right to the notion of second nature*" (1996, 95; emphasis added). It's just as "natural" for our mental lives to be constitutively semantic as it is for the central nervous system to work as it does.

It seems clear, though, that it does not address the issues typically raised by Fodor et al. simply to help ourselves to this idea of "naturalness"; this seems, indeed, to represent a question-begging assertion that there just isn't a problem here. To be sure, McDowell does not propose the idea of "second nature" as *solving* the kinds of problems posed by cognitive-scientific philosophers of mind; it is, in fact, particularly at this juncture that McDowell is most apt to characterize his as the kind of Wittgensteinian "therapeutic" exercise that aims to show the demand for a "solution" to be misguided.[22] That McDowell himself has nevertheless elaborated a position with essentially metaphysical entailments is most clear, I think, at the points where his project seems to make contact with characteristically cognitive-scientific proposals—points, that is, where he attempts most explicitly to distinguish his concerns from those of cognitive-scientifically inclined philosophers and to indicate which of the positions of the latter he does or does not mean to exclude.

For example, McDowell ventures that he is "rejecting a picture of a mere animal's perceptual sensitivity to its environment: a picture in which the senses yield content that is less than conceptual but already such as to represent the world. What I am rejecting is a picture of what perceptual states and occurrences are *for an animal*" (1996, 121). This effectively raises what has been called the *problem of infralinguals*—the problem that despite the neurobiological and other continuities between higher apes and humans (not to mention those between human infants and adults), the account of intentionality here on offer "seems to introduce a fundamental ontological and methodological discontinuity where there ought to be continuity" (Garfield 1988, 72). This problem, indeed, is often taken to represent one of the principal considerations in favor of physicalist accounts of the mental.[23]

The difficulty of these considerations makes it all the more striking that immediately after claiming to reject "a picture of what perceptual states are *for an animal*," McDowell nevertheless claims to have "said nothing about how things look when someone tackles scientific questions about how an animal's *perceptual machinery* works." He allows that it's hard to imagine addressing scientific questions about this "without exploiting an idea of content that represents the world but cannot be conceptual in the demanding sense I have been using"—hard to imagine, that is, "since no animal's perceptual machinery (not even ours) possesses the spontaneity of understanding." Given, however, his emphasis on the ineliminably "spontaneous" character of human understanding, it sounds like a non sequitur when McDowell concludes these reflections by insisting that "I do not mean to be objecting to anything in cognitive science" (1996, 121)—and indeed, by allowing that it would "be dangerous to deny, from a philosophical armchair, that cognitive psychology is an intellectually respectable discipline, at least so long as it stays within its proper bounds" (1996, 55).

McDowell thus thinks that we can uphold the sui generis character of conceptual mental content—the kind "that belongs with the capacities exercised in active self-conscious thinking"—and still allow "the respectable theoretical role that non-conceptual content has in cognitive psychology" (1996, 55). Reflecting what I take to be a significant tension running through the foregoing remarks, McDowell nevertheless holds that we cannot understand our distinctively conceptual capacities as "a welling-up to the surface of some of the content that a good psychological theory would attribute to goings-on in our cognitive machinery" (1996, 55). Particularly, however, insofar as a great many projects in "cognitive psychology" would have us understand our conceptual capacities precisely in terms of a "welling-up to the surface" of subpersonal processes, it's not at all obvious at these junctures in McDowell's thought just what he would have us think are the limits of cognitive psychology's disciplinarily proper "respectability."

How exactly would McDowell have us understand the relation between our "perceptual machinery" and the "spontaneity of understanding"? He seems in remarks such as the foregoing to allow that there *is* some such relation, but with his emphasis on the Kantian idea that the sui generis character of the space of reasons is aptly characterized in terms of "spontaneity" (in terms, that is, of its *resisting* causal explanation), it's reasonable to wonder how or whether neurocognitive goings-on could be enabling conditions of—how, indeed, they could be *in any way related to*—the intentionality of the mental as McDowell would have us understand that. Notwithstanding, then, McDowell's Wittgensteinian confidence that he has exorcized philosophical anxieties, it's reasonable to think he still owes us an account of just the kind he thinks is unnecessary; "without something like a *theory* of second nature," as Robert Pippin expresses this concern, "it is not hard to imagine all sorts of bald naturalists nodding in agreement, convinced that the 'training up' of 'neural nets' can handle second-nature considerations just fine" (2002, 65).[24]

Particularly in light of such misgivings about his project, it's worth highlighting some passages in his corpus where McDowell can be taken to allow that his position does, after all, entail metaphysically significant conclusions—that if what he says about our conceptual capacities is right, then certain claims (characteristically physicalist claims, e.g., about causal efficacy as the criterion of the real) *cannot be true*. Thus, "If we can rethink our conception of nature so as to make room for spontaneity, even though we deny that spontaneity is capturable by the resources of bald naturalism, we shall by the same token be rethinking our conception of what it takes for a position to deserve to be called 'naturalism'" (1996, 77).[25] To the extent that McDowell's appeal to second nature thus serves not only as an assertion that it's "natural" for human understanding to exhibit spontaneity but also as a check on scientistic understandings of "naturalism," the idea may not, after all, beg the questions at issue; McDowell's claims regarding second nature may, rather, be valuable not just as a therapeutic reminder but as rejecting the view that "causal relations 'must ultimately be supported by a characterization of the world as the domain of physical natural fact'" (McDowell 2009, 139, quoting Friedman 1996).[26]

Elaborating what I take to be an essentially metaphysical conclusion, McDowell says of the view he thus rejects that "physicalism about causal relations reflects a scientistic hijacking of the concept of causality, according to which the concept is taken to have its primary role in articulating the partial world view that is characteristic of the physical sciences, so that all other causal thinking needs to be based on causal relations characterizable in physical terms." This is, he continues, a defensible view of causation only insofar as there is any "reason to credit physical science with a proprietary capacity to penetrate to the real connectedness of things. But I follow Gadamer in holding that there is no such reason" (McDowell 2009, 139).[27] The strong conclusion McDowell here embraces—the conclusion that characteristically physicalist understandings of causation cannot be exhaustive—is entailed, I have been arguing, by his case for the ineliminably conceptual character of perceptual experience. The "scientistic hijacking" of the notion of causality—the claim, we might say, that only *efficient* causal relations are finally real and that only the kinds of things that enter into such relations can therefore be thought really to exist—is ontologically incomplete (representing only a "partial world view"); this is because we can make sense of the intentionality of the mental only by making reference to the "logical space of reasons." What McDowell thus refuses with his characterization of them as "scientistic," then, is just those scientific accounts that "claim to contain all the real objects there are" (1998b, 473n).[28]

The ineliminable character of our conceptual capacities thus demands that we not take causal relations to consist only in "relations characterizable in physical terms." With respect, then, to the concern—expressed by Boghossian and noted at the beginning of chapter 2—that affirming the ineliminably normative character of mental content seems to commit one, "implausibly, to the essential incompleteness of physics,"[29] we might take the lesson from McDowell to be that it's only mistakenly that we could ever have assumed the *completeness* of physics in the first place.[30] On this reading, McDowell's argument for the ineliminable character of our conceptual capacities (of our "faculty of spontaneity") just is, among other things, a transcendental argument against physicalism—one that can be taken to show that it's a condition of the possibility of experience's objective purport that *causation cannot be exhaustively describable in the terms of physics.*

On the complete picture I have aimed to elaborate following McDowell, then, the argument is not only that our experience can have "objective purport" only insofar as experience always already involves our conceptual capacities (only insofar as perceptual content is essentially the kind of thing one might take as *true*); he is also, I'm now emphasizing, committed to arguing that insofar as we thus cannot make sense of our experience except as having a conceptual dimension, any understanding of causality that renders this problematic cannot be right. Thus, it is finally a condition of the possibility of our "having the world in view"—of our having the kind of mental lives and experience that we do—that causation cannot be exhaustively described in the terms typically favored by physicalists. If he says anything at all by the claim, then, McDowell says something quite significant in saying that "we need not see the idea of causal linkages as the exclusive property of natural-scientific thinking" (2009, 258).

If it's right thus to take McDowell as making essentially metaphysical claims at these junctures, it's not immediately clear how different the resulting picture finally is from the basically dualist kind of account one can take from Kant.[31] While it is not the point of their projects to warrant the conclusion that consciousness or subjectivity represents an ontologically distinct kind of "stuff," for both McDowell and Kant it seems we may still have the kind of "dual-aspect" view according to which we are asked to accept that there are two fundamentally distinct levels of description (call them *causal* and *intentional*) that make sense of human being—and for both thinkers, the question of how or whether these levels of description relate to each other is meant somehow to be ruled out. This foreclosure of the question of their relation need not, however, be understood in terms of the familiarly Kantian reference to constitutively unknowable "things-in-themselves." The real insight may be not that there is a mysteriously but essentially unknowable "other side" of reality, but that *there is nothing it could look like* to answer the question of how these levels of description relate—that nothing could count as explaining how reasoning "really works" (how it *causally intervenes* in the world), since the very idea of there being some way reason "really works"—something else (something "natural") that our responsiveness to reasons *really* consists in—could only be the idea of it as something other than reasoning.

It is, in other words, only *under the right description* that it could in any case be our conceptual capacities that we are talking about; it's only *as conceptual* that intentionality can be individuated, only as semantically contentful that it could be someone's reasons-for-acting that we are talking about. The demand that we show what these "really" are is incoherent as long as it's thought that it can be met only by indicating something not itself conceptual or intentional; it makes no more sense to think we could thus reduce epistemic to nonepistemic facts than it does to say we might *know* something unknowable. Indeed, the very distinction between the "logical space of reasons" and that of "nature" is itself internal to the space of reasons; our *knowing* anything at all about this always already subsumes the very divide that seems to present a problem.

Philosophical intuitions tend to diverge sharply over whether this is a significant point; it's not immediately clear whether it's a truism (one to the effect that we can only think about things *as thought-about-by-us*) or whether instead it discloses a logically or metaphysically significant constraint. While he is, to that extent, here unlikely to move those who are strongly inclined to take the point as vacuous, I take it that it is this broadly Hegelian thought that McDowell elaborates when he revisits the themes of *Mind and World* in his 1998 Woodbridge Lectures.[32]

Among the recurrent images in *Mind and World* is that of our conceptual capacities as somehow extending "all the way out"[33]—an image evidently meant to suggest that we cannot make sense of the world itself as what is on the "other side" of our conceptual capacities, as constraining the latter *from the outside*. Despite, however, his own indebtedness to Sellars in developing this thought, McDowell comes, in his Woodbridge Lectures, to convict Sellars himself of smuggling in a form of just the sort of "givenness" he so influentially criticized; fairly or not, McDowell thus reads Sellars's commitment to critical realism as itself involving a finally scientistic stance.[34] McDowell embraces Sellars's guiding thought that a "conceptual episode's being intentionally directed toward an element in the real order is analogous to, say, a linguistic episode's containing an expression that functions as a name of an element in the real order"; but he resists the view (also found in Sellars, he thinks) that "this 'aboutness' must not be conceived as a relation between an element in the conceptual order and an element in the real order" (McDowell 1998b, 479).[35] According to this reading of Sellars, it must be something from the world *under a true scientific description* that finally constrains thought. According to McDowell, then, Sellars finally thinks Kant ought to have "cast the objects of the scientific image, which are distinct from the objects of the manifest image, in the role of things in themselves" (1998b, 469n23).[36] On this reading, Sellars's point is that certain scientifically described facts about the world finally represent the real conditions of the possibility of our having the kind of experience we do.

One version of the kind of view McDowell is here concerned to reject—and we can set aside the question of whether it's really Sellars's view—is the idea that the posited scientifically describable constraints on experience are precisely such as can supersede (can *explain away*) even the fact of our knowing them. This is the idea that the scientifically describable facts represent, in other words, "what there really is" *instead of* the kind of first-personal experience we seem to ourselves to have (even where it is the experience *of adducing those scientific facts* that we are talking about). McDowell argues that this kind of view cannot coherently be thought to get, as it were, "behind" the kind of experience we are trying to understand, just insofar as such facts are only accessible to us as already the content of just such experience; against, then, Sellars's supposedly scientific-realist construal of Kant, McDowell urges that "for Kant objects as they appear in the scientific image would be just another case of objects as they appear, with a transcendental background for that conception just as necessary here as anywhere. Sellars's attempt to be responsive to Kantian transcendental concerns goes astray in his idea that an appeal to science could do the transcendental job" (1998b, 469n23).[37]

McDowell thus argues that we cannot make any sense of the idea of *explaining* our conceptual capacities in terms of anything that is not itself already the content of those very capacities; just insofar as we *think* any such explanation, thought already sublates the very distinction between thought and reality that we would thus claim to have invoked. Wary, perhaps, of the variously egregious excesses of Hegel, McDowell suggests that "Tarskian semantics points to a sober interpretation"[38] of the clearly Hegelian point he is making here (1998b, 489). McDowell thus invokes Alfred Tarski's "Convention *T*," which specifies that in order for any theory of truth to be adequate, it must entail that for every sentence *P* of any language, "*P*" is true if and only if *p*—as, on a canonical example, " 'Snow is white' is true if and only if snow is white." Here, it's important to appreciate that the seemingly tautological repetition on the right-hand side of such statements represents something essentially abstract—the *proposition*, for example, that is expressed by the natural-language phrase on the left-hand side. This distinction is obscured, however, by the fact that we can only *express* propositions in natural-language sentences. McDowell's Hegelian turn can be characterized as emphasizing just this point; thus, he comments that "we have to *use* the words on the right-hand side of semantical statements" (1998b, 489; cf. 2009a, 63).

If I rightly understand him, the point is that we cannot suppose the proposition on the right-hand side amounts to an *explanation*, from essentially outside semantic space, of how the sentence on the left-hand side means what it does; Tarski's point in deploying this apparatus, rather, is itself intelligible only given the essentially semantic character of *both sides of the equation*. With respect, then, to the essentially Sellarsian thought that "the categories of intentionality are, at bottom, semantical categories pertaining to overt verbal performances" (Sellars 1956, 94), McDowell is here arguing—against what he takes to be Sellars's own finally scientistic compromising of a properly transcendental insight—that it matters that "we have to *use* the words that figure in specifications of what nonovert conceptual episodes are intentionally directed toward. In statements of meaning and aboutness, we relate the conceptual order to the real order, mentioning elements of the real order by making ordinary uses of the words on the right-hand sides of these statements" (1998b, 489; cf. 2009a, 63). The logical space of reasons (to return to the image from *Mind and World*) goes "all the way out," then, in the sense that anything we could know or think about "the other side" of that space would, ipso facto, already be within it.[39]

The logical space of reasons, on this account, is thus ineliminable—which is also to say that our conceptual capacities are ineliminable, that epistemic facts cannot be "analyzed without remainder into non-epistemic facts"—in the sense that anything we could *know* about what explains this would already be itself "contained" therein. There is, then, nothing it could look like to *know* that, say, intentionally describable states like knowing or believing might "really" be something else, or that our conceptual capacities are explicable in terms of things that are not themselves conceptual; just insofar as this could be *known* (could be an object of thought), it would be known "without moving outside the conceptual order—without doing more than employing our conceptual capacities" (McDowell 1998b, 489; cf. 2009a, 63).

A NECESSARY COMPLEMENT TO MCDOWELL'S ARGUMENT: WHAT KANT'S SECOND *CRITIQUE* ADDS TO HIS FIRST

Insofar as it thus involves reflection on *what we are doing* in knowing (or arguing for) the truth of any position, the foregoing nicely introduces an argument that seems to me a necessary complement to the account so far developed—an argument for thinking that the ineliminable character of our conceptual capacities imposes a metaphysically significant constraint on our thinking about intentionality, and that the problems with reconciling certain kinds of causal accounts with our first-personal experience of intentionality should finally be thought to count against the former rather than against the latter. The argument I here have in mind centers on what I follow Kant in calling *practical rationality*, and is to the effect that the physicalist's own demand—the demand, in the face of the difficulties it raises regarding mental causation, that we justify our commitment to the ineliminably "spontaneous" character of conceptual thought—is itself intelligible only given the truth of the claim being challenged.

The complementary argument from practical reason is significant, I think, insofar as it can reasonably be thought possible to reverse the argument so far developed following McDowell—possible, that is, to concede McDowell's point that conceptual and causal descriptions are irreconcilable, but to conclude that this is just so much the worse for descriptions of us as ultimately responsive to reasons. The position I have reconstructed following McDowell—according to which any understanding of causality on which our conceptual capacities becomes problematic cannot, ipso facto, be the right account—is finally only as strong, then, as our commitment to the reality of what McDowell calls the "epistemic position we are manifestly in." The argument so far developed shows, in other words, that we could only *be* in this situation if, inter alia, our experience is not exhaustively describable in causal terms. But if one is prepared to deny that we really *are* in the epistemic situation McDowell takes it we are manifestly in, then the fact that some account of causal relations—one that assumes the completeness of physics, for example—is irreconcilable with a purported condition of the possibility of our being so can be thought to count not against our understanding of causation, but *against our really being in the situation we think we're in.*[40]

To conclude this, one would have to have good grounds for thinking it is particularly the *causal* description of us that is to be preferred in case of conflict between that description and how things seem to us. The present argument thus focuses on the question whether we really are entitled to think this kind of "theoretical" description more likely true than is *what it seems like to reason about it*. That we are *not* so entitled is what Kant argues in his *Critique of Practical Reason*, in which (Kant says) he is concerned "merely to show *that there is pure practical reason*" (1788, 3). Thus to show that reason is "practical," on this account, is just to show that reason is "concerned with the determining grounds of the will" (1788, 12)—that explanations of what we do must include some reference to our *reasons* for doing so and, conversely, that our reasons for acting have some role in explaining how we act. More precisely, Kant's question (as we saw in the first section of chapter 2) is "whether pure reason of itself alone suffices to determine the will or whether it can be a determining ground of the will only as empirically conditioned" (1788, 12). In aiming, then, to show "that there is pure practical reason," Kant particularly has it in mind to show only that we are (as McDowell regularly puts the point) *responsive to reasons as such*—that it is *as semantically contentful* (and not as empirically conditioned) that reasons must figure in a complete account of what we are like.

That reason *is* "practical" in this sense is just what is denied by those who hold that it's only under some other description—only, for example, as represented in brain states—that reasons can be thought to figure in psychology. On one widely entertained version of this denial that reason is really "practical," the "common-sense" view of the mental—the view, in effect, that reason *is* "practical"—really amounts to a *theory* (often characterized as "folk psychology"). The point of saying so is that it's in the nature of theories to admit of alternatives; to characterize our first-personal sense of ourselves as *doing things for reasons* as "theoretical," then, is to suggest that this is essentially comparable to theoretical posits like phlogiston and ether—and that our sense of ourselves may, to that extent, be altogether superseded.[41] While we may, that is, subjectively experience ourselves as responsive to reasons, it's conceivable that a complete scientific description of our cognitive machinery will, though making no reference at all to items such as "reasons" and "beliefs," nevertheless capture everything there is to understand about the mental. It's against such views that Kant aims to show that our responsiveness to reasons as such is *ineliminably* among the "determining grounds of the will"—that human action cannot be exhaustively described without reference to the semantic content of reasons and beliefs.

It's important to emphasize that for reason thus to be among the "determining grounds of the will" is (perhaps notwithstanding Kant's image of a "grounding" relation) precisely *not* for it to be understood as *causally* intervening in our actions; it is only under the right description that it could be our reasoning that we have in view, only *as semantically contentful* that it could be someone's reasons-for-acting that we are talking about. This point is reflected in comments from Elizabeth Anscombe, who brings together the sense of "intentionality" in play throughout this book—the sense in which an *intentional* level of description is involved in experiencing someone who is speaking as not just making noises but as *saying* something—with the garden-variety sense in play when we talk of someone's *intending* to do something. The latter idea, Anscombe says, "would not exist if our question 'Why?' did not. It is not that certain things, namely the movements of humans, are for some undiscovered reason subject to the question 'Why?' "[42] Her point is that "the description of something as a human action could not occur prior to the existence of the question 'Why?', simply as a kind of utterance by which we were *then* obscurely prompted to address the question" (1963, 83).

It is, in other words, intelligible that reasons as such might be among the "determining grounds" of any action just insofar as it's the kind of action regarding which it makes sense to ask the agent *why* she did it. That the agent in such a case is responsive to reasons as such is not to be known, then, by (for example) inferring from the action that it must have been *caused* by the having of a reason; rather, there is something more like a logical or conceptual relation (an *internal* relation) between any action and the reasons that may be taken as among its "determining grounds."[43] The very idea that someone might have acted *intentionally* (in the garden-variety sense of that word) emerges, then, only insofar as we already find intelligible the demand for justification; we *discover* our responsiveness to reasons as such simply in our already understanding what we are being asked when we are called on to justify anything we have done or claimed. Making just this point, Kant urges that "morality first discloses to us the concept of freedom"; it is, he says, "*practical reason* which first poses to speculative reason" the possibility of our freedom, practical reason that has "come in and forced this concept upon us" (1788, 27). The moral idea of freedom that Kant chiefly meant to advance in terms of conceptual "spontaneity" consists, then, at least in our finding "Why?" questions intelligible.

For Kant to show, in light of this, merely "*that there is pure practical reason*"—that our responsiveness to reasons as such must remain part of a complete account of what we are like—is therefore to show simply that we find demands for justification intelligible, and that the aspects of our being that can only be individuated relative to that fact drop out of view if it's denied that reason really *is* thus "practical." This point is not understood, moreover, as long as we persist in thinking it must mean that reasoning is *causally* efficacious—a point McDowell expresses as the thought that "the way certain bodily goings-on *are* our spontaneity in action, not just effects of it, is central to a proper understanding of the self as a bodily presence in the world" (1996, 91n). For a "faculty of spontaneity" always already to be in play *just is* for us to find it intelligible that we can individuate certain of our actions by entertaining the question whether they are as we *ought* to have done—a fact that cannot be individuated without reference to the logical space of reasons.

What Kant's second *Critique* most significantly adds to the understanding of freedom that can be had following the first, then, is an argument to the effect that if any of the foregoing still seems problematic—if, that is, our interlocutor persists in thinking that it finally counts not against the completeness of our understanding of causation, but against the individuation of actions *as* "intentional" that the latter can only be effected relative to the semantic content of demands for justification—it is nevertheless a condition of the possibility of *arguing* so that the space of reasons already be in play. As Kant says to this effect, "if as pure reason it is really practical, it proves its reality and that of its concepts by what it does, and all subtle reasoning against the possibility of its being practical is futile" (1788, 3). Any argument for the finally eliminable character of reason's *being* "practical," then, is only intelligible given the idea of *arguing* for it; just to that extent, though, the fact that our reasoning has some role to play in our behavior is not something that can coherently be denied, since it is only *by reasoning* that one could do so. There is no making sense of the idea of anyone's hoping to persuade us, in effect, that acts of *persuading* are not really real.

What the argument from practical reason develops, then, is a cogent claim to the effect that we not only *can* conceive of reason's really having a place in understanding what we are like but also that we inexorably *do*—even in the very act of arguing against that conclusion. This is why it makes sense for Kant to conclude that while "speculative reason" could put forward the idea of freedom "only problematically, as not impossible to think, without assuring it objective reality" (1788, 3), it can now be appreciated that "practical reason of itself, without any collusion with speculative reason," gives more reality to the idea of freedom than is given by the arguments of the first *Critique*, establishing "by means of a fact what could there only be *thought*" (1788, 5). As he also puts the point, "the moral law thus determines that which speculative philosophy had to leave undetermined" (1788, 42). That is (to demystify Kant's reference here to the "moral law"), the inexorable fact of our responsiveness to reasons as such means that regardless of what it seems our best theories would have us think in this regard, in cases of conflict between any such theories and what we manifestly *do* in entertaining (thinking about, arguing for, knowing the truth of) them, it's the latter that must provide the operative constraint. It cannot coherently be thought that theoretical reason is to be privileged over practical reason, then, just insofar as it can only be *by engaging in reasoning* that any of the theoretical options could constitute the content of our claims.

This, finally, is the kind of argument that I take Dharmakīrti's Mīmāṃsaka and Mādhyamika critics most cogently to press against him. These Indian critics of Dharmakīrti, we will see in chapter 6, can be taken similarly to press the point that reason really is "practical," variously advancing arguments to the effect that we cannot make sense of our *knowing* of seemingly intentional actions (actions like *arguing for reductionism*) that they "really" are explicable in exhaustively causal terms. To raise the question whether this is so is already to engage in *reasoning* on the subject, already to step back from the situation and ask whether things might be other than they seem to us to be; to step back thus from one's immediate situation, though, just is to evince a responsiveness to reasons as such. If, then, we are to find the physicalist's engagement in the argument intelligible, it must be that she finds intelligible the idea of persuading her interlocutor of the truth of her claim—and unless we can give a causal account *of the intelligibility of that way of understanding the conversation*, there cannot, ipso facto, be an exhaustively causal account of the intentionality that is on display in the physicalist's reasoning for her case.

CONCLUSION: RATIONALITY AND THE FIRST-PERSON PERSPECTIVE

Reason's being "practical" is thus shown finally to be a condition of the possibility of its also being "theoretical." This point makes sense of G. F. Schueler's claim (noted in chapter 2 with regard to Dennett's "intentional stance" strategy) that there is necessarily "a 'non-theoretical' element at the heart of reasons explanations, namely the way I understand my own case when I act for a reason" (2003, 160). To argue, in other words, that any account of intentionality (even one that would explain it away) is itself intelligible only as the content of the constitutively *intentional* activity of reasoning about it is, among other things, to argue that our first-personal experience of rationality is logically basic and ineliminable; for me to understand anyone as responsive to reasons is finally to understand them, that is, in terms of *what I am doing when I experience myself as acting for a reason.*[44] Insofar, then, as we cannot finally go any "further down," in understanding or attributing rationality, than to our own first-personal experience thereof, to argue (with Kant) that "there is pure practical reason" is also effectively to argue that an exhaustively *impersonal* account of the mental is finally unintelligible. To the extent, though, that we accept McDowell's arguments that our first-personal awareness must nevertheless be constitutively *of* a world, to argue for the logical priority of the first-personal understanding of rationality is not to push toward solipsism; it is, indeed, the basis for what is arguably the best account of the objectivity of our knowledge. (Dignāga and Dharmakīrti, we will see in chapter 5, come to a different conclusion, based on considerations involving the first-personal character of experience.)

We now have a complete argument to the effect that in reflecting on the nature of intentionality, we cannot coherently eliminate the point of view from which we must do so. The common-sense experience of the mental is therefore not to be understood as analogous to a theory, insofar as it is not, in fact, open to us to accept or reject the very fact that it is only *as reasoning* that it makes sense to think about what "reasoning" might be. Any thought we could have on this or any other subject must, that is, be such as could in principle be expressed as the content of Kant's "I think" ("I think *that* intentionality is causally explicable")—and we have now followed a chain of argument to the effect that this just is to say that anything that could be the content of our theorizing must be conceptually articulable (must be "in" the logical space of reasons), and that this finally entails that putatively exhaustive understandings of causation cannot be right.

If, at the end of the day, it nevertheless seems intelligible that our responsiveness to reasons as such might admit of an alternative explanation (one according to which conceptual thought is finally constrained by something altogether outside of conceptual space), we have now seen that *this cannot be right just insofar as we understand what it would mean to argue for that very view.* To give up the idea that it is thus significant what we manifestly *do* in reasoning about this, as Lynne Rudder Baker says in concluding a transcendental argument of just the sort elaborated here, is "to give up the point of view from which thinking about anything, meaning anything, or doing anything intentionally is possible. To abandon the common-sense conception of the mental would be to relinquish the point of view from which the idea of making sense makes sense" (1987, 173).[45]

Whether or not the line of argument I have thus developed following Kant, Sellars, and McDowell is finally judged cogent, the point for our present concerns is that this line of argument cuts not only against cognitive-scientifically inclined physicalists but also against Buddhists like Dharmakīrti. Despite the extent of Dharmakīrti's own interest in refuting physicalism, the foregoing argument against physicalist attempts at "naturalizing" intentionality is not only one that it is not open to Dharmakīrti to make; it can also be enlisted to identify and characterize philosophical problems with Dharmakīrti's own project. To that extent, Dharmakīrti's own account of intentionality may finally have something essentially in common with the kinds of physicalist accounts he so unambiguously eschews.

In particular, what Dharmakīrti shares with contemporary physicalists is the conviction that efficient-causal efficacy is the criterion of being real and that only the kinds of things (viz., unique particulars) that have such identity criteria are therefore to be admitted into a final ontology. Having concluded, then, our philosophical excursus on some modern and contemporary ways of characterizing the issues in philosophy of mind with a case for the ineliminably *conceptual* character of the mental, we return now to a thinker who, though adamantly opposed to physicalism, is at least as strongly opposed to the reality of just the kinds of things that thus figure in the logical space of reasons. We will first consider, in the next chapter, Dharmakīrti's attempt, in his elaboration of the *apoha* doctrine, to explain the kind of conceptual mental content that has figured so prominently in the foregoing arguments.

4

The *Apoha* Doctrine

DHARMAKĪRTI'S ACCOUNT OF MENTAL CONTENT

A theory of meaning for a particular language should be conceived by a philosopher as describing the practice of linguistic interchange by speakers of the language without taking it as already understood what it is to have a language at all: that is what, by imagining such a theory, we are trying to make explicit.

—Michael Dummett

INTRODUCTION: *APOHA* THEORY AS A NONINTENTIONAL ACCOUNT OF MENTAL CONTENT

We saw in chapter 1 that Dharmakīrti elaborated an epistemological project with affinities to the empiricism of modern philosophers such as John Locke. Attending, in particular, to the extent to which his critique of physicalism is focused by the question of what *causes* cognitions, we saw that Dharmakīrti—advancing what subsequent Indian philosophers would take to be the Buddhist position on the matter—held that only perception (*pratyakṣa*) and inference (*anumāna*) have the status of epistemic criteria (*pramāṇas*); all other ways of arriving at knowledge are reducible to one of these criteria. Of these two, perception is the privileged criterion for Dharmakīrti, given that the contrast between perception and inference can itself be characterized in terms of perception's being, uniquely, causally describable; insofar as he takes causal efficacy as the criterion of the real, Dharmakīrti can therefore think that causally describable perceptual cognitions uniquely afford epistemic contact with *what there really is*. (In the next chapter, we will see that when Dharmakīrti lays his Yogācāra cards on the table, the claim that only causally efficacious particulars are real will look rather different; his will become the position that only causally unfolding mental events finally exist.)

Taking these two *pramāṇas* to have as their respective objects two fundamentally different kinds of existents, Dharmakīrti held, we saw, that a "perceptible" is to be understood as what "causes the content of awareness to track its own presence and absence"—and, in contrast, that anything that could be the content of a conceptual awareness is characterized by its "lacking the capacity for projecting its nature directly into thought."[1] Structuring his ontology around this contrast, Dharmakīrti further held that "ultimately existent" (*paramārthasat*) things are just those that can causally interact with other particulars (and that can, therefore, *produce* perceptual cognitions); in contrast, "everything general, because of its being without suitability for causal efficacy, is not really a thing (*avastu*)."[2] Closely related to these empiricist intuitions are the commitments in virtue of which other Indian philosophers could reasonably characterize Dharmakīrti as an upholder of epistemological representationalism (*sākāravāda*)—the view, as one famous doxographical text puts it, that external objects are only *inferred* from the mental representations (*ākāra*) that, caused by the impingements of the world upon our sensory faculties, are themselves the direct objects of awareness.[3]

Dharmakīrti's characteristic emphasis on causal explanation will look, I've said, rather different when we take into account the idealistic Yogācāra position he finally upholds—though we will see in chapter 5 that Dharmakīrti all along aims to exploit the extent to which epistemological representationalism already recommends idealist conclusions. For now, it's enough to have emphasized Dharmakīrti's characteristic emphasis on causal explanation, in virtue of which Dharmakīrti, like contemporary proponents of the philosophical program of "naturalizing" intentionality, is himself vulnerable to those arguments against physicalism that focus on intentionality. It is because of their common commitment to causal explanation that, notwithstanding Dharmakīrti's emphatically not being a physicalist, intentionality is commonly problematic for cognitive-scientifically inclined philosophers of mind and for Dharmakīrti.

Now, the claim that an Indian Buddhist philosopher is at pains to account for the intentionality of the mental might give pause; surely Indian philosophers, Buddhist and non-Buddhist alike, took something like Brentano's idea of "aboutness" or "reference to a content" to distinguish mental events. This is reflected in standard pairs of Sanskrit terms typically denoting what might generally be called "subject" and "object"; Indian philosophers commonly talk of *viṣayin* and *viṣaya* ("one who has a cognitive object" and the "cognitive object" she has), or of *grāhaka* and *grāhya* (cognitive "apprehender" and "apprehended"). Similarly, the Buddhist Abhidharma tradition standardly defined *vijñāna* ("cognition" or "awareness") as "a specific representation of an object" (*viṣaya-prativijñapti*, or *vijñaptir viṣayasya*)—a definition Dharmakīrti himself affirms at *Pramāṇavārttika* 2.206, where he says the defining property of cognition is "apprehension of an object" (*viṣayagrahaṇam*).[4] What's more, a famous Ābhidharmika debate, concerning whether the past and the future should be thought really to *exist* in any sense, was framed by the dictum that "cognition functions only when there is some content thereof, not when there is none."[5] Based on this idea, some Buddhists proposed that if we are to imagine *thinking about* past or future events, we must suppose these are somehow real, since otherwise there would be nothing such a thought could *be* about.[6]

Buddhist and other Indian philosophers well understood, then, that it's distinctive of cognition to have some content, to represent or be about objects or states of affairs. Even when Buddhist philosophers of an idealist stripe argue against the idea that awareness ultimately has an intentional structure—as many Yogācāra philosophers seem to argue in claiming that the "apprehender-apprehended" duality is ultimately unreal—they nevertheless argue from the recognition that this is surely at least how it *seems* to us. While there may, then, have been influential Buddhist thinkers who were in the business of arguing that intentionality was not finally an *ultimately real* fact, it seems that Buddhist philosophers nevertheless accepted that something like what Brentano identified as "intentionality" is at least among the things we need to explain. Indeed, a predominant theme of Paul Griffiths's *On Being Mindless* (1986) is that the Buddhist tradition's own recognition that *vijñāna* definitively consists in "representation of an object" (that it is definitively *intentional*) occasioned problems for Yogācāra philosophers, who were hard-pressed to explain certain facts about the continuity of awareness by positing seemingly *non*intentional kinds of awareness like (paradigmatically) *ālayavijñāna*.[7]

Particularly, then, in light of the Buddhist tradition's own emphasis on the constitutively intentional character of awareness, it could seem that Buddhist philosophers are well positioned to account for intentionality. We saw in chapter 3, however, that there is a case for thinking of intentionality as essentially involving *conceptual* capacities—for thinking, as on Sellars's elaboration of the Kantian line of thought that recommends this conclusion, that "our original idea-contents turn out to be the sort of thing which serve as the senses of linguistic expressions" (1967, 66). Particularly insofar as there are good reasons for holding such a view, Dharmakīrti may be at pains to account for intentionality; owing, indeed, to his characteristic focus on causal explanation, he may be vulnerable to arguments, pressed by critics both Brahmanical and Buddhist, whose basic logic is comparable to chapter 3's argument against physicalism: the argument that an *intentional* level of description, in the sense developed there, is ineliminable from any complete account of the mental just insofar as such a level of description necessarily figures in the making of any argument that could be advanced on the topic. With an eye toward appreciating the points at which he thus presupposes the very things he aims to explain, we will in this chapter consider the *apoha* doctrine as Dharmakīrti's proposed explanation of the content of thought—an explanation, on my reading, meant as a *non*intentional account of intentionality, resembling, in this respect, the contemporary project of "naturalizing" intentionality.

Apoha simply means "exclusion," and the doctrine centering on this notion is typically (and not inappropriately) characterized as the signal Buddhist contribution to India's philosophically sophisticated preoccupation with language.[8] The *apoha* doctrine represents, in this regard, an alternative to the kinds of realism about linguistic universals variously exemplified by Brahmanical schools of Indian philosophy. Most basically, Buddhist proponents of the *apoha* doctrine aimed to argue that the semantic contentfulness of terms can finally be accounted for without reference to really existent universals[9]—in particular, that the referents of words can be accounted for in terms of "exclusion." On a canonical example of the doctrine, the referent of the word *cow* can be explained simply as excluding whatever is *not a non-cow*. The sense it makes to say this is complex and can be variously understood; the bottom line, though, is that against the kind of view epitomized by proponents of Pūrva Mīmāṃsā—for whom language as such (and Vedic texts, in particular) was eternal—Buddhists were commonly concerned to argue that linguistic items are fundamentally relative to varying and episodic human interests, and that language is therefore to be explained with reference to thought, rather than (as for Mīmāṃsakas) the other way round.

There are many reasons why Indian Buddhists would find it important to take such a position. Ideologically speaking, Buddhists were surely concerned to undermine the authoritative status of the Vedic corpus that provides the basis for Brahmanical social formations. In this regard, the characteristically Mīmāṃsaka claim that the Vedic texts are transcendently authorless or "impersonal" (*apauruṣeya*) paradigmatically lends itself to the sort of analysis characteristic of Pierre Bourdieu, for whom "every established order tends to produce (to very different degrees and with very different means) the naturalization of its own arbitrariness" (1977, 164). The Mīmāṃsaka position, that is, has the effect of masking the interested character of Brahmanical claims, "giving an historical intention a natural justification, and making contingency appear eternal."[10] In this light, Buddhist arguments for the contingent character of language surely reflect a concern to deflate Brahmanical status by developing, as Sheldon Pollock says, "a wider-ranging understanding of contingency or conventionalism in human life"—an understanding that "stood in radical opposition to the naturalism of the *vaidika* thought world" (2006, 52). Buddhist "conventionalism," Pollock urges, is paradigmatically reflected in a view of language that "contrasts as profoundly as possible with Mīmāṃsā postulates of a primal, necessary, and nonarbitrary relationship" between language and nonlinguistic fact (2006, 53).

While Buddhists surely aimed to advance such concerns by elaborating the *apoha* doctrine, what is of interest for us is the philosophical issues motivating the doctrine. In general, characteristically Buddhist claims regarding the status of linguistic universals can be taken to reflect an overriding preoccupation with the constitutively Buddhist doctrine of *selflessness*. Buddhist proponents of *apoha* can thus be understood to have recognized that the kinds of abstractions that figure in the analysis of language are conceptually similar to the abstraction (of governing importance for Buddhists) that is a "self"; linguistic universals therefore should not be allowed into a final ontology for the same kinds of reasons that reference to *selves* does not belong in an ultimately true account of what there is.[11] But there is a more specific set of issues that make it imperative, perhaps especially for Dharmakīrti, to offer the kind of account he does in elaborating the *apoha* doctrine that he takes over from his predecessor Dignāga—issues centering on Dharmakīrti's emphasis on the nonconceptual character of perception. It is, then, particularly owing to the sharpness with which Dharmakīrti distinguishes *perceptual* from *conceptual* awareness that he is ever at pains to bridge the gap between these—and the doctrine of *apoha*, as he elaborates it, can be understood as meant precisely to accomplish this task.

To say of perception that it is essentially nonconceptual is to say, among other things, that perceptual awareness does not (indeed cannot) by itself have the kind of content that makes perceptions intelligible as giving *reasons* for acting one way or another—the kind of content, "suitable for association with discourse,"[12] that is involved in *judgments*. On this kind of view, it would seem that what is given to us in bare perceivings is nothing but uninterpreted sense data; as soon as one attends to the content of perception *under any description*, awareness further involves something other than immediately present perceptibles. Among the problems this picture raises is that insofar as perception's privileged status is a function of its having been caused by its object, and insofar as discursive cognitions are *not* so constrained, it becomes hard to see how the latter could possibly relate to the former—hard to see, that is, how the content of our *reasons* could be thought to involve the same world given to us in perception.

How, in other words, do we get *from* (nonconceptual, causally describable) perception *to* the kind of semantically contentful thought for which that is supposedly foundational? As we saw in chapter 3, Sellars and McDowell take the Kantian lesson in this regard to be that just insofar as there *is* no way to get from nonconceptual perception to conceptually expressible thought, it must therefore be the case that perception essentially involves conceptual capacities from the start. Insofar, however, as that is just what Dharmakīrti denies with his characteristic emphasis on perception's nonconceptual character, it becomes necessary to argue that semantically contentful thought can, after all, be "gotten out of" (can be *explained in terms of*) awareness that is not, initially, itself semantically contentful.

Among the problems in play is that it would seem that perception, even by Dharmakīrti's lights, could not itself count as a *pramāṇa* except insofar as the gap can be bridged in this way. Thus, Dharmakīrti takes any cognition's role in informing fruitful activity as essential to its status as a *pramāṇa*.[13] But on the view that perception is nonconceptual, perceptual awareness cannot by itself be thought to yield the kind of epistemic content with respect to which we purposefully act; indeed, insofar as our activity typically engages what we take to be temporally enduring macro-objects, and insofar as the fleeting particulars given to us in perception appear to us under that description only as conceptually elaborated, there seems to be no avoiding the conclusion that (as Georges Dreyfus says) "for Dharmakīrti perception is not by itself fully cognitive and intentional" (2007, 107). This problem led the commentator Dharmottara, for one, to argue that it is only insofar as any instance of perception comes to "fruition" (*phala*) in an epistemically contentful *judgment* that it can really be thought a *pramāṇa*; something such as this, Dreyfus allows, is as Dharmakīrti must say, since "it is simply not possible to explain intentionality in the full-blown sense of the word without having recourse to conceptuality."[14]

In terms of Dharmakīrti's characteristic understanding of Buddhist "two truths" talk, it's therefore necessary to explain the kind of conventionally existent (*saṃvṛtisat*) phenomena that motivate activity with reference only to such *ultimately* existent (*paramārthasat*) things as figure in Dharmakīrti's account of perception; otherwise, the contrast between perceptual and conceptual thought cannot do the philosophical heavy lifting that Dharmakīrti invokes it to do. Dharmakīrti elaborates the *apoha* doctrine, then, to show how the kinds of things that figure in Sellars's "logical space of reasons" can be explained given the resources of an ontology according to which only causally efficacious particulars are finally real. In terms of my guiding concerns, Dharmakīrti's point is thus to explain *intentionality* (insofar as that is essentially *semantic*) in terms of a finally nonintentional, nonsemantic level of description. In terms suggested by our consideration, in chapter 2, of Jerry Fodor's project, the doctrine of *apoha* aims to explain the very idea of *meaning* simply in the (as it were) "syntactic" terms of causally describable transactions among unique particulars.

If his account is to succeed, Dharmakīrti cannot presuppose a semantic level of description—a level at which notions like "meaning" and "truth" are in play—since that is just what he aims to explain. His success in this regard is surely debatable; the *apoha* doctrine is complex and in many ways promising, and cogent arguments were developed both for and against it. What I am driving at in this chapter is the point that arguments for the doctrine depend at some points on a related pair of questions that proponents of *apoha* do not, so far as I can see, satisfactorily address. These questions concern the initial *devising*, by hitherto nonlinguistic beings, of a system of linguistic "conventions" (*saṃketa*), and any individual's first *acquisition* of a language so devised. These issues are recurrently conflated, in Dharmakīrti's elaboration of *apoha*, with insights about *using* an already available language; this conflation is exploited to obscure what is arguably among the most basic difficulties in giving a finally nonintentional account of semantic content.

A related observation was ventured by Georges Dreyfus, whose discussion of Dharmakīrti's account of *apoha* (like Dharmakīrti's account itself) "does not intend to illustrate how we acquire language in general but how we learn a particular concept" (1997, 227). Noting that "the question of how language is acquired is not addressed by Buddhist epistemologists" (1997, 515n32), Dreyfus cites some pertinent observations from Sellars, who should be understood (Dreyfus says) as pointing out "the fallacy of placing the learning person in [a] universe of already categorized objects" (1997, 515n32). As Sellars says in the passage to which Dreyfus thus refers, the real test of a theory of language lies in its "account of those occasions on which the fundamental connection of language with non-linguistic fact is exhibited"; many seemingly nominalist accounts, Sellars says, "turn out to be quite 'Augustinian' when the scalpel is turned to their account of [this]" (1956, 65).

Sellars here refers, no doubt, to the passage from Augustine in terms of which Wittgenstein famously begins the *Philosophical Investigations*—a passage, we saw in chapter 2, regarding whose significance Fodor sharply disagrees with Wittgenstein.[15] Among the salient points of Augustine's account of language acquisition, on Wittgenstein's reading, is that insofar as we imagine *becoming linguistic* to consist simply in learning the names of things, we are not getting at what "having a language" really consists in; such an account presupposes, rather, the very thing we are trying to understand when we investigate our being linguistic, which is the idea of *meaning* anything. The present chapter explains, in effect, what I take Sellars to mean by his allusion to this discussion; following Dreyfus's suggestion in referring to it, I want to show that Sellars's point may shed light on some interesting problems with Dharmakīrti's project. When we consider, in particular, Dharmakīrti's own references to "those occasions on which the fundamental connection of language with non-linguistic fact is exhibited," we can see that he presupposes precisely the sort of thing Wittgenstein takes Augustine to presuppose. To get at this, however, it's useful to begin with the rather different account of the *apoha* doctrine first elaborated by Dharmakīrti's predecessor Dignāga.

DIGNĀGA'S ACCOUNT OF *APOHA*: CONCEPTUAL CONTENT AS DEFINED BY INFERENTIAL RELATIONS

The doctrine of *apoha* was first elaborated by Dharmakīrti's predecessor Dignāga, whose *Pramāṇasamuccaya* ("Compendium on *Pramāṇas*") is the work on which Dharmakīrti's *Pramāṇavārttika* is ostensibly a commentary. Notwithstanding, however, a long-attested tendency (traditional and modern) to see these thinkers as exemplifying a unitary school of thought, *apoha* is chief among the issues regarding which we can appreciate the sometimes significant divergence between them. Their different elaborations of the doctrine reveal something of the significance of Dharmakīrti's peculiar focus on causal explanation; for while causal efficacy is for Dharmakīrti the criterion of *being ultimately existent*, that axiom does not obviously figure in Dignāga's development of the Buddhist project.[16] While these Buddhists commonly aim, then, to develop the *apoha* doctrine as an alternative to characteristically Brahmanical realism about linguistic universals, it's clear that Dharmakīrti's elaboration of the doctrine (but not Dignāga's) further amounts to an attempt at an exhaustively causal account of mental content. That this is an apt way to characterize Dharmakīrti's understanding of *apoha* can usefully be brought out by appreciating some of the differences between his understanding of it and that of Dignāga.

Dignāga argued (as Dharmakīrti would follow him in doing) that only perception and inference finally have the status of *pramāṇas*, and that none of the other epistemic criteria that Indian philosophers proposed as *pramāṇas* count as such just insofar as they are demonstrably reducible to one of these two. Among the various epistemic criteria that were candidates for the status of *pramāṇa*, those Brahmanical thinkers intent on defending the authority of the Vedic corpus took the status of linguistic cognition (*śābdajñāna*) to be particularly significant. Brahmanical thinkers were variously concerned to argue that the epistemic reliability of the testimony of "scripture" or "tradition" (*āgama*) was somehow basic—that there is, indeed, something ineliminably and irreducibly *linguistic* about knowing and that linguistic cognition therefore counts somehow as a *pramāṇa*. Against such intuitions, Dignāga and Dharmakīrti commonly argued that instances of linguistic cognition do not count as *pramāṇas* just insofar as language is, in fact, somehow reducible to inference.

This might most naturally be understood as the claim that one reasonably credits any instance of testimony as epistemically reliable just insofar as one can infer that the source of the utterance is reliable; knowing something linguistically, that is, essentially involves inferentially taking the measure of some speaker.[17] That is not, however, precisely how either Dignāga or Dharmakīrti understood the claim. On Dharmakīrti's account, we will see, the point is that upon encountering any utterance, one is entitled only to infer that some speaker's *intention* has been expressed—where, significantly, it is a peculiar sense of "intention" that Dharmakīrti must, in virtue of his central commitments, have in view. Dignāga, on the other hand, had in mind yet another way to understand linguistic awareness as reducible to inference, and it is with this that he begins his elaboration of the *apoha* doctrine in chapter 5 of his *Pramāṇasamuccaya*: "Linguistic [cognition] is not a *pramāṇa* distinct from inference, since, just as in the case of [an inferential sign] like 'being made,'[18] [it] designates its proper referent by excluding what is other."[19] Dignāga's point in thus affirming that linguistic cognition is not a *pramāṇa* distinct from inference seems to be simply that language and inference both, as it were, *work the same way*.

Shoryu Katsura and Richard Hayes have suggested in this regard that Dignāga be understood to have elaborated the *apoha* idea as effectively thematizing the logic of inferential relations. Dignāga's account of inferential relations was (Hayes suggests following Erich Frauwallner) thus distinguished from its predecessors by the recognition that "inference was based not upon an appeal to causal relations between the inferential sign (*liṅga*) and the thing inferred from it, but rather upon the relative scopes of concepts, whereby wider concepts could be inferred from narrower but not vice versa" (1988, 24). While we will see that Dharmakīrti is concerned to offer an explanation of how conceptual mental content is constructed just from the causally describable inputs to awareness, Dignāga's elaboration of *apoha* doctrine, in contrast, evinces little concern with how linguistic items "make contact" with the world of really existent particulars. Instead, his arguments address only the *relative* determinacy of conceptual content—the conceptual scope or richness of terms only insofar as they are relative to the other terms in a system.

Dignāga's development of the doctrine well exemplifies what Hayes takes to be "the basic claim behind the *apoha* theory of meaning": that "every symbol divides the universe into two and only two mutually exclusive classes" (1988, 211).[20] Specifically, every concept divides the universe into the class of all things that come under that concept and the complementary class of *everything else*. When the matter is thus understood, the question to be answered will always simply be: at what level of generality has this division been made? Dignāga's insight is that the answer to this question can be expressed (and accordingly, that relative conceptual determinacy can be explained) entirely in negative terms—which is to say, without having positively to specify really existent universals of any sort. The relative determinacy of concepts like "tree" and "maple," then, can be precisely expressed without reference to timeless properties like *being a tree* or *the set of all trees*; rather, the term "tree" excludes from its purview everything there is that does not properly come under the concept "tree," while the term "maple" excludes exactly that much *plus* all nonmaples within the category "tree." The greater determinacy of the category "maple" is thus a function of its excluding a larger domain—one whose scope is constrained by the immediately superordinate category in an ascending hierarchy of increasing generality.[21]

Dignāga concisely expresses this idea of a hierarchy of concepts at *Pramāṇasamuccaya* 5.35: "[The properties] 'being a tree,' 'being earthen,' 'being a substance,' 'being existent,' and 'being knowable' are, [respectively,] the basis of four, three, two, and one [degrees of] certainty; taken in the opposite order, [they are the basis of just as many degrees of] doubt."[22] That is, these properties constitute an ascending hierarchy of increasing generality, with the most general level ("being knowable") representing the least conceptually determinate; it is the basis, Dignāga suggests, of only one "degree" of certainty.[23] While *concepts*, by definition, never have the concreteness that characterizes spatiotemporally determinate objects—a hierarchical account such as Dignāga's, Jonardon Ganeri aptly says, is "asymptotic, reaching ever nearer, but never actually touching the world of objects" (2001, 109)—the most determinate conceptual level (the one with the most precisely specifiable content) will be, on this account, *the one with the greatest exclusion range.*

Dignāga can be understood thus to have characterized what Dharmakīrti will call the *tādātmya*, or "identity," relation. Dharmakīrti will subsequently elaborate, then, the idea that only two kinds of relations can obtain between any terms: the *causal* relation—that of *tadutpatti*, or "arising from that"—that obtains between, say, fire and smoke; and the *tādātmya* relation, which obtains between precisely such conceptual levels ("being a tree" and "being a maple") as we have here seen Dignāga address.[24] On Dharmakīrti's later treatment, these two kinds of relations correspond to two fundamentally different kinds of reasons (*hetu*) such as can provide entitlement to any inferential conclusion. Thus, when a reason consists in the *effect* (*kāryahetu*) from which one infers the presence of its cause (as when inferring the presence of fire from seen smoke), the *tadutpatti* or "causal" relation is in play; inferences, in contrast, that trade simply on the relative scopes of concepts—as when one knows, based on something's being a *maple*, that it is therefore also a *tree*—involve the *tādātmya*, or "identity," relation.

It should be clear that there is a difficulty with thinking of the latter case as involving *identity* relations, since if we think of "maple" and "tree" as strictly identical we lose the asymmetry that characterizes inferential relations; unlike identity relations, that is, this inference only works in one direction—we are not entitled to the claim that because something is a *tree* it must therefore be a *maple*, since not all trees are maples.[25] Indeed, what Dignāga has elaborated, with his development of the *apoha* doctrine, just is an account of conceptual relations as defined by inferential asymmetry—as defined by the fact that relations among conceptual levels license inferences in one direction but not the other. In the characteristically elliptical terms of Sanskrit verse texts, then, Dignāga has made a point almost precisely like one advanced in Robert Brandom's account of the relation *being inferentially weaker or stronger than*:

> The sentence *q* is inferentially weaker than the sentence *p* just in case everything that is a consequence of *q* is a consequence of *p*, but not vice versa. . . . The negation of a claim is its inferentially minimal incompatible: ~*p* is what is entailed by everything materially incompatible with *p*. These underlying incompatibilities induce a notion of inferential weakening: "Thera is a dog" incompatibility-entails, and so is inferentially stronger than, "Thera is a mammal," because everything incompatible with "Thera is a mammal" is incompatible with "Thera is a dog," but not vice versa. . . . It follows that incompatibility-inferentially weakening a negated claim incompatibility-inferentially strengthens the negation. "It is not the case that Thera is a mammal" is incompatibility-inferentially stronger than "It is not the case that Thera is a dog," just because "Thera is a mammal" is incompatibility-inferentially weaker than "Thera is a dog."
>
> (2000, 147)

So, too, on Dignāga's account, "this is a maple" is inferentially stronger than "this is a tree" just insofar as everything that is incompatible with "this is a tree" is also incompatible with "this is a maple" but not the other way round. This gives us a way *negatively* to specify the different scope of concepts, whose relative determinacy is expressible simply in terms of their exclusion of all the other members of a branching categorial hierarchy—just as "tree" excludes "chariot" but not "maple" or "oak," while "maple" excludes not only chariots (and everything else in the world that is not a tree), but additionally *all trees that are not maples*.

With regard to Indian debates about the ontological status of linguistic universals, the point is that it's thus possible to account for the *relative contentfulness* of concepts without having to specify in what, precisely, their content "really" consists; we can account for the inferential asymmetry that defines the place of any concept (say, *tree*) in a larger scheme without having positively to specify either the intension ("being tall and leafy") or the extension ("the set of all woody perennial plants") of the concept. This is a desideratum, for Buddhists, since the kinds of things we could positively specify in this way are not really *real* in anything like the same way as, say, particular trees that one can actually chop down and use for wood. Given such an understanding, it's rather beside the point to fault the doctrine of *apoha* (as many Brahmanical critics did) on the grounds that what is phenomenologically present to someone who is thinking of maples is nothing like "all trees that are not nonmaples."[26] Dignāga's is, rather, a strictly formal account of the constitutively inferential logic of the kinds of things that figure in Sellars's "logical space of reasons."

ON LEARNING CONVENTIONS: DIGNĀGA'S "AUGUSTINIAN" PRESUPPOSITIONS

Even if it's allowed, however, that it cogently accounts for the relative determinacy of conceptual content, the foregoing account nevertheless raises an obvious question: how do we know *which* things properly come under any of the concepts whose content can be thus delimited? To say that the concept "tree" divides the universe into the class of *all things coming under that concept* and the class of *everything else*, it seems, is to presuppose that we already know what the concept "tree" picks out—and one could reasonably suppose that's just what the proponent of *apoha* needs to explain. Dignāga's account may indeed be vulnerable, then, to one of the standard objections to *apoha* doctrine, which is that insofar as it presupposes just what it purports to explain, it fundamentally begs the question. This objection can be straightforwardly expressed (as it frequently was by the Mīmāṃsaka Kumārila Bhaṭṭa) in terms of double negation; if the referent of the word "cow" is really to be understood in terms of the exclusion of everything that is "*not a non-cow*," the double negation entails that this is no different from the referent's being *cow*. But if we know, in this way, that the referent of "cow" is, after all, *cow*, it seems that we cannot avoid saying we are thus acquainted with some kind of universal.[27]

With respect to this problem, we can usefully introduce one of the most interesting ways in which Dignāga's account of linguistic meaning dovetails with his account of inference: while his account of inference centrally involves (like all Indian discussions of the matter) the relations of *anvaya* and *vyatireka*—terms most often represented as concerning the logical relations of positive and negative "concomitance"—it matters that it's particularly the Sanskrit grammarians' usage of these terms that informs Dignāga's presentation. When the same terms, in the senses they have for the grammarians, come into play when Dignāga addresses the question I have just raised, their use can be seen as problematic in a way that precisely parallels what many take to be the basic problem in Dignāga's account of formally stated inferences. It is, then, pertinent to say a bit more about Dignāga's account of inference.

Offering an unprecedentedly formal account of the conditions to be met in order for any inference to entitle us to its conclusion, Dignāga influentially specified three conditions (the *trairūpya*) that must be met in this regard.[28] These conditions involve possible relations among three terms: the "locus" in question (*pakṣa*); the property, present at that locus, from which we infer something else (i.e., the *hetu* or "reason"); and the property whose presence in the locus is just what is inferred (*sādhya*) from the "reason" property. The first of these conditions is called *pakṣadharmatā* ("being a property of the locus") and consists simply in the fact that the "reason" property—on the canonical example of inferring from smoke that there is fire on a mountain, this would be the mountain's *being smoky*—really is present in the relevant locus (here, the mountain). The relation of *anvaya* then specifies, as the second condition, simply that there is *at least one other thing*[29] in the induction domain—at least one among all things other than the locus in question—that exemplifies the co-occurrence of the probative and inferred properties, one other case of something's being both smoky and fiery. The relation of *vyatireka*, finally, specifies that there is nothing in the induction domain possessing the *hetu* ("being smoky") without also possessing the property to be inferred therefrom ("being fiery").

Clearly, knowledge of the last condition is problematic. While a subject can be in a position to know that *pakṣadharmatā* obtains (that some mountain, e.g., really is smoky) and also that the relation of *anvaya* applies (that there is at least one other known case of something's being at once *smoky* and *fiery*), only an omniscient subject could have knowledge to the effect that *nothing in the world has been smoky without also being fiery*.[30] It's at this point, then, that modern expositors of Dignāga will point out that his remains a finally inductivist model of inference and that Dignāga's account of reasoning is therefore vitiated by the limitations inherent in such a model.[31] *Vyatireka*, on this account, represents something other than the logical contraposition of *anvaya*, and Dignāga can reasonably think it not redundant for a formally stated inference to make reference to both;[32] but while reference to both is therefore not redundant, the same requirement nevertheless reflects the extent to which (as Jonardon Ganeri says) Dignāga "could not quite free himself from the old model of inference from sampling" (2001, 21).

Be that as it may, Hayes suggests that we can better see that it's not redundant to refer to both *anvaya* and *vyatireka* if we appreciate that Dignāga particularly presupposes the Sanskrit grammarians' understanding of these terms; this is because "in the usage of the grammarians, *anvaya* and *vyatireka* are logically independent rather than being contrapositive propositions" (1988, 119).[33] For thinkers in the Sanskrit grammatical tradition, the same terms figure in an account of the conditions under which the meanings of words are learned; specifically, they refer (George Cardona says) to conditions for determining "the constant co-occurrence (*sāhacarya*) of a linguistic item (*śabda*) and a meaning (*artha*). A meaning is not understood unless the item expressing it occurs; if an item occurs a meaning is understood, and when that item is absent the meaning attributed to it is also absent" (1967–1968, 345).

Corresponding to each of Dignāga's three conditions for a successful inference, then, there is a precisely analogous rule (also expressible in terms of *anvaya* and *vyatireka*) for determining the proper use of a word. Corresponding to the requirement of *pakṣadharmatā*, there is the rule simply that "the word must be applicable to the subject of discourse"; that is, the meaning of a word can be learned only if it's appropriately applied at least to the particular thing referred to on the occasion of learning. The semantic analogue of the requirement of *anvaya* then specifies that the word "must be applicable to objects other than the subject of discourse that have that which is to be learned through the word"; that is, it can only be a semantically contentful *word* or *concept* that is being explained (as contra the unique ostension of some particular) if there is at least one other example of something appropriately referred to thereby. Finally, the *vyatireka* condition here takes the form of knowledge to the effect that the word is "restricted in application to that which is to be learned through it"; that is, rightly understanding the learned word consists partly in recognizing when it is *not* appropriately used—recognizing when it would be wrong (as when one says "horse" while pointing at a cow) to use the word.[34]

Here is what these requirements look like in Dignāga's verse statement of the issue at *Pramāṇasamuccaya* 5.34:

> Since we don't observe [the use of] a word in regard to a contrary sense, [and] since we do observe [the use of it] in regard to the portion which is its own sense, the word's connection is easy to indicate, and there is no errancy.[35]

Dignāga's autocommentary elaborates:

> A word expresses its referent by means of *anvaya* and *vyatireka*. These [consist, respectively, in] applying to what is similar, and not applying to what is not similar. In this regard, it's certainly not said that [a word is known to] apply to *every* similar case (though it does to some), since the expression of an unlimited extension is impossible. But simply insofar as it's not observed in connection with what is dissimilar—even though that, too, is unlimited—it is possible to say that it doesn't apply to the latter.[36]

The point of Dignāga's here saying that one needn't know every particular in the extension of a concept is exactly the same as the requirement of *anvaya* in the case of inference; the account requires (and explains conceptual determinacy partly by virtue of the fact) only that there be *at least one other* particular thing to which the word is appropriately taken to refer—one needn't be in a position to specify all such things.

It is, however, really the *vyatireka* condition on the learning of a word that is doing the work here; while it's necessary to be acquainted with a few tokens of the kinds of things appropriately referred to by a word, we don't really get any purchase on the *normative* character of its use until we also know what is *not* appropriately referred to thereby.[37] And just as in Dignāga's account of formally stated inferences (which requires knowledge to the effect that nothing in the world has the probative property without also having the property proved thereby), it's this condition that is most problematic; indeed, at this juncture Dignāga arguably begs just the question at issue. In regard, then, to his claim that it can be known that there are no relevantly *dissimilar* particulars to which a word is appropriately taken to refer, Dignāga's concession ("even though that, too, is unlimited") is revealing; for if it's true that the relative scope of concepts can be specified in terms of their exclusion ranges, it nevertheless remains the case that one cannot know that a word is *inappropriately* applied without knowing, thereby, something more than that some particular is excluded from the range of the term in question. As we have seen following Paul Boghossian,[38] what is most difficult to specify, on the sort of dispositional account Dignāga can here be said to suggest, is *what it is in virtue of which* anyone could be judged wrong in using a word—and the relevant criterion is not a matter of how individuals *do* use words but rather how they *ought* to. To that extent, though, Dignāga's appeal to the *vyatireka* condition here is no more helpful than it is when he suggests, by his use of the same terms in formalizing inference, that a non-omniscient person could know nothing in the universe to be smoky without also being fiery.

In both of the cases in which Dignāga appeals to *vyatireka*, then, it seems that what we need to know in order to be entitled to the conclusion—whether the conclusion is that there must be fire on some mountain or that we understand what the word "fire" appropriately refers to—is just what the proponent of *apoha* needs to explain. It seems, in other words, that we again face a circularity problem: to know there is nothing *dissimilar* that is rightly picked out by a term just is, it seems, to know what *is* rightly picked out. Dignāga responds, at this point, with something of a retreat, effectively saying (according to Hayes) "that the universal property that is shared by a group of particulars and that serves as the basis for grouping those particulars is simply the fact that all those particulars are members of the set of things to which a specified word is applicable. That by which I know of a fire that it is a fire is simply the fact that I readily apply the word 'fire' to it" (1988, 187). As Dignāga expresses the point, "In this regard, the word itself is the thing that objects have in common."[39]

But in that case (and this is chief among the points I've been aiming to make about his account), Dignāga's elaboration of the *apoha* doctrine finally presupposes an intentional level of description; insofar, that is, as his account cannot avoid reference to an already available and intelligible system of linguistic conventions, Dignāga presupposes, to recur to Lynne Rudder Baker's words, that we already know "how one thing (some mental item) *can mean or represent or be about* some other thing (for example, some state of affairs)—[that we already] understand how anything can have content."[40] In order, that is, to learn from the observation of linguistic practice how any *particular* words are appropriately used, one must already have, we will see the Mīmāṃsakas argue, what the *apohavādin* most needs to explain; *the very idea of meaning something* (and not just the meanings of particular words) is the problem that the initial acquisition of a language most basically represents, and Dignāga's appeal (in the contexts of formalizing inferences and of accounting for language learning) to *anvaya* and *vyatireka* gives us no purchase on that problem.

One might reasonably rejoin on Dignāga's behalf that the whole point of his approach just is to suggest that "there is not necessarily a basis in reality for our conventions being as they are" (Hayes 1988, 208). Whether or not that's a satisfying answer, we here begin to glimpse the problem that will come more sharply into relief given Dharmakīrti's clearly different ambitions for the *apoha* doctrine: insofar as Dignāga has said we learn which things in the world fall under which concepts just by observing how people use an already given language, this invites the counterargument that *that fact* is not something that can itself be explained in nonsemantic terms. It's at just this point, then, that we can usefully turn to Dharmakīrti's peculiarly causal elaboration of the *apoha* doctrine; while Dignāga may not aim to explain, in nonsemantic terms, the point at which language makes contact with nonlinguistic reality, this is just what Dharmakīrti seems to be after.

DHARMAKĪRTI'S ACCOUNT OF *APOHA*: CAUSALLY LINKING PERCEPTS AND CONCEPTS

We might say, in terms suggested by Frege, that if Dignāga's account of *apoha* chiefly concerns the *sense* of terms, Dharmakīrti's account instead concerns their *reference*;[41] that is, what Dharmakīrti can be taken to add to the picture sketched by Dignāga is chiefly an account of how linguistic items can be understood to make some kind of contact with the unique particulars that alone ultimately exist. If Dignāga's elaboration of the *apoha* doctrine is finally unhelpful in determining how we know *which particulars* are rightly brought under any concept (however cogently he has explained the relative scope thereof), something precisely like this seems to be what Dharmakīrti aims for. We might also say that if Dignāga's account can be understood as characterizing the inferential asymmetry that defines what Dharmakīrti would call the *tādātmya* relation,[42] Dharmakīrti's elaboration of the *apoha* doctrine instead centers on the *tadutpatti* ("causal") relation, insofar as the account of reference he offers is an eminently *causal* one. On Dharmakīrti's understanding of the doctrine, then, *apoha* is proposed as addressing the problem I characterized in beginning this chapter—as explaining how we get *from* causally describable perceptions (which must be what we start with since these alone contact real existents) *to* the semantically contentful thought on which perception is supposed to provide some constraint.

Chief among the difficulties here is that the transition from one level of description to the other can itself be causally described, it seems, only insofar as conceptual capacities will finally admit of causal explanation (and we saw, in chapter 3, a case for thinking they will not)—while if the transition is *not* itself causally describable, then it is hard to see how the privileged status that goes with *perception's* being so can be transmitted to (can be a constraint *on*) the semantically contentful awareness we are here trying to understand.[43] While we saw in chapter 3 that the intractability of this problem can be taken to recommend the conclusion that conceptual capacities must therefore be in play from the start (and that there is thus no "transition" in need of explaining), Dharmakīrti's commitment to the view that only causal relations are finally real inclines him, rather, to attempt a causal explanation of the bridging of this gap. Thus, Dharmakīrti holds that while the propositional contents of thought are constitutively erroneous insofar as they involve unreal abstractions, they are not groundless; rather (as Georges Dreyfus says in summarizing his account), "they arise as results of the indirect causal connection between real things, our perceptions of them, and our thoughts. There is no connection between perceptions and universals, the objects of concepts, for those are of two different orders, but experiences and concepts are connected and thus provide a bridge between the two realms (the conceptual and the real)" (1997, 226–227). To make good on the promise of such an account would be to give a finally nonintentional account of what Sellars refers to as "the fundamental connection of language with non-linguistic fact." Examining Dharmakīrti's elaboration of the *apoha* doctrine, we will see that he may not be able to make a non-question-begging case for the kind of explanation thus required.

The commentator Manorathanandin introduces one expression of the problem here at issue by asking, "If existents have, in every case, a nature that is distinct (*vyāvṛtta*),[44] there is no generality (*sāmānyam*) among them; so how is there the idea of generality [we have when we imagine particulars to exemplify properties like] 'being a cow'?"[45] The verses from Dharmakīrti that are so introduced read:

> Existents that are intrinsically distinct appear as though non-distinct, with some form [not really their own. This is because] their plurality is obscured by that veil (*saṃvṛti*) which is thought—which is based on distinct existents, but whose phenomenal content (*pratibhāsa*) is a unitary object—that obscures with its own form a form that is other than it. Based on the intention (*abhiprāya*) of that [thought], a generality (*sāmānyam*) is said to exist; but that [general form] ultimately doesn't exist in the way imagined by that thought.[46]

That is, all that really exists (as what can present itself to perception) is unique particulars (*this* colored shape and *that* one), but we typically experience these manifold particulars under some description—as examples of familiar *kinds* ("I see some cows"). When we thus experience what are really irreducibly unique particulars instead as tokens of familiar types,

Dharmakīrti is here saying, our thought is really *about* something that does not ultimately exist—namely, the concepts that we take to be commonly exemplified by what are really particulars, whose irreducible plurality is thus "obscured" (*saṃvriyate*)[47] by conceptual thought. What, then, could be the relation between percepts and concepts, such that they can be as sharply distinct from one another as Dharmakīrti here suggests, but such that our trade in concepts nevertheless facilitates our getting by in the world of really existent particulars?

In order to link perceptions with semantic mental content, Dharmakīrti needs something that is at once a causally describable particular, *and* somehow contentful in a way that gets us closer to (what we are here trying to understand) the kind of contentfulness exhibited by things like overtly expressed sentences. Here, it's important to recall (from chapter 2) Schueler's comment on the difference between true or false claims and "the *things* ('mental states') that *have* these true or false contents" (where the latter, we saw, do all the explaining for philosophers such as Fodor).[48] Just the same distinction is integral to Dharmakīrti's approach here; for Dharmakīrti, too, "concepts as real mental events are to be distinguished from concepts as content" (Dreyfus 2011, 217).[49] Dharmakīrti urges, then, that mental representations—variously referred to as "aspects" (*ākāra*), "reflections" (*pratibimba*), and "appearances" (*pratibhāsa*)—provide the necessary link between perceptual and conceptual content. While these representations can be thought to exhibit the property of intentionality—surely, after all, mental representations should be said to "mean or represent or be about" other things—they are themselves *particulars* that are causally produced by perceptual cognitions.

Emphasizing as much, Dreyfus says Dharmakīrti's view is that "in perception a representation, that is, a reflection or an aspect, stands for a real individual object in a one-to-one, direct causal correspondence" (1997, 229).[50] Insofar, that is, as they originate from perceptual encounters, particular mental representations are undeniably real and must therefore be distinguished from whatever semantic content they might be said to "bear" or otherwise explain. "Even a universal," the commentator Manorathanandin thus explains, "is admitted as being a particular insofar as it is the aspect (*ākāra*) of a cognition"; universality enters in, he adds, by virtue of the phenomenal *content* of these mental aspects ("by virtue of the form to be cognized, which is being ascertained"), "but not by virtue of there being an aspect of thought."[51] "Aspect," then, refers on Dharmakīrti's account to really occurrent mental representations, regardless of their content.

Insofar, however, as such representations are themselves particulars, we are still owed an account of how these can yield the specifically *semantic* content they seem to have; if mental representations are themselves particulars, how can they any better explain semantic contentfulness than other causally describable particulars? This is the point of departure for Dharmakīrti's elaboration of the *apoha* doctrine; his idea is that while these images do not themselves count as concepts, they are the bases of the "exclusions" (*apoha*) through which concepts gain their contentfulness and hence serve to bridge the gap. On one characteristically elliptical expression of the picture on offer, Dharmakīrti says that "even though without basis for distinguishing the capacity of an external object, expression (*śruti*) of that [i.e., of an external object] is connected to conceptual reflections (*vikalpa-pratibimba*) that are [themselves] based on that [external object]."[52] That is, the names of objects are not themselves among the things produced by the "capacity" (*śakti*)—that is, the causal efficacy—of the real objects supposedly referred to thereby; nevertheless, words are associated with "conceptual reflections" (or "aspects," *ākāra*, per Manorathanandin's gloss) that *are* themselves so produced. In particular, Manorathanandin explains, words are thus associated "at the time of the convention" (*saṃketakāle*)—a crucially indeterminate notion to which we will return shortly.[53]

What happens at "the time of the convention" here invoked can itself be explained in terms of "exclusions" that Dharmakīrti understands in a peculiarly causal way. He obliquely expresses this by way of answering the objection that insofar as only particulars are real, they cannot be taken to constrain the kind of discursive thought that, on Dharmakīrti's account, essentially involves unreal things. "This is not a problem," he answers:

> Ordinary discursive transactions (*vyavahārāḥ*) involving linguistic items[54] pertain to the object that appears in cognition (*jñānapratibhāsiny arthe*). Such cognition—stemming from latent dispositions (*vāsanā*), which are deposited by [the kind of perceptual] experience that apprehends the nature of things—is conceptual. Though it does not [really] have those [particulars] as its objects, it seems as though it has these as its objects; its form is to [seem to] exist as those, in the way imagined, because its nature is to originate from the latent dispositions deposited by experience of them. As though it were apprehending nondistinct objects, [this cognition thus] has an aspect (*ākāra*) that is the same in regard to [objects] that ultimately have a difference from those [having a comparable effect], because of its production from things whose effects are indistinct.[55]

The subjective representations produced by our perceptions, Dharmakīrti thus argues, serve as links to universals insofar as the cognitions produced by objects—reckoned by Dharmakīrti as among the *effects* thereof—appear to a subject as similar to one another. To that extent, reference particularly to the "object that appears in cognition" (*jñānapratibhāsiny arthe*) represents the point at which Dharmakīrti brings in the kind of "sameness" that necessarily figures in linguistic universals. While the particulars that seem to us to be represented in cognition are in fact irreducibly unique, he thus allows that there is at least *phenomenal* similarity in the mental representations thereof—representations, he here emphasizes, that are themselves a function of "latent dispositions" (*vāsanā*) that are "deposited" (*āhita*) in our mental continua by our initial, causally describable encounters with particulars.

Of particular importance is the point Dharmakīrti introduces at the end of this passage: the strictly phenomenal similarity he thus allows is itself to be described in causal terms. Thus, what is "excluded" from the range of things to which any concept refers is *all those particulars that do not produce the same effect*. As Dharmakīrti puts the point earlier in the same section of his text, it is "by virtue of having the same effects and causes" (*ekasādhyasādhanatayā*)—and by virtue, as well, of the latent dispositions (*vāsanā*) we have to imagine and exploit useful cognitive regularities—that distinct existents can and do fruitfully appear to cognition as examples of the same kinds.[56] As Manorathanandin says to similar effect in another discussion of the same issues, "There isn't *really* (*na khalu*) any being the same, i.e., being one; rather, there is the similarity of being a single effect (*ekakāryatāsādṛśyam*)."[57]

Dharmakīrti's idea here has affinities with some moves made by Jerry Fodor, who similarly argues that the "sameness" that essentially characterizes concepts can be explained in causal terms. We saw in chapter 2 that if Fodor is willing in some of his later work to back away from the appeal to "narrow content" as best accounting for mental causation, he is nevertheless willing to allow that "broadly" contentful awareness—awareness, that is, taken as representing states of affairs external to the subject thereof—can nevertheless accommodate mental causation only insofar as broad content, too, will finally admit of causal explanation. In the course of his case for that conclusion, Fodor says: "Suppose there is some bundle of dispositions D such that, according to The One True Informational Semantics, [concept] C applies to Xs just in case I bear D to Xs. Then, for C to be one of my functional concepts *just is* for me to bear D to Xs (not in virtue of the similarity of their microstructures but) *in virtue of the similarity of their effects and causes*" (1994, 31). Dharmakīrti similarly suggests that if there is any "sameness" involved in the individuation of real existents as coming under concepts, it is explicable simply in terms of subjectively occurrent dispositions to respond similarly to such particulars as are capable of causing comparable effects.

This appeal to "sameness of effects," however, could reasonably be thought not to advance Dharmakīrti's case; the appeal to the capacity of various unique particulars to produce comparable effects remains vulnerable to the charge of circularity often brought against proponents of *apoha*—a point surely invited by Dharmakīrti's recurrent reference to its being the causal "nature" (*prakṛti*) of particulars to cause this or that effect. If it's held that some domain of particulars is usefully demarcated as sharing "the same causal capacity," do we not thus have recourse to precisely the sort of abstraction that the *apoha* doctrine purports to explain? This is a particularly problematic charge insofar as it is precisely the circularity objection that Dharmakīrti is evidently trying to circumvent with his causal account of "sameness."[58]

Dharmakīrti's idea comes through in an example recurrently adduced to address this concern: that of such medicinal herbs (*oṣadhi*) as are commonly prized for things like their fever-reducing effects (*jvarādiśamana*).[59] What is picked out when there is reference to such herbs is just what cannot be excluded as producing the common effect of fever reduction—and grounding the account in the herbs themselves short-circuits circularity, since *what* it is to which one's activity is directed on these occasions of use is always *some particular* instance of the herb in question (and not to an abstraction like "being an herbal remedy"). If, in other words, there remains doubt about whether "sameness of effect" amounts to something just as unreal as the universals supposedly explained thereby, one can always check to see whether the thing picked out by discourse actually produces the desired effect—and it can only be *as a particular* that it does so, since only particulars are causally efficacious.

So, to the anticipated charge that a shared causal capacity just amounts to a universal,[60] Dharmakīrti elliptically responds:

> Since there is no distinction [between occurrences of a universal], there is no universal [present in these herbs to explain their common effect], because [otherwise there would be] the unwanted consequence of non-distinction, even given the differences in the fields [from which they were harvested], etc.—and because [a universal is] not the performer of any function, owing to its permanence.[61]

That is, universals are characterized precisely by their lack of identity criteria and their consequent inability to *do* anything; but what one encounters upon picking some medicinal herbs that produce particular effects is *some particular plant*, distinguished both by its having been found in some particular place (in just *this* field, not over there) and by the fact that it really does ameliorate fever. The reason Dharmakīrti can think his account served by the appeal to causal capacities, then, is that it is precisely the possession of such a capacity that defines something as *real*—and any time discursive practice thus comes to rest in the discovery or realization of such a capacity, one has, ipso facto, encountered a really existent, unique particular. Dharmakīrti thus thinks he here appeals to something essentially different from the kind of "sameness" (*sāmānya*) that characterizes concepts.

If, however, this example gives us a good way to imagine *finding out* whether some instance of conceptual activity has successfully directed us to such real particulars as can further the aims we meant to have advanced, it clearly does not give us any purchase on the problem Dharmakīrti is supposedly addressing; this doesn't obviously help us understand the kind of sameness involved not in evaluating the *outcome* of any instance of discourse, but in understanding *what* we are talking about in the first place. To urge, in other words, that some range of particulars is usefully individuated in terms of their commonly causing fever reduction is to give no help in understanding the very idea that "commonly causing fever reduction" could in the first place be the kind of thing *meant* by something said. The *apoha* theory is proposed as explaining what it is in virtue of which we understand the meanings of utterances—and while the causal or pragmatic efficacy of the things to which we are directed by discourse may very well constitute good evidence of our *having understood* what was meant, it gives us no purchase on the conceptually prior question of *what is understood* by the utterances in virtue of which we found some particular plants in the first place.

Moreover, Dharmakīrti's appeal to "sameness of effect" turns out to be significantly complicated by a point that may in any case undermine the intuitive plausibility of the example of fever-reducing herbs. We might concede that the account so far elaborated in terms of "sameness of effects" shows at least that what is picked out by kind terms varies as a function of our contingent and episodic desires and interests—*what* it is that we exclude when we think of *not a non-cow* will vary (and the content of the explained concept will accordingly differ) depending upon whether, e.g., it is *milk* that we want ("not a nonproducer of the effect that is milk") or fuel ("not a nonproducer of the effect that is manure"). Surely this idea suggests, at least, that the referents of words are not as stable as Mīmāṃsakas, among others, would urge. Things like "milk" and "manure" are not, however, finally the kinds of "effects" that Dharmakīrti really has in mind; it makes a difference that he proposes, rather, that the "sameness of effect" thus produced by sensible particulars consists in *the cognitions they cause.*

The basis, that is, for the "exclusions" in virtue of which semantic content emerges is ultimately just subjectively occurrent representations that are taken *by a subject* as *phenomenally* similar. Thus, Dharmakīrti (here as elaborated by Manorathanandin) says at *Pramāṇavārttika* 1.109: "Even if each individual is distinct, nevertheless, because of being the cause of a unitary judgment (*ekapratyavamarśa*), the thought [produced by individuals] is said to be without difference, i.e., one; and by virtue of [their] being the cause of a unitary thought of this kind, individuals [themselves are in turn] said to be without difference."[62] Again, Dharmakīrti explains that the singular "effect" that, say, various examples of the same kind of tree relevantly produce is, in fact, "a unitary image, which is a recognition."[63] If there is room for doubt about whether the idea of sameness of effect really circumvents the problem Dharmakīrti means to address, it is in any case more significant that Dharmakīrti's account of the reference of words is thus finally based in something eminently subjective.

So, contrary to the Kantian intuition that the conceptual order is to be understood precisely as making possible the objectivity of knowledge, Dharmakīrti argues that the explanation of the constitutively intersubjective phenomenon of language must be based in (what is finally subjective) the psychological; the conceptual order is here to be explained in terms of the intrinsic workings of individual minds, whose contents are ultimately intelligible without reference to anything external to them.[64] While the direction of explanation, according to the argument we developed in chapter 3, ought to be from the conceptual order to the objectivity of knowledge, the direction of explanation for Dharmakīrti is instead *from* impersonally described subjective events *to* the conceptual order.[65] Insofar as the subjective, for Dharmakīrti, is finally all that is indubitably known—is intelligible (we'll see with the next chapter's consideration of *svasaṃvitti*, "self-awareness") without reference to a world—the conceptual elaboration of a world must therefore be explicable in terms of the mental.

Georges Dreyfus rightly takes Dharmakīrti to argue, in this way, that "similarities do not exist 'out there,' but are the products of our interactions with the world. There is no such thing as real similarities between shapes or colors, as we tend to think, but only *evaluations of similarity* between shapes or colors that provide the basis for our conceptual elaborations" (2011, 213; emphasis mine). Dreyfus's reference to "evaluations of similarity"—to what we saw Dharmakīrti refer to as "unitary judgments" (*ekapratyavamarśa*)—reflects the fact that the bases of Dharmakīrti's "exclusions" must themselves be *judgments* if semantic content is to get off the ground. To claim, however, that these lower-level judgments are themselves causally describable particulars is to beg just the question at issue; this amounts to simply asserting that notwithstanding Dharmakīrti's guiding commitments, there are some cognitions that are causally constrained but that manage nonetheless to be *judgments*—and whether anything will admit of both descriptions is just what was in question. If, in other words, particular mental events ("aspects") are causally relatable to the particulars they represent, we are entitled to ask how *these* causally describable particulars can, exceptionally, be capable of giving rise to the kinds of "judgments" whose resistance to causal explanation is just what is at issue.

Dreyfus says in this regard that Dharmakīrti's reference to "evaluations of similarity" picks out something "of a lower order than full-blown predicative judgments"; these "are not the products of a higher level of conceptualization but *are directly caused by our experiences*" (2011, 214; emphasis mine). It's no help, however, to characterize these supposed judgments as of a "lower order" and to assert that they are "directly caused by our experiences"; it's no easier to understand how these "lower-order" cognitions could be at once causally describable and epistemically contentful than it is to understand how Fodor's "narrow content" could be. What we are trying to understand *just is* how (or whether) perception can represent a constraint on semantic content despite its being essentially nonconceptual—how, that is, *perception* can be described in causal terms yet stand in some kind of relation to the kind of conceptual awareness that Kant characterized as constitutively involving "spontaneity." Simply to assert that there are some perceptions (those that issue in the recognition of phenomenal sameness) that do so is not to answer that question; nevertheless, this is just as Dharmakīrti does when he urges, as we've seen, that cognitions can do so simply insofar as they are based on "latent dispositions, which are deposited by [the kind of perceptual] experience that apprehends the nature of things."[66]

PROBLEMS WITH THE FOCUS ON INWARDNESS: DHARMAKĪRTI ON "SPEAKER'S INTENTION"

The significance of Dharmakīrti's thus appealing, by his reference to "sameness of effects," to subjectively occurrent mental events can be brought sharply into relief by returning to the issue with which we began our consideration of Dignāga; the picture so far elaborated can thus shed some light on Dharmakīrti's different account of the sense in which linguistic awareness is finally reducible to inference. Interestingly, we can begin by noting the verse—quoted from a tenth-century commentary on the work of the grammarian Bhartṛhari—with which Peter Scharf frames his essay "Early Indian Grammarians on a Speaker's Intention"; in my translation, the verse says: "Language is an epistemic criterion with regard to that object which appears in thought, which is the speaker's object of engagement; it is not grounded in the reality of the object [itself]."[67] Not inappropriately, Scharf takes this verse to reflect the Indian grammatical tradition's recognition that what utterances (and by extension, the thoughts expressed thereby) are about is logically independent of *what there is*; after all, we are sometimes *wrong* about how things really are, and our thoughts and utterances therefore sometimes fail to track reality.

I suggest, though, that the unattributed quotation from which Scharf takes his bearings gains new significance when we realize that it's from Dharmakīrti.[68] In the context of Dharmakīrti's project as here elaborated, I take it that the passage expresses a rather more radical point than Scharf's; Dharmakīrti's point is that thoughts can only finally be *about* the uniquely particular representations that are indubitably known to a subject through introspection (through, that is, *svasaṃvitti*, which we will consider in the next chapter). Everything about semantic contentfulness (and about our knowledge of what there is) is thus to be explained with reference to *intra*-subjective psychological events rather than the other way round. This, finally, is the context for understanding Dharmakīrti's argument that linguistic cognition (*śābdajñāna*) doesn't count as a *pramāṇa* just insofar as it is reducible to inference.

Recall, here, that Dignāga's point in making the same claim was that the semantic content of words can be accounted for in terms of *the same asymmetry that essentially characterizes inferential relations*. For Dignāga, the point of the *apoha* doctrine was that the semantic scope of words reflecting different levels of abstraction (such as *tree* and *maple*) can be negatively characterized as a function of the fact that everything excluded by "this is a tree" is also excluded by "this is a maple" but not the other way round—just as one is entitled to the inference that "this is a tree because it's a maple" but not conversely. Dharmakīrti, in contrast, holds that linguistic cognition is reducible to inference just insofar as one can infer, from any encounter with an utterance, *that* some speaker's intention has been expressed. As he says at *Pramāṇavārttika* 1.213, "Since words have no inherent connection with things, there is no proof of objects based on them; they express a speaker's intention."[69]

This is not an unfamiliar or, perhaps, obviously problematic claim; indeed, Dharmakīrti's thought here again converges with that of some modern and contemporary upholders of Fodor's "representational theory of mind." Thus, for Locke, too, "Words in their primary or immediate Signification, stand for nothing, but the Ideas in the Mind of him that uses them" (1689, 405). Fodor, we saw in chapter 2, similarly said—in arguing for the "asymmetrical dependence" of all meaningful utterances upon causally describable episodes—that while *some* tokens of the word "slab" must carry "information" about (that is, *be causally relatable to*) actual slabs, many if not most particular uses of the word are *not* causally relatable to slabs; "if anything," he added parenthetically, "*they carry information about wants*; viz., the information that a slab is wanted" (1990, 97–98; emphasis added).[70] Surely it's plausible thus to suppose that what is *immediately* expressed by any subject's utterance is just what that subject *intends* to express, and that what a subject thus wants can to some extent float free of states of affairs in the world; while any subject may be wrong in thinking her requests for slabs likely to be satisfied, she cannot be wrong in thinking that *that is what she wants*.[71]

This idea is problematic, however, to the extent that it's invoked as *explaining* semantic contentfulness as such; the plausible intuitions here do not warrant the conclusion that the right direction of explanation is from autonomously intelligible "intentions" to the meaningfulness of language, rather than conversely. The problem becomes clear when we consider just what Dharmakīrti understands by a speaker's "intention" (*vivakṣā* or *abhiprāya*), which is suggested in passages such as the following:

> These [viz., the usefully efficacious particulars picked out by discourse] can be expressed by one word, or by many; the speaker has autonomy in this regard (*svātantryam atra vaktuḥ*). Insofar as it is owing to the intention of a speaker (*vaktrabhiprāyavaśāt*) that a single expression refers to many things, one cannot object [to someone's so using words]. And it's not the case that this reference is impossible because of [its] being dependent upon [the speaker's] desires; for if the [language-]user does not have a desire, how could he refer even to one thing?[72]

Dharmakīrti thus concludes that since a speaker cannot refer to anything at all except insofar as she *intends* to, we should hold that any expression's picking out particulars is finally based on considerations internal to the speaker. The really striking point is that we are encouraged to overlook the difference between a speaker's desires as causing *particular utterances*, and such desires as themselves creating the *conditions of the possibility of any such utterance*. While a speaker might indeed be thought to "choose" the right words for some occasion, this is not at all the same thing as saying she could choose what (much less *that*) her words mean—and it is, significantly, precisely these levels of description that Dharmakīrti and his philosophical heirs recurrently conflate in their discussions of language use.[73]

That Dharmakīrti is inclined to conflate these follows, however, from the peculiarly causal sense in which he understands the "intentions" we have seen him refer to. It's important, then, to appreciate that the "speaker's intention" (*vaktrabhiprāya*) recurrently invoked by Dharmakīrti is to be understood not in terms of the semantic *content* the speaker means to communicate; it consists, rather, in a particular mental event such as can be understood to *cause* an utterance. Thus, for example:

> An utterance is impelled by an intention regarding a particular point; for one who knows that this [utterance thus] comes from that [intention], the point expressed [by the utterance] is the phenomenal appearance (*ābhāsa*) which is its proper cause (*svanidāna*). Hence, there is a cause-effect relation (*janyajanakabhāva*) between [an intention] whose form is mental, and its expression in speech.[74]

This is as Dharmakīrti must hold, since on his account of linguistic awareness as reducible to inference, the inference from utterance to speaker's intention is finally understood as an inference based on a *kāryahetu*—based, that is, on a "reason" (*hetu*) that consists in the "effect" (*kārya*) from which one is entitled to infer the presence of its cause.[75] Insofar, then, as only particulars (*svalakṣaṇa*) are, for Dharmakīrti, causally efficacious, it must finally be particulars that Dharmakīrti has in mind as "causing" any utterance—specifically, the particular mental events (the "appearances" or "aspects") that are indubitably known only to the subjects thereof.

All one is finally entitled to infer from any utterance, then, is *that* some speaker's "intention" has been expressed—where that is to say only that some particular, first-personally experienced mental event has caused the speaker to give utterance. Determining *what* that intention *is*—insofar as that means understanding the semantic content of the utterance—is not explained at all by Dharmakīrti's account of the sense in which linguistic cognition is reducible to inference. Not only, then, do we have all over again the problem of how causally describable particulars can be thought to yield semantic content; we further have the problem of explaining how the constitutively social, intersubjective character of semantic content is to be understood in terms of mental events that are immediately known only to the subjects thereof. Dharmakīrti's prima facie plausible contention that linguistic cognition "is an epistemic criterion in regard to that object which appears in thought," and that what thus appears in thought alone is "the speaker's object of engagement," can now be seen to raise some difficult problems.

The problems turn on the question of how or whether the normative, social character of language ultimately represents a constraint on the thought of individuals—or whether, instead, the psychological processes of individuals must be able to explain the normative character of thought. According to Scharf, the Sanskrit grammarians who quoted Dharmakīrti on language's reference to the object "which appears in thought" held, despite the possibility of understanding Dharmakīrti's claim as just elaborated, that essentially social conventions should be understood finally to constrain any speaker's intention (*vivakṣā*): "Although the principle of *vivakṣā* allows grammarians to account for usages inconsonant with the state of affairs described, they do not consider that a speaker's intention is individual whim. Linguistic convention limits the scope of a speaker's intention" (Scharf 1995, 67).[76] Given the intuitions we have so far seen him develop, it should not be surprising that Dharmakīrti, in contrast, is committed to *deriving* the normativity of linguistic conventions from individual speakers' intentions; for Dharmakīrti, it is *conventions* that are constrained by *intentions*.

The problems with this crystallize around the question of how essentially social conventions (*saṃketa*) can figure in the picture we have been sketching following Dharmakīrti. On the account of *apoha* as so far developed, then, Dharmakīrti's attempt at a finally nonintentional account of semantic content has taken the form of an argument involving mental representations (*ākāra*, etc.)—representations taken by Dharmakīrti as the *effects* produced by perceptual encounters with the world, and as nevertheless exhibiting the phenomenal similarity that make them a suitable basis for the kind of "exclusion" (*apoha*) that he takes to explain semantic content. Supplementing this with the version of the doctrine elaborated by Dignāga, we can thus say that the contentfulness of concepts is explicable in terms of how much is excluded from coming under any one of these—where what is excluded, Dharmakīrti adds, is just whatever does not cause relevantly similar effects.

Insofar, however, as this "sameness of effects" turns out to involve only the *phenomenal* sameness that a subject takes various of her own cognitions to have—and insofar, therefore, as the "intentions" we are thus entitled to infer from utterances consist just in mental representations whose phenomenal character is really known only to the subjects thereof—we still need to know how the utterances thus described can participate in eminently social, *intersubjective*, conventions.

We still need to know, that is, how the subjectively known "sameness" posited by Dharmakīrti relates to—how or whether it can *explain*—the *objective* sameness in virtue of which innumerable utterances of (say) the word "cow" can commonly be taken by innumerable subjects as picking out the same things. What is it, then, in virtue of which Dharmakīrti's first-personally known, phenomenal "sameness" can be a constraint on the objectively normative character of linguistic conventions? Just as in our elaboration, in chapter 2, of the philosophical project of Jerry Fodor, Dharmakīrti's *apoha* doctrine as so far developed brings us to the point where it is necessary to consider those practices that, Fodor said, "fix the extensions of our predicates" (1990, 97). It's now pertinent, in particular, to consider Dharmakīrti's recurrent references to *saṃketakāla*, the "time of the convention" to which we saw Manorathanandin appeal above.[77] The "convention-setting" occasions thus referred to represent, finally, what we saw Sellars characterize as those "occasions on which the fundamental connection of language with non-linguistic fact is exhibited"—and it's with respect to these that Dharmakīrti's account most clearly turns out to be, as Sellars leads us to expect, "Augustinian" in the sense found problematic by Wittgenstein.

DHARMAKĪRTI ON CONCEPTUAL THOUGHT AS ESSENTIALLY MNEMONIC

We saw in chapter 2, with regard to those "practices that fix the extensions of our predicates," that what is most significant for Fodor is the initial *application* of terms: "Some of our linguistic practices presuppose some of our others, and it's plausible that practices of *applying* terms (names to their bearers, predicates to things in their extensions) are at the bottom of the pile" (1990, 97).[78] The same thought, I suggest, underlies Dharmakīrti's references to *saṃketakāla*. This Sanskrit compound refers to "the time (*kāla*) of a convention (*saṃketa*)"; as on Fodor's account, this is ambiguous between the time of the *creating* of any convention and the time of any subject's *learn-*

ing some already created convention. Strikingly, Dharmakīrti often seems to have the former in mind; either way, though, his account of the "computation" of utterances—of the transition from a *perceptual* experience of anyone as making noises to the semantic understanding of them *as saying something*—essentially involves reference to the agent's memory of the prior occasions thus invoked. The important question is whether these moments—the one that is "the time of the convention" (*saṃketakāla*), and the one consisting in the *memory* thereof—will themselves admit of a nonintentional description.

We have seen that conceptual cognitions, for Dharmakīrti, are distinguished from perceptual cognitions partly by their essentially involving reference to something not actually present—that, for example, a semantically contentful thought like "this is a dog" involves reference (not only to some perceived particular but also) to things like the concept *being a dog*, the conventions for the use of the word "dog," etc. Among the salient points about such things, for Dharmakīrti, is that any entertaining of a discursive thought necessarily involves our *remembering* them. Not only, then, do semantically contentful thoughts involve something not "really present" insofar as the concepts involved therein are purportedly reducible in the ways so far considered; insofar as semantically contentful thoughts further involve conventions governing the sounds that express the concepts so described, there must also be reference to some necessarily prior occasion that is taken somehow to have "fixed the extensions of our predicates."

Dharmakīrti can, then, highlight the immediacy that characterizes perception by thus elaborating on what it lacks: "How can [verbal conception]—which consists in association with [a word previously] experienced, and which has as its mode recollection of a convention—occur in a sensory [cognition], given that the latter lacks any reflection on prior and subsequent?"[79] That is, among the respects in which perceptual cognition is uniquely immediate is that it is *temporally* so; perceptual cognition involves only what is temporally present. Among the reasons, then, why it cannot be thought that perception is conceptual is that this would essentially be to say that its objects are *mediated* by the kind of memory that essentially figures in conceptual awareness; as Dharmakīrti says at *Pramāṇaviniścaya* 1.5, "If sensory thought were dependent on a relation to language,[80] which involves memory, then even given application to an object, that object would be obscured."[81] That is, the kind of *presence* that essentially distinguishes perceptual objects for Dharmakīrti would be compromised by any concession that perception is conceptual, since, among other things, conceptual thought involves memory—and this because conceptual thought is intelligible only with reference to no-longer-present occasions of "convention-setting."

Dharmakīrti refers to such convention-setting occasions in thus elaborating, in his autocommentary, on the foregoing: "Application [of a word] to that [object of awareness] is impossible without remembering the discursive universal (*abhilāpasāmānyam*) that was brought into being (*bhāvitam*) at the time of the convention (*saṃketakāla*)." If, as frequently in Dharmakīrti's discussions of the issue, there is ambiguity regarding the convention-setting occasion thus referred to, the word *bhāvita*—from the causative stem of one of the verbs for "to be," hence (on my rendering) *brought into being*—can be taken to suggest the radical idea that what is recalled is someone's *creating* the convention in question. Whatever the case, Dharmakīrti adds that what is thus recalled is to be understood in terms of finally *inner* processes: "And without an interior transformation (*asaty āntare vikāre*) which was created in proximity with an object, memory in regard to a particular word doesn't make sense."[82]

The point, for Dharmakīrti, is that recollection of a governing convention is possible only insofar as there was, on a previous occasion, some "proximity with an object"—which is to say, some causally describable perceptual encounter with a particular such as can effect the kind of "interior transformation" that, we've seen, Dharmakīrti takes to provide the ultimate constraint on the development of concepts. Of the ultimately perceptual occasions on which these inner events are produced, in contrast, Dharmakīrti emphasizes that "because of the absence of any other memory of discourse when the arising of a thought is produced by proximity to an object, it is established that perception is nonconceptual."[83] Just as on Fodor's account, Dharmakīrti too aims to ground recalled conventions in a causal chain linking any use of a term to a *first* use that is itself causally describable with reference only to immediately present particulars—the point of which, Fodor could just as well have been saying of Dharmakīrti's account as of his own, is to explain semantic content "without resort to intentional or semantic idiom."[84] The possibility of conceptual thought is thus said to depend on *non*conceptually describable occasions—on occasions of perceptual proximity such as can produce the "interior transformations" that must be *recalled* for conceptual faculties to come into play.

Reference to the recollection of convention-setting occasions also figures interestingly in some passages from Dharmakīrti's commentator Dharmottara, who raises the question of how we are to understand the movement from a perceptual encounter with someone who is making noises to the conceptual understanding of them *as saying something*. Here it's important to stress that any particular utterance of a word or sentence—insofar as that consists in a unique, perceptible acoustic event—is the kind of thing of which we can have a wholly nonconceptual perception. Given, then, that the perception of an utterance can appropriately be described as not essentially different from (say) the hearing of thunder, among the things that needs to be explained on Dharmakīrti's account is how in one such case (but not the other) the perceived sound can also be taken to *mean* something—and again, the question is how (or whether) the transition from one level of description to the other can itself be described in the nonintentional terms that Dharmakīrti's *apoha* account requires.

The problem thus raised is closely related to what, in chapter 2, we saw Jerry Fodor identify as the "disjunction problem." This is, recall, a problem that turns on the differences between what Fodor distinguished as *meaning* and *information*: "Information is tied to etiology in a way that meaning isn't. . . . By contrast, *the meaning of a symbol is one of the things that all of its tokens have in common, however they may happen to be caused. All* 'cow' tokens mean *cow*; if they didn't, they wouldn't be 'cow' tokens" (1990, 90).[85] The problem, then, is how to tell a finally causal story about meaning while allowing that what thus distinguishes the "meaning" relation just is its "robustness," or apparent lack of causal constraint. The problem Fodor thus characterizes, I'm now suggesting, is closely related to the problem of how innumerable uniquely particular acoustic events—those that occur, for example, when countless speakers of English make the sound conventionally represented by the letters *c-o-w*—can commonly be taken as utterances *of the same word* ("cow").

Insofar as any such utterance can be understood as a perceptible particular, the problem is, again, how to relate a causal level of description to the intentional description of someone as *understanding a sentence*. Dharmottara anticipates this question in commenting on verse 5 of the first chapter of Dharmakīrti's *Nyāyabindu*—the verse in which Dharmakīrti stipulates that the "conceptual thought" (*kalpanā*) of which perception is constitutively devoid consists in "a thought whose phenomenal content (*pratibhāsa*) is suitable for association with discourse."[86] With this reference to *suitability* for association, Dharmakīrti significantly revises Dignāga's earlier characterization of conceptual thought simply as the (presumably explicit or actual) "association with name and genus and so forth"; Dharmakīrti's alternative definition makes it possible to infer conceptual thought even in pre- or nonlinguistic creatures—even, that is, in the absence of any *actual* use of language.[87]

It raises various questions, though, to argue in this way that *thought* (particularly insofar as that is imagined in terms of language) can be inferred even in the absence of any overt use of language; Dharmottara thus sketches one of the situations that Dharmakīrti's definition brings into view:

> There are some thoughts whose phenomenal content (*ābhāsa*) is [actually] associated with discourse, such as the conception of a jar on the part of someone by whom the [relevant linguistic] convention has been learned—[such a thought is one] whose phenomenal content [actually] involves the word *jar*. But some [thoughts] have phenomenal content that is [simply] *suitable* for association with discourse, even though [they are in fact] unassociated with discourse—like the conception of a child by whom the [relevant linguistic conception] has not been learned.[88]

Both a prelinguistic subject and an already linguistic one, that is, can commonly have in mind the *kind* of generality that is picked out by words (a "generic image" of a jar)—and thus can experience what is really a unique particular instead as a *token* of some *type*—independently of their having a word for the thing in view. To that extent, Dharmottara here suggests, it makes sense to say that both subjects entertain a *conceptual* thought, even though the thought of only one of them can take explicitly linguistic form ("here's a jar"). Here, then, reference to a subject's having learned (or not learned) a relevant convention is made in order to distinguish the content of two thoughts that are, Dharmottara emphasizes, nevertheless commonly conceptual.

Dharmottara recurs to the difference it makes to have learned a linguistic convention when, a few pages later, he anticipates the objection I've been scouting: "An auditory cognition" (*śrotrajñāna*)—that is, a sensory perception of the auditory sort—"apprehends a unique particular which is a sound (*śabda-svalakṣaṇa*). And since some audible particulars are *referents* and some are *signifiers*,[89] [it therefore follows that cognition of an audible particular] could be one whose phenomenal content is suitable for association with discourse—and thus, that it would be *conceptual*."[90] The objection is that as a unique, perceptible acoustic event, any particular utterance would seem to count as the kind of thing (a *svalakṣaṇa*) that can be the object of a constitutively nonconceptual perception; but insofar as it is *words* that are uttered, it seems we would have to allow that even though thus describable as a perception, the cognition thereof is nevertheless *conceptual*. In order to finesse this, Dharmottara must keep these two descriptions of the same event distinct from each other (so that the true "perception" of the utterance can, as Dharmakīrti's definition of perception requires, still count as nonconceptual)—but in a way that allows us nevertheless to understand how, as users of language, we effortlessly go from the perceptual to the semantic (the *conceptual*) description of the same event.[91]

This is, then, another case of the same problem that recurrently bedevils Dharmakīrti's philosophical program: how to bring these two sharply distinct levels of description together while insisting on their distinctness. With regard to the problem as here stated, Dharmottara elaborates the following account:

> This is not a problem. Even if a unique particular can be a referent or a signifier, the unique particular can be apprehended as referent or signifier [only insofar as it is] being apprehended as having been experienced at the time [when one learned the relevant linguistic] convention (*saṃketakāla-dṛṣṭatvena*). And a thing's being an object of experience does not now exist as occurring at the time [when one learned the relevant linguistic] convention (*saṃketakāla*). And just as the perception that existed at the time [one learned the relevant linguistic] convention has now ceased, in the same way a thing's also being an object of that [experience] does not now exist. Thus, a [purely perceptual] auditory cognition, not experiencing the fact of having been previously seen (*pūrvakāladṛṣṭatvam apaśyat*), does not [itself] apprehend a signifier-signified relation.[92]

Dharmottara thus says we can appropriately distinguish the two opposed descriptions of the experience of an utterance—the perceptual experience of it as a noise and the conceptual experience of it as meaning something—by appealing to the same temporal dislocation we saw in Dharmakīrti's characterizations of conceptual thought as essentially mnemonic. It's only with reference to a necessarily prior occasion of convention setting that the conceptual description of the event is possible—and recollection of that prior occasion is not to be confused with the perceptual description of the same event, since the latter description picks out only features of the immediately present occasion.

The foregoing passages address what is one of the most strikingly recurrent issues in Husserl's *Logical Investigations*: "What in general is the surplus element distinguishing the understanding of a symbolically functioning expression from the uncomprehended verbal sound?" (1970, 567). What is it, that is, in virtue of which a perceptually describable encounter with an utterance can be experienced as *understanding what someone says*? While Husserl's is a chiefly phenomenological insight,[93] he argues that this nevertheless puts a significant constraint on our theorizing about the nature of reference:

> The ideality of the relationship between expression and meaning is at once plain in regard to both its sides, inasmuch as, when we ask for the meaning of an expression, e.g. "quadratic remainder," we are naturally not referring to the sound-pattern uttered here and now, the vanishing noise that can never recur identically: we mean the expression *in specie*. "Quadratic remainder" is the same expression by whomsoever uttered. The same holds of talk about the expression's meaning, *which naturally does not refer to some meaning-conferring experience.*
>
> (1970, 284; EMPHASIS ADDED)

It is chief among the recurrent concerns of Husserl's *Logical Investigations* thus to urge that *meaning*—the kind of semantic content, that is, whose structure and relations represent the constitutive concern of logic—cannot be given a finally psychological explanation; for insofar as any such explanation would have us attend to causally describable particulars ("the acts constituting the expression as a physical object," the production of a "vanishing noise that can never recur identically"), it necessarily leaves out the essentially "ideal" sort of thing that is just what semantic content consists in. To that extent, the semantic content that essentially figures in *understanding* therefore cannot be explained by *any* particular "meaning-conferring experience."[94] Whatever the merits of Husserl's critique of psychologism (and it is perhaps clear that I'm generally sympathetic), it seems apt to say that what Dharmakīrti and Dharmottara are essentially referring to, with their recurrent invocations of "the time of the convention" (*saṃketakāla*), *just is* "some meaning-conferring experience."

CONCLUSION: *SAṂKETAKĀLA* AS "MEANING-CONFERRING EXPERIENCE"

Thus, what ultimately grounds the account of meaning in which the *apoha* doctrine centrally figures is these recalled occasions—the convention-setting occasions on which the extensions of our predicates are first fixed—in virtue of which a present perception can give rise to conceptual thought.

As so often with the *apoha* doctrine, though, the point at which meaning thus comes into play is just deferred by the appeal to these occasions. It's here important to ask, of the supposedly causally describable occasions thus recalled, just what happens that makes *these* "meaning-conferring"; just what is it that are we to suppose *happens* "at the time of the convention" (*saṃketakāle*)? Can these occasions themselves be described without resorting to intentional or semantic idiom? Or must such an idiom come into play at this point?

Consider, in this regard, an exemplary passage from Dharmakīrti:

> The same expression (*samā śrutiḥ*)—[pertaining] to different [things] whose effect is the same, based on the exclusion of what does not have that effect—was created by forebears in order to show the effects of these [different particulars] (*tatkāryaparicodane . . . kṛtā vṛddhair*); [forebears did this] because of the impossibility (owing to the excessive difficulty) and the pointlessness of naming [each] different [thing]. [Hence, they did] not [apply these expressions] to anything real, since every existent is distinguished by a unique nature.[95]

While this passage clearly reflects the characteristically causal version of the *apoha* doctrine elaborated by Dharmakīrti, it also affords a glimpse of his presupposed picture of the practices by which the extensions of our predicates are first fixed—practices, it's clear from passages like this, that do not so much explain as *presuppose* that we know how meaning is thus conferred. It is, then, important to ask whether there is a way to explain this bygone "creation" of expressions by the "forebears" here invoked; can we imagine, in nonintentional terms, what *they* did?

While the salient point of this passage, for Dharmakīrti, is just the now-familiar one that the contentfulness of expressions is explicable in terms of exclusion of things in terms of their "effects," what is thus laid bare by this apparent reference to the initial application of terms is Dharmakīrti's presupposition that we already find intelligible the idea of *meaning* something. Here, we can appreciate that the conceptual problems involved in accounting for the first *acquisition* of a language parallel those involved in giving an account of first *creating* one; both situations basically represent Sellars's "occasions on which the fundamental connection of language with non-linguistic fact is exhibited." And just as in his problematic appeal, above, to a speaker's "autonomy" (*svātantryam*),[96] here, too, Dharmakīrti suggests that neither of these cases significantly differs from that of *using* a language—

that intuitions regarding an individual speaker's agency in using an already available language can be invoked to get us off the hook, as well, with regard to the conceptually prior question of our having the idea that utterances can *mean* anything in the first place.

Again, Dharmakīrti explains that "this apprehension of singularity with respect to [many particular] things is a false construction; the seed of this is the difference of one from another, *for the purpose of which there is signification* (*saṃjñā yadarthikā*)."[97] That is, the experience of many particular things as being tokens of a single type (hence, of their "singularity") involves reference to unreal abstractions—and it is really based on our attending to the relevant *differences* (viz., in causal capacities) that discursive practices can involve such abstractions. But is this "signification" (*saṃjñā*) just there for the taking? John Dunne—following the commentary of Śākyabuddhi, who glosses Dharmakīrti's *saṃjñā* with *saṃketakriyā* (the "activity" or "making of conventions")[98]—translates this last verse in a way that clearly discloses Dharmakīrti's problematic presupposition: "The seed of this conceptual cognition is each object's difference from this and that other object; *one engages in the formation of linguistic conventions* (saṃjñā) *for the purpose of knowing that difference*" (2004, 343–344; emphasis added). Dharmakīrti's autocommentary (also here in Dunne's translation) elaborates: "*One forms linguistic conventions* in order to have a cognition of a certain type of difference such that, having known that things which have nondifferent effects are different from those which do not have those effects, persons who understand those conventions act by avoiding those things that do not have the aforementioned effect" (Dunne 2004, 344; emphasis added).[99]

Characteristic passages like these virtually cry out for an answer to the question: *who* thus "forms" these? Can it really be thought that individuals, in using any particular language, are thereby doing something comparable to *devising* language as such? Will these "occasions on which the fundamental connection of language with non-linguistic fact is exhibited" really admit of the same explanation Dharmakīrti gives for the contentfulness of *already intelligible* concepts?

What is at issue is not the formation of *particular linguistic items* (e.g., the coinage of technical terms or neologisms) but of language as such—of the very idea that the utterance of a sound could *mean* something, which is an idea presupposed by the intelligibility of any particular coinage *as* linguistic. If we keep in mind this form of the question of the fundamental connection of language with nonlinguistic fact, the recurrent passages in Dharmakīrti's account where these distinct levels of description are conflated begins to sound obviously problematic. "For example," Dharmakīrti says, "when there is the possibility of expressing, with respect to things like the eye (whose result is a single cognition of form),[100] their having that effect as their nondistinction, *someone can create a conventional expression* (*kaścit sāṃketikīṃ śrutim kuryād*) for the sake of an understanding of all [such cognitions] at once—even without a separate universal as the form of that."[101] Of the crucially indeterminate "someone" (*kaścit*) who, we are encouraged to accept, thus decides that whatever "commonly produces the effect of cognition of form" will be called "eye," Manorathanandin says: "someone who has a desire for discursive commerce to be created (*sandheyavyavahāraruciḥ*) could form a conventional expression for the sake of an understanding of every instance of sight, etc., all together."[102]

And again: "Therefore, at the time of [the formation of? the learning of?] the convention, too, exclusion of what is other, joined to an indicated object—which results in a thought of itself—is connected to the expression."[103] The same account, that is, that Dharmakīrti has proposed as explaining semantic content, in general, is thus taken to explain, as well, what happens on the particular occasions when we first fix the extensions of our predicates—occasions, it seems, characterized by the perceptible *pointing out* of "indicated objects" (*nirdiṣṭa-artha*), which are, as for Augustine, thus "shewn by their bodily movements, as it were the natural language of all peoples." Regardless of how cogent we judge Dharmakīrti's account of reference to be—of whether, for example, we take it that his characteristic appeal to "sameness of effects" non-question-beggingly explains the kind of sameness that essentially characterizes semantic content—it's clear that we are here being asked to accept an account of the scope of semantic content as an account, as well, of *how we come to have the very idea thereof*. Manorathanandin's comment makes this conflation clear: "Since, at the time of usage (*vyavahārakāle*), there is understanding, based on language, that discriminates what is other, therefore, at the time of the [formation of? learning of?] the convention, too, exclusion of what is other is bound to the expression as being expressible—nothing else."[104] The same account proposed as explaining *what is understood* by language is thus taken also to explain the creation thereof.

That it is the *creating* of conventions here explained is made explicit by the commentator Prajñākaragupta; commenting on the same verse, he says that "in making a convention, too, the maker of a convention (*saṃketakāra*) does not make the convention by means of a rule (*vidhimukhena*); rather, it is just by means of exclusion, since even at the time of [the making of] the convention, only exclusion of what is other is connected to the expression, not a thing."[105] The activity of a "convention maker" (*saṃketakāra*) is thus represented by Prajñākaragupta as intelligible without reference to a "rule"—though we might also render *vidhi* as "affirmation," in which case the point is that convention setting is intelligible without the (positive) affirmation of a really existent universal.[106] Either way, the point is that the *vidhi* here eschewed in favor of *apoha* would be something that preexists the would-be creator of a convention; no such thing is required, Prajñākaragupta avers, insofar as the activity of first *instituting* conventions no more requires reference to intentional idiom than does an account of the content thereof.

What I'm pressing here is the question of whether Dharmakīrti and his commentators are really entitled to help themselves to the idea that we already understand what it would be thus to "create" a convention. On my reading, what is presupposed by Dharmakīrti's recurrently expressed thought in this regard—the thought that *creating* linguistic conventions is as readily intelligible as *using* them—is just what the proponent of *apoha* most needs to explain. Dharmakīrti's recurrent appeal to a bygone *saṃketakāla* does not "resolve the question of meaning itself" (as Bernhard Weiss says of the approach of Paul Grice, who also tried to explain semantic content in terms of speakers' intentions); it just "reduces linguistic meaning to mental meaning plus convention" (Weiss 2010, 57).[107] This presupposes, however, that we already understand how mental events can *be* semantically contentful—and that is just what was in question.

Jerry Fodor's recognition of the same problem, we saw in chapter 2, motivates his argument for a "Language of Thought." Of his own preliminary account of the practices that fix the extensions of our predicates, Fodor acknowledged that "none of this is of any use to a reductionist"; to invoke bygone convention-setting occasions, he allowed, just is to invoke further linguistic practices, themselves dependent, ipso facto, on linguistic *policies*—and insofar as "being in pursuit of a policy is being in an intentional state," this gives no help with "the naturalization problem" (1990, 98).[108] It's similarly reasonable to doubt whether Dharmakīrti's elaboration of *apoha* doctrine—his account of how conceptual thoughts can in any sense be about (can *mean*) what is given to us in perception—is advanced by claims to the effect that conceptual thought essentially involves the recollection (contra Husserl) of "some meaning-conferring experience."

This question, we will see in chapter 6, is effectively pressed by Mīmāṃsaka proponents of an argument whose purchase with respect to the *apoha* doctrine has not been much appreciated. Before turning to that, however, let us complete the case for taking Dharmakīrti's approach to exemplify the kind of "solipsistic and causalist position in the philosophy of mind" that Vincent Descombes characterized as *cognitivist.* Having reached a point in elaborating Dharmakīrti's *apoha* doctrine that is analogous to the point at which Fodor finds it necessary to posit a "Language of Thought"—something essentially *internal to a subject* that finally explains how thought can be semantically contentful—let us turn in the next chapter to Dharmakīrti's doctrine of *svasaṃvitti,* or "self-awareness." We will see how the kinds of commitments here elaborated relate to Dharmakīrti's arguments for the "methodologically solipsistic" view that cognition is autonomously intelligible—that, in other words, the character of awareness is intelligible simply in terms of intrinsic properties thereof and that nothing about awareness requires, therefore, that it be constitutively *of* the kind of world we typically take it to be of.

5

The *Svasaṃvitti* Doctrine

DHARMAKĪRTI'S "METHODOLOGICAL SOLIPSISM"

The seeing of objects is not established for one whose apprehension thereof is itself imperceptible.

—Dharmakīrti

INTRODUCTION: *PERCEPTUAL* AND *CONSTITUTIVE* UNDERSTANDINGS OF SELF-AWARENESS

In the last chapter, we saw that for Dharmakīrti it matters that the mental representations (*ākāra*) in terms of which semantic content is to be explained are themselves particulars. As particulars, they are causally describable (they are the *effects* of perceptual encounters); as *representations*, they are also phenomenally contentful, and it's only at this level of description that Dharmakīrti allows for the kind of "sameness" seemingly necessary to get semantic content off the ground. Thus, Dharmakīrti's account has it that what is excluded from coming under any concept is just whatever particulars do not produce "the same effect"; the *effects* in view are particular mental representations, taken as phenomenally similar to other such effects. This advances Dharmakīrti's guiding intuition that the sameness that essentially characterizes universals does not really obtain "out there" in the world to which these are taken to apply; what is the same, rather, is finally just the phenomenally recognizable character of first-personally experienced mental events.

We saw, though, that this account is fraught with the kinds of problems typically attending psychologistic explanations of semantic content. Insofar as his account appeals to some kind of sameness, Dharmakīrti is vulnerable to the charge that he presupposes (what he had set out to explain) just what essentially characterizes universals; still more difficult for him to account for is the eminently social (the *intersubjective*) character of semantic content. Dharmakīrti is, then, hard-pressed to explain how his psychologically explained concepts come to be expressible in terms of intersubjectively available "conventions" (*saṃketa*)—how mental particulars, fully intelligible with reference just to individual minds, can themselves explain something that is in principle available to innumerable other minds.

The problems are on display, we saw, in his recurrent sleights-of-hand involving "speaker's intention" (*vaktṛ-abhiprāya*). Thus, we are recurrently required by Dharmakīrti's account to imagine that the plausible sense in which some speaker's intention "causes" any utterance also explains the very possibility of that utterance's meaning anything—that a speaker's intention explains not only what her utterance means but even *that it means something*. The problems come into sharper focus when we notice that Dharmakīrti recurrently conflates intuitions regarding individual agency in the *use* of language with intuitions regarding what is involved in first acquiring or even *creating* language—a conflation that masks the extent to which Dharmakīrti must somewhere along the way presuppose experiences that are just intrinsically "meaning-conferring." Thus, a language user's moving from nonconceptually perceiving particular noises to *understanding a sentence* is explained, for Dharmakīrti, in terms of a subject's recollection of some bygone *saṃketakāla*—but how we are to describe what happened on these recalled occasions (whether these occasions themselves can be explained nonsemantically) is left obscure.

That Dharmakīrti's account thus presupposes (and therefore cannot *explain*) "meaning-conferring experiences" is also clear, we saw, from another of the cases involving reference to "speaker's intention"—from Dharmakīrti's understanding, that is, of the sense in which linguistic cognition is finally reducible to inference. What we are really entitled to claim from encountering any utterance, on Dharmakīrti's view, is only *that some agent's intention has been expressed*. Insofar as this is imagined by Dharmakīrti as an inference from effect (utterance) to cause (speaker's intention), the "intention" thus inferred cannot be understood to consist in the semantically contentful claim the speaker means to communicate; rather, the "intention" here must itself be a particular, since only particulars, for Dharmakīrti, can cause anything. What is really known from linguistic cognition is therefore just that a first-personally known mental event has caused somebody to give utterance; what that utterance *means*, though, is indubitably known only by the utterer—a view reflected in the recurrent passages where Dharmakīrti suggests that it's up to a speaker what she means by what she says.

The foregoing dimensions of Dharmakīrti's doctrine commonly reflect, I suggest, the guiding thought that first-personally experienced mental particulars can by themselves explain the essentially intersubjective "logical space of reasons" that we have been trying to understand. That Dharmakīrti's *apoha* doctrine thus grounds out in first-personally known episodes of experience is suggested by Tom Tillemans, who thus states what he takes to be Dharmakīrti's "fundamental position" on speakers' intentions: "words are used according to the speaker's wishes and designate anything whatsoever which he might intend. The speaker is thus an authority as to what he is referring to in that he can ascertain his own intention by means of a valid cognition (*pramāṇa*), viz., reflexive awareness (*svasaṃvedana*)" (2000, 163).[1]

Tillemans here invokes the other of the two doctrines I've all along had in mind in characterizing Dharmakīrti's (like Fodor's) as a basically *cognitivist* understanding of the mental—the doctrine of *svasaṃvedana* (often equivalently referred to as *svasaṃvitti*). That this doctrine relates closely to Dharmakīrti's *apoha* doctrine is suggested by the fact that Buddhist thinkers typically took the arguments for *svasaṃvitti* to advance the case for *sākāravāda*—for, that is, a representational theory of mind on which it is only of "aspects" or (we might also say) "representations" (*ākāra*) that we are immediately aware. Like the *apoha* doctrine, then, *svasaṃvitti*, too, essentially involves reference to subjectively experienced *ākāras*; on one understanding of the doctrine here in view, these are just what *svasaṃvitti* is *of*. However, rather than render *svasaṃvitti* (with Tillemans) as "reflexive awareness," I would leave open the possibility of this doctrine's being understood in at least a couple of distinct ways; thus, I will render *svasaṃvitti* (when not leaving it untranslated) more straightforwardly as "self-awareness," which retains the ambiguity of the Sanskrit compound. (Does the compound "self-awareness," e.g., involve a subjective or an objective genitive? In English as in Sanskrit, both are possible—"one's own awareness," "awareness of oneself"—and yield different senses.)

Dharmakīrti's doctrine of "self-awareness" might, then, be understood as picking out a particular *kind* of awareness—one distinguished by its having "oneself" (or one's own mental states) as its content. But it might also be understood as picking out something more like a defining characteristic of any "awareness" that is rightly so called.[2] Tillemans's reference to *svasaṃvitti* particularly in the context of understanding Dharmakīrti's semantics—his suggestion, that is, of the idea that first-personally experienced mental events finally explain meaning just insofar as "self-awareness" is a uniquely authoritative epistemic criterion (*pramāṇa*)—suggests that *svasaṃvitti* can be understood in ways congenial to Dharmakīrti's basically empiricist account of the mental. The claim that self-awareness is distinctive among *pramāṇas* might, on such a view, be understood as advancing a point familiar to students of Locke, Descartes, and Brentano: that insofar as our acquaintance with our own mental states is uniquely indubitable and immediate, this must somehow be reckoned the basis of any other convictions we could be entitled to. Among other things, this is to affirm that cognition is autonomously intelligible—that, as McDowell says of the view Hume inherits from predecessors like Locke, "no experience is in its very nature—intrinsically—an encounter with objects" (1998a, 344).[3]

I will follow Akeel Bilgrami in taking the latter, peculiarly epistemological appeal to *svasaṃvitti* to reflect an essentially *perceptual* understanding of self-awareness. In developing his own attempt to capture the distinctive character of self-awareness, Bilgrami considers what he takes to be the Cartesian view thereof as similarly holding that self-awareness essentially consists in "a form of infallible (inner) *perception* of one's mental states" (2006, 12). In addition, Bilgrami suggests, the Cartesian view also has it that self-awareness has a "*constitutive* role in the very idea of what it is knowledge of, i.e., in the very idea of a mental state" (2006, 12). Thus, it is somehow *constitutive* of "knowing," as such, that it involve this perceptual relation to itself.

Bilgrami affirms, however, that chief among the upshots of a constitutive view of self-awareness is that "our very notion of a mental state requires that mental states lack an independence from our capacity for knowing that we have them" (2006, 17). More clearly, what mental states lack is "precisely the independence possessed by the things *of* which we have perceptual knowledge, *from* that perceptual knowledge, i.e., the independence from perceptual knowledge that objects and facts in the external world possess" (2006, 29). Properly perceptual cognition is thus defined by its being independent of the things it is *about*; anyone's perceptually apprehending something in the vicinity is not constitutive of that thing's *being* there. A tree's being situated somewhere doesn't consist in its being the object of a proximal agent's awareness (its *being* is not the same as its *being known*); for a cognition to occur, in contrast, just is for the subject thereof to be aware of it.

In light of this difference from perceptual awareness, Bilgrami takes it that among the problems with the Cartesian view is that it incoherently holds a *constitutive* view of self-awareness together with a *perceptual* view thereof. Against this, Bilgrami's own case for a constitutive view of self-awareness takes its bearings from a "governing disjunction": "Only one of the two models, perceptual or constitutive, can be right" (2006, 28). If that is right, then it would seem that Dharmakīrti and other Buddhist proponents of *svasaṃvitti* must hold *either* a perceptual *or* a constitutive view—which would seem to mean that if we can appropriately attribute a constitutive view of *svasaṃvitti* to them, we would have to judge them wrong to have characterized it all along as also "perceptual" (*pratyakṣa*).

From Dharmakīrti's perspective, though, Bilgrami would surely be thought to beg one of the questions centrally at issue. Insofar, that is, as Dharmakīrti argues finally for an idealist position, his whole point—we will see in following his arguments regarding *svasaṃvitti*—is that even an avowed realist must finally allow that perceptual awareness in general is *not*, in fact, ultimately distinguishable from self-awareness. While, then, for Bilgrami a constitutive view of self-awareness is to be characterized chiefly in terms of its contrast with perceptual awareness, it's just insofar as he is an idealist that Dharmakīrti could reasonably reject Bilgrami's governing disjunction between perceptual and constitutive understandings of self-awareness.[4]

That questions of idealism are in play here is clear from the presentations of *svasaṃvitti* elaborated both by Dignāga and Dharmakīrti, who may here (in contrast to the case of the *apoha* discussion) be rather closer together; indeed, Georges Dreyfus and Christian Lindtner have opined that in their accounts of *svasaṃvitti*, the works of Dignāga and Dharmakīrti basically represent the "products of a unified intention" (1989, 27). Whether or not that's right, it is surely the case that a central preoccupation of commentators on both thinkers has been to characterize the arguments regarding *svasaṃvitti* as alternately representing what they take to be (in traditional doxographical terms) "Sautrāntika" and "Yogācāra" perspectives—as saying something about *svasaṃvitti*, that is, from (respectively) the point of view of an empiricist sort of representationalism, and from that of the full-blown idealism typically taken to be characteristic of Yogācāra.[5]

As noted in chapter 1, John Dunne characterizes the first of these doxographical perspectives as reflecting "External Realism"—as reflecting, that is, an affirmation of external reality. In contrast, the Yogācāra perspective—which Dharmakīrti maintains "consistently only in one significant section of his *Pramāṇavārttika*" (Dunne 2004, 59)[6]—is to be understood as "Epistemic Idealism," by which Dunne means the view that "All Entities are Mental."[7] On my reading, though, reference to "epistemic idealism" fails to distinguish Sautrāntika from Yogācāra; indeed, *epistemic* idealism is just the view these positions share. I thus take both Dignāga and Dharmakīrti commonly to argue that proponents of Sautrāntika and Yogācāra are alike committed to the view that *what we are immediately aware of*—which is distinct from the ontological issue of *what there is*—is only things somehow intrinsic to cognition. Dharmakīrti's "Yogācāra" move is just to make explicit that this is all that need be said, epistemologically, to recommend idealism. The difference between Sautrāntika and Yogācāra does not lie, then, in their epistemologies, since the Sautrāntika too can hold that we are *immediately* acquainted only with the contents of our own awareness; rather, the difference lies in the metaphysical arguments that (the idealist takes it) additionally show that only such mental things as sense data *could* be real.[8] What distinguishes the "Yogācāra" section of Dharmakīrti's text, then, is simply his making explicit that the "Sautrāntika" epistemological commitments he has all along been elaborating are already compatible with full-blown idealism.

Despite the eminently epistemological character of this line of argument—and despite the extent to which Dharmakīrti might accordingly be thought to hold a perceptual view of self-awareness—there is reason to think the doctrine of *svasaṃvitti* was nevertheless elaborated, at some points, in ways that reflect what Bilgrami calls a constitutive view of self-awareness. In this regard, it has been suggested by Paul Williams (1998) that the Indian Buddhist tradition attests two broad streams of interpretation concerning *svasaṃvitti*—that the doctrine has not only been invoked as a uniquely indubitable sort of awareness but also as saying something important simply about what awareness *is*. Williams aptly takes Śāntarakṣita (c. 725–788) as the chief exemplar of the latter sort of view. In a passage much quoted and discussed by later commentators, Śāntarakṣita affirmed in this vein that "cognition is distinct from insentient forms; it is just this self-awareness (*ātmasaṃvitti*) which is cognition's not being an insentient form."[9]

On this view, *svasaṃvitti* is something like a criterion for individuating tokens of the type "cognition"—a view that has affinities with Kant's transcendental unity of apperception. Thus, Śāntarakṣita suggests that it can be *cognition* that we're talking about only if it's identified under a description such as his; even *denying* of cognitions that they are finally subjective requires first having individuated them—and it will not be *cognitions* of which one denies this if they are not individuated with reference to the subjective perspective from which they are had. But of course, Kant takes the transcendental unity of apperception as the basis for inferring that epistemically contentful experiences are always necessarily *conceptual*; by invariably discussing *svasaṃvitti* particularly in the context of treating perception (*pratyakṣa*), in contrast, Buddhist proponents of the doctrine commonly argue that self-awareness represents a constitutively—indeed, perhaps a uniquely—nonconceptual sort of acquaintance.

In order to see how, with respect to alternative interpretations like these, we might reasonably take Dharmakīrti to have understood *svasaṃvitti*, it will be useful to begin (as we did in considering *apoha*) with his predecessor Dignāga. In first introducing the doctrine, Dignāga sketches most of the significant intuitions about *svasaṃvitti* in just a few verses and thus gives us in fairly brief scope some grip on the various claims and arguments here in play. The options thus introduced can then be fleshed out with reference to Dharmakīrti, whose most influential argument for *svasaṃvitti*—the so-called *sahopalambhaniyama* argument (see pages 175–83, below)—seems interestingly to involve both *perceptual* and *constitutive* understandings of self-awareness. This argument is, on the one hand, characterized by something like the mode of necessity (as that can similarly figure in Śāntarakṣita's view); it can also, though, be understood as the kind of eminently epistemological argument that McDowell characterizes as appealing to a "highest common factor"[10]—an argument, in effect, for the autonomously intelligible character of awareness. It is just this point that Dharmakīrti takes to warrant the conclusion (contra Bilgrami's "governing disjunction") that perceptual content is not, after all, distinct from self-awareness.

We will then conclude this chapter with some consideration of how Dharmakīrti's understanding of *svasaṃvitti* dovetails with his characteristic emphasis on causal explanation. One way to bring this out (and to get some critical purchase on the doctrine) is to consider the tenth-century Śaiva Siddhāntin thinker Bhaṭṭa Rāmakaṇṭha, who elaborated a promising critique of *svasaṃvitti*. Rāmakaṇṭha is interesting in this regard since, in fact, he appropriated the Buddhist doctrine of *svasaṃvitti* for his own project; this requires, however, that he specify the problematic misstep (as he takes it) owing to which Buddhists like Dharmakīrti could think it reasonable to enlist the doctrine in the service of an account of selflessness (*anātmavāda*). Arguing instead that *svasaṃvitti* reveals precisely that there is something essentially *continuous* about cognition, Rāmakaṇṭha considers whether Dharmakīrti's commitment to causal explanation—and particularly to the concomitant claim that this must involve only momentary terms—can be reconciled with the phenomenology of temporality. To the extent that his critique hits its mark, Rāmakaṇṭha's reading of Dharmakīrti affords an illuminating perspective on (among other things) the question of whether or how ontological explanations should be constrained by phenomenological considerations.

We turn, however, first to Dignāga.

DIGNĀGA ON *PRAMĀṆAPHALA* AS *SVASAMVITTI*

Svasaṃvitti is introduced in chapter 1 of Dignāga's *Pramāṇasamuccaya*, the chapter on perception. First appearing in this chapter's sixth verse, *svasaṃvitti* is introduced as somehow subsumed under the category of *mānasapratyakṣa*, "mental perception." So, having begun the chapter by elaborating the constitutively nonconceptual character of *pratyakṣa* in general, Dignāga specifies in verses 6 and 7 that there are two other significant instances of such nonconceptual awareness (two instances, that is, other than sensory perception): *mānasa-* and *yogi-pratyakṣa*.[11] *Svasaṃvitti*, it seems we are to understand, somehow relates to the former; in Masaaki Hattori's translation, Dignāga says: "there is also mental [perception, which is of two kinds:] awareness of an [external] object and self-awareness of [such subordinate mental activities as] desire and the like, [both of which are] free from conceptual construction" (1968, 27; all insertions original). Masatoshi Nagatomi—whose own approach to the verse, as with many scholars writing before the recent availability of a useable Sanskrit text of Dignāga, was by way of Hattori's translation from the Tibetan—observed in regard to this verse that it is "in fact so elliptical that no two post-Dharmakīrti commentators reached an exact consensus on the reading of it" (1980, 255–256).[12]

A straightforward reading of Dignāga's limited commentary on this is, I think, indeterminate with respect to the most puzzling issues: "Mental [perception], too, is nonconceptual, having as its content (*ālambana*) objects (*viṣaya*) like form and so forth, engaging aspects (*ākāra*) of experience; and self-awareness with regard to such things as pleasure, because of its being independent of the senses, is mental perception."[13] If it's clear that Dignāga here introduces *svasaṃvitti* as an instance or aspect of "mental perception," it is not altogether clear just what it would mean to say so. Does self-awareness occur, for example, only with regard to "such things as pleasure"? Even if it does, is it nevertheless to be imagined as somehow present in *every* awareness? (Is the reference to affective responses simply meant, that is, as exemplifying *any* of the constitutively subjective aspects that characterize every instance of awareness?) Is *svasaṃvitti* to be understood as a particular *kind* of "mental perception," distinguished by its special sort of object or content? Or as a way of talking about what *mānasapratyakṣa is*?

We saw in chapter 1 that *mānasapratyakṣa* is akin to the Ābhidharmika idea of *manovijñāna*; indeed, when he discusses *mānasapratyakṣa* in his *Nyāyabindu*, Dharmakīrti actually calls it *manovijñāna*.[14] The latter, recall from chapter 1, names a kind of awareness whose content is the outputs of the five "form-possessing" or *material* sense faculties; the outputs of the latter, on this view, are not themselves really "cognitive" except as the content of a mental cognition (*manovijñāna*).[15] Here it's worth noting that when the Mādhyamika Candrakīrti later presses a critique of Dignāga, he will invoke *manovijñāna* to undermine Dignāga's case for the constitutively nonconceptual character of perception. This is because Dignāga had supported his own characterization of perception by invoking an Ābhidharmika passage according to which "someone endowed only with visual cognition senses blue, but not *that* it is blue."[16] Hattori expresses the obvious point of Dignāga's quotation of this: "The expression '*nīlaṃ vijānāti*' implies that one has an immediate awareness of the object itself. On the other hand, '*nīlam iti vijānāti*' implies that one forms a perceptual judgement by associating a name with the object perceived. Thus, the . . . Abhidharma passage expresses the thought that perception is free from conceptual construction" (1968, 88n1.36).

As Candrakīrti will rightly argue, though, the passage does not in fact support Dignāga's characterization of perception; the point of the text, Candrakīrti says, is "not to state a definition of *pratyakṣa*, but is simply that of demonstrating the insentience of the five material senses."[17] Candrakīrti thus takes the passage to express only the point that the outputs of the material senses are not themselves contentful—that they are, rather, the content *of* the *manovijñāna*.[18] Not only, then, does the passage quoted by Dignāga not obviously support his characterization of perception as nonconceptual—it suggests, indeed, that *manovijñāna* is precisely that *conceptual* sort of faculty which knows *that* things are as represented by the material senses. If this is the sort of thing Dignāga has in mind when he introduces *mānasapratyakṣa*, then his claim (at *Pramāṇasamuccaya* 1.6) that *svasaṃvitti* is somehow related to *mānasapratyakṣa* might be taken to advance an idea expressed by Paul Williams; stating what he takes as one of the two main interpretations of *svasaṃvitti*, Williams says that "in order for knowing that one knows to occur and therefore, it is maintained, for a proper perceptual act to take place, it is argued that . . . [a first-order awareness of, say, something's being blue] has to become the object of an awareness *that* it is an eye-consciousness with an aspect of blue" (1998, 7).

As we saw in chapter 3, however, what is individuated by "that"-clauses such as this can only be states of affairs under some description; but in that case, to attribute to Dignāga an understanding of *svasaṃvitti* such as Williams here suggests is to imagine *svasaṃvitti* as somehow conceptual—as the faculty, for example, for producing perceptual judgments.[19] While there is, though, much that is unclear in Dignāga's opening discussion of self-awareness in relation to *mānasapratyakṣa*, it cannot be doubted that Dignāga means to emphasize the perhaps uniquely nonconceptual character of *svasaṃvitti*. Notwithstanding the kind of view stated by Williams, then, Dignāga means to emphasize that *svasaṃvitti* is not a faculty that yields perceptual or any other judgments; he argues, rather, that even though such judgments turn out themselves to be "perceptual"—in the sense, at least, that *acts* of judging are themselves things we are immediately aware of—it is precisely *not* in their capacity *as judgments* (not *as having semantic content*) that they are so.

Dignāga says as much in responding to the anticipated objection that insofar as we are thus "self-aware" even with regard to our conceptual thoughts—are immediately aware *of having them*—reference to *svasaṃvitti* turns out to undermine the distinction between perceptual and conceptual thought. Embracing the point, Dignāga answers by explaining why it doesn't represent a problem for his account; thus, in the second half of his verse 6, Dignāga allows that "even conceptual thought is admitted [as being perceptual] in terms of self-awareness—but not," he continues, "with respect to its content (*artha*), because of the conceptual construction of that."[20] Dignāga thus allows that in *svasaṃvitti* we are perceptually (which is to say *nonconceptually*) aware *of* our own (conceptual) acts of judging, but emphasizes that it's not with respect to the *content* of these judgings that this immediacy obtains; rather, the really immediate apprehension here concerns only the character of the judging *as mental event*.

Dignāga can here be taken to express one of the guiding intuitions of such representational theories of mind, generally characteristic of empiricism, as we have seen exemplified by Fodor and Dharmakīrti: namely, that we can think of the *things* ("mental states") that *have* content—Locke's "Ideas," Dharmakīrti's *ākāras*—as autonomously intelligible just *as particular occurrents*. In initially discussing *svasaṃvitti*, then, Dignāga thus suggests that any awareness to the effect *that* things in the world are thus and so—even simply *that* I perceive a tree—is, ipso facto, a conceptual (i.e., semantically contentful) awareness. This would seem to imply that only when cognition is aware *of itself*, of its own occurrence, can it really be said to be genuinely "nonconceptual"—and hence, for Dignāga, properly *perceptual*. On one reading of the trend of thought Dignāga here initiates, then, only *svasaṃvitti* therefore finally counts as perception—a view surely congenial to characteristically Yogācāra commitments. What is "ultimately" knowable, on such a view, is only something about the character of awareness itself and not about the world that awareness seems to us to disclose; for we are *indubitably* acquainted only with the fact that awareness itself occurs.

However he understands the idea first introduced and characterized as we have so far seen, Dignāga most significantly argues for *svasaṃvitti* at *Pramāṇasamuccaya* 1.8cd–10.[21] He does so by way of elaborating the claim—characteristic of the school of thought that begins with him, although quite variously understood—that by the word *pramāṇa* we cannot really refer (as the word-form suggests) to the epistemic "instruments" of our awareness; rather, all that can finally be in view is the cognition generally imagined as *resulting* from the exercise thereof—the *pramāṇaphala*, the result or "fruit" of a *pramāṇa*.[22] Introducing this claim, Dignāga asserts at *Pramāṇasamuccaya* 1.8d that perceptual awareness is "actually a *pramāṇa* only as result" (*pramāṇaṃ phalam eva sat*).[23]

Dignāga's understanding of this claim as dovetailing with the case for *svasaṃvitti* can be brought out by briefly noting the later commentator Dharmottara's very different understanding of the same claim. In commenting on passages in Dharmakīrti's *Nyāyabindu*, Dharmottara ventures an understanding of the *pramāṇaphala* doctrine that concerns just the kind of problem I've taken to be addressed by Dharmakīrti's *apoha* doctrine; specifically, Dharmottara takes the claim regarding *pramāṇaphala* to be that it's only insofar as any instance particularly of perception (*pratyakṣa*) comes, we might say, to "fruition" (*phala*) in an epistemically contentful *judgment* that it can really be thought a *pramāṇa*. On Dharmottara's reading, the *pramāṇaphala* doctrine thus concerns Dharmakīrti's basic problem of getting from perceptual awareness to the "logical space of reasons"—a problem in this case addressed by arguing (notwithstanding Dharmottara's claim as an avowedly faithful interpreter of Dharmakīrti to be allowing nothing of the sort) that perception does, after all, involve something like a conceptual dimension.[24] Perception comes to "fruition" as an epistemic criterion, on Dharmottara's account, only insofar as it yields the constitutively conceptual awareness *that* such-and-such is the case.

While Dharmottara's elaboration of the *pramāṇaphala* doctrine thus makes no reference to *svasaṃvitti*, it is, in contrast, just the point of Dignāga's seminal elaboration of the *pramāṇaphala* claim to advance a line of argument centrally involving *svasaṃvitti*—which is (we've seen) nothing if not nonconceptual. Dignāga begins this trend of argument by thus explaining the claim that it's "only as result" that perceptual awareness is a *pramāṇa*:

> For in this regard, the result is not, as for realists (*bāhyaka*), something other than the *pramāṇa*; rather, in virtue of just this cognition's occur-

> rence (existing as a result) as being contentful (*viṣayākāratayā*), there is the conception of it as having a function. Based on that conception, being a *pramāṇa* is figuratively predicated (*upacaryate*), even though really without function.[25]

Reference to *pramāṇas*, then, encourages us to imagine that we might distinguish something essentially *precognitive* as a constraint on the determinacy of cognitions—something not itself contentful that is nevertheless "instrumental" in the realization of cognitions. But anything we could thus indicate, Dignāga here suggests, is always already accessible to us only given a complete and contentful act of cognition; there is no access to anything somehow given to us before cognition, since it can only be through already constituted cognitions that we can "get at" anything at all. It's therefore only figuratively that we can refer to *pramāṇas*, since all we can really have in view is the kinds of already contentful cognitions that *pramāṇas* themselves are supposedly invoked to explain; thus, Dignāga here says it is just "in virtue of cognition's occurrence as being contentful" (*jñānasya viṣayākāratayā utpattyā*) that we can in the first place take there to be anything we might refer to as "instrumental" in the realization thereof.

Dignāga's commentator Jinendrabuddhi (710–770)[26] elaborates, with regard to this verse, on what we are entitled to think is picked out by the characterization of anything as "instrumental" (*sādhanam*): "The expression 'instrument of an action' (*kriyāsādhanam*) should not [be understood to refer to] every instrument of every action, or [to mean that] every action is to be accomplished by all; rather, the instrument of an action, *x*, is that instrument immediately (*avyavadhānena*) owing to which *x* reaches completion."[27] We should not, that is, suppose that all of the factors conducing to anything are rightly thought "instrumental" in its realization or that every action will have the same range of factors; rather, only that factor "immediately" (*avyavadhānena*) owing to which an act is realized is appropriately characterized as "instrumental" (*sādhanam*) in bringing that about. This gives us a way to understand why Dignāga is entitled to think that cognition's "being contentful" (*viṣayākāratā*) is finally all that one could refer to as "*pramāṇa*": it is "immediately" owing to *its being contentful* that cognition is determinate in the peculiarly strong sense that goes with identity—the identity, in effect, of cognition's *being* and its *being known*.

Explaining as much, Jinendrabuddhi thus characterizes the "nature" (*svabhāva*) in virtue of which cognition itself is all that could be thought "instrumental" in its own realization:

> In this regard, with respect to an accusative[28] such as form, a cognition (which consists in resemblance) must have a nature (*svabhāva*), comparable to an instrument (*karaṇabhūta*),[29] as being experience—[an experiential nature] owing to which there is effected an ascertainment of various cognitions as distinct, such that we can be aware: "this is a cognition of blue, this of yellow."[30]

Among the things Jinendrabuddhi here makes clear is that we are after a criterion for first-personally individuating cognitions—something in virtue of which we can take cognitions to *be* phenomenologically distinct, such that we know of our own experience when it is of one thing and when of another. Jinendrabuddhi here entertains the possibility that factors like the acuity of the senses provide the requisite constraint—that, in other words, it's our sensory interactions with things in the world that are "instrumental" in producing contentful cognitions. But he says these cannot be thought "instrumental" in the realization of determinate cognitions "because of their not being of the nature of cognition (*ajñānasvabhāvatvāt*), and because, rather, of their being the *causes* of all cognitions."[31] His point, I take it, is that the one thing in virtue of which we can take cognitions to *be* phenomenologically distinct, and which we are therefore entitled to take as "instrumental" in the realization thereof, is something intrinsic to awareness—specifically, the first-personally known fact of any cognition's seeming as it does, which (on the view that it's constitutive of cognition that it be so known) just is to say *the very fact of cognition's occurrence*.

Nothing, that is, but cognition's occurrence *as seeming some way* is so "immediately" (*avyavadhānena*) related to its first-personally known character; indeed, insofar as a constitutive view of self-awareness has it that cognition's *being* is coextensive with its *being known*, these are identical—for a cognition to be contentful for a subject *just is for a cognition to occur*. This is why it makes sense to say that anything we might refer to as "instrumental" to the realization of cognition (anything we might call "*pramāṇa*") must finally be identical with the "resulting" cognition. Dignāga makes the same point when he proceeds to claim, at verse 1.9a, that the "result" (*pramāṇaphala*) he has been discussing is *svasaṃvitti*: "Now in this case,[32] self-awareness is the result."[33] Together with the view we've just considered—the view that "*pramāṇa*" can really refer only to "*pramāṇaphala*"—this would seem to suggest that the *pramāṇa* that is perception is to be understood as finally consisting in *svasaṃvitti*; for if perceptual cognition is "actually a *pramāṇa* only as result," and if "result" here refers to self-awareness, it would seem to follow that perceptual cognition counts as a *pramāṇa only as self-awareness.*[34]

There is some question, however, about the force of Dignāga's disjunctive *vā*, which I perhaps fudged in the preceding paragraph; I rendered it as "Now" at the beginning of the passage ("Now in this regard . . . "), but it usually means *or*. Thus, Dignāga could well be saying: "*Or* self-awareness is the result"—in which case, it seems, it would only be within certain parameters that self-awareness is thus to be understood as what is referred to by the word *pramāṇa*. This reading represents one of the bases for taking Dignāga here to be alternately giving accounts of what might be said on either of the perspectives traditionally characterized as "Sautrāntika" and "Yogācāra." On one such interpretation, Dignāga's verse 1.8d—"[cognition] is a *pramāṇa* only as result"—can be thought to concern the case where it's an external object that a "resultant" cognition is of; whereas he here (1.9ab) considers instead what we should say said if it is cognition itself that the "resultant" cognition is of.[35]

While readings that thus emphasize the apparent disjunction of Dignāga's claims are not without basis, this obscures the point I take to be chiefly advanced in these verses: that it is with *svasaṃvitti* that the epistemological common ground of these doxographically characterized Buddhist perspectives most clearly emerges. The trend of the ensuing arguments, then, is that no matter how one finally *explains* the contentfulness of cognition (whether in terms of really existent external objects or not), the very fact of *its being contentful* should be reckoned as both intrinsic to cognition and explanatorily basic. Dignāga is further concerned, I think, to argue that the occurrence of a contentful cognition just is the occurrence of a subjectively experienced cognition; anything *known* can finally be only *first-personally* known. Proponents of characteristically "Sautrāntika" and "Yogācāra" views can (and must) alike accept this point; whether or not one is inclined finally to advert to external objects, it is incontrovertible that it's only *as known* that it makes sense to say that even these are accessible.

Dignāga suggests as much at verse 1.9b: the reason why *svasaṃvitti* is what is meant by *pramāṇaphala* is that "judgment regarding an object (*arthaniścaya*) has [self-awareness] as its form."[36] Introducing this claim, Dignāga invokes the category of *ābhāsa*, "appearance," which has much the same sense as *ākāra*. Thus, the point he is making here is that "cognition arises having two appearances: the appearance of itself, and the appearance of an object. It is its [i.e., cognition's] self-awareness, having both appearances, which is the result."[37] On my reading, Dignāga's expression thus involves a subjective genitive ("*its* self-awareness, having both appearances");[38] he says, then, not that *svasaṃvitti* is *of* both these aspects (in the way, e.g., that perceptions are *of* trees), but rather that cognition *has* the quality of self-awareness—which is so, Dignāga is here emphasizing, regardless of how we explain its content. Cognition has the property of being first-personally known, that is, *however* its content be characterized—whether as having "the appearance of an object" or just "the appearance of itself."

Jinendrabuddhi reads Dignāga as here pressing the point that "there can be no awareness (*saṃvitti*) of anything apart from cognition."[39] Anything known, that is, can be known only *as* given in some cognition. Jinendrabuddhi continues: "Suppose there are external objects; even so, an object of awareness (*viṣaya*) is ascertained only according to experience (*yathāsaṃvedanam eva*), so it makes sense to say that just this is the result (*phala*)"; there is, he emphasizes, no "experience of an object as it is in itself (*yathāsvabhāvam*)."[40] With respect, then, to the apparently contrasting "Sautrāntika" and "Yogācāra" perspectives supposedly in play, the point is that "*whether or not* external objects are present, cognition, having both appearances, is sensed; that which is its [cognition's] self-cognition, i.e., its experience of itself, that will be the result"[41]—will be, that is, the result (*pramāṇaphala*) that alone can be referred to by the word "*pramāṇa*," regardless of how we explain what awareness is finally of.

This reading is consistent with what Dignāga says in the course of introducing and elaborating the remainder of his verse 9 (1.9cd, here italicized), where he again makes reference to the fact of cognition's "being contentful":[42]

> For when cognition, along with all its content,[43] is the object, then one knows the object as desired or not desired only in conformity to self-awareness; but when it is an external object being known, then *just its [i.e., cognition's]*[44] *being contentful is the pramāṇa.* For in that case, disregarding that its nature is self-cognized by awareness, just its [i.e., cognition's] being contentful (*arthābhāsatā*) is the *pramāṇa*, since that content (*artha*) is *known through that.*[45]

The contrast apparently drawn here is not nearly so sharp as Dignāga's disjunctive syntax might suggest; indeed, it seems to me that the alternatives proposed here are to be understood as finally amounting to the same thing.

The apparent contrast makes it easy to suppose that Dignāga's reference to what counts as a "*pramāṇa*" in this case represents an alternative to what he said in the first half of the verse (1.9a, where it was claimed that "self-awareness is the result")—that, in other words, he is no longer advancing the same point in the second half of the verse. On such a reading of the verse's two claims as independent of each other, the text's references to what counts as "*pramāṇaphala*" and what as "*pramāṇa*" are to *two really different things*. Insofar as one reads the text this way, one might then see problems arising with regard to Dignāga's subsequent verse (*Pramāṇasamuccaya* 1.10), which is traditionally read as reflecting a Yogācāra perspective: "That [cognition] whose appearance is *x* is the thing known (*prameya*); but being the *pramāṇa* and the result thereof belong, respectively, to the subjective aspect (*grāhakākāra*) and to [*sva-*]*saṃvitti*—hence, these three are not separate."[46]

Thus, from the "Sautrāntika" perspective taken to be expressed in 1.9cd, it is (we saw) cognition's *being contentful* (*viṣayābhāsatā*) that we are to imagine as "*pramāṇa*." In verse 10, however, Dignāga says instead that it is cognition's *having some content* (its being *yadābhāsam*, "that whose appearance is *x*")[47] that is to be reckoned as what is known (*prameya*), its "subjective aspect" (*grāhakākāra*) that is to reckoned as the "*pramāṇa*," and *svasaṃvitti* that represents what we are to imagine as brought about by the operations of these (*pramāṇaphala*). Thus, it seems that the Sautrāntikas (at 1.9cd) call *pramāṇa* what Yogācāras (in verse 10) call *prameya*—and that what Yogācāras (again in verse 10) call *pramāṇa* (the "subjective aspect") is altogether missing from the Sautrāntika picture.

This would seem, among other things, to recommend the impression of these doxographically described perspectives as significantly different, precisely in regard to *svasaṃvitti*. While that conclusion is not without basis, though, it obscures the extent to which it is precisely the *svasaṃvitti* doctrine that Dignāga takes to *unite* the "Sautrāntika" and "Yogācāra" perspectives; the apparent tension between 1.9cd and 1.10 looks rather different if we keep in mind that *all* of Dignāga's claims here are made in the context of his overarching claim (at 1.8d) that by "*pramāṇa*" we really refer only to the "*pramāṇaphala*." Dignāga's reference to the seemingly contrastive case "in which it is an external object that is to be known"—the case where *being contentful* is what is referred to by "*pramāṇa*"—is not to be read, then, as supporting a different understanding of *svasaṃvitti*; indeed, he just is explaining *why it makes sense* to hold that self-awareness is the *pramāṇaphala* regardless of how one would explain the contentfulness of cognition. Dignāga thus argues that even if we want to account for cognition's being contentful with reference to external objects, it remains the case that it is only *through cognition*—and, insofar as all cognitions are first-personally known, therefore only through *svasaṃvitti*—that there can be any access to them.

The claim (at 1.9cd) that cognition's "being contentful" (*viṣayābhāsatā*) is the only thing worth the name "*pramāṇa*" does not, then, amount to the claim that this is something over and above the "*phala*" that is self-awareness; on the view I take Dignāga to be pressing, the right account of cognition's often seeming to represent external objects is just that cognition sometimes has this sort of *phenomenal content* (*ābhāsa*). But that is just to make a phenomenological point (not an ontological or metaphysical one): that cognition *seems to be of things*. Regardless of how one would *explain* this strictly phenomenological fact (whether, e.g., in realist or idealist terms), the fact itself, *as* phenomenological, concerns something intrinsically known to the subject thereof. To the extent, then, that contentful cognition is defined (is *constituted* as such) by its *svasaṃvitti*, Dignāga can therefore find epistemological common ground for Sautrāntika and Yogācāra: regardless of what we think cognition is finally *of*, it is only as first-personally known, only as internally related to an act of cognition, that its content is accessible. This is finally why I said above (at page 172), of the apparent contrast in terms of which Dignāga introduces 1.9cd, that what might seem to be proposed as alternatives may in fact amount to the same thing.

With respect, then, to Dignāga's verse 10 (which could be supposed in tension with 1.9cd), the salient point on the present interpretation is Dignāga's conclusion: "hence, these three are not distinct."[48] If we take Dignāga still to have in view the overarching claim (made at 1.8d) that by "*pramāṇa*" we can only refer to what is really the *pramāṇaphala*—the claim that any of the various terms thought to be in play in acts of knowing are only "figuratively referred to" (*upacaryate*), with its really being only through already constituted (and first-personally experienced) cognitions that any of these can be individuated—it's not a problem that *viṣayābhāsatā* is figuratively referred to at 1.9cd as "*pramāṇa*," while the equivalent fact that cognition "has as its appearance *x*" (*yadābhāsam*) is, in contrast, figuratively referred to at 1.10 as the "thing known" (*prameya*). This apparent divergence isn't a problem because Dignāga's point all along has been that there really aren't two different things here to *be* referred to; *pramāṇa* and *prameya* are just figuratively invoked, since it's only the *results* of *pramāṇas* (*pramāṇaphala*) that can really be in view. This is because it's only as internally related to acts of cognition that anything at all can be experienced by us; "self-awareness" is just the manifestness of the cognitions in which everything that is present to us shows up. This is why it makes sense to say that *svasaṃvitti* is the *pramāṇaphala* regardless of our ontological commitments.

DHARMAKĪRTI'S CULMINATING ARGUMENT FOR *SVASAṂVITTI*: "*SAHOPALAMBHANIYAMA*"

Chief among the concerns of Dharmakīrti's arguments regarding *pramāṇa-phala* and *svasaṃvitti* is similarly to argue for epistemic idealism—for the view that cognition is intelligible apart from any consideration of its semantic content, apart from its being *of a world*. Of Dharmakīrti's arguments to this effect, the so-called *sahopalambhaniyama* argument—one to the effect that even perceptual objects are most significantly characterized by "the constraint" (*niyama*) that is their being accessible only "together with the apprehension [thereof]" (*sahopalambha*)[49]—was taken by subsequent Indian philosophers to represent the most significant argument for *svasaṃvitti*; we turn now to this culminating argument to see how some of Dignāga's claims were elaborated and how Dharmakīrti's elaboration of the doctrine reflects his essentially cognitivist approach.

Dharmakīrti can be understood as here advancing the kind of argument that John McDowell characterizes as involving appeal to a "highest common factor."[50] Dharmakīrti is concerned to show that insofar as it can only be *through awareness* that we have access even to the contrast between perceptual and other kinds of objects of awareness, it makes sense to say it's in virtue of something intrinsic to awareness that even perceptual cognitions seem to us as they do. This intrinsic property thus represents the "common factor" in virtue of which, for example, nonveridical cognitions can be phenomenologically indistinguishable from veridical ones; to that extent, the direction of epistemological explanation ought therefore be from *seeming* to *being*. Just as Dignāga argues that the bare fact of cognition's *being contentful* (*viṣayābhāsatā*) is all we can really have in view in referring to a criterion or "instrument" of knowledge (a *pramāṇa*), so Dharmakīrti will argue that it's only in virtue of intrinsic properties of awareness that perceptual objects can *seem* in the first place to be distinguished by their independence from awareness.

It is this line of argument that cuts most clearly against Bilgrami's "governing disjunction." Of the two basic models of self-awareness here invoked for thinking about how to understand *svasaṃvitti*, Bilgrami affirmed, we saw, that "only one of the two models, perceptual or constitutive, can be right"[51]—and this because for a cognition to occur just is for the subject thereof to be aware of it, whereas the things *of* which we have perceptual knowledge are, in contrast, independent of the perceptual knowledge thereof. We also saw, however, that Bilgrami characterizes the latter fact as "the independence from perceptual knowledge *that objects and facts in the external world possess*"—and it's precisely the point of Dignāga's and Dharmakīrti's arguments for epistemic idealism to deny the significance of this apparent contrast.[52] To that end, the *sahopalambhaniyama* argument would show that insofar as we cannot have anything but *cognitive* access even to this contrast, the difference between perceptual awareness and the objects thereof amounts only to a *phenomenal* contrast—hence, a contrast that can itself be accounted for with reference to something (viz., *its being contentful*) intrinsic to awareness. This recommends the conclusion that awareness itself is known prior to and independent of our knowing a world.

Insofar as Dharmakīrti can be taken thus to argue that the contrast invoked by Bilgrami is itself intrinsic to awareness, it makes sense that Dharmakīrti's arguments concerning *svasaṃvitti* would, like Dignāga's, be represented by commentators in terms of a debate between proponents of the "Sautrāntika" and "Yogācāra" perspectives. In introducing, then, what was credited by generations of Indian philosophers as Dharmakīrti's most compelling argument for *svasaṃvitti*, we can begin by considering something of the Sautrāntika-Yogācāra debate that Dharmakīrti frames in setting up one statement of the *sahopalambhaniyama* argument. More clearly than in Dignāga, we can see here that the trend of these doxographically characterized discussions is to emphasize that characteristically "Sautrāntika" epistemological commitments already amount to an *epistemic* (as contra metaphysical) case for the idealism of Yogācāra.

Having, then, first elaborated (in verses 301–319 of the "perception" chapter of his *Pramāṇavārttika*) the *pramāṇaphala* doctrine sketched above following Dignāga, Dharmakīrti entertains questions naturally raised by that view: What, finally, is it reasonable to think we are aware of when we thus experience any seemingly contentful awareness? Is it, indeed, right to think that experience thus consists in awareness *of* anything at all? Or do the arguments for the *pramāṇaphala* doctrine entail the view that awareness can be exhaustively described as consisting in mental events that are just intrinsically characterized by their seeming to have content? And, if the latter is the recommended conclusion, does it any longer make sense to distinguish, as it were, the mental "vehicles" of epistemic content from the content borne thereby? Given what I take to be the Yogācāra view finally on offer, such questions will be seen as rhetorical; this is a view on which there is nothing for awareness to *be* "of," insofar as causally describable occurrences of awareness are all that finally exist. What Dharmakīrti's Yogācāra proponent wants to argue, though, is only that the basically empiricist commitments characteristic of "Sautrāntika" can be taken already to have paved the way for that conclusion.

It might seem that it would be difficult to motivate such a claim, particularly given the basis for the Sautrāntika position's intuitive plausibility. The Sautrāntika epistemologist is committed, we saw in chapter 1,[53] to the not implausible view that perceptual cognition is distinguished not only by its representing some object but by its causal connection with that object—a view, one could think, that points precisely away from idealism, for what could better show something's being "objective" than its actually *causing* the operation of the transducers that are one's senses? Dharmakīrti's Yogācāra proponent suggests at *Pramāṇavārttika* 3.323, however, that something like the same intuition can be retained even on the view that only mental events finally exist: "If it's agreed that the mark of being cognizable is *resemblance of* and *causal relation to* something, even so, an immediately antecedent cognition (*samanantaram vijñānam*), having the same content, could be what is known (*saṃvedyam*)."[54] Dharmakīrti's Yogācāra proponent thus appeals to the standard-issue Buddhist analysis of the causal conditions of any moment of awareness—in particular, to the idea that among the causes of any cognition is an immediately preceding moment of cognition (*samantarapratyaya*).[55] The point ventured here is that the same idea can satisfy the Sautrāntika's criterion of a causal constraint on perceptual cognition; even, that is, if there existed only mental events, it would still be the case that such events are causally constrained by *what there is*, simply insofar as mental events themselves occur in causally regular ways.

Dharmakīrti anticipates the Sautrāntika rejoinder that this misses the mark, insofar as the salient point of the Sautrāntika's view is that perceptual cognitions are causally constrained by what they are cognitions *of*—and surely no one would say that an "immediately preceding moment of awareness" is itself the *content* of any awareness. Unpacking Dharmakīrti's expression of this likely objection, the commentator Manorathanandin says that "an experience is of that regarding which there arises a thought of ascertainment—'this was seen,' or 'this was heard'—not of anything else. And there is no ascertainment of something seen or heard, etc., with regard to an immediately preceding moment of awareness (*samantarapratyaya*)—so this is not what is apprehended."[56] The Sautrāntika's objection thus raises precisely the issues (sketched in chapter 1) considered in Dignāga's *Ālambanaparīkṣā*[57]—in particular, that of how or whether an impersonal, causal description of awareness can be reconciled with the first-personally known content thereof.

Dharmakīrti's idealist responds by acknowledging that of course, phenomenologically speaking, it *seems* to us that the content of experience represents something external to awareness—but how we are (metaphysically or ontologically) to *explain* this strictly phenomenological fact is just what's in question. Thus, at verse 3.334 Dharmakīrti's Yogācāra proponent allows that "thought possesses a specific aspect (*buddhir ākāraviseṣiṇī*), i.e., it's connected with a particular aspect of blue or non-blue, etc.; but it's worth considering whether that thought could arise from an external object, or from something else, i.e., from the constraint of a latent disposition (*vāsanā*)."[58] *Vāsanās*, recall from Chapter 4, are the lingering "traces" of mental activity, variously posited to explain the many occasions on which the effects of *karma* are realized only well after the relevant action, as well as things like our beginningless disposition to recognize and exploit phenomenally similar cognitions.[59] The salient point is that *vāsanās* are essentially *mental* items, and the Yogācāra proponent thus advances the claim that we cannot finally know anything beyond such mental items to constrain our awareness.

The reason for this, Dharmakīrti and Manorathanandin continue, is that "there is no object at all, possessing a distinction from thought (*buddhivyatirekin*), which is apprehended as being the cause (*hetutayā-upalabhyate*)." The deceptively straightforward point of this claim, I take it, is that anything cognitively "apprehended" as a cause is, ipso facto, internally related to an act of awareness; to that extent, however, what is immediately *known*, when one knows anything to be a constraint on awareness—the content of this very act of knowing—could never have the property of "possessing a distinction from thought." Hence, as Manorathanandin says in unpacking the Yogācāra's point, no object apart from thought itself can be known as the cause "because of the awareness of nothing but the form of cognition."[60] We can only experience things, Dharmakīrti here clearly emphasizes, *as experienced by us*—as the content of (hence, as internally related to) awareness itself.

Dharmakīrti elaborates on this in what is a lesser-known statement of his distinctive *sahopalambhaniyama* argument—which can here be seen to represent an argument that is in fact familiar from Dignāga's *Pramāṇasamuccaya* 1.9, with its claims that "self-awareness is the result, since judgment regarding an object has the form of that"[61] and that "just cognition's being contentful (*viṣayābhāsatâiva*) is the *pramāṇa*, since content is known through that."[62] With similar intuitions in view, then, Dharmakīrti's *Pramāṇavārttika* 3.335 expresses an argument that Manorathanandin elaborates thus:

> In regard to this, because of the nonapprehension of things like blue apart from the qualification (*upādhi*) which is awareness—and because of the apprehension of blue only when there is apprehension of that [i.e., of the qualification which is awareness]—perceiving (*darśana*), whose content is things like blue (i.e., whose aspect is blue), is based on awareness of the blue and of the thought *only together* (*sahâiva*).[63]

The one thing we cannot doubt with respect to any occurrent awareness, Dharmakīrti thus argues, is the fact—itself *constitutive of awareness*—of its *seeming* some way to a subject; there is no awareness lacking this property or "qualification" (*upādhi*). This means, however, that the property of thus *seeming*, phenomenologically, to have content is *intrinsic* to cognition; that is, indeed, just what it means to say there can be no awareness without this property.

Only the intrinsic property of cognition's *seeming* some way, then, is indubitable; just to that extent, awareness itself must be reckoned as epistemically basic. If, in other words, we have (based on our experience) the idea that things out there in the world exhibit such properties as *being blue*, that can finally be the case only insofar as we have the logically prior experience of its *seeming to us* that such things are the case. This is just the point I take Dignāga all along to have been after in arguing that *the seeming itself* (*viṣayābhāsatā*) is the only *pramāṇa*; this is why Dharmakīrti can similarly conclude (as he does in the last quarter of his verse 3.335) that experience is therefore intelligible without reference to external objects. As Manorathanandin says in elaborating this conclusion, "It's only that there are no external objects (things like colors), since what is sensible (*adhyakṣa*)—which is what is accepted [by the Sautrāntika] as being probative of external objects—does not have the capacity"[64]—does not have the capacity, I take it, for warranting conclusions about what might be the case apart from awareness.

We can get the same conclusion out of the most widely quoted statement of Dharmakīrti's *sahopalambhaniyama* argument, which comes not from the *Pramāṇavārttika* but from the *Pramāṇaviniścaya*. At verse 1.54a–b of that text, Dharmakīrti says: "Owing to the constraint [according to which anything is known only] together with the apprehension thereof, there is no difference between *blue* and the *cognition* thereof."[65] Among the points Dharmakīrti makes in elaborating on this half-verse is that "when there is non-apprehension of the aspect of one of these two, there is no apprehension of the other, either—and this doesn't make sense if there is a difference in nature (*svabhāvaviveke*), since there is no cause of the connection between them."[66] That is, without some *awareness* of blue, there can be no epistemic access to the "blue itself," either—and if, conversely, there is thought to be some access to the "blue itself," that can only be insofar as there is some *awareness* thereof. Emphasizing that it follows that these are therefore *identical*, Dharmakīrti explains that this invariable concomitance is tantamount to the two terms having the same "nature" (*svabhāva*).[67] This is, Dharmakīrti suggests, because there is nothing that could be thought of as *causing* such a connection; anything that could be *known* as doing so would, ipso facto, already be internally related to an act of cognition just such as we had been aiming to explain.

With regard to this claim, Dharmakīrti entertains an objection such as might be raised by a Sautrāntika, for whom contentful cognition is to be understood as constrained, in the first instance, by sensory outputs that, while themselves of the nature of *vijñāna*, are produced by contact with objects in the world—the objection, in other words, that what causes this connection is just the operation of such factors as sensory contact with objects in the world. On such a view, "first there is apprehension (*upalambha*) of an object, owing to its proximity as being the cause of cognition; subsequently, of the awareness (*saṃvedanasya*) [thereof]."[68] The interlocutor's point is that there can be contentful cognition only insofar as there are *inputs* to cognition—and if it's characteristic of the cognition thus produced for it to be first-personally known by the subject thereof, it must nevertheless be the case that only a cognition so occasioned could present itself to a subject in the first place. The direction of explanation, this interlocutor objects, should thus be from *world* to *awareness*.

It is this objection that elicits Dharmakīrti's argument for the initial claim that perceptual objects are characterized by the "constraint" (*niyama*) that is their being knowable only "together with the apprehension thereof" (*sahopalambha*); while that point, then, has already been adduced as a reason for thinking there is finally no difference between "blue itself" and the cognition thereof, Dharmakīrti now gives a reason for thinking this constraint to obtain in the first place. Why should it be thought, that is, that self-awareness is in this sense explanatorily prior to awareness of objects? Concluding his verse 1.54, Dharmakīrti answers: "The seeing of objects is not established for one whose apprehension thereof is itself imperceptible."[69] Reading from the Tibetan translation of Dharmakīrti's text, Georges Dreyfus and Christian Lindtner rather differently translate thus: "[*If you do*] *not* [*accept that only*] *perception is perceived, the perception of an* [*external*] *object can never be proved*" (1989, 47). Particularly their second insertion suggests that the point of the passage is that cognition can only finally be "of" itself. While this may be as Dharmakīrti finally thinks, I take it he is making a more limited and conceptually basic point: there cannot be any state of *cognizing* that is not experienced as such by the subject thereof—and only given such an awareness can there be any acquaintance even with perceptual objects. This is, as Dharmakīrti immediately elaborates, because "there is not awareness of an object simply in virtue of there *being* an object; rather, [there is awareness of an object] by virtue of there being an *awareness* thereof."[70]

So, while cognition's really being *of an object* can coherently be doubted, *there being such a cognition* cannot itself be thought to require demonstration; this is immediately manifest without any need of a further epistemic criterion (*sā câprāmāṇikā*).[71] There being some occurrent awareness is simply the self-evident basis of all our transactions, none of which can get off the ground except through such epistemic access as cognition alone affords.[72] There is, then, nothing more certain than the occurrence of cognition itself; any cognition's being known by the subject thereof must therefore be reckoned, epistemically and conceptually, as the most basic fact of all—as uniquely indubitable or immediate. While a realist will take himself to claim not (with Dignāga and Dharmakīrti) that cognition *seems* to be of a world but that it *is* so, Dharmakīrti is here arguing that before a realist can make sense even of his own claim, he must first allow at least that it *seems*, phenomenologically, to be so.

Dharmakīrti further emphasizes that this conceptually basic fact concerns something intrinsic to awareness, since otherwise an infinite regress ensues. Thus, considering again the view that "first there is apprehension of an object, owing to its proximity as being the cause of cognition; subsequently, of the awareness,"[73] Dharmakīrti says:

> Awaiting the end of a series of apprehensions, a person does not comprehend any object, because of the non-establishment of all cognitions when there is non-establishment of one [i.e., of a first-personally known one]. And since there is no end of the arising of apprehensions, the whole world would be blind and deaf. If there is to be any termination to the series, cognition must intrinsically apprehend itself and the aspect of an object simultaneously (*svayam ātmānaṃ viṣayākāraṃ ca yugapad upalabhate*).[74]

We cannot, that is, be said to have any epistemic acquaintance with something we are not *aware* of—and since to be aware just is to be *first-personally* aware, that means there can be no epistemic acquaintance with anything at all until there is a cognition essentially characterized by *svasaṃvitti*. This means, however, that cognitions must themselves be known by the subjects thereof from the get-go—they must be, as it were, *reflexive all the way down*—since otherwise there would be no way to bridge the gap between first being somehow *non*cognitively acquainted with the world, and then cognitively so; indeed, Dharmakīrti's point is that there is nothing it could look like to *be* "noncognitively" aware of anything.

It cannot be the case, then, that our first-personal acquaintance with our own mental lives is parasitic on a world of objects that are themselves intelligible apart from our awareness thereof, since this very fact could be *known* by us only through a cognition whose character as a cognition already constitutively involves its being known by the subject thereof. Dharmakīrti thus argues not only that the doctrine of *svasaṃvitti* does not (contra many of the doctrine's Indian critics) open up an infinite regress, but that it represents the only way to *foreclose* a regress; only cognitions that are *intrinsically* reflexive could be thought to disclose anything at all, quite independently of what we say about what is thus disclosed.

Among other things, this all suggests that Dharmakīrti's idea may not be that *svasaṃvitti* represents one among several *kinds* of awareness (viz., that kind which is *of* our own mental states); rather, it here seems to pick out the intrinsically reflexive character in virtue of which the subject of any cognition knows her own cognition to be contentful.[75] This, finally, is why Dharmakīrti thinks it right to say that the most salient characteristic *even of perceptual objects* is the constraint (*niyama*) that is their being experienceable only "together with the apprehension thereof" (*sahopalambha*). Contra views like Bilgrami's, then, Dharmakīrti clearly aims to argue that perceptual awareness is *not* to be distinguished from self-awareness in terms of the latter's lack of the "independence possessed by the things *of* which we have perceptual knowledge, *from* that perceptual knowledge." On Dharmakīrti's view, rather, it turns out that perceptual objects, too, finally lack this independence; perceptual objects are *not*, in fact, intelligible apart from *the perceptual knowledge thereof.*

Dharmakīrti concludes from this that we should therefore embrace precisely the conclusion that Sellars took to be problematic:

> "Awareness" seems that way because of its nature (*tādātmyāt*); it is not *of* anything other than itself, just like self-awareness. Because of this, it doesn't make sense that it be with regard to another object than itself.

> But given that things like colors are not objects apart from experience, what exists with these as its nature just manifests (*prakāśate*) that way; hence (*iti*), *there can be the experience of things like color*.[76]

It is, in other words, only indubitably owing to properties intrinsic to awareness that "there can be the experience of things like color"—which is almost precisely to say, contra Sellars, that "*x is red* is analyzable in terms of *x looks red to y*" (Sellars 1956, 36).[77] Dharmakīrti's point is that it cannot be held that cognition is constitutively *of* a world, since it is just cognition itself (and not what cognition seems, phenomenologically, to represent) that must finally be reckoned as basic. Cognition is, to that extent, autonomously intelligible—we can make sense of its being the kind of thing it is quite independently of whether it is of a world.

SVASAMVITTI AND CAUSAL EXPLANATION

One might reasonably object that the foregoing argument involves an insignificant truism; *of course* we can only know things *as known* by us—how else? But Dharmakīrti could reasonably rejoin that his claim nevertheless has the property, typically exhibited by truisms, of being true—indeed, incontrovertibly so. The mode of *necessity* that arguably thus figures in Dharmakīrti's position may reflect the extent to which it is not only a perceptual but also a *constitutive* understanding of self-awareness that is here in play. Insofar, that is, as it's constitutive of acts of cognizing for them to be first-personally experienced—insofar, indeed, as that is something of what cognizing *is*—it is just true by definition that anything *known* can only be *first-personally* known. The first-personally known fact of any cognition's seeming as it does, then, is all that we could really refer to as "*pramāṇa*," for the same reason that even perceptual objects are not finally distinct from the perceptual awareness thereof; just as the phenomenological contrast between perceptual and other cognitions is itself accessible only *as experienced*, so, too, it's possible to individuate the "*pramāṇas*" instrumental in realizing cognition only through already constituted, first-personally known cognitions.

The indubitable fact that thus figures in Dharmakīrti's argument may make it difficult to refute. In an illuminating essay on the *sahopalambhaniyama* argument, Arindam Chakrabarti says to similar effect that "realists in the West have tried to undermine the argument by labeling it 'the egocentric predicament,' but for all its egocentricity, it nevertheless remains a predicament for even the rank realist that a person cannot sincerely say 'p' without at the same time showing that he or she believes 'p.' Or as Bradley put it, '. . . you cannot find fact unless in unity with sentience'" (1990, 17). The challenging question is just what, if anything, follows from this; while we can thus appreciate that Dharmakīrti's *sahopalambhaniyama* argument for *svasaṃvitti* is logically distinctive, it's reasonable to ask just how much this argument can really be thought to do for him.

That there are limits in this regard can be brought out by attending to the relation of Dharmakīrti's *svasaṃvitti* doctrine to the account of semantic content (the *apoha* doctrine) considered in the last chapter. Thus, at the beginning of the present chapter I introduced Dharmakīrti's idea of self-awareness as finally making sense of his problematic commitments regarding the significance of "speaker's intention"; Tillemans, we saw, said in this regard that Dharmakīrti's fundamental position is that "words are used according to the speaker's wishes and designate anything whatsoever which he might intend" (2000, 163). This is so, Tillemans said, insofar as the speaker of any utterance is uniquely authoritative regarding her own intention; only she can finally ascertain that "intention"—which, recall, consists for Dharmakīrti not in the semantic content of her claim but, rather, in the first-personally known mental particular that really explains (read: *causes*) her utterance.

I have in this chapter been aiming to suggest that Dharmakīrti's thus grounding his account of semantics in subjectively known particulars relates closely to his case for *svasaṃvitti*; indeed, insofar as his arguments for *svasaṃvitti* amount to a case for the autonomously intelligible character of awareness, Dharmakīrti is committed to understanding his account of meaning, in just the way suggested by Tillemans, as coming to rest with *svasaṃvitti*. With his development of the *svasaṃvitti* doctrine, then, Dharmakīrti has elaborated the kind of view on which (as John McDowell says) "the 'inner' role of [e.g.] colour concepts is autonomously intelligible, and . . . [we can] explain their 'outer' role in terms of the idea that for an 'outer' object to fall under a colour concept is for it to be such as to cause the appropriate visual 'inner experience'" (1996, 30). McDowell thus characterizes a view precisely such as that of Fodor, for whom (we saw in chapter 2) a commitment to "methodological solipsism" is similarly recommended by the need for a kind of "narrow content"—for a constitutively nonsemantic sort of representing that itself explains the "broad" (i.e., *semantic*) content that figures in the logical space of reasons. Thus, Fodor's idea is that what properly *explains*—where again that means *causes*—any agent's behavior is only propositional attitudes under "referentially opaque" construals; how things *seem* to an agent explains her actions quite apart from what it would mean for it to be *true* that things are as they seem to her.

Among the problems we noted regarding Fodor's proposal is that there is no reason to think a referentially opaque construal of mental content also individuates (what Fodor is really after) causally efficacious particulars inside the skull; it's not obvious, I thus argued in chapter 2, that *epistemically* "narrow content," just because it reflects the subject's own perspective on what she believes, gets us any closer to brain events than wide content does. The problem with thus exploiting an intentional level of description to individuate narrow content is that this still keeps in play what Fodor ultimately thinks he is *explaining*: the contentfulness of thoughts. It's not clear, to that extent, that we are (as McDowell says of such a view) "entitled to characterize inner facts in content-involving terms—in terms of its seeming to one that things are thus and so—at all" (1998, 243).

Similarly, we can ask of Dharmakīrti's position, as elaborated in this and the preceding chapter, whether it really is intelligible, after all, to think that cognition could *be* semantically contentful on the kind of view we have here seen him elaborate—whether, indeed, one could so much as have the idea of cognition's being contentful apart from its being, essentially, *of a world*. By this I mean to suggest that Dharmakīrti's thought that awareness is autonomously intelligible—that we are, he says, only immediately acquainted with awareness's having "the qualification which is awareness"[78]—may itself presuppose the kind of view he finally aims to demonstrate.

To appreciate this, we can invoke not Bilgrami's "governing disjunction" but the disjunction that (we saw in chapter 3) McDowell takes as the point of departure for his transcendental argument—the disjunction between views on which cognition is *essentially* of a world, and views according to which it is so much as intelligible that it might not really be so.[79] These are disjunctive, McDowell takes Sellars to have shown, since there is no way to get *from* the second of these to the first—no way to get from its just *seeming* that anything is so to the idea of its really *being* so, since if one accepts as intelligible the idea that cognition merely *seems* to have objective purport ("although that is not how things are," McDowell says), the consequent skeptical problems make problematic any understanding of the possibility that it *does*. Given this line of thought, it might be said of Dharmakīrti that he advances his case by exploiting epistemological intuitions that are not, after all, innocent of the view he means to support thereby; he may not, then, be entitled to think cognition could *be* contentful, on his view that mental content is autonomously intelligible, unless he already holds (what as an idealist he aims to show) that awareness is not constitutively *of* a world.

In this regard, we can, perhaps counterintuitively, best understand the doctrine of *svasaṃvitti* as problematic in the same ways as Fodor's methodological solipsism if we briefly consider (what would seem most sharply to divide Dharmakīrti from physicalists like Fodor) something of what the doctrine of *svasaṃvitti* might look like if it is taken as finally integral to a case for metaphysical idealism—as part of a doctrine, that is, according to which the most fundamental existents are mental events that are not, finally, *about* anything but themselves. Fittingly, we can here take our bearings from Dharmakīrti's familiar passage (considered in chapter 1) regarding causal efficacy as the criterion of the real: "Whatever has the capacity for causal efficacy (*arthakriyā*)"—or, one could also translate, the capacity for *pragmatic* efficacy, for *achieving a goal*—"is ultimately existent; everything else is conventionally existent."[80] The appeal to (what is among Dharmakīrti's principal terms of art) the notion of *arthakriyā* here is pivotal; for this idea will admit of either a *teleological* or an *efficient-causal* reading, depending on which of two lexically possible senses we take *artha* to have.[81] Given the first of these senses, *arthakriyā* is plausibly understood to denote the eminently teleological idea of "action (*kriyā*) with respect to a goal (*artha*)." On this reading, Dharmakīrti's claim—that only those particulars having the capacity for facilitating this should be judged real—could be taken to recommend the commonsensical thought that whatever advances our purposeful interventions in the world is to be judged "real."

But note that on this reading *arthakriyā* has a chiefly epistemic significance; something's being "pragmatically useful" amounts to *evidence* of its being real (it might justify someone's believing so), but doesn't shed any light on what its *being real* (or what a belief's being true) consists in.[82] Complementing, then, this epistemic sense of *arthakriyā*, there is also something like an *ontological* sense of the term—a sense having to do with what it is in virtue of which anything might *be* "pragmatically useful" in the first place. Given this sense, *arthakriyā* can be taken to denote the efficient-causal idea of the "action of a thing"; the point is that it's finally just those things having *this* capacity that turn out to be pragmatically useful—being causally efficacious, that is, *explains* anything's being pragmatically useful. While John Dunne (2004, 260) is right, I think, that Dharmakīrti's works don't decisively settle things in favor of one or the other of these understandings of *arthakriyā*, both of which are in play at various points, it seems to me that the general trend in Dharmakīrti's thought is finally away from the "teleological" reading. It is, I think, finally the extent of Dharmakīrti's focus on something like efficient-causal explanation that saddles him with philosophical problems just such as Fodor's project faces. On this understanding of *arthakriyā*, Dharmakīrti's statement of one of his guiding intuitions may attribute causal efficacy finally just to existents of a very different sort than the kinds of things that figure in our ordinarily purposeful activity.

The centrality of *svasaṃvitti* is important to seeing this. Dunne suggests, in this regard, a "speculative interpretation" according to which it's particularly in the doctrine of *svasaṃvitti* that the efficient-causal reading of *arthakriyā* comes to the fore; it's especially in the case of *svasaṃvitti* that "the notion of *arthakriyā* may be applicable only in terms of sheer causal efficiency, since it is difficult to see how practical action (*vyavahāra*) makes sense within this context" (2004, 260). Given Dharmakīrti's basic commitments, the "ultimacy" of *svasaṃvitti* thus consists in its revealing "the mere fact of experience, which is the same as saying that it reveals the mere causal efficiency (*arthakriyā*) of awareness" (Dunne 2004, 276).[83] Thus, at the level of description where *svasaṃvitti* discloses, to the subject thereof, nothing more than the causally describable (because essentially episodic) occurrence of her own cognitions, it is difficult to account for the kinds of things that a subject might take as her *reasons for acting*. But of course, we saw in chapter 4 that it is just the point of Dharmakīrti's *apoha* doctrine to give a finally nonintentional account of the kinds of things that figure in the logical space of reasons. To the extent, then, that he finally means precisely to argue that "reasons explanations" will admit of an altogether different description, Dharmakīrti's *sahopalambhaniyama* argument can be understood as advancing the case for the view that all we know indubitably is *that there are causally describable cognitions*.

The late eighth-century commentator Prajñākaragupta lends credence to this strong reading of Dharmakīrti as finally meaning to show that all there really is to cognition is its own causally describable occurrence. In the context of commenting on the opening verses of the *pramāṇasiddhi* chapter of the *Pramāṇavārttika*, Prajñākaragupta elaborates on the consequences of the verse (considered in chapter 4) in which Dharmakīrti ventures that "language is an epistemic criterion with regard to that object which appears in thought."[84] Prajñākaragupta takes Dharmakīrti to say, just two verses later (at *Pramāṇavārttika* 2.4–5), that only *svasaṃvitti* finally counts as a *pramāṇa*—and that the sense in which *pramāṇa*-talk has to do with the furtherance of goals is therefore just conventional, and hence explicable in terms of an ultimately true description that makes no reference to the other level. He explains: "There is intrinsically understanding only of its [cognition's] own form, not of anything else. For perception is immediate understanding (*sākṣād gatiḥ*), and immediate understanding is of its own form—not of the form of anything else, which has a different time of obtaining."[85]

Prajñākaragupta thus invokes the perennially vexed time-lag problem—the problem, arising as soon as one explains perception with reference to intermediating representations, of cognition's never being present at the same time as what it is putatively *of*[86]—to argue that no cognition that is "of" anything other than itself could have the kind of immediacy (the kind of *identity* between how it seems and what it is of) that alone qualifies awareness as properly perceptual. As we saw in the second section of this chapter, Jinendrabuddhi argues to similar effect that all that "immediately" (*avyavadhānena*) figures in the phenomenologically distinct character of cognitions is the first-personally known fact of their seeming as they do. The fact of being a *pramāṇa*, Dharmakīrti says in the passage Prajñākaragupta is here explaining, therefore finally obtains only conventionally; Prajñākaragupta thus states the conclusion he takes Dharmakīrti thereby to affirm: "By teaching that being a *pramāṇa* is just conventional (*sāṃvyavahārikaṃ prāmāṇyaṃ*), it's said that ultimately there is only the perception which is self-awareness."[87]

On such a reading, the thought chiefly advanced by the *svasaṃvitti* doctrine is that all we are ultimately entitled to claim—all that is known indubitably, all that is *paramārthasat*—is *that cognition occurs*. Insofar, though, as it is thus to count as real, *that cognition occurs* must itself exhibit the kind of causal efficacy (*arthakriyāsāmarthya*) that is Dharmakīrti's criterion of the real. What is disclosed by our indubitable first-personal acquaintance with our own experience must, to that extent, be just mental particulars, since on Dharmakīrti's account only these could have the capacity to *do* anything. To the extent, moreover, that *svasaṃvitti* ultimately discloses nothing more than the causally describable occurrence of experience, it must thus disclose something essentially *momentary*, since only essentially *changing* things can have causal efficacy.[88] Surely Dunne is right that "it is difficult to see how practical action makes sense within this context"—difficult, that is, to see how the causally explicable occurrence of fleeting moments of experience could alone make sense of the *contentfulness* in terms of which our first-personally experienced awareness affords reasons for belief and action.

ON WHAT DHARMAKĪRTI'S ARGUMENT GETS US: RĀMAKAṆṬHA ON THE PHENOMENOLOGY OF TIME-CONSCIOUSNESS AND THE LIMITS OF CAUSAL EXPLANATION

Given, then, Dharmakīrti's understanding of the momentary character of the real—and hence, *of the mental*, as that alone is indubitably known—it becomes relevant to ask whether he rightly characterizes the temporality of experience. Here, it's important to ask not only whether his account of fleeting series of mental particulars gets the phenomenology right but also whether, in light of his other commitments, Dharmakīrti *can* get the phenomenology right—whether, that is, the phenomenological character of experience *could be* as it is on Dharmakīrti's account. Particularly with the latter formulation of the problem, I mean to suggest that the chiefly epistemological case Dharmakīrti makes for *svasaṃvitti* (and the largely perceptual understanding he has thereof) may finally make him vulnerable to a transcendental argument that is not constrained by a prior commitment to causal explanation—that, conversely, properly attending to what is constitutive of experience might show that it's a condition of the possibility thereof that it cannot be such as to admit of the kind of causal explanation Dharmakīrti would finally offer. Here I have in mind a line of argument that Alex Watson has explicated following the tenth-century Śaiva Siddhānta thinker Bhaṭṭa Rāmakaṇṭha, who argues on phenomenological grounds that self-awareness *doesn't* show the momentary character of cognition, and (we can say) on transcendental grounds that it *couldn't*.[89]

It's important to recognize, with regard to the issues here introduced, that a properly transcendental argument does not need to show that the transcendental claim at issue is itself (as Mark Sacks says) "part of what is given as the content of our perceptual experience"; such an argument is, rather, concerned to show that certain facts "are required for experience to have the structure it does—even if those facts cannot be read off directly from the content of our perceptual experience of [the] world" (2005, 450). Thus, on Sacks's reconstruction of Kantian transcendental arguments, "it is not that our point of view is tainted by a particular cognitive structure that we bring with us, but that it is the notion of a situated thought, the mere notion of experience as being from a point of view, that itself imposes the relevant structure" (2005, 455). Transcendental arguments, that is, essentially involve what might be characterized as a *phenomenological* step—the initial step, in particular, in which one is encouraged to attend to what

Sacks characterizes as the "phenomenologically embedded and directed" nature of claims regarding experience. (Comparable here is Dharmakīrti's encouraging us first to recognize that we can only know anything *as first-personally known by us*.) The initial phenomenological observation is not, however, itself the transcendental argument; rather, the argument proper consists in showing what must be the case in order for that to *be* the phenomenological character of experience. The question answered by such an argument consists, that is, in showing what "imposes the relevant structure" on the phenomenology.

The same dialectic is on display in the arguments of Rāmakaṇṭha, whose critical appropriation of Dharmakīrti's doctrine of *svasaṃvitti* involves both phenomenological and transcendental considerations. Indeed, Rāmakaṇṭha's treatment of *svasaṃvitti* involves a line of argument that is in many respects almost precisely like Kant's argument, contra Hume, for the transcendental unity of apperception.[90] To that extent, Rāmakaṇṭha's arguments seem to me cogently to undermine particularly Dharmakīrti's strongly held commitment to the momentary, causally explicable character of first-personally known mental events—though whether these arguments also cut against Dignāga (who did not share Dharmakīrti's strong commitment to momentariness)[91] and whether they can really be thought to warrant (what Rāmakaṇṭha chiefly wants) anything like a doctrine of *ātmavāda* (of a really existent "self") seem to me to remain reasonable questions.

It is, as Watson emphasizes, important to recognize that Rāmakaṇṭha's doctrine of *ātmavāda* was distinct among Brahmanical versions thereof, insofar as he eschews "the existence of a self over and above consciousness"; on Rāmakaṇṭha's view, rather, "The self just *is* consciousness" (2010, 298). Rāmakaṇṭha is thus able to begin his account by making common cause with the Buddhists, enlisting characteristically Buddhist arguments against any view according to which an enduring and autonomous *ātman* is supposed to be related to (but not identical with) our manifestly episodic experience. Buddhists are typically apt, in this regard, to take the episodic character of experience to be clear from the manifestly evanescent *content* thereof—from the fact, that is, that what we are aware of is continuously in flux, giving our experience the character of a constitutively temporal flow of momentary events. Rāmakaṇṭha's view, however, is that even the episodic character of experiential *content* is only intelligible against the background of a unitary, synthesizing *perspective*—against the background, that is, of *svasaṃvitti*, which he effectively understands as a condition of the possibility of cognition's being contentful in the first place.

Insofar, then, as Rāmakaṇṭha shares the Buddhist view that there is no *ātman* over and above what can be found in experience, he is chiefly interested in showing that *svasaṃvitti* cannot, after all, be understood as momentary; as Watson puts it, "the way to discover who is correct about whether consciousness is momentary or enduring is to focus on our self-awareness, and see if consciousness appears in it as momentary or enduring. We do not need logical arguments here, but rather a kind of phenomenological observation of our ongoing *svasaṃvedana*" (2010, 299). Rāmakaṇṭha thus argues, in a strictly phenomenological key, that while the content of experience is indeed episodic, "the perceiver of those objects appears to us, through self-awareness, as always the same. We never lose a sense, after all, that it is me who is experiencing the objects" (2010, 299). Among the points Rāmakaṇṭha offers in support of the intuition thus expressed by Watson is that any moment of experience is characterized by its "having no sense of its non-existence before it [comes into being] or non-existence after it is destroyed even in all three times."[92] Later alluding to the same point, Rāmakaṇṭha further argues that "the ceasing of the perceiver is not sensed in any of the three times. For something which had prior non-existence is said to have arisen; something which undergoes cessation is [said to] be destroyed; but when there is no consciousness of something at some previous or subsequent extremity of it, it cannot be said to arise and cease in every moment."[93] Its *having just arisen* and its being *just about to cease* are not, that is, part of the phenomenal content of any putatively momentary instance of awareness; rather, awareness is phenomenologically characterized by temporal extension (by *continuity*).

The same idea is concisely stated by Charles Peirce, who thus introduces some problems in the mathematical representation of continuity as they arise particularly with regard to the "subjective now": "We are conscious only of the present time, which is an instant if there be any such thing as an instant. But in the present we are conscious of the flow of time. There is no flow in an instant. Hence the present is not an instant" (1976, 127).[94] Subjectivity is, in other words, a constitutively *present* phenomenon, in the sense that consciousness is experienced with subjective immediacy only in the present—a fact that emerges when one reflects on the phenomenological difference between any present moment and one's own past experiences as presently available to memory; the past experiences are now available as *the content* of reflection, but there is subjective immediacy only *in the present remembering*. Despite, however, the fact that the subjectively immediate "now" of experience would seem to represent (as Peirce aptly says) "an instant if there be any such thing as an instant," the phenomenologically salient feature of present experience strikingly seems to be its *non*momentary character; the present is experienced as continuous.

While it surely complicates things thus to attend to the phenomenologically continuous character of what could seem (particularly for someone who takes her bearings from the episodic character of experiential content) like the paradigm case of a "moment," Dharmakīrti can (as Rāmakaṇṭha himself recognized) nevertheless concede the foregoing phenomenological point; indeed, a Buddhist would surely urge that the entire Buddhist project is called for in the first place just insofar as we are seduced by the *phenomenologically* continuous character of awareness into supposing that awareness must therefore *really* belong to something (a "self") finally enduring. Rāmakaṇṭha and his Buddhist opponents disagree, then, not chiefly in regard to the foregoing phenomenological description but in regard to how we are to *explain* that's being the phenomenological character of subjective immediacy.

The situation is thus very much like that of Dignāga's and Dharmakīrti's cases for idealism; in that case, too, these Buddhists can concede that it *seems*, phenomenologically, like experience is of a world of external objects—their challenge, rather, is to *explain* (in terms that are phenomenologically counterintuitive) how the phenomenological facts can be as they are. As for the explanation they offer, Rāmakaṇṭha not unreasonably attributes to his Buddhist interlocutors an account strikingly like the one we saw Hume offer of the same phenomenological facts; Buddhists like Dharmakīrti, as Rāmakaṇṭha reads them, thus explain the phenomenologically unitary and continuous character of awareness as a function of "conceptualization" (*vikalpa, kalpanā*), which distortedly represents what should really be understood as causally continuous series of essentially momentary events. Sketching Rāmakaṇṭha's presentation of the Buddhist alternative he refuses, Watson says: "What actually presents itself is a sequence of momentary perceivers, but because of the rapidity with which they succeed each other, and the likeness of each to the previous one, we superimpose permanence on to them, we mistake them for being one lasting thing rather than many momentary things" (2010, 300). In chapter 3, we saw Hume say to similar effect that "it can only be from the resemblance, which this act of the mind bears to that, by which we contemplate one continu'd object, that the error arises."[95]

Here, it becomes significant that *svasaṃvitti* can be taken to pick out the fact of experience's being from a seemingly continuous point of view. Thus, the particular respect in which we are here to understand "the likeness of each moment to the previous one" is that of their being taken as experiences *had from the same perspective*—and it may be just this perspectival character that is thematized in the *svasaṃvitti* doctrine, insofar as experience's being constitutively perspectival is tantamount to its being known by the subject thereof. Dharmakīrti will not allow, however, that *svasaṃvitti* is implicated in the conceptually distorted synthesis of episodic experiences; for him, indeed, *svasaṃvitti* represents the paradigm case of a constitutively *non*conceptual acquaintance. Thus, Watson (2010, 301) says,

> The debate between Rāmakaṇṭha and Buddhism . . . ceases to be about whether we experience our consciousness as momentary or enduring. The crucial issue now is whether our sense of our consciousness as enduring is a case of *svasaṃvedana* or is a *vikalpa* (conceptual cognition). The reason that so much hangs on this question of whether or not something is *svasaṃvedana* is that both sides hold *svasaṃvedana* to be necessarily valid.

While Dharmakīrti can, then, concede Rāmakaṇṭha's strictly phenomenological point about the phenomenally continuous character of awareness, he cannot concede that this describes the phenomenal content particularly of *svasaṃvitti*; to allow that it is *svasaṃvitti* itself that exhibits this would be to allow that this continuity has precisely the indubitability that goes with its being immediately, nonconceptually known—which would of course be to concede Rāmakaṇṭha's point that this is real.

It's at this point that Rāmakaṇṭha's becomes a transcendental argument; his move at this juncture is to argue, in effect, that it's a condition of the possibility of *the phenomenology's being as it is* that the Buddhist explanation thereof cannot be right. Against Dharmakīrti's view that conceptual superimposition accounts for the phenomenological sense of cognitive continuity, Rāmakaṇṭha argues that the very idea of superimposition here already presupposes something *non*momentary, since nothing momentary could be thought to "do" the superimposing that we are here asked to imagine: "since [for Dharmakīrti] everything is momentary, nothing could do the joining. That is precisely why even several momentary conceptual cognitions in sequence could not superimpose."[96] The point is that no two *successive* states of awareness could ever be judged *the same*—in the respect, that is, of seeming to be commonly the states *of the same subject*—unless they could be held together in one state somehow comprising both; a *succession of experiences* doesn't constitute or explain the *experience of succession*.

Watson credits Rāmakaṇṭha with thus raising the question: "In a Dharmakīrtian universe, in which all things, both perceivers and perceived objects, are momentary, where could anyone ever have experienced something enduring, in order to acquire the concept of duration such that they are then able to superimpose it?" (2010, 301). The trend of Rāmakaṇṭha's argument here can, I think, quite effectively be glossed by returning to Kant: "There must therefore be something that itself makes possible this reproduction of the appearances by being the *a priori* ground of a necessary synthetic unity of them . . . one must assume a pure transcendental synthesis of this power, which grounds even the possibility of all experience (as that which the reproducibility of the appearances necessarily presupposes)."[97] The very ideas of reproduction and recognition only make sense, that is, relative to a unifying point of view—relative, that is, to *svasaṃvitti*, which must therefore genuinely disclose the essentially unitary character of awareness. On Rāmakaṇṭha's view, cognition can thus seem as it does only given the unitariness—which is among other things to say the nonmomentariness—of the perspective *from which* it must be had if it's so much as to count as "cognition."

CONCLUSION: DHARMAKĪRTI'S COGNITIVISM

The purchase of Rāmakaṇṭha's arguments against Dharmakīrti might be said to involve the former's holding a basically *constitutive* view of self-awareness; for the most cogent of Rāmakaṇṭha's claims, I think, is that cognition cannot so much as *seem* as it does (where its seeming some way to a subject is constitutive of it *as* a cognition) unless its phenomenologically continuous character somehow reflects something real. Further, Rāmakaṇṭha would deny the idealist conclusions that Dharmakīrti and his fellow travelers take to be recommended by *svasaṃvitti*; Rāmakaṇṭha is, indeed, a direct realist, and one of the things suggested by his appropriation of the doctrine is that *svasaṃvitti* is logically independent of the epistemological representationalism (*sākāravāda*) that some Buddhists regarded as virtually co-extensive with the idea of self-awareness.[98] While Dignāga and Dharmakīrti clearly took their view of *svasaṃvitti* to dovetail, then, with a case for thinking of cognition as essentially involving intermediary "representations" (*ākāra*), Rāmakaṇṭha thinks the reflexive character of awareness is compatible with the view that an external world is immediately present to cognition. Insofar as he steers clear of idealism, it seems Rāmakaṇṭha would share Bilgrami's conviction (contra Dignāga and Dharmakīrti) that the distinction between perceptual objects and the perceptual knowledge thereof is therefore not just phenomenal but *real.*

If Bilgrami is right, however, that "only one of the two models, perceptual or constitutive, can be right," then Rāmakaṇṭha himself may yet run afoul of Bilgrami's governing disjunction; for while he clearly aims to refute aspects particularly of Dharmakīrti's perceptual understanding of *svasaṃvitti*—chiefly, those centering on the case for epistemic idealism—Rāmakaṇṭha can nevertheless be said to enlist a perceptual understanding of self-awareness when it suits him. We can, in this regard, pose for Rāmakaṇṭha the same kinds of questions noted in chapter 3 with respect to Kant; even allowing, then, that Rāmakaṇṭha has cogently argued for the ineliminable continuity of a first-person perspective, and allowing also for that's being inexplicable in exhaustively momentary terms, we can still ask whether he is entitled to think he has thereby shown the reality of anything worth the name *ātman.* While Rāmakaṇṭha may have given good reasons for thinking that a continuous first-person perspective represents the irreducible horizon of experience, it's not clear that it follows from this that such a perspective must therefore consist in the kind of empirical existent that could exhibit *temporal* continuity—and that is just what Rāmakaṇṭha suggests in claiming that (Watson says) "*svasaṃvedana* occurs all the time; it 'accompanies' the self permanently, even in deep sleep, *even after death and before the next incarnation*" (2010, 310; emphasis added).[99]

Even if one can show, then, that there is an irreducibly unitary character to awareness, that is not to have shown that awareness must therefore involve some temporally enduring *thing*; something's being *temporally* enduring is as surely an empirically applicable criterion of identity as its being involved in causal transactions, and Rāmakaṇṭha's argument therefore seems to compromise the properly transcendental character of the argument. To the extent that the purchase of his argument against Dharmakīrti derives particularly from Rāmakaṇṭha's *constitutive* view of *svasaṃvitti*—and to the extent, as well, that Rāmakaṇṭha is averse to the idealism of his Buddhist opponents and therefore apt to share Bilgrami's governing disjunction—it would seem he cannot say that recognizing the constitutively perspectival character of awareness represents anything like *a perceptual encounter with one's "self."* That would appear, however, to be just the sort of thing he claims when he nevertheless concludes that *svasaṃvitti* is the kind of thing that continues after death.

Nevertheless, I think Rāmakaṇṭha is to be credited with advancing a cogent and interesting critique of Dharmakīrti's doctrine of *svasaṃvitti*, even as he recognized the importance for his own project of the basic insights he took his Buddhist interlocutor to have elaborated. We have seen that Dignāga and Dharmakīrti alike elaborated the *svasaṃvitti* doctrine as advancing a case for what I have called epistemic idealism—for the "Yogācāra" view that the epistemological representationalism typical of empiricism (of "Sautrāntika") already amounts to the most that can be said, epistemologically speaking, in favor of full-blown idealism. This claim amounts, I have been saying, to the thought that awareness is autonomously intelligible—to the idea that its being *of a world* is not among the things we indubitably know about awareness, whose bare occurrence is itself uniquely known with the "immediacy" that essentially characterizes perceptual acquaintance.

Chief among the arguments to that effect was Dharmakīrti's *sahopalambhaniyama* argument, which can be seen to elaborate intuitions already in play in Dignāga's relatively brief introduction of the doctrine. Thus, we saw Dignāga claim that we can really individuate *pramāṇas* (factors "instrumental" to the realization of veridical awareness) only with reference to what is ordinarily regarded as the "fruition" thereof (*pramāṇaphala*); this is to say that it is only *through* already constituted, first-personally known cognitions (hence, "through" *svasaṃvitti*) that we can think there are *pramāṇas* explaining these, just as it's only through self-awareness that we can have epistemic access even to perceptual objects. Dharmakīrti's definitive argument for *svasaṃvitti* presses, to similar effect, the point that it is only *as known* that anything can be experienced by us—and that we must, to that extent, reckon cognition itself to be explanatorily basic. He argues that we must therefore hold (contra Sellars and McDowell) that the idea of anything's *seeming* to be the case is prior to and independent of the idea of its really *being* so.

Particularly in light of Dharmakīrti's further commitments—in light, chiefly, of his commitment to causal efficacy as the criterion of the real and to the consequent momentariness that necessarily characterizes all real existents—the view that cognition alone is indubitably *known* (regardless of whether or not Dharmakīrti's view is finally that only cognition therefore *exists*) can be understood as furthering a project with deep affinities to that of Jerry Fodor, as that was considered in chapter 2. Understood this way, the *svasaṃvitti* doctrine can be taken as basically meant to provide a level of "representing" that is not itself *conceptual* or *linguistic* representing but that somehow *explains* the kind of semantic content that characterizes these other ways of representing—a sort of "narrow content" that grounds the kind of "wide content" that essentially figures in the logical space of reasons. It is, on this reading, *svasaṃvitti* that finally grounds semantic content.

The *svasaṃvitti* doctrine turns out, then, to be closely related to Dharmakīrti's understanding of the *apoha* doctrine, as considered in the previous chapter. There we saw that it's finally just subjectively occurrent, uniquely particular representations (*ākāra*) that constitute the bases for the "exclusion" that is meant to explain conceptual content—that what is excluded from coming under any concept just is whatever does not produce the same effects, where the "effects" in question are just these mental representations. In this way, Dharmakīrti allows only that the sameness that essentially characterizes universals is *phenomenal* (there are no real similarities in the world, only *subjective* similarities)—a view, we saw, that has him hard-pressed to account for the essentially *intersubjective* character of the conventions expressing concepts. Thus, Dharmakīrti's elaboration of the *apoha* doctrine finds him recurrently referring to bygone "convention-setting occasions" (*saṃketakāla*), which we are left to imagine as just intrinsically "meaning-conferring" experiences. Dharmakīrti refers, as well, to the "intentions" (*abhiprāya*) of speakers as though these explained not only particular utterances but also (the same thing he defers to the mysterious convention-setting occasions) *the very possibility of utterances as meaning anything*.

This characteristically psychologistic account of meaning, we are now in a position to appreciate, is finally of a piece with the kind of view Dharmakīrti has developed in arguing for *svasaṃvitti*. Thus, it's just because he takes his bearings from the thought that awareness itself is uniquely indubitable that Dharmakīrti is finally committed to saying, problematically, that the "intentions" expressed by linguistic acts are indubitably known *only by the subjects thereof*—that, in other words, there is nothing more to the *content* of anything said than can be explained in terms of the mental particulars that are first-personally experienced by the speaker. Just as on Fodor's account, though, there is a real question whether Dharmakīrti can reconcile the causal description of the mental particulars in terms of which he would explain semantic content with what is phenomenologically accessible to a subject; it's hard to see how essentially momentary mental particulars could so much as "conceive" themselves as resembling one another, let alone how they could explain semantic content.

Elaborating that thought, we have concluded our consideration of Dharmakīrti's *svasaṃvitti* doctrine with a brief look at Bhaṭṭa Rāmakaṇṭha's transcendental argument to the effect that cognition could not so much as *seem* as it does given Dharmakīrti's account. Thus having concluded what I hope is a full picture of Dharmakīrti's essentially cognitivist account—of his as the kind of "solipsistic and causalist position in the philosophy of mind" according to which it follows, from taking causal efficacy as the criterion of the real, that the content of awareness must be fully explicable in terms of factors somehow internal to a subject—we finally turn, in chapter 6, to some other Indian critics of Dharmakīrti's philosophical project. We will next consider, then, the extent to which a Mīmāṃsaka argument for the eternality of language can be understood to cut particularly against Dharmakīrti's deferral of the genesis of meaning to unexplained "convention-setting occasions." We will also consider the extent to which Mādhyamika critiques particularly of causal explanation strike at the heart of Dharmakīrti's presuppositions. Both of these lines of argument, I suggest, are conceptually similar to the broadly Kantian argument whose purchase against physicalism I sketched in chapter 3. Let us see, then, how Mīmāṃsakas and Mādhyamikas might help us understand what is philosophically problematic about Dharmakīrti's project.

6

Indian Arguments from Practical Reason

MĪMĀṂSAKAS AND MĀDHYAMIKAS CONTRA COGNITIVISM

The self is not other than its appropriated basis, nor is it itself the basis, nor does it exist without basis—nor, though, is there any certainty that "it doesn't exist."

—Nāgārjuna

INTRODUCTION: DHARMAKĪRTI ON PRACTICAL REASON

The commentator Prajñākaragupta, we saw, summarizes Dharmakīrti as saying that except for the case of *svasaṃvitti*, "being a *pramāṇa* is just conventional" (*sāṃvyavahārikaṃ prāmāṇyaṃ*)—a point also expressed conversely as the claim that "ultimately there is only the perception which is self-awareness."[1] On one understanding of what it means for "conventionally" real epistemic practices thus to be contrasted with "ultimately" real ones, the point is that the latter somehow *explain* what is conventionally experienced. There is more to be said on the "conventional" status of *pramāṇas*, again with reference to Prajñākaragupta and Dharmakīrti, when we turn (in the fourth section of this chapter) to a Mādhyamika line of argument that can be enlisted against Dharmakīrti; there we will see that Dharmakīrti makes a significant concession (hitherto suppressed) with regard to the "conventional" status even of our supposedly privileged epistemic practices, and that in doing so he affords an opening for the Mādhyamika critique of his project. For now, I just want to elaborate on what it would mean for Dharmakīrti to characterize all *pramāṇas* other than self-awareness as "conventional."

On Dharmakīrti's understanding of the two truths, *reasoning itself* is among the things to be characterized as "conventional." Indeed, we have seen by our attention to his *apoha* doctrine that the kinds of things (*conceptual* things) that figure in the logical space of reasons are, by Dharmakīrti's lights, paradigmatic of things that do not ultimately exist; these must therefore be finally explicable with reference only to momentary mental particulars, insofar as those alone are indubitably known to be real. The kinds of things that figure in the *content* of our reasoning, then, are on this account to be explained in terms of causally describable psychological processes. The salient point of this, from the perspective of a rationalist critic of psychologism, is that it is thus only under a different description that our "reasons" really turn out to do anything; the *content* of our reasoning needn't finally figure in a total account of our acting, only the momentary mental states that "have" this content. To that extent, Dharmakīrti effectively denies (what Kant affirms) *that there is pure practical reason.*

Recall from chapter 3 that to characterize it as "practical" is just to say (with Kant) that reason is "concerned with the determining grounds of the will"—that human persons are ineliminably responsive to reasons as such, and that this is not understood as long as it's supposed that reason's *being* "concerned with the determining grounds of the will" could only consist in its being somehow *causally* efficacious. With respect to Kant's guiding question—"whether pure reason of itself" belongs in accounts of what we are or whether instead reason really figures "only as empirically conditioned"[2]—it should be clear that Dharmakīrti can be understood to affirm the latter. Denying that it is *as semantically contentful* that reasons ultimately figure in accounts of our actions, Dharmakīrti affirms instead that it's only as consisting in fleeting mental particulars that reasoning actually involves anything real, that it *does* anything. Dharmakīrti's claim that *pramāṇas* are just "conventional," and that they will therefore admit of explanation simply in terms of what is disclosed by *svasaṃvitti*, thus amounts in Kantian terms to a claim that *theoretical* reason trumps *practical* reason; for Dharmakīrti, a philosophically motivated redescription of reasoning explains what that *really* consists in, regardless of how it seems to us to reason.

To the extent that this aptly characterizes something of Dharmakīrti's project, it seems he would therefore be vulnerable to the kind of argument I have elaborated on the basis of Kant's *Critique of Practical Reason*—vulnerable to the argument that reason's *being* "practical" is not, in fact, something that can coherently be denied, insofar as it is only *in terms of reasoning* that such a denial is even intelligible. In this chapter, I want to develop another angle on the aptness of my characterization of Dharmakīrti's philosophical project—one afforded by sympathetic reconstruction of some of the critiques of Dharmakīrti elaborated by other first-millennium Indian philosophers. My characterization of Dharmakīrti vis-à-vis contemporary cognitivism, I am thus arguing, is partly warranted by the extent to which some classical Indian arguments against him turn out to exemplify basically the same logic as the argument from practical reason.

Arguments ventured by Mīmāṃsakas and Mādhyamikas, in particular, can be understood to exemplify basically the same reasoning I have taken to advance a cogent critique of physicalism—notwithstanding that in targeting Dharmakīrti, these classical Indian critics were not arguing against a physicalist. That such arguments have purchase against both physicalists like Fodor and idealists like Dharmakīrti suggests that the seemingly sharp divergence between the projects of these thinkers belies the significance of their shared presuppositions: that causal efficacy is the criterion of the real, and that everything about the mental can (indeed *must*) therefore be explained in terms of efficient-causal interactions among particulars. In some Mīmāṃsaka arguments for the eternality of language, and in some Mādhyamika arguments concerning the nature and limits of causal explanation, we see cogent challenges to precisely these presuppositions.

MĪMĀṂSĀ: PRACTICAL REASON AS *LINGUISTIC*, LANGUAGE AS TIMELESS

The first argument I want to reconstruct was elaborated by proponents of the Brahmanical tradition of Pūrva Mīmāṃsā.[3] Arguably the most orthodox of all the Brahmanical schools of thought, this tradition has as its constitutive concern the interpretation and right application of Vedic injunctions—particularly those of the earlier portions of the vast corpus of texts styled "Veda," centering on the texts (called *Brāhmaṇas*) that describe and enjoin the performance of Vedic rituals.[4] The enjoined ritual acts, on the Mīmāṃsaka account, are required for the realization of *dharma*, which Mīmāṃsā's foundational text—the *Mīmāṃsā Sūtras*, attributed to a certain Jaimini (c. 25 C.E.)—indicates as the guiding topic for this tradition of thought.

While early Mīmāṃsakas said little more about this *dharma* than that it is what "connects a person with the highest good,"[5] the salient point for us is that it denotes an always *still-to-be-realized* state of affairs—*dharma*, Mīmāṃsakas say, is always *bhaviṣyat*, "going to be," which reflects (among other things) a guiding commitment to the view that Vedic injunctions essentially enjoin the ongoing *bringing into being* of a ritual world that must continually be renewed; it's insofar as no one ever *finishes* bringing this world into being that its realization is always still to come. Most significantly for us, the perennially subjunctive character of Mīmāṃsā's summum bonum means that it is essentially inaccessible to perception; only language can inform us of things not (yet) present. Proponents of Mīmāṃsā thus had a strong stake in a robust realism about linguistic universals. Among the expressions of this is their view that the relations between language and nonlinguistic fact are eternal. Insofar, then, as Mīmāṃsakas held there to be something ineliminably unique about how linguistic items relate to their referents, linguistic relations cannot be thought to have a first beginning; to think otherwise just is to think these relations reducible to whatever state of affairs obtained at that moment.

This claim relates closely to the characteristically Mīmāṃsaka view that the Vedic texts themselves are authorless and eternal—that they are "not of persons" (*apauruṣeya*), which requires among other things that we make sense of the idea that *language*, insofar as it is constitutively independent of any particular speakers, might itself "speak" a text. While that claim about the Vedic texts is one that few non-Mīmāṃsakas are apt to credit, proponents of this tradition of thought nevertheless elaborate, in their arguments for it, profound intuitions about (we might say) *the essentially semantic character of the mental.* When Jaimini seminally affirms (in the fifth *Mīmāṃsā Sūtra*) that "the relation between word and referent is eternal,"[6] he is, inter alia, getting at something significant about the conditions of the possibility of mind. It's worthwhile to ask how this could be a reasonable thing to think.

Appreciating the Mīmāṃsaka insight here depends, of course, in part on just what we take this "relation" (*sambandha*) to consist in. Indeed, it's reasonable to ask whether there could *be* any real "relation" between words and their referents; what *kind* of relation could it be?[7] Canvassing the possibilities (causal relations, containment relations, etc.) and finding them all wanting, early Mīmāṃsaka commentators urged that the relation in question is sui generis—there being a relation between language and nonlinguistic fact is just an irreducible fact about the world, and that relation is therefore to be taken as explanatorily primitive. That this relation cannot be explained in terms of the kinds of relations obtaining among spatiotemporally determinate particulars is, indeed, just as we should expect; the relations in question are among such essentially abstract things as *what it is in virtue of which we understand someone's meaning.* We here have in view the kinds of things that figure in the level of description that Ferdinand de Saussure referred to as *langue*, not those figuring in what he referred to as *parole*—*langue* being the synchronically conceived system of abstract signs in virtue of which any utterances are meaningful and not particular occasions of utterance themselves.[8] Just, then, as with Saussure's familiar terms "signifier" and "signified,"[9] relations among the universals whose reality Mīmāṃsakas affirm as part of their account of language—such as the "genus" (*jāti*) or "form" (*ākṛti*), which is what any noun essentially picks out[10]—are relations among things with no spatiotemporal identity criteria; there is nowhere or nowhen that these *are*, which is all that it means to characterize them as "universals." The *semantic* character of reality, on the Mīmāṃsaka view, is essentially timeless.

To affirm this is to affirm that linguistic universals cannot be finally explained with reference to particular occasions of language use or with reference to the psychological goings-on of particular subjects. Proponents of Mīmāṃsā are therefore strongly inclined to resist the accounts of those (chiefly Buddhists and Naiyāyikas) committed to thinking of language as essentially arbitrary or conventional. Buddhists like Dharmakīrti, we've seen, held that the "relation" between language and nonlinguistic fact is just whatever was arbitrarily assigned on some past convention-setting occasion; it's particularly against such accounts that proponents of Mīmāṃsā argued for the eternality of the language-world relation. Some of the Mīmāṃsaka arguments on this score can be understood particularly to target the coherence of the very idea of a bygone *saṃketakāla* such as Dharmakīrti can only presuppose as "meaning-conferring"; Mīmāṃsaka arguments for the eternality of linguistic relations cogently question this idea of particular baptismal tokenings as somehow getting language going. The argument to this effect can be generalized, I propose, as one to the effect that *intentionality is ineliminably semantic*.

The argument I have in mind can be gleaned from the oldest extant commentary on Jaimini's *Mīmāṃsā Sūtras*—that of Śabara (c. 4th century C.E.), who himself quotes extensively from the anonymous author of an earlier commentary.[11] Śabara includes an unusually lengthy extract from the latter in elaborating on Jaimini's affirmation (in the fifth *Mīmāṃsā Sūtra*) that the relations between words and referents are eternal. Here, the unnamed commentator, entertaining the objection that convention theories of language undermine the Mīmāṃsaka claim, identifies a significant problem for those who would appeal to particular convention-setting occasions—and takes this to recommend the conclusion that linguistic relations must therefore be timeless:

> There was never any time without a relation between words and their referents, no time at which not a single word was related to any referent. How so? Because the very act of making a relation does not

> otherwise stand to reason. Some language (*kenacic chabdena*) must be used by the one who is creating the relation; who created the relations constitutive of that language by which he would thus do so? If that was done by someone else, then who created linguistic relations for him, and who, in turn, for him? There's no coming to rest. Therefore, anyone creating any linguistic relation must presuppose some words whose relations are unmade, already available to us through the usage of forebears (*vṛddhavyavahārasiddhā*).[12]

The argument is that the creation of what Sellars referred to as "the fundamental connection of language with non-linguistic fact"[13]—here imagined in terms of a convention-setting act such as that consisting in the utterance "*this* [accompanied by an act of pointing] *is called a cow*"—cannot coherently be imagined *except as itself an essentially semantic act*. But the possibility of a semantic level of description is just what was supposed to be explained by the posited act of creation.[14] Hence, "the very act of creating such a relation" (*saṃbandhakriyâiva*)[15] does not stand to reason unless we presuppose that both the agent and the audience of this act already have (what we were here trying to understand) the idea of *meaning* something.

To presuppose the intelligibility of meaning here is effectively to presuppose (as we have seen Wittgenstein argue) that the audience for this act of creation "already had a language, only not this one."[16] The unnamed Mīmāṃsaka commentator quoted by Śabara makes just this point by urging against his conventionalist opponent that "some language must be used by the one who is creating the relation." The challenge that this Mīmāṃsaka's Wittgensteinian point poses for the aspiring nominalist is significant: What must be imagined is how anybody could *explain* to someone, how they could *tell* them, what it means to mean something. This must be imagined, moreover, without presupposing that the parties to this eminently intentional act can already *think*; for thinking is itself a notion one is not yet entitled to at this stage of the argument, insofar as that means (with Wittgenstein) something like *talking to themselves*. Insofar as it is among the conditions of the possibility of thought that our experience of the world always already be semantic, thought's *being* essentially semantic in character is not something that could be explained with reference to any particular occasions of "meaning-conferral"; the very thought necessary to *realize* any occasion as such must itself be already semantic in character.

Among the Mīmāṃsaka insights here, as suggested by the above passage's concluding reference to "the usage of forebears," is that there is something essentially *social* about the semantic; to emphasize, with Mīmāṃsakas, that language is always already "available" or "well known" (*siddha*) is, among other things, to say that it has reality apart from individual language users. That something essentially social thus represents a condition of the possibility of individuals' being *minded* is shown, as Émile Durkheim argued to similar effect, by the "irreducibility of reason to individual experience" (1995, 16).[17] Mīmāṃsakas similarly urge that the intelligibility of meaning necessarily requires reference to things that essentially transcend individual thought—a community of language users, for example, in which (Mīmāṃsakas say) a language is already "manifested."

The argument thus preserved in Śabara's commentary represents one of several for the eternality of language, and Śabara does not add anything of note to it. However, this thread of argument is picked up by Kumārila (who was roughly contemporaneous with Dharmakīrti), whose *Ślokavārttika* includes a diffuse but interesting chapter entitled "refutation of critiques of relation" (*saṃbandhākṣepaparihāra*). This chapter lays out Kumārila's responses to critics of the claim that the relation between words and their referents is essentially timeless. Kumārila begins by canvassing and rejecting such alternatives as a "contract" or "convention" account of linguistic relations, which he represents thus: "Expressive capacity (*śaktatvam*) does not intrinsically belong to the pair of signified and signifier; rather, comprehension could be based only on human convention (*puṃsāṃ samaya*)."[18] His case is then framed by negative arguments against the intelligibility of various ways to make sense of that thought; raising doubts in order to refute the appeal to arbitrary conventions, Kumārila asks: "Is this convention specific to each person (*pratimartyam*), or to each utterance? Or did someone make it all at once, at the beginning of the world?"[19]

The chapter early on considers the position (the *pratimartyapakṣa*) according to which—as Dharmakīrti recurrently suggests—the relation between word and referent is a function simply of the "intentions" of individual language users. Against this, Kumārila emphasizes the intersubjective character of linguistic understanding; thus, if all of the auditors of any utterance do not understand *the same relation* (between word and world), it could not be said that what the auditors understand is in any way the same as what the speaker intended—where, clearly, Kumārila understands a speaker's "intention" as consisting in *the semantic content thereof* (and not, as for Dharmakīrti, in a particular mental state such as might cause someone to give utterance). If mutual intelligibility were a function of innumerable, essentially private transactions, it could not make sense to think (among other things) that one could be right or wrong regarding *what is being talked about*, and ordinary discursive commerce (*vyavahāra*) would therefore be impossible.[20]

The eminently social character of speech acts, which constitutively involve a speaker and potentially innumerable auditors, nicely serves Kumārila's point, showing why linguistic relations necessarily precede all of the individual agents of any speech situation—and hence, precede *any particular speech act*. Pressing the point familiar from Śabara's quotation from the anonymous commentator, Kumārila asks: "In order to create a relation for the hearer, what relation would the speaker use? If it's by one that is already understood, then he doesn't make it for the hearer; if it's a new one that he makes, it could not be seen to bring about understanding."[21] To suppose, that is, that particular word-meanings are explained with reference to an already available idea of *meaning* something is just to take the Mīmāṃsaka position; if, on the other hand, it were part of any speech act to create the conditions for its own intelligibility as such, it could not already *be* a speech act, and there could be no understanding of it. The essentially social nature of any speech act thus requires that its terms already be available to all of the parties to that act—in which case, no particular speech act can itself be that which (by creating the idea of *meaning* something) creates the possibility of all speech acts.

Explaining why the speaker in this situation could not use hitherto "unavailable" (*asiddha*) terms,[22] Kumārila's commentator Pārthasārathimiśra effectively relates the issue here to intentionality more generally: "The creator of a relation, his activity preceded by thought (*buddhipūrvakārī*), does not make something completely new, its capacity uncognized."[23] It is, in other words, precisely insofar as any would-be creator of linguistic reference is herself engaged in an intentionally describable act—it's insofar as her activity is *preceded by thought*—that this effort has as a condition of its possibility the constitutively social fact (*language*) whose creation is supposedly being explained. How else are we to imagine this creator's *thinking* about his goal if not (with Wittgenstein) in terms of that agent's "talking to himself"? For any act of *saying what something means* to *be* deliberative (for it to be preceded by thought), then, just is for it already to be semantically describable—and how that could be so is just what the proponent of the convention theory was supposed to be explaining.

Kumārila resumes this thread of argument at chapter's end, saying: "An inference regarding the creation of linguistic relations is contradicted by there being no way [to establish the relation without presupposing what is to be explained], but an inference to [the effect that there is ultimately] no discourse is contradicted precisely by what is seen."[24] Kumārila here suggests a reason for thinking that the relation between language and nonlinguistic fact must be simply sui generis; insofar as there undeniably *is* a relation between language and reality, and insofar as no available model of relations makes sense of that fact, it's necessary to posit linguistic relations as just metaphysically basic. That this kind of relation cannot be imagined on the model of any other kinds of relata cannot, then, be thought to count against the reality of linguistic relations—cannot be thought to count in favor of (what is the same thing) an account that reduces these to some other kind of relation. On the contrary, what the impossibility of showing linguistic relations to be reducible to other relations shows is just that the relation of language to reality is a metaphysically primitive fact. Pārthasārathi comments:

> The supposed maker of a relation cannot have, for creating the relation, a sentence with unestablished meanings; but it *is* possible for a sentence with established meanings to explain the relation [that already obtains], since the sentence is established for the explainer. If it's said that, for understanders to whom the meanings of words are completely unfamiliar, there is no way that the understanding of meaning based on utterance is possible—well, this contradicts what is seen.[25]

Thus, while we cannot (for the kinds of reasons so far scouted) coherently posit a first creator of linguistic reference, that fact cannot be taken to count against the reality and success of discourse; *that there is meaning*, and that we therefore should not credit any account on which that fact turns out to be problematic, cannot coherently be denied, since any expression of denial could only be a discursive act.

Kumārila urges, then, that "the comprehension of elders being seen again and again is the way [to explain all this]; there is abandonment of this possible explanation for one whose understanding is unestablished."[26] We just *see* that, generation after generation, children acquire a native language from seeing its use exemplified by their elders—an observation that, like Mīmāṃsaka epistemology, can be understood to express what is simply our common-sense understanding.[27] It's not possible, that is, to explain (what is surely seen all the time) anyone's learning a first language except insofar as language learners *already have* the very idea of a relation between language and reality; this relation must therefore obtain independently of anyone's first learning a language. This cannot, moreover, be explained with reference to (putatively sense-conferring) *gestures*—with reference, that is, to an account based in bodily movements that are not themselves linguistic but that rather represent (with Augustine) "as it were the natural language of all peoples." Against this idea,[28] Kumārila argues that "a method such as hand gestures is not available to us on the first occasions of making [a relation]; for its signifying capacity cannot be known without other language users (*vinânyair vyavahartṛbhiḥ*)."[29] If we are in pursuit of the origin of linguistic rules, it will not do to stop at behaviors that themselves presuppose such rules—and this is the case even for gestures, at least insofar as these are to be intelligible as laying down linguistic policies.

Jerry Fodor, we saw in chapter 2, makes an argument precisely like the one here in view; Fodor could, indeed, be stating the Mīmāṃsakas' guiding premise when he avers that "one cannot learn that *P* falls under *R* unless one has a language in which *P* and *R* can be represented."[30] Considering the threat of regress intolerable, Fodor takes this point to recommend the conclusion that the nature of linguistic relations must therefore consist in something *in the brain*—a "language of thought," which he posits as a regress-stopping condition of the possibility of acquiring a first natural language. We have seen, though, that there are problems with the kind of psychologistic accounts encouraged by Fodor's methodological solipsism. Instead taking their bearings from the constitutively social character of language, Śabara and Kumārila can be seen to conclude—from a premise shared with Fodor—that linguistic relations must therefore obtain altogether independently of individual language learners.

IS LANGUAGE MIND-INDEPENDENT?

It's clear, I think, from their still-vexed character that the problems that come into view when we sympathetically assess the Mīmāṃsakas' insight—which, I've been suggesting, is most basically that we cannot, as the sapient beings we are, imagine ourselves creating what are conditions of the possibility of our being so—are profound. This is suggested by the extent to which Fodor and the Mīmāṃsakas can make what is effectively the very same argument ("one cannot learn that *P* falls under *R* unless one has a language in which *P* and *R* can be represented") while yet diverging sharply over what it shows. Some theistic Indian philosophers also credited this argument; while, like Fodor, they found the regress intolerable, they instead took that as among the reasons for positing the existence of God (*īśvara*). Naiyāyikas like the tenth-century theist Udayana thus argued that insofar as we cannot coherently imagine linguistic conventions to have been created by prelinguistic persons, we must suppose that God created the relations obtaining between words and their referents. Jonardon Ganeri credits these Naiyāyikas with recognizing at least that linguistic terms "function *as if* they had been introduced by acts of divine will" (1999b, 38).

This is why it's relevant for Kumārila's *Sambandhākṣepaparihāra* chapter to comprise (as it does) several critiques of theism; here, it is particularly as a rival explanation of the Mīmāṃsaka account of linguistic relations that theism is to be refuted. It's worth noting, in this regard, that the critiques of theism ventured by Kumārila are in fact very similar to arguments that Dharmakīrti makes.[31] The observation that these sharply divergent thinkers had a common interest in refuting theism can serve to introduce a point that it's surely important to acknowledge: Buddhists, like Mīmāṃsakas, upheld a view of the world and its processes as beginningless (*anādi*) and uncreated; to that extent, Buddhists could (and did!) also say that the phenomenon of language acquisition is beginningless. Recall, in this regard, that Dharmakīrti invokes the idea of our beginningless "dispositions" (*vāsanā*) to reify phenomenal sameness;[32] there was, Dharmakīrti too can say, never a time when we first started to conceptually structure our experience in all the ways that, on his account, lead us astray. Mightn't it be thought, then, that these seemingly contrary accounts really come to the same thing?

What is different here is that the Mīmāṃsakas take this process to be without beginning insofar as they take there to be, irreducibly, something *essentially semantic* about thought; that it is semantic, in other words, is not, on the Mīmāṃsaka view, something incidental to our having the kind of experience we do. For Dharmakīrti, in contrast, it may be true that beings have without beginning been prone to experience the world semantically, but that fact is, for him, finally adventitious. Dharmakīrti allows, then, that our tendencies for linguistic abstraction may be without beginning, but he holds that they are nevertheless eliminable—that is, indeed, just what he argues with his *apoha* doctrine. Notwithstanding, then, his sharing with Mīmāṃsakas the view that human being in the world is without beginning, the relevant one among Dharmakīrti's guiding convictions is that it's possible to eliminate the conceptualization of reality—that it makes sense to think of our experiencing a world thus shorn, in effect, of *meaning*, which is surely among the upshots of thinking that a Buddha's knowing how things really are consists (as Buddhists often urge) in "nonconceptual awareness" (*nirvikalpakajñāna*).

This, then, is why the Mīmāṃsaka argument we have been scouting has purchase even given the Buddhist appeal to beginninglessness. Let us recall, here, the point to which we developed Dharmakīrti's account of mental content in chapter 4: We saw that in his arguments for *apoha*, Dharmakīrti recurrently defers the dawning of meaning to unspecified convention-setting occasions—to a bygone *saṃketakāla* that is, we are left to suppose, just intrinsically "meaning-conferring." It's precisely with reference to these points in Dharmakīrti's argument that the considerations here advanced by Mīmāṃsakas have some purchase against Dharmakīrti's *apoha* doctrine; arguing for the eternality of linguistic relations, then, Mīmāṃsakas like Kumārila effectively argue that Dharmakīrti's unspecified "convention-occasions" (*saṃketakāla*) will not themselves admit of a nonintentional explanation—which, recall, is what Dharmakīrti must produce if his appeal to convention-setting occasions is to ground his causal redescription of mental content. Indeed, at just the points where he appeals to bygone convention-setting occasions, Dharmakīrti can be seen most clearly to presuppose that we already understand what it would be for some mental event to *be* semantically contentful—which is just what the *apoha* doctrine was supposed to explain.

Mīmāṃsakas take this fact to show that there is an ineliminably semantic character to the way things are—that *meaning* cannot, in principle, be explained with reference to goings-on in any particular heads or to any other essentially nonsemantic factors; it is, we might say they mean to affirm, *mind-independently* true that there are relations between language and world. Any particular *use* of language, any particular *event* of its being understood, discloses something (its *meaning*) that cannot depend for its intelligibility on any particular act of thought—not even on the very act first to express that meaning. In this regard, though, we can note a significant slippage; there is a difference between the claim that the reality of language is independent of *any particular minds* and the claim that it is independent of *all* particular minds. The Mīmāṃsaka arguments may be said to show the former; they clearly think themselves entitled, however, to conclude that the reality of language obtains independently not just of any but of *all* particular minds, and it's reasonable to doubt whether this makes sense.

It should be allowed, however, that the difference between these two claims—the fact, if it is one, that one of them is true (language *is* real, independent of any particular minds) and the other false (it cannot be independent of *all* of them)—turns out still to be difficult to account for. In contemporary terms, this can be brought out with reference to what was referred to in chapter 3 as the "problem of infralinguals." Thus, to the extent that the Mīmāṃsaka argument can be generalized as making a point about the ineliminably semantic character of intentionality, many would worry that this picture renders acute a problem that arises, as well, for McDowell: the problem that it introduces profound discontinuity (where much about our best theorizing on the subjects suggests there should be *continuity*) both between infants and adult humans, and also between, say, primates and humans (though first-millennium Mīmāṃsakas would not, of course, have been troubled by the latter case); surely all of these beings exhibit "intentionality," even though only some are linguistic. And surely some such nonlinguistic beings must somewhere along the way have contrived language.

The significance of the problem of infralinguals can surely be taken as good evidence that the Mīmāṃsaka view cannot be right. But the issues are difficult on *any* of the available positions, and the argument here sketched following the Mīmāṃsakas turns out to identify problems that are no less thorny for accounts on which convention-setting is to be explained with reference to an evolutionary timescale. Mīmāṃsakas might in this regard be taken to have grasped a problem that Clifford Geertz expressed thus: "We need to be able both to deny any significant relationship between (group) cultural achievement and innate mental capacity in the present, and to affirm such a relationship in the past" (1973, 65). It seems, that is, that we cannot conceive that the constitutively social facts that are among the present conditions of the possibility of our *being minded* are themselves the products of individual minds—but that we must, nevertheless, suppose just such a state of affairs to have obtained in the past. Surely, though, Mīmāṃsakas would argue that it's just as unclear how persons in the remote past could at any particular point first have "conferred meaning" on the world as it is hard to imagine in the present what it could look like to do that now; the appeal to an evolutionary timescale does not eliminate the difficulty.[33] It's not for nothing, then, that Durkheim was led to characterize the social as essentially "emergent" in the same way some philosophers of mind take the mental to be; *the social*, he argued, cannot be explained with reference even to *aggregated* individuals—it consists, rather, in "something other than a mere epiphenomenon of its morphological base, just as individual consciousness is something other than a mere product of the nervous system" (1995, 426).[34]

It thus remains a challenge to explain how language could be real independently of *any* particular minds, without allowing its reality independently of *all* of them. Against, then, precisely the kind of account that finds Dharmakīrti harking back to bygone convention-setting occasions, Mīmāṃsakas elaborated a profound insight concerning our linguistic being: knowing a language (*being linguistic*) involves much more than simply "knowing the names for things"; it involves, more basically, having a grasp of the meaning of *meaning*—of the idea that the unique acoustic events that are human utterances can, like thought itself, be *about* states of affairs. And Mīmāṃsakas can be said to have understood that that idea—the very idea, in effect, of intentionality, insofar as that is to be understood as semantic—is a constitutively social one; insofar as language necessarily precedes and exceeds any individual language user, the realm of the semantic (the logical space of reasons) is, among conditions of the possibility of thought, one that cannot itself be explained in terms of any particular person or speech act.

DHARMAKĪRTI'S CONCESSION: PRACTICAL REASON, CAUSAL EXPLANATION, AND THE MADHYAMAKA IMPULSE

Now, insofar as it's taken to warrant the conclusion that language must therefore be eternal, the foregoing Mīmāṃsaka argument might be thought to represent a *reductio ad absurdum*—might be thought, that is, to issue in a truistic conclusion ("we can only talk about language *in language*!") and therefore to show nothing more than the limits of this kind of argument. Surely our best *theory* of the matter would have it that the origin of linguistic conventions can be given a broadly bioevolutionary explanation. We might, accordingly, take it that the Mīmāṃsaka argument shows only that it *seems* to us—as a matter, say, of practical reason, or of our first-personal experience of ourselves as reasoning—impossible to *imagine* the first devising, by hitherto nonlinguistic beings, of linguistic conventions. (Perhaps this is impossible for us to imagine in something like the same sense in which it is impossible for us to imagine our own deaths.)[35] But that is only a fact (if it is one) about what epistemically limited beings like us find *conceivable*; what basis have we for supposing that limits on conceivability entail any limits on what can *be*?[36] One might thus suggest that the Mīmāṃsaka argument reveals only facts about us, about our epistemically finite situation, and not about what is mind-independently true. Surely we understand, in this case, what it means to think there is thus a *theoretical* level of description—one that provides an impersonal perspective on the truth about what exists—at which the facts' *seeming* some way to us is just wrong.

Whatever one finally concludes in the case of this argument's deployment to support the claimed timelessness of language, though, it's important to appreciate that there may be cases where it is our theoretical descriptions that should be constrained by what is "practically" true, rather than the other way round. Consider, for example, the kind of theoretical claim made by those reductionists for whom the common-sense view of the mental is finally to be understood as a *theory* ("folk psychology"), such as can in principle be superseded by the rival theory that is reductionism. (The common-sense view's thus *being* eliminable is just the point of its being likened to a theory.) Such a claim amounts to a denial that reason really *is* practical in our sense; for the "theory" of us as responsive to reasons as such, on this account, yields to an alternative theory that finally makes no reference to the content of our reasons—an alternative account proposed as *explaining*, in altogether different terms, what is really the case and why things could have seemed as they did.

Against the intelligibility of this kind of reductionist conclusion, however, it can be urged that intentionality represents the paradigm case of a situation where the perspective of practical reason (the perspective *from which* we reason) necessarily constrains our theories, and not the other way round. The way we understand ourselves when we reason for or against theories should itself be understood as something that our theoretical commitments must take account of, such that its incompatibility with any theory is to be taken as evidence (not of the problematic character of reasoning but) *of the theory's failure*. On this kind of view, as contra Dharmakīrti's, in cases of conflict between how we *experience* reasoning and any proposed *explanation* thereof, it's the former that should trump the latter. This thought can be expressed as the point that our first-person perspective on reasoning is not, in fact, analogous to a "theory" at all—is not, that is, something that it's open to us to adopt or not adopt; it is, rather, something that is forced upon us by the way things are, and reference to it therefore cannot be superseded in the way that theoretical commitments essentially can.[37] Insofar as any theoretical commitments we could entertain are, ipso facto, always already embraced by the logical space of reasons, there can be no outstripping reason, no seeing it, as it were, *from the other side*.

Noting that the foregoing considerations represent what is "widely taken to constitute an insuperable difficulty for reductionism about persons," Mark Siderits has indicated a precisely similar trend of argument as relevant for the context of some Indian Buddhist discussions (2009, 66). Scouting the question of whether a project such as Dharmakīrti's involves self-reflexive incoherence (insofar, that is, as the project's own claims turn out to be inexpressible), Siderits identifies just the problem that I have been characterizing in terms of relations between "theoretical" and "practical" reason—though the issues are framed by Siderits, in characteristically Buddhist terms, in terms of the relation between what is "ultimately true" (*paramārthasat*) and what is "conventionally" so (*saṃvṛtisat*). The problem, in these terms, is that the reductionist redescription of experience is claimed as *ultimately true*, but *the entertaining of that claim*, as something intelligible only at an intentional level of description, can itself be only conventionally real. How, then, are we to make sense of any claim to the effect that *ultimately an intentional level of description is unreal*, when it is only *at* such a level of description that the claim itself is intelligible?[38] One solution to the problem, Siderits suggests with reference to various Buddhist takes on it, is the kind of "metalinguistic" strategy I said above could be deployed vis-à-vis the Mīmāṃsaka argument; that is, the apparent incoherence might be explicable with reference to "facts about creatures like us," such as that we are, epistemically, profoundly finite.

It's with respect to this move that Siderits effectively states the argument I have charted following Kant. Showing, then, the difference it makes when a reductionist account bears (not on ordinary medium-sized dry goods but) particularly on the kind of *personal* level of description that I have been characterizing with reference to intentionality, Siderits says of a metalinguistic strategy like the foregoing that it "requires that we bring in facts about 'creatures like us.'" The problem is that if, as the reductionist about persons argues, "there ultimately are no such creatures, then no ultimately true statement can invoke facts about their interests and cognitive limitations and their resulting speech habits" (2009, 66). Intentionality is not *explained*, that is, by an account that is itself intelligible only with reference to an intentional level of description.

That this problem does indeed represent an "insuperable difficulty for reductionism about persons," I now want to argue, is just the point that proponents of the Buddhist Madhyamaka tradition of thought can be taken to have pressed against co-religionists like Dharmakīrti. In thus elaborating what I take to be the most significant point that some Mādhyamikas aimed to advance, I am eschewing a route it might have been expected I would take. Having reconstructed a Mīmāṃsā line of argument as having purchase particularly against Dharmakīrti's account (with the *apoha* doctrine) of mental content, I might now be expected to take up Madhyamaka as offering arguments bearing on the other of the two Dharmakīrtian doctrines I've developed, that of *svasaṃvitti*; influential Mādhyamikas (particularly Candrakīrti) were, after all, highly critical of that doctrine. However, Mādhyamika arguments in this regard are not particularly distinctive; indeed, along with

Mīmāṃsakas like Kumārila, Candrakīrti advanced what was basically the standard Sanskritic critique of *svasaṃvitti.* On this argument, the problem with *svasaṃvitti* is that we are asked to imagine that the same thing could be at once *agent* and *patient* of the same act; but awareness cannot be *of* itself, Indian critics are fond of saying, any more than a sword edge can cut itself or a fingertip touch itself.[39]

Among the points worth noting about this critique is that it seems to target only the kind of *perceptual* understanding on which self-awareness is *of* one's own mental states in the same way that perceptions are *of* things like trees. If, though, *svasaṃvitti* is understood not as a *kind* of intentional awareness but as something more like a defining characteristic thereof, this critique may not hit its mark—which is perhaps not a problem, since it's hard to see what stake Mādhyamikas might have had in refuting *svasaṃvitti*, at least insofar as one has a constitutive understanding thereof.[40] While it's perhaps easier to see why a thinker like Candrakīrti might have a stake in refuting a *perceptual* understanding of self-awareness—on such an understanding, the doctrine is most likely to figure as providing our epistemically foundational contact with reality, and this is emphatically not how Mādhyamikas imagined anyone's knowing the ultimately real (*paramārthasat*)—I would emphasize a still more basic point: what Mādhyamikas above all resisted was any idea of "ultimate truth" as affording ultimate explanatory purchase. Thus, what is most apt to have rankled Mādhyamikas about *svasaṃvitti* is any variation on the thought that it shows awareness to be, uniquely, *autonomously intelligible*; awareness would be, on any such view, a counterinstance to the one point Mādhyamikas are most intent on making, which is that all explanatory terms turn out to be relative not only to all manner of other such terms but also to *the very phenomena on which they supposedly give us purchase.*

The guiding intuition for Mādhyamikas, I thus take it, is that rightly understanding the Buddhist doctrine of selflessness could not consist in specifying what *really exists* instead of the "selves" we take ourselves to be. In light of this conviction, the claim that self-awareness is autonomously intelligible can look like the claim—just the one Dharmakīrti seems to have intended all along—that in knowing simply *that* there are episodic cognitions, we know all that can be indubitably known, and therefore all that we are entitled to think of as *paramārthasat*. On such an understanding, what belongs in a final ontology (what is "ultimately real") turns out to be just episodic cognitions—enumerable, particular *existents*, that is, of the sort with which we might be perceptually acquainted. Insofar as we typically ("conventionally") experience the world as consisting of temporally enduring macro-objects, what is ultimately true thus turns out to be the world (and particularly *ourselves*) under a completely different description than is ordinarily in view.

Against such views, the whole point, for proponents of Madhyamaka as I understand them, is that *there is no such set of ontological primitives*, nothing we could point to as *what there really is*. There is nothing, more precisely, that is essentially apart from, nothing *more real than*, the "conventional" perspective from which questions about ontology must themselves be framed—though I submit that it nevertheless makes sense to say it is *really true* that this is the case. (More on this below.) Against, then, views on which what it is to *know* something will (as Dharmakīrti aimed to show with his *apoha* doctrine) finally admit of a wholly impersonal description, proponents of Madhyamaka can be taken to affirm that any such redescription turns out to be intelligible only as itself dependent on *the perspective from which explanations must be offered*. Mādhyamika thinkers like Nāgārjuna and Candrakīrti thus argued for the irreducibly *conventional* character of, well, anything at all that we could know or think. Whether that is a sensible claim depends, of course, on just what "conventional" here means; I suggest that in thus arguing that a "conventionally true" level of description is ineliminable, these Mādhyamikas effectively argue for the ineliminable character of an *intentional* level of description.

This can be expressed as the point that any supposedly privileged, nonintentional level of description—particularly the *causal* level of description that figures centrally in Dharmakīrti's project—necessarily involves (as Siderits puts it) "elements of intentionality or conceptual construction" (2003, 131). Insofar as that can sound like an idealist sort of claim—like the claim that *all there is* to causation (or anything else) is our imagining thereof—it's important to be clear about what it means thus to affirm the ineliminable character of intentionality. We can begin to get at this by noting that it only makes sense to think of causal relations as obtaining *among events under some description*; it is, in other words, only *as picked out* in terms of some explanatory interests that anything can so much as *be* individuated as causally related to anything else—a fact that is problematic for anyone who would enlist causal relations in order to explain such constitutively intentional phenomena as *our individuating events*. How are we to finesse the fact that causal explanations are necessarily offered from some perspective, particularly in the case where it is *having such a perspective* that we aim to explain in causal terms?

The difficulty of the question was appreciated by Hume, whose arguments regarding the limits of causal explanation were coupled with his own *appeal* to causal relations as explaining the unity of consciousness. Thus, I have recurrently referred to Hume's famous arguments to the effect that we cannot claim to know *causation as such*, but only that we have observed regularities that it's conventionally useful to exploit. But, much like Dharmakīrti, Hume (we saw in chapter 3) also *invoked* causal relations among particulars to account for the phenomenal sense of unity that Kant, in contrast, characterized as transcendental.[41] What is hard to explain on Hume's account, we saw, is the eminently conceptual *taking* of discrete mental states as phenomenally similar to one another; the difficulty, again, is in giving a causal account of intentionality.

Strikingly conceding the intractability of the problem, Hume allowed, in the fascinating appendix to his *Treatise*, that "I find myself involv'd in such a labyrinth, that, I must confess, I neither know how to correct my former opinions, nor how to render them consistent" (1739, 633). The problem centered, Hume saw, on his appeal to causal series of discrete mental states as explaining phenomenal unity—an appeal that forced him to confront "two principles, which I cannot render consistent; nor is it in my power to renounce either of them." These principles are "*that all our distinct perceptions are distinct existences*"—that, in other words, a causal-atomistic account makes the best sense of the episodic character of perceptual experience; and "*that the mind never perceives any real connexion among distinct existences*" (1739, 636). That Hume could not see how to reconcile these points—could not see how finally to *explain* that our taking ourselves as unified subjects *really* consists in Hume's "bundle of perceptions"—vexed him considerably; for insofar as one aims to explain what our *taking* things some way or another ultimately consists in, it makes a difference whether we are really in a position to think our proposed redescription more secure than the practical reason (more secure than the perspective *from which* we reason) supposedly explained thereby.

Interestingly, Dharmakīrti himself entertained such worries, and we can usefully introduce the Mādhyamika arguments I want to elaborate by first noting what he says on this score; from the perspective of someone whose philosophical sympathies are with Madhyamaka, Dharmakīrti will here seem to expose himself to just the critique Mādhyamikas would advance. At the beginning of this chapter, we revisited Prajñākaragupta's comments on the merely "conventional" status of all other *pramāṇas*, and I said his account of the unique purchase afforded by *svasaṃvitti*—his claim that this is finally the only ultimately valid *pramāṇa*—brings to mind another discussion centered on Dharmakīrti's *Pramāṇavārttika*. I was thinking of Dharmakīrti's often-cited expression of the claim—first noted in chapter 1,[42] where it's adduced as evidence of his taking causal efficacy as the criterion of the real—that "whatever has the capacity for causal efficacy is ultimately existent." What I have so far suppressed, in my recurrent attention to his thus privileging causal explanation, is a significant concession that Dharmakīrti makes immediately after saying as much—a concession strikingly like Hume's.

Having affirmed that causal efficacy (*arthakriyāsāmarthyam*) is the criterion of being "ultimately existent" (*paramārthasat*), Dharmakīrti anticipates the objection that what are typically characterized as causal relations may amount to nothing more than observed regularities—that we are not, in other words, entitled to attribute to the things involved in such regularities anything like a causal "power" or "capacity" (*sāmarthyam* or *śakti*).[43] A further objection is thus expressed by Manorathanandin (here sounding very much indeed like Hume): "The relation of effect to cause is established only customarily (*vyavahāramātrataḥ*), not ultimately (*na paramārthataḥ*)."[44] We cannot, that is, be said ever to *perceive* "the causation" that supposedly occurs in cases of causal relations; indeed, insofar as causal relations are constitutively sequential, it could only be with reference to *memory* that such relations are even posited. Insofar, however, as reference to memory is, by Dharmakīrti's own lights, chief among the things that distinguish conceptual awareness from perceptual—perceiving something *as* a tree, recall, involves remembering past experience of the use of the word "tree"—Dharmakīrti's own account of the privileged status of perception turns out, it seems, to depend upon precisely such epistemically deficient procedures as perception is supposedly privileged to lack.

Given the importance of the difference between "ultimately true" and "conventionally true" descriptions for Dharmakīrti—and given, especially, the work this contrast does for his epistemology, according to which perception is to be privileged over discursive awareness just insofar as the former (but not the latter) is causally describable and thus uniquely in contact with *ultimately existent things*—the objection that Dharmakīrti's defining contrast is *itself* just conventionally true could seem to be serious. It's striking, then, that Dharmakīrti responds to this anticipated objection by conceding the point: "Fine," he says; "let it be that way."[45]

Dharmakīrti thus thinks this line of objection doesn't count against his project; "worldly discourse," the commentator Manorathanandin is therefore willing to allow in elaborating the concession, "is achieved based on agreement regarding correspondence of discourse concerning such things as explanans and explanandum, in reliance upon the cause and effect relation (*kāryakāraṇabhāvam āśritya*), *even though the latter is conventional* (*sāṃvṛtam api*)."[46] Dharmakīrti thus allows that we cannot have epistemic access to *the very fact of causation* apart from the same cognitive tools available to us in articulating any account thereof—even though these are eminently *conceptual* tools, and conceptual elaboration is just what perception was supposed to lack. What is thus allowed is effectively that anything we could be said to know about the ultimately existent character of perceptibles, simply insofar as it is an instance of *knowing*, could not itself be "ultimately true," on Dharmakīrti's understanding thereof.[47]

Faced with this worry, Dharmakīrti embraces the point, blithely disavowing any claim to offer anything more than a "conventionally" valid account of our epistemic practices. The Mādhyamika arguments I want to reconstruct are usefully introduced by asking whether Dharmakīrti is really entitled to concede this—whether, indeed, Dharmakīrti's claim to offer what is only a conventionally valid account of intentionality could be coherent even with his own aims. This is among the questions that Mādhyamikas are most apt to press, and it represents a way to get at the more general point they aim (on my reading) to advance: that an intentional level of description is ineliminable from any account of what there is. Understanding why Mādhyamikas thus think Dharmakīrti's concession problematic, then, is key to understanding why proponents of this school of thought can think theirs the right course for preventing the Buddhist doctrine of selflessness from becoming an instance of *ucchedavāda*, or "eliminativism." Let us see, then, whether there are good Mādhyamika arguments for thinking that Dharmakīrti's concession is incoherent.

THE "CONVENTIONAL" AS THE "INTENTIONAL": MADHYAMAKA ARGUMENTS FOR THE INELIMINABLE CHARACTER OF THESE

Proponents of Madhyamaka, I've been suggesting, characteristically argued that there is something irreducibly "conventional" (*saṃvṛtisat*) about the way things are—that, for example, just such causal explanations as Dharmakīrti would give *of* intentionality are themselves intelligible only relative to (what is an eminently intentional sort of thing) the explanatory interests of beings like us. I have also suggested that Mādhyamikas advanced this point chiefly out of a concern (generally shared by Buddhists) that the cardinal doctrine of selflessness not be understood as an *eliminativist* one. It's relevant to note, in this regard, that in styling the school that develops from Nāgārjuna's works the *madhyamaka*, or "middle way," proponents of the so-named school of thought exploited a long-invoked Buddhist trope. Traditional accounts of the life of the Buddha characterize him as having struck a "middle way" between the extravagant courtly life available to him as a prince and the self-mortification he is said first to have tried in his pursuit of transformative insight; philosophically, the relevant extremes between which Buddhist accounts of the person aim to steer are *eternalism* and *eliminativism*.

"Eternalism" (*śāśvatavāda*) names the view that there are enduring existents, of which the self is the chief example; "eliminativism" (*ucchedavāda*) names the contrary extreme, according to which intentional actions (*karma*) have no ethical consequences. (It's as an *ethical* problem that this extreme is perhaps most keenly felt in the tradition.) Understood in terms of the eliminativist extreme, the doctrine of selflessness would amount to the claim that there really *are* no agents of actions or consequences—a claim that can, among other things, be thought to entail the conclusion that ethical considerations about *karma* and the like do not really belong in a final account of things. Given their guiding Buddhist concern to refuse the existence of an ultimately existent "self," it's clearly the eliminativist pole that proponents of Madhyamaka must particularly work to avoid; avoidance of the other extreme just goes with being Buddhist. The sense in which proponents of Madhyamaka can coherently claim to avoid *both* of these extremes (as most Buddhists will also claim to do) is central to understanding the distinctive character of their thought.

Significantly, the concern to avoid charges of nihilism (leveled alike by Brahmanical and other Buddhist interlocutors) represents one of the most recurrent preoccupations of Nāgārjuna and the philosophers who follow him. This concern has to be understood with reference to the Buddhist doctrine of two truths—with reference, that is, to the same idea in terms of which Dharmakīrti specified that causal efficacy is the criterion of the real (of the *paramārthasat*). Among the salient points of Dharmakīrti's unpacking of the two truths doctrine, we've seen, is that it warrants the conclusion that we can specify just what kinds of things (namely, perceptible particulars) we are entitled to think *really* exist. The important thing is that there are thus taken to be *ultimate existents*; this, and not "ultimate *truth*," is what *paramārthasat* really means. For proponents of Madhyamaka, in contrast, whether there is anything it could look like for something thus to *be* "ultimately existent" is just the point at issue; they challenge the very idea that anything could be thought to afford "ultimate" explanatory purchase.

In doing so, Nāgārjuna takes his bearings from the thought that the cardinal Buddhist doctrine of dependent origination (*pratītyasamutpāda*)—the doctrine that is the flipside of selflessness and that Dharmakīrti not unreasonably elaborated as amounting to causal reductionism—represents the most basic of the Buddhist tradition's insights; *that everything is dependently originated*, on his view, is what the Buddha taught. Nāgārjuna can be said to have recognized, in this regard, that anything posited as ontologically primitive—anything taken as the point at which explanations must come to rest—could *have* explanatory purchase only insofar as it represents an exception to what Nāgārjuna thus takes to be the governing rule. Dependently originated existents would be "ultimately explained," that is, only by something that does not itself require the same kind of explanation—and the Mādhyamika's point just is that there can *be* nothing that is not itself dependently originated. Nāgārjuna thus emphasizes that "*all dharmas*"—*all* of the kinds of things (*skandhas*, *svalakṣaṇas*, etc.) that other Buddhist thinkers had proposed as ultimately existent—are themselves "empty."

What even such supposedly "ultimate existents" are empty *of* is an "essence," as we might not unreasonably render *svabhāva*; the point, it's clear however we unpack that idea, is that all existents are without the very kind of existence (*being paramārthasat*) that Dharmakīrti attributes to *svalakṣaṇas*.[48] Among the points Nāgārjuna most recurrently clarifies is that this is just to say that even the supposed explanatory primitives of Buddhists like Dharmakīrti are themselves *dependently originated*. I take it that the point in provocatively characterizing this fact in terms of the "emptiness" of existents—and thus inviting the kind of objection, always dependent on the thought that "empty" means *nonexistent*, that provides the recurrent occasions for Nāgārjuna's clarifying that—is a rhetorical one; the point is to emphasize that things are dependently originated, as it were, *all the way down*.[49] "Emptiness" thus amounts to the fact that there is no point at which it uniquely makes sense to think that something has been finally explained, that there is nothing it could look like to say, of any conventionally described phenomenon, what it "really" is.

Here, however, it makes a difference that the conventionally described phenomena paradigmatically in view are *persons* or *selves*; the difference this makes, indeed, is just what I'm trying to bring out by suggesting that we understand "conventionally described" here to mean, above all, *intentionally* described. Thus, while it's clear that there are cases where, in fact, we *can* say what some conventionally described thing "really is"—surely there's no problem in saying, for example, that sunrise and sunset *really* consist in facts about the earth's rotation—the situation is essentially different when the explanandum is intentionality. In the case where we want to understand something precisely like *what it is to understand something*, it cannot coherently be held that the explanation might do without the very perspective from which that idea makes sense; the perspective from which we reason is not the kind of thing of which we could coherently say that it is *really* something else. To avoid the extreme of *ucchedavāda* or "eliminativism," on the Madhyamaka view, is to affirm that "conventionally real" (*saṃvṛtisat*) things are ineliminable from a complete understanding of what there is and what we are like—and I'm suggesting that this is effectively to argue for the ineliminable character of an intentional level of description.

That it's reasonable thus to reconstruct Mādhyamika arguments can be appreciated by considering why thinkers like Nāgārjuna and Candrakīrti are apt to hold that Dharmakīrti cannot, in fact, coherently say that he offers only a conventionally true account of our experience—by considering the sense it makes to say that Dharmakīrti's specification of ultimately real existents has no explanatory purchase *on* the conventional just insofar as it turns out to be *shot through* with that. Dharmakīrti is not, to that extent, entitled to claim that causal efficacy is the unique criterion of the real. Nāgārjuna's commentator Candrakīrti argues in just this way that one cannot admit the conventional status of causal explanations without at the same time admitting the other things that are *conventionally said* to enter into such relations—such as that they obtain not among momentary particulars but among ordinary objects of experience. One is not, after all, entitled to think one's account "conventionally true" if it's inconsistent with what is conventionally said in the matter; indeed, what is *conventionally true* would seem to be just our conventions, and it's incoherent to claim to offer a conventionally valid account of these while at the same time eschewing what are precisely the conditions for the intelligibility of such an account.

Candrakīrti argues thus not against Dharmakīrti (with whom he was roughly contemporaneous but whose work he seems not to have known), but against Dignāga. In an engagement I've treated before,[50] Candrakīrti imagined Dignāga claiming, just as we've seen Dharmakīrti concede, that his redescription of our epistemic practices is to be taken simply as a conventionally valid account; Candrakīrti's whole ensuing engagement with Dignāga's epistemology consists just in his challenging the coherence of that claim. Candrakīrti particularly seizes on the two correlated terms that structure the epistemological commitments Dignāga shares with Dharmakīrti:

pratyakṣa ("perception") and *svalakṣaṇa* ("unique particular"). Candrakīrti takes it that on Dignāga's usage (as, more clearly, on Dharmakīrti's), the latter refers to the ultimately existent particulars that are given to us in perception; Candrakīrti rightly argues that this is not, in fact, the primary sense of the Sanskrit word *svalakṣaṇa*. That word conventionally means not (as for Dignāga) "unique particular" but something more like "defining characteristic"—as, for example, when people (those who know Sanskrit, anyway) familiarly say that fire's *svalakṣaṇa* is *being hot*, earth's is *being resistant*, etc. "Defining characteristics," though, are not particulars; indeed, as shared by every instance of whatever they define, they represent precisely the sort of thing that Dignāga and Dharmakīrti would call a universal. Candrakīrti is right, then, to think that Dignāga would be hard-pressed to use the word as he does while still making sense of such conventional expressions as "earth's *svalakṣaṇa* is being resistant."

It's an important fact about the conventional usage, moreover, that it necessarily involves a relationship; it is incoherent to suppose that these are not the "characteristics" *of* anything, since the conventional understanding of the term "*svalakṣaṇa*" constitutively involves a relationship between a characteristic (*lakṣaṇa*) and something *characterized* (*lakṣya*) thereby. Dignāga cannot concede this, since his position requires that there be no further *kind* of existent to which *svalakṣaṇas* could belong; these are meant, rather, as ontological primitives. Candrakīrti represents Dignāga as wanting, then, to maintain that the perceptible objects he takes the word to denote are simply *self-characterizing*—that they are given to perception simply as self-identical particulars. It's precisely this requirement that is at odds with the conventional usage of the word; what *svalakṣaṇa* conventionally refers to (viz, "defining characteristics") is just the sort of thing in virtue of which things are always experienced *under some description*.

This argument clearly counts against the claim that perceptual cognition affords access to uninterpreted data. Among the points that Candrakīrti thus makes by urging that "defining characteristics" are necessarily related to some *lakṣya* (some "bearer" of the defining property in question) is that it's not possible to perceive any instance of, say, earth without at the same time perceiving *its being resistant*. This is tantamount to arguing, against Dignāga and Dharmakīrti's guiding claim to the contrary, that perception—as "conventionally," or (I'm here suggesting) *intentionally*, described—always already involves our conceptual capacities. The logical space of reasons, as we might more tendentiously put the point, always already *sublates* our perceptual relation to the world; the latter, it follows, therefore cannot be thought to afford any privileged epistemic purchase, cannot be thought itself to *explain* our conceptual capacities.

Candrakīrti's critique of Dignāga, redolent of ordinary-language philosophy, typifies Mādhyamika arguments, which are generally to the effect that anything one could posit as *explaining* something will turn out itself to be "empty" (where that just means *dependently originated*) in just the same way as the phenomenon it supposedly explains. The point at stake, for proponents of this tradition of thought, is always finally that the analytic categories stemming from the Buddhist Abhidharma tradition (a tradition with which Dharmakīrti's thought is continuous) cannot coherently be thought "more real" than the conventionally existent entities they are invoked to explain. An exemplary case of Mādhyamika arguments to this effect centers on the relation between *fire* and *fuel*. It's particularly clear in Nāgārjuna's handling of this case that the arguments it typifies can be generalized as urging the ineliminable character of an intentional level of description; indeed, it is not without basis that in his commentary Candrakīrti extends Nāgārjuna's point, taking the consideration of fire and fuel to tell us everything we need to know about "self" and "selflessness," on the Mādhyamika understanding thereof.

As throughout Nāgārjuna's work, the guiding question here is whether these relata (fire and fuel) are intelligible as such apart from each other, or whether instead it is only *as related* that they can come into view as the kinds of things they are taken to be.[51] Exemplifying the same logic evinced by Candrakīrti's ordinary-linguistic critique of Dignāga, Nāgārjuna chiefly challenges the idea that either "fire" or "fuel" could be autonomously intelligible; if, that is, the terms of the relationship are intelligible as such *only insofar as they are related*, what can it mean to ask what either of them "really is" apart from the relation? The point Nāgārjuna would thus have us understand about all such relata is that it is only *as* related that any of them can come into view as the kinds of things whose relations we could think requires explanation in the first place; "fire" and "fuel" cannot be individuated *as* the relata we are explaining, except under a description on which they are already related.

Now, this might, as I allowed of the Mīmāṃsaka argument for the eternality of language, be thought a rather underwhelming argument; surely, one might object, this amounts only to the insignificantly *notional* sort of point that "fire" and "fuel" are just *defined* in terms of each other and that it therefore tells us nothing of existential significance.[52] The point can look rather different, however, when it bears on the relation between what is taken to be the "self" and the various impersonal categories adduced by some Buddhists as explaining that; as noted above with reference to Mark Siderits, it makes a difference when it is a reductionist account particularly of *persons* that is at issue.[53] It's easy, in this regard, for Nāgārjuna (as Candrakīrti says in introducing verse 10.15) to "extend" his point about the fire-fuel relation as one that is relevant particularly for getting clear on the question of *selves*; as Nāgārjuna says, "the whole order (*krama*) of [the relation between] the self and its basis (*upādāna*)"—between, we might say, an intentional perspective and the impersonally described existents from which that is supposed to emerge—"is completely explained based on fire and fuel."[54]

Nāgārjuna here exploits a Sanskrit lexical point: the word *upādāna*, which can mean *fuel*, also refers (and this is perhaps the primary resonance for a Buddhist philosopher) to any of the various impersonal existents proposed as what is really "taken" for a self—any of the kinds of things, e.g., that Ābhidharmika philosophers proposed as ultimately existent *dharmas*.[55] Etymologically denoting any act of "appropriating" or "taking up," the word *upādāna* thus also refers to whatever *gets taken up*—to the "material out of which anything is made,"[56] or (as with fuel) what is "consumed" by the "appropriator" that is fire. It is, then, easy for a Sanskritic Buddhist to say the self's relation to its basic parts is just like that of fire to fuel; selves and fires, indeed, are commonly said to be the "appropriators" (*upādātṛ*) of their proper fields or "fuel" (*upādāna*).

By referring to the proper "order" or "sequence" (*krama*) of these relata, I take it that Nāgārjuna raises the question of their logical or conceptual priority—the question of which of these (appropriator or appropriated) is reasonably thought to *explain* the other. This can be generally understood as the question of what we are to say of the relation between conventional and ultimate truth; does the latter, in particular, *explain* the former? Or can the explanatory terms—those, for Dharmakīrti, distinguished by their causal efficacy as "ultimately existent" (*paramārthasat*)—themselves come into view only relative to the *intentional* level of description putatively explained thereby? It is, of course, the latter conclusion that Nāgārjuna advances by his characteristic critiques of basic categories. Just, then, as fire and fuel can only be individuated as such insofar as they are already relative to each other, so, too, the supposed ontological primitives to which Buddhists like Dharmakīrti would reduce the self—any of the kinds of things that can generally be referred to as *upādāna*—are themselves intelligible only relative to the very phenomenon they are posited to help us understand. With respect, then, to the question of which of these levels of description should be taken to have explanatory priority, Candrakīrti emphasizes Nāgārjuna's answer: "neither of them."[57]

The supposedly privileged, impersonal level of description—generally referred to as *upādāna*—is only intelligible, Nāgārjuna thus suggests, relative to the *personal* level of description (the one involving "selves") putatively explained thereby. This point is advanced, I suggest, by Nāgārjuna and Candrakīrti's characteristic deployment of one of their central terms of art, *upādāya prajñapti*. This term involves the idea that everything that can come into view is (as many render this) a "dependent designation," or as I have rendered this before (trying to avoid the idealist connotations of the first) a "relative indication."[58] Reference to this expression follows naturally from Nāgārjuna's invocation of *upādāna*, since the expression involves a gerund form (*upādāya*) of the same verbal root; the "*prajñapti*" in question can thus be understood as significantly qualified—as *having*, in some sense, *been appropriated*, having been "taken up."[59]

Taking seriously the root sense of *prajñapti* (from the causative stem of a verb meaning "know"), we can say the point is that any "making known" is always relative to some "taking up" of the matter—that anything's *coming into view* is always *relative to some perspective*. The force of the infinite verbal form *upādāya*, I would venture, is thus to suggest the always already "taken" character of anything we could want to explain; it is only *from some perspective*, only under some description, that anything can be individuated as "appropriator" and "appropriated." Insofar, however, as anything can thus be *taken* only as under one description or another (events don't describe themselves), any attempt to explain *our so taking things* is always already outstripped, already sublated, by the very thing (the very *taking*) we are trying to understand.

On this way of talking, the salient point of reference to a "taker" or "appropriator" (*upādātṛ*), as one among the constituents of any act of or appropriation or "taking up" (*upādāna*), is that this is something essentially subjective—something, more precisely, like *the perspective adopted* on whatever act of "appropriating" we are talking about, the perspective *from which* (for example) it makes sense to say it is just *this act of burning wood* whose realization is in view. Fire is the "appropriator" of fuel, then, in the sense that fuel only comes into view, is only "made known" (*prajñapyate*), from a perspective for which *fire* is also already in view. I'm thus suggesting that the point in similarly imagining the emergence of "selves" on the model of acts of "appropriating" is finally to emphasize that an intentional level of description is *always already* in play, is already "happening," in the very attempt to find out what intentionality really consists in.

Nāgārjuna can be understood to make just this point near the end of his foundational text, where, again ringing the changes on "appropriation," he concludes: "Thus, the self is not other than its appropriated basis (*upādāna*), nor is it itself the basis, nor does it exist without basis—nor, though, is there any certainty that 'it doesn't exist.' "[60] The first three alternatives are untenable for the same kinds of reasons seen in the fire-and-fuel discussion; insofar as these categories can come into view in the first place only *as related*, questions about *how* they are related—insofar as such questions presuppose, on Nāgārjuna's view, that the terms are autonomously intelligible—are already on the wrong track. But Nāgārjuna concludes by emphasizing that the right conclusion is not that the self therefore does not exist at all; insofar, rather, as it's only with reference to the perspectives that are "selves" that we could individuate anything as the *parts* thereof, reference to selves is unavoidable if we would make sense *even of these other things*—even if we would make sense, that is, of talk of Dharmakīrti's finally impersonal terms of analysis.

Expressing just this point, Candrakīrti thus elaborates the striking conclusion to Nāgārjuna's verse:

> How could that which is made known relative to (*upādāya*) the aggregates "not exist"? For the son of a barren woman, insofar as there is no such thing, is not made known relative to the aggregates; how, when there *is* a basis, does it make sense to say there is no appropriator? Therefore, its not being existent doesn't make sense, either; because of this, the judgment "there isn't a self" doesn't make sense, either.[61]

The twice-occurrent expression "made known" here renders Candrakīrti's *prajñapyate*, a verbal form of the same root that gives us *prajñapti*; the point is that the kinds of things that are such that they can be "made known" (can *come into view*) relative to other things are essentially different from altogether *nonexistent* things. Indeed, to *be* the sort of thing that could come into view under the right conditions, Candrakīrti suggests with his characteristic appeal to the phrase *upādāya prajñapti*, just is to exist as "really" as anything *can* exist. Nothing, then, that could be adduced as impersonally explaining persons could be thought more real than these, since it is only relative to persons that anything could so much as be individuated *as explaining them*; and "how, when there is a basis, does it make sense to say there is no appropriator?"

So, with respect to any candidates for the status of *upādāna*—for the status of an impersonal "basis" such as Buddhists like Dharmakīrti take to be what is *really* available to be "taken up" as a self—the Mādhyamika point is always that these are intelligible only relative to some "appropriator" (*upādātṛ*), relative to some *perspective on* whatever is being taken some way. And the point in emphasizing, as Nāgārjuna does, that there is no way to get "appropriator" and "appropriated" *into* relation unless they are already so—in emphasizing that what emerges, rather, is always *upādāya prajñapti*, an always already present "coming into view" that is relative to some already-in-play "taking" of things—is, on this reading, to emphasize the irreducibly dynamic character of all this. If it makes sense to individuate various impersonal goings-on (neurophysiological events, say) as figuring in a subject's perceptual experience of a sunflower—as, that is, the *upādāna* for this experience—the description of such goings-on will no longer be a description *of the same thing* if there is no reference also to the intentional level of description (the level that involves *somebody's seeing a sunflower*) supposedly explained thereby. There can therefore be no making sense of any claim to the effect that *ultimately an intentional level of description is unreal*, insofar as it can only be *at* such a level of description that the claim itself is intelligible.

The upshot of this is that while proponents of Madhyamaka surely mean (simply insofar as they are Buddhists) to have us understand ourselves very differently than we ordinarily do, they do not think it right to say that doing so could coherently consist in our understanding what there "really" is *instead of* the kind of thing we take ourselves to be. On the kind of noneliminative understanding of selflessness I thus take Mādhyamikas to advance, the point is neither that selves exist *nor* that they do not exist; properly understood, selves will be seen, rather, as the constitutively relative and dynamic kinds of thing of which neither affirmation makes sense. What it ought to mean, therefore, to say (with Siderits) that causation "necessarily involves elements of intentionality or conceptual construction"[62] is not that causality obtains only insofar as we think it does (only, that is, in our minds); it is to say, rather, that it cannot coherently be thought that enumeration of the episodic causes of any experience could tell us *what experience really is*, where intentionally describable experience—experience like *that of enumerating episodic causes!*—is itself constitutively *less real than* (is *explained by*) the causal factors thus specified. The reason for this, Nāgārjuna and Candrakīrti argue, is that it's just as true that any causal factors one could specify can themselves "come into view" only relative to the self as it is that the latter emerges only relative to the former; neither level of description can coherently be thought to have explanatory priority.

CONCLUSION: HOW TO THINK IT *REALLY TRUE* THAT THE LOGICAL SPACE OF REASONS IS INELIMINABLE

I've been arguing that some quintessentially Mādhyamika arguments can be understood as exemplifying the same basic logic as that evinced by what I have characterized as the argument from practical reason. Like the Mīmāṃsaka argument considered in the first half of this chapter, the Mādhyamika arguments show not only that something like a semantic or intentional level of description is ineliminable from any final account of what there is and what we are like, but particularly that this is shown by the performatively incoherent character of any claim to the contrary. These Mādhyamika arguments are generally to the effect that the claim from Dharmakīrti with which I introduced our consideration of Madhyamaka—the claim that he is entitled to think there are explanatorily primitive "ultimate existents," even though it's only from the point of view of the reduced level that he can say so—is performatively incoherent in just the way exploited by the Kantian argument.

On the Mādhyamika view of the matter, then, Dharmakīrti cannot coherently allow that his is just a conventionally true account and at the same time maintain that causal efficacy is the unique criterion of the real (and that the logical space of reasons must therefore be finally explicable in causal terms). As Candrakīrti argued with respect to Dignāga's peculiarly technical usage of ordinary words, it's incoherent to claim to offer a conventionally valid account while at the same time eschewing the conditions for the intelligibility of such an account—just as, on the argument from practical reason, it's incoherent to think we might explain away (with claims about the reducibility of intentionality) the very perspective from which such claims make sense. Mādhyamika arguments against the coherence of any supposed explanatory primitives thus aim to show that one cannot, without self-contradiction, say *what there really is* instead of the reasoning persons we take ourselves to be.

That the arguments considered in this chapter following some Mīmāṃsakas and Mādhyamikas are significantly similar is reflected by the extent of their commonly having purchase against Dharmakīrti's project.

Indeed, it has all along been among the points of my appeal to the Kantian idiom of McDowell to help us see, of these Indian arguments offered in support of totally different commitments, that they can usefully be characterized as similarly arguing that *theoretical* reason cannot coherently be thought to trump *practical* reason. They commonly recommend, that is, variations on the conclusion that performatively ineliminable features of practical reason are constitutively different from theories; as stances that it's not open to us to adopt or not adopt, they *cannot* be superseded in the way that theoretical commitments can be.

Insofar as these arguments commonly urge, in effect, that the direction of explanation is from *practical* reason to *theoretical* reason—that, in other words, we can have no more secure understanding of what *acting for reasons* is than we have in our own experience of ourselves as doing so—they can further be said to pick out something of the logical priority of the first-person perspective. The appeal to "practical reason," in other words, amounts to the thought that we cannot finally know anything more real about what reasoning is, about what it "really is" for a person to *take* things to be some way or another, than we already do in knowing this first-personally. No theoretical redescription can coherently be thought to supersede that, insofar as it is only with reference to our first-personal experience of reason that we can entertain the truth of any theory in the first place. The basic logic of these arguments, then, is to show that in attempting to *explain* something like practical reason—to explain our being linguistic, our having semantically contentful thought—we are, necessarily, always already exemplifying it.

Thus, the Mīmāṃsaka argument for the eternality of language exploits the paradoxical fact that we cannot imagine, first-personally, what it would be like to have nonconceptual, non*linguistic* experience—despite the fact of our all having *been* non- (or at least pre-) linguistic beings! Indeed, it's a striking fact that linguistically competent adults not only cannot remember but cannot *imagine* the phenomenology of a two-year-old.[63] There is something, then, *horizonal* about our linguistic being, to invoke a term from J. J. Valberg; what always necessarily transcends (encompasses, sublates) any account of semantic content, Valberg says, is "the fact that there *is* such a subject matter as our system of language-games." (Recall, here, Mīmāṃsaka claims about the always already *siddha*, "available," character of language.) Like subjectivity itself, this fact is essentially unlike other things we can know; to "discover" this is nothing like perceptually encountering particulars, insofar as what is here in view (Valberg continues) is "the existence of *that from within which* any such possibility holds: the 'horizon' (we shall say) of conceptual possibility" (2007, 10). It's an intuition like this, I think, that really lends the Mīmāṃsaka argument whatever cogency it has; Mīmāṃsakas can thus be said to have identified (with George Steiner) "the problems posed by the indissoluble bond of the examining process with the examined, the dynamics of instability which result from the need to use language in order to study language—these are very probably resistant to rigorous, let alone exhaustive, construction. This dilemma is at the root of epistemology" (1998, 115).

Surely the Mādhyamika point about the ineliminable character of conventionally real existents—the ineliminable character of existents as always *under some description*, as always *taken* from some conventionally experienced perspective—similarly amounts to the recognition that it can only be *from* a first-person perspective that one could know anything at all about what having such a perspective "really" consists in. The arguments I've sketched following some Mādhyamikas, then, can be thought to get a measure of cogency from the basic fact that no explanation *of* our first-personally taking things as some way or another could ever be more secure than *the very experience of so taking them*; this, finally, is the sense it makes to argue, with Mādhyamikas, that no explanation could tell us what experience (quite apart from how it seems) *really* is. Note, however, that thus to give up on saying what experience "really" is is not necessarily to give up on saying anything true in the matter; indeed, I suggest that Mādhyamikas are entitled to claim it is *really true* that there are no ultimately real (*paramārthasat*) existents. "The ultimate truth," as I've concurred with Mark Siderits in saying of the Madhyamaka view, "is that there *is* no ultimate truth." Just what this claim comes to, though, depends on how one explains its not being contradictory.

Siderits favors what he characterizes as a "semantic antirealist" reading of Madhyamaka, in support of which he accounts for the noncontradictory character of his signature formulation with reference to its involving an equivocation; the two iterations of "ultimate truth" here refer, that is, to two different kinds of things. On Siderits's semantic antirealist reading, these are: "ultimate truth$_1$: a fact that must be grasped in order to attain full enlightenment"; and "ultimate truth$_2$: a statement that corresponds to the ultimate nature of mind-independent reality." The basic claim of Madhyamaka then becomes that "the ultimate truth$_1$ is that there is no ultimate truth$_2$" (2007, 202)—that, in other words, the ultimate "fact that must be grasped" is that there is no "*statement that corresponds to the ultimate nature of mind-independent reality*." This can be taken to recommend the conclusion that proponents of Madhyamaka therefore do not affirm any claim about what is really the case, since there seems to be a contradiction involved in making a *statement* to the effect that there can be no "statement that corresponds to the ultimate nature of mind-independent reality." Siderits's is an antirealist interpretation, then, in the sense that he takes Mādhyamikas chiefly to deny that there is anything "really existent" such as could *make our statements true*; the focus on statements, I take it, is what it means that this is a *semantic* antirealism.

On my understanding of Mādhyamikas as most concerned to counter an *ontological* understanding of the "two truths"—as targeting particularly the Ābhidharmika sort of view on which these consist in conventionally and ultimately real *existents*—the claim I've endorsed following Siderits ("the ultimate truth is that there *is* not ultimate truth") looks rather different. In particular, Siderits's "ultimate truth$_2$" picks out, on my reading, not a kind of *statement* but a kind of *existent*. The formula would then be taken to assert not (as Siderits has it) that there can be no "*statement that corresponds to the ultimate nature of mind-independent reality*"; the formula says, rather, that it cannot make sense that there be ontological primitives, that there be anything that is what it is apart from everything else. I don't see that there are any obvious semantic problems in saying, then, that the ultimate "fact that must be grasped" is that *there can be no ontological primitives.*[64]

On my interpretation, Siderits's felicitous formulation still involves an equivocation, as the two iterations of "ultimate truth" refer to different things (it *really is the case* that there are no *ultimate existents*). The significant difference, as I see it, is that there is nothing that would tempt us to suppose there is any antirealism, on the part of Mādhyamikas, with regard to *the truth of their claim*. Rather than concede the term "realism," then, to those who posit explanatorily basic ontological primitives, and rather than argue that Mādhyamikas are therefore "antirealist" in countering thinkers like Dharmakīrti, I prefer to think of Mādhyamikas as challenging the very idea that truth could be grounded in causal constraint—and as doing so not in order to jettison the category of truth but only *that understanding thereof.* Insofar as Mādhyamikas thus refuse the kind of semantics presupposed by Dharmakīrti, there is no reason to think they have any special explaining to do in making sense of the possible truth of their own claims; to the extent, indeed, that a realist conception of truth is surely what is *conventionally* in play in all our discursive transactions, I see no reason to grant the "realist" characterization to Dharmakīrti and his ilk, or any reason to think it problematic for Mādhyamikas to hold that it is *really true* that there are no ultimately real existents.

More important for present purposes, though, is that Siderits takes the "realism" that Mādhyamikas supposedly eschew as defined chiefly in terms of "mind-independence"; ultimate truth, we saw him say above, is on the realist understanding to be defined in terms of correspondence with "mind-independent reality."[65] To the extent that satisfactory characterizations of the positions in play (as, e.g., "realist" or not) remain elusive, the tricky point may be the nature and status of this "mind-independence" criterion. If we grant this as the principally defining feature of realism, it may seem obviously to follow that of course Mādhyamikas are antirealists; for I have been arguing all along that the claims Mādhyamikas are finally most interested in are claims about *what persons are like*, and that their point about such claims just is that there is nothing it could make sense to say that persons, mind-independently—independently, I've been saying, of an intentional level of description—"really are."

This can, I concurred with Siderits in saying, be expressed as the point that even supposedly impersonal explanations thus turn out invariably to have "elements of intentionality or conceptual construction." I emphasized, however, that such a statement should not be confused with idealist claims to the effect that the world is just "conceptual constructions" all the way down; the context, rather, in which this characterization of Madhyamaka makes sense is precisely that in which we are asked to entertain reductionism not mainly about medium-sized dry goods but about *persons*. Just to the extent that the Madhyamaka project is as I have characterized it—just insofar as Mādhyamikas argue that the doctrine of selflessness is wrongly understood if taken to entail that an intentional level of description is eliminable—their point is that there *can be* nothing that experience "really is" apart from how it seems to us, apart from its always already being *taken* some way. The fact, however, that Mādhyamikas thus tackle claims particularly about intentionality does not entail that they are not entitled to think their own conclusions in this regard really true; Mādhyamikas effectively jettison the "mind-independence" criterion of truth not because they have given up on thinking their own claims *really true*, but precisely because the claims they are most interested in are claims *about persons*. There is, then, no incoherence in thinking it ultimately true that "there *is* no ultimate truth"; the fact that an intentional level of description is not, in principle, the kind of thing of which one could say *what it really is* is itself a fact about the way things really are.

But if we can thus make sense of Mādhyamika claims as *really true*, it nevertheless remains the case that philosophical intuitions differ regarding the significance of arguments to this effect, and one might reasonably wonder just what they get us. Just what kinds of conclusions are warranted by these various arguments from practical reason? In chapter 3, I concluded that the sense of John McDowell's characteristic position—the sense of his claim, e.g., that the logical space of reasons goes "all the way out"—comes down to the basically Hegelian point that anything we could know or think about "the other side" of that space would, ipso facto, already be within it. The same logic, I'm suggesting, is basically on display in the foregoing Mīmāṃsaka and Mādhyamika arguments; these Indian critiques of Dharmakīrti, too, effectively press against Dharmakīrti the point that anything he could say by way of explaining away our conceptual capacities can only be affirmed (in McDowell's words) "without moving outside the conceptual order—without doing more than employing our conceptual capacities."

Our resistance to the conclusion (*that language has no beginning*) Mīmāṃsakas drew from such considerations might encourage us, though, to ask whether that is a significant conclusion—or whether, e.g., it simply states a fact, irrelevant when one is theorizing about what really exists, about our essential epistemic finitude. Just what are we to suppose is the philosophical significance of the claim that practical reason trumps theoretical reason? To the extent that this amounts (as I've suggested) to a claim about the logical priority of the first-person perspective, mightn't this amount simply to the truistic claim that anything we could know can only be known *as known by us*?

To the extent that the foregoing Mīmāṃsaka and Mādhyamika arguments will admit of this restatement, their point might, among other things, be taken as very much like the point advanced by Dharmakīrti's *sahopalambhaniyama* argument. Nevertheless, there is an important difference. The self-awareness (*svasaṃvitti*) whose explanatory basicness Dharmakīrti takes to be shown by the *sahopalambhaniyama* argument is understood by him as eminently *nonconceptual*; he takes it that self-awareness immediately discloses something essentially momentary and hence causally describable. The Mīmāṃsaka and Mādhyamika arguments, in contrast, can be taken to show (albeit in very different ways) precisely that the *conceptual* realm—variously understood as (for Mīmāṃsakas) a realm of timeless linguistic relations or (for Mādhyamikas) as the "conventionally" described world than which there is nothing more real—is finally ineliminable from any account of what we are like, and that we are not entitled to think that efficient-causal explanations alone can tell us what is *really* existent. If there is a common and philosophically interesting discovery here—one such as possibly places a metaphysically significant constraint on "theoretical" reason—perhaps it has most basically to do with what Mark Johnston calls "the realm of sense, the realm of that in virtue of which things are intelligible" (2009, 128).[66]

There are, to be sure, many ways one might account for the ineliminable character of the "realm of sense." Mīmāṃsakas embrace an ontologically realist explanation, forcefully arguing that linguistic items and their relations to the world *really exist*. Mādhyamikas are, no doubt, up to something very different in arguing for the ineliminably *conventional* character of reality—though it is among the upshots of this, I've been urging, that they argue particularly for the ineliminable character of existents as always *under some description*, as always *taken* from some conventionally experienced perspective that is such that there can be no saying what it "really" is. The antireductionist arguments of these Mīmāṃsaka and Mādhyamika critics of Dharmakīrti, importantly divergent though they are in many respects, can nevertheless be understood as commonly representing different ways to argue that it's *really true* that there can be no "explanation" of the logical space of reasons—really true that reason is sui generis and ineliminable.

Whether, then, the claim is (with Mīmāṃsakas) that real universals belong in a final ontology or (with Mādhyamikas) that there cannot, in principle, *be* a final ontology specifying what there "really" is instead of persons, in either case we have claims—proposed as really true—to the effect that Dharmakīrti's cognitivist account of *what it is to be a reasoning person* cannot be correct. The arguments elaborated in this chapter converge, to that extent, on the thought that what it is to reason about any theory at all is just not the kind of thing about which one can coherently say that it is *really* something else—a point, I've been arguing all along, that cuts as much against Dharmakīrti as it does against contemporary physicalists.

Concluding Reflections

RELIGIOUS STUDIES AND PHILOSOPHY OF MIND

IN THE introduction, I noted a basic divide among philosophers of mind over whether the questions of their field are essentially *empirical* or *metaphysical* in character. Among the points centrally at issue in philosophy of mind has thus been whether the findings of cognitive-scientific research count as *answering* basic questions in philosophy of mind (such that with recourse to this research we might see, as in Dennett's provocative 1991 title, *Consciousness Explained*)—or whether, instead, essentially philosophical questions about mind are such that they will not, in principle, admit of *that kind* of answer. It has been among my concerns in the foregoing chapters to make a case for the reasonableness of the latter view—for the view that insofar as the project of "naturalizing" intentionality consists in advancing essentially causal explanations of the contentful character of thought, there is something about intentionality that *cannot* be accounted for thereby. What necessarily goes missing, on purportedly exhaustive causal accounts of the mental, amounts to a condition of the intelligibility of the accounts themselves; the facts that we can *mean* something by any of our claims, and that we can find ourselves persuaded of their *truth*—facts that are necessary conditions of any account's making sense—are essentially irreducible to causally describable functional states. Whether that be characterized in terms of Kantian "spontaneity," the normative character of meaning, or really existent linguistic universals, the fact remains that the logical space of reasons is sui generis—something compellingly reflected in the fact that any denial of this claim can itself be made intelligible only *within* the space of reasons.

Just what we are to conclude from the irreducibly semantic character of intentionality is, to be sure, a difficult question. This clearly does not warrant, for example, conclusions (surely at stake for some critics of physicalism) such as that we have souls that survive death, or that there exists a supernatural realm essentially beyond the purview of scientific inquiry. This is not, then, a critique of physicalism such as could advance Dharmakīrti's case for the reality of rebirth (though it's not mutually exclusive thereof, either). Insofar, rather, as the semantic character of intentionality represents an essentially *transcendental* condition of intelligibility—the logical or conceptual horizon of any conceivable act of inquiring about anything at all—it's not obvious just what constraints this imposes on our theorizing about what there is or what we are like.

I suggest that it does, however, tell us at least that any philosophical account on which *meaning* is not real cannot, ipso facto, be a complete account. Among the upshots of this is that any account on which causal efficacy is the unique criterion of the real—any account on which, as for physicalists, all that is real is spatiotemporally determinate particulars—cannot, in principle, capture everything there is to understand about us. One might conclude from this that we must (with the Mīmāṃsakas) admit linguistic abstractions into a final ontology, or (with Nāgārjuna and Candrakīrti) that the aspiration to enumerate all "real" existents cannot, in principle, be realized—or, as both of the foregoing entail, that we just do not understand causation, at least insofar as the supposed causal completeness of physics is integral to our idea thereof.[1] What cannot be doubted, in any case, is *that there is meaning*; this necessarily figures in our reasoning about anything at all (in our *being minded*) and is to that extent as certain as anything could be. Insofar as this fact essentially resists efficient-causal explanation—insofar, that is, as conceptual relations (not only *have* not but) *cannot* be reduced to causal transactions among particulars—any project that presupposes an ontology consisting only of such things cannot be made coherent.

To the extent, though, that philosophical intuitions sharply diverge over the significance of arguments to this effect, it's unlikely that the foregoing chapters will have been persuasive to, e.g., intransigent empiricists who are unmoved by transcendental arguments (though whether they are persuaded is, of course, logically independent of whether the arguments are sound). Nevertheless, one of my central aims in this book can have been achieved whether or not one is finally persuaded of the cogency of these arguments; that they commonly have purchase against physicalists like Fodor and idealists like Dharmakīrti is what I have been most concerned to show. Despite the seemingly sharp divergence between the projects of these thinkers, the significance of their shared presuppositions is considerable—a fact that surely reveals something interesting both about Dharmakīrti and about cognitive-scientific physicalism.

Thus, while Dharmakīrti takes the Buddhist project (and the possibility, in particular, of the Buddha's fathomless compassion) to require the reality of rebirth—which means, Dharmakīrti argues, that mental continua are not interrupted by bodily death, insofar as moments of mind cannot be thought to depend upon physical events—and while Fodor, in contrast, holds that intentionality is cognitive-scientifically explicable in terms of brain events, both thinkers evince what I have characterized as *cognitivist* views of the mind. Among the salient aspects of both projects, then, is the view that the mental will (indeed, *must*) admit of an exhaustively causal explanation—and, insofar as efficient-causal relations are local, that everything about the mental must therefore admit of characterization in terms of factors somehow internal to the subject. It is owing to this that these projects are commonly at pains to account for intentionality—and given this, the widely noted convergence of Buddhist and cognitive-scientific concerns may be so much the worse for some Buddhist philosophers.

Note, however, that thus to press against Dharmakīrti a cogent critique such as can also be directed at cognitive-scientistic philosophy of mind is not, ipso facto, to argue against Buddhist thought per se or even particularly against the Buddhist doctrine of selflessness (*anātmavāda*); while Dharmakīrti was taken by many subsequent Indian philosophers to epitomize "the Buddhist position" in matters philosophical, the fact that his is not the only reasonable working out of basic Buddhist commitments is compellingly reflected in my having been able to enlist, among his critics, his co-religionists Nāgārjuna and Candrakīrti. *That an intentional level of description is ineliminable*, then, does not necessarily count against the cardinal Buddhist commitment to selflessness; indeed, just insofar as they are Buddhists, Nāgārjuna and his philosophical fellow travelers mean for their arguments to be not only consistent with but to be *elaborations of* that commitment. The Mādhyamika recuperation of "conventional truth"—of the perspective from which it's possible to *mean* anything by Buddhist claims—cannot, to that extent, be understood as tantamount to the concession that there are, after all, selves.

Among the points to be made in understanding Madhyamaka as consistently elaborating Buddhist commitments is that Nāgārjuna's may not, after all, make sense as a Buddhist account just by itself; rather, the Madhyamaka project itself may be constitutively relative to the Abhidharma project against which it is framed. Suggesting just this point, many proponents of traditional Buddhist scholastic curricula held that one can grasp the Mādhyamika point *only after having entertained the Abhidharma project*; before it makes sense to appreciate the necessarily "empty" character even of the Buddhist tradition's explanatory primitives, one first has to have seen that what is ordinarily thought of as one's "self" will indeed admit of reductive analysis in terms of these.[2] Only having thus understood the failure of the concept of "self" can one entertain Mādhyamika critiques of these supposed ontological primitives in such a way as to appreciate what is the real point of Madhyamaka arguments—which is not only that we could not be "selves" but also that *nothing at all* could count as answering the question of what being a person "really is." Not only, then, are the foregoing engagements with Dharmakīrti in light of cognitive-scientistic philosophy not proposed as arguments *against basic Buddhist commitments*; they can, indeed, be taken to support the Mādhyamika case for thinking that the only thoroughly consistent elaboration of the Buddhist tradition's fundamental insight—the only one that fully takes account of what it means that really *everything* is dependently originated—is one, such as Nāgārjuna's, that recognizes that there can be no sense in saying what there *really* is instead of "selves."

While the arguments advanced here should not, then, be understood to cut against Buddhist thought per se, they do have purchase with respect to some recent trends in religious studies. In this regard, recent decades have seen an often salutary turn away from (what many take to be a characteristically Protestant) preoccupation with *doctrine* as the preeminently significant category for organizing religious phenomena. There are many reasons for this and many different things it has looked like thus to eschew questions of religious belief; the broadly Wittgensteinian thought that "being religious" (or using religious language) essentially consists in something other than assenting to certain propositions, for example, surely represents one influential impulse behind this trend, as do the increasingly voluminous reflections on the emergence of "religious studies" (and of the very category of *religion*) out of particular Euro-American theological and political agendas.[3] Then, too, there is the burgeoning discourse of cognitive-scientific studies in religion, many proponents of which aim to explain characteristically religious beliefs as epiphenomenal artifacts of the evolutionary history of mind.

Studies in the latter vein, of course, most explicitly involve the kinds of issues that have concerned us here. Representative in this regard is Ilkka Pyysiäinen, whose work, though much influenced by that of Pascal Boyer, appears to be more grounded in the literature of religious studies than Boyer (who, like many exponents of the cognitive-scientific program here, has no particular expertise in religious studies). But despite Pyysiäinen's evident familiarity with the literature in the field—his *Supernatural Agents: Why We Believe in Souls, Gods, and Buddhas* (2009) contains a fifty-one-page bibliography reflecting many of the seminally framing debates of religious studies and includes three pages' worth of editions and translations of Indian Buddhist texts—his work most saliently involves a battery of concepts that will be familiar to readers of Boyer and other cognitive-scientifically inclined critics of religion. Thus, characteristically religious beliefs are to be explained chiefly with reference to various cognitive "modules" or "mechanisms"—HADD ("hyperactive agent detection device"), for example, and HUI ("hyperactive understanding of intentionality")—that are evolutionarily advantageous insofar as they make humans inordinately inclined to imagine "agentive" causes of prima facie inexplicable events.

These cognitive-scientific posits represent a way to update an argument that is essentially the same as one ventured in Hume's 1757 *Natural History of Religion*; for Hume, too, insofar as "the *causes*, which bestow happiness or misery, are, in general, very little known and very uncertain, our anxious concern endeavours to attain a determinate idea of them; and finds no better expedient than to represent them as intelligent voluntary agents, like ourselves" (1757, 152). Run through the apparatus of current thinking in evolutionary biology and "social neuroscience," this becomes, in Pyysiäinen's hands, the argument that "religion is only a by-product of evolved cognitive mechanisms" (2009, 186)—that it's evolutionarily advantageous to be excessively apt to suppose that, say, rustling bushes signal predators (since the cost of being wrong here is lower than the cost of failure to detect threats), and that it's insofar as our neurocognitive architecture reflects that evolutionary fact that we spin the kinds of tales that get elaborated into full-blown religious traditions.

Whatever else might be said about Pyysiäinen's deployment of this idea to explain all manner of religious phenomena, the arguments of the foregoing chapters surely cut against presuppositions that are central to his approach. Revealingly, one of the most recurrent words in Pyysiäinen's

Supernatural Agents is "trigger"—as, for example, in the claim (made of one theologically abstract idea seemingly far removed from the "folk-psychological" notions that Pyysiäinen takes to underlie all religious ideas) that "'God is the ground of being' is a cognitively costly representation because it does not immediately *trigger any automatic inferential system* in a person's mind" (2009, 4; emphasis added). The reason, that is, why complex theological notions like Paul Tillich's idea of God as *the ground of being* are not widely found compelling is that these do not readily elicit the kinds of responses that go with such innate capacities ("HADD," etc.) as give rise to the "folk-psychological" intuitions that are more immediately compelling—and that ultimately underlie, Pyysiäinen holds, even such ramified developments as Tillich's theology.

The idea, however, that we know what it is for an "inferential system" thus to be "triggered"—an idea that recurrently figures, too, in Pascal Boyer's work[4]—is a sleight of hand; given the scientistic presuppositions characteristic of this work, what "triggered" really means is *caused*.[5] Reference, then, to the "triggering" of our conceptual capacities amounts to a promissory note to the effect that a causal account *of reasoning* can be given. Pyysiäinen makes, however, a significant concession in this regard: he allows, of "the received view in cognitive science"—the view that "conceptual knowledge is somehow transduced from sensory representations of experience in the brain"—that there is the problem that "so far no account of the possible mechanism of this transduction has been specified" (2009, 28). If the arguments of the foregoing chapters have any purchase, though, there is reason to think not only that no such account *has been* given but that none *could be* given; there is nothing it could look like to show, e.g., that *what Pyysiäinen is doing in arguing for his claims* will itself admit of the kind of causal explanation he is all about—not, at least, if we are to find intelligible the very idea of anyone's *being persuaded* by it.

But it's not only the patently scientistic program of Pyysiäinen, Boyer, et al. that invites this line of critique; Terry Godlove has argued that recently influential books like Talal Asad's *Genealogies of Religion* (1993) and Mark Taylor's *Critical Terms for Religious Studies* (1998) reflect a "new materialism in religious studies"—that there is, in these various approaches to religious phenomena, something conceptually similar to precisely such physicalist philosophies of mind as have focused our concerns here. The problem with these, Godlove argues, is their incoherent denial of the logical priority of *belief*. Whether, then, the relevant causes are taken to consist in psychosocial conditioning, economic pressures, the experienced naturalness of hegemonic representations, evolutionary trends, or events in the central nervous system, any purportedly exhaustive causal account of religious phenomena undermines its own entitlement to be taken as *true*; insofar as it's claimed that the semantic content of *religious belief* is demonstrably epiphenomenal, there can be no making sense, either, of the scholar's own belief in the truth of the analysis. This is not to say that all (or even most) of the things religious persons do are done *for reasons*; it is, rather, to argue (in terms suggested by the foregoing chapters) that characteristically religious activities, like all purposeful human actions, count as the kinds of thing they are only in virtue of its being at least *intelligible* that the agents thereof could attend to them under some reasoned description.

However well motivated the turn away from doctrinal studies in religion has been, then, that trend becomes incoherent if taken to show the eliminable character, in effect, of *an intentional level of description*. With respect, for example, to the reductively behavioristic "ritual studies" of Catherine Bell, Godlove says: "I do not see how—except by taking the agent herself to be taking herself to be pursuing religious ends—to situate her movements in a specifically religious context, and so to see her movements as religious" (Godlove 2002, 21–22). His point is the same one developed in the foregoing chapters: "intentionally" describable events (thinking, reasoning, experiencing, uttering a sentence, *performing a religious rite*) cannot be understood *as* what they are except in intentional terms. It surely picks out something significant to say, of someone who is uttering sentences, that she is producing acoustic disturbances by means of muscular movements, controlled breath, etc.—but we would not be understanding her *as* uttering a sentence so long as we do not also have the idea of her *meaning* something; similarly, the phenomena generally of interest to scholars of religion could not be the *kinds* of things they are except insofar as it is possible for the agents thereof to *take themselves* as acting under some description.

To the extent, however, that anybody's so taking herself necessarily implies the logically basic propositional attitude of *belief*—to act deliberately is, ipso facto, to *believe* that certain things are the case (that this is an act worth undertaking, that there are better and worse ways to do it, that it may contribute to one's salvation)—this category cannot coherently be thought eliminable from any complete understanding of *homo religioso*. While belief needn't be the organizing category for all projects in religious studies, it's incoherent to suppose there could be exhaustive understanding of human religious being without some reference to the content of religious beliefs;

to suppose otherwise is to jettison the conditions of the intelligibility of the scholar's *own* belief that she says something true.

The line of argument, then, that commonly cuts against Dharmakīrti and against contemporary physicalists is also illuminating with respect to recent trends in religious studies. While there may, to be sure, be something of value in cognitive-scientific and other programs of research in religion,[6] and while (I have emphasized) philosophical intuitions regarding the significance of this book's line of argument surely differ, it's clear at least that these deep-running philosophical issues are sufficiently far from settled that an overweening confidence in the explanatory power of cognitive science is altogether unwarranted. Indeed, the foregoing consideration of some arguments from first-millennium India, read in light of some modern discussions in philosophy of mind, suggests that notwithstanding staggering advances in the understanding of the human brain, it's still not entirely clear, when it comes to philosophy of mind, just what it is that we're talking about. When we have a thought that means or represents or is about something—about the Pythagorean theorem, about the current state of affairs in the Middle East, about how much we like the latest Wilco record, about whether *being religious* is an important (or worthwhile, or problematic) way to be—that thought is not *about* the proximate causes thereof, not *about* neurological events, visible marks on a page, or the acoustic waves that impact our sensory transducers. That we still do not have a clear understanding of just how that can be so should, I think, occasion astonishment.

Notes

INTRODUCTION

1. Brooks (2008); all quotations from Brooks are from this article. See also Dawkins (2006). The additional literature that could be cited in this vein is vast, but see especially Dennett (2006); Newberg, d'Aquili, and Rause (2001); Boyer (2001); and, for a critical assessment along lines that will be developed in the present book, Godlove (2002).
2. See, e.g., Lopez (2002, 2008a, 2008b); McMahan (2004, 2008).
3. See Smith (2008), which is framed in terms of Boyer (2001), as well as Smith (2009). For an overview of the Immanent Frame thread (collectively entitled "A Cognitive Revolution?"), see Cho (2008).
4. Carey (2005); further quotes here are from this article.
5. Brent Field's (2008) contribution to the Immanent Frame thread invokes this divide against Brooks: "For both pragmatic and philosophical reasons . . . it is clear that Brooks granted neuroscience an undeserved authority over metaphysics."
6. George Steiner makes the same point with respect to language and linguistics, which (we will see) involve questions inextricably related with questions in philosophy of mind; for Steiner, too, cognitive-scientific accounts of language represent "an empirical and not, necessarily, analytic step. We do not know *what* it is we are talking about, though our discourse may induce profitable, experimentally verifiable techniques of treatment" (1998, 298).
7. There is an increasingly voluminous literature in this vein. Among the most prolific contributors has been B. Alan Wallace (e.g., 2007); other exemplary (and highly various) contributions to this discussion include Lutz, Dunne, and Davidson (2007); deCharms (1998); Mansfield (2008); Davidson and Harrington (2002); Varela,

Thompson, and Rosch (1991). The Web site of the Mind & Life Institute (http://www.mindandlife.org) provides information on many publications, events, and conferences on the subject. We might also note Owen Flanagan's *The Really Hard Problem: Meaning in a Material World* (2007, esp. chap. 4); for my inquiry, too, the category of "meaning" (particularly as that figures in the idea of linguistic items as *meaning* what they are about) will turn out to be a "really hard problem," though my sense is that this is particularly so for cognitive-scientifically inclined philosophers such as Flanagan.

8. See chap. 1, note 11, for textual details.
9. Siderits reflects contemporary philosophical usage in urging that we distinguish "physicalism" from *materialism*, insofar as the latter also suggests "the view that the only worthwhile goal for persons is the attainment of material possessions and wealth. Physicalism makes no such claim, for it is not a theory about the good for humans. Physicalism is a strictly metaphysical view, namely that all that exists is physical in nature" (2001, 307–308). I follow this usage throughout the present book, though some of the thinkers to whom I refer instead say "materialist."
10. Siderits himself begins his piece by noting, "Indian Buddhism is decidedly anti-physicalist in outlook" (2001, 307).
11. The scare quotes flag the misleading character of this term; the prefix "re-" suggests," as in many Hindu versions of this idea, that some one thing (a self!) repeatedly undergoes the process of birth. On a Buddhist version of this idea, the point is that the causally continuous series of mental events is not interrupted by the death of the physical body and that this mental continuum can become associated, in future "lives," with all manner of different bodies. This idea is central to Siderits's proposed reconstruction of Buddhist thought in physicalist terms; invoking the computer metaphor that drives so much contemporary cognitive-scientific thought, he suggests that "rebirth might be the organic equivalent of using a Zip drive just before the final crash of the old computer, then installing selected files on a new machine" (2001, 310–311). Daniel Dennett suggests something like the same point: "If what you are is that organization of information that has structured your body's control system (or, to put it in its more usual provocative form, if what you are is the program that runs on your brain's computer), then you could in principle survive the death of your body as intact as a program can survive the destruction of the computer on which it was created and first run" (1991, 430).
12. For textual details, see chap. 1, note 5.
13. Urging an important distinction between "the scientific program and the philosophy that, according to some, supports it or, according to others, merely accompanies it," Descombes thus distinguishes between the *cognitive sciences* and *cognitivism*; the latter, he argues, "has been derived not from cognitive psychology but . . . from a particular philosophy" (2001, 66–67). For another nuanced characterization and critique of cognitivism, see Haugeland (1998, 9–45).
14. A case in point is the decades-long discussion initiated by Hilary Putnam's "Twin Earth" thought experiment; see Pessin and Goldberg (1996).

15. The centrality of *belief* among the propositional attitudes is reflected in the titles of many contributions to contemporary discussions in philosophy of mind—e.g., those of Stich (1983), Baker (1987; this gives Godlove the title for his 2002 reflections on the "new materialism in religious studies"), and Garfield (1988).
16. Sellars recognizes as much: "If we take seriously the idea that one and the same content can exist in many representings by many minds . . . we introduce a platonic theme—the contrast between a *one* which is shared and the *many* which share it" (1967, 62).
17. For Fodor, it is in a brain; Dharmakirti's account is harder to pin down, but he comparably holds (we will see in chapter 5) that cognition is autonomously intelligible.
18. For critical reflections on the sense of "naturalistic" conditions here, see Gasser (2007). As we will see in chapter 3, the question of what properly counts as "natural" is among the things centrally at issue in much of the contemporary debate.
19. See, for example, Siderits (2003, 157), *et passim*.
20. Note 13, above.

1. DHARMAKĪRTI'S PROOF OF REBIRTH

1. On Dignāga, see Hayes (1988); for overviews of Dharmakīrti's thought, see Dreyfus (1997), Dunne (2004), and Eltschinger (2010).
2. There is no complete translation of the *Pramāṇavārttika* into any modern language, and basic text-critical questions like the correct order of chapters remain open (see note 5, below); together with the fact that Dharmakīrti addressed intrinsically complex philosophical topics in the elliptical way typical of Sanskritic philosophy, this means consideration of Dharmakīrti's thought is unusually dependent on recourse to commentaries. I chiefly follow Manorathanandin's (fl. c. 950), largely owing to its availability in Sanskrit; Dunne (2004) excavates the earlier commentaries (extant only in Tibetan translation) of Śākyabuddhi and Devendrabuddhi, on whom Manorathanandin clearly relied. Unless otherwise noted, all translations from Dharmakīrti are my own.
3. Franco (1997, 132) comments to similar effect that Dharmakīrti's arguments for rebirth are chiefly "based on the nature of causality." My consideration of Dharmakīrti's arguments for rebirth owes much to Taber and Franco, as well as to Hayes (1993).
4. See note 13 of the introduction.
5. With many contemporary scholars, I follow Gnoli (1960, xv–xvi) in thus taking the *Pramāṇṇavārttika*'s order of chapters: (1) *svārthānumāna* ("inference for one's own sake"); (2) *pramāṇasiddhi* ("proof of *pramāṇa*"); (3) *pratyakṣa* ("perception"); (4) *parārthānumāna* ("inference for the sake of another"). This is counterintuitive, since (e.g.) it doesn't track the order of chapters in Dignāga's *Pramāṇasamuccaya* (on which the *Pramāṇavārttika* is ostensibly a commentary). Many modern editions—Sāṅkṛtyāyana (1938–1940), Shastri (1968), Miyasaka (1971–1972), Pandeya

(1989)—therefore follow some traditional authorities in reshuffling the chapters to align with the expected order; according to these editions, chapter 1 is *pramāṇasiddhi*, followed by the chapters on perception, inference for one's own sake, and inference for the sake of another. Though mostly citing Shastri (1968), I will number Dharmakīrti's chapters per Gnoli; this explains discrepancies with respect to two translations of the *pramāṇasiddhi* chapter from which I have benefited—those of Hayes (2004) and Franco (1997, 159–321). My own references to verses in this chapter correspond exactly to Franco's, but are off by two verses vis-à-vis Hayes—who, using an edition that takes *pramāṇasiddhi* as chapter 1, includes the *Pramāṇavārttika*'s two dedicatory verses at the beginning of this chapter.

6. Commentators take the *pramāṇasiddhi* chapter to be structured as elaborating the epithets with which the beginning of Dignāga's *Pramāṇasamuccaya* glorifies the Buddha; on this, and on possible senses of the characterization "*pramāṇabhūta*," see Franco (1997, 15–43).
7. See, e.g., *Nyāyabindu* 1.4 (Malvania 1971, 40).
8. At *Nyāyabindu* 1.5 (Malvania 1971, 47), Dharmakīrti defines the "conception" (*kalpanā*) that perception lacks as "thought whose phenomenal content (*pratibhāsa*) is suitable for association with discourse."
9. Against the characterization of Dharmakīrti as an empiricist of the kind I take him to be, see Dreyfus (1996). Tillemans (2003, 101–102, 121n31) questions Dreyfus's interpretation here along lines that I, too, would press; see, e.g., chapter 4, note 14.
10. Regarding Dharmakīrti's revisions of Dignāga's thought, consider Hayes's survey (1988, 15) of views that many modern scholars have followed Th. Stcherbatsky in mistakenly attributing, based on reading Dharmakīrti, to Dignāga.
11. *Pramāṇavārttika* [3].3 (Shastri 1968, 100). We will see, in the fourth section of our chapter 6, that Dharmakīrti himself importantly qualifies this point—and that whether he can coherently do so is debatable.
12. Translated from the Sanskrit in Steinkellner (1967, 1:37); for Steinkellner's German translation of the same, see 2:37.
13. See, e.g., Jackson (1985).
14. See, inter alia, Boucher (1991), who gives a Pali version of this famous utterance at 7.
15. See, inter alia, Houben (1995, 257–262); Halbfass (1992, 91–92). Thus to credit universals with *upacārasattā* is not, for Bhartṛhari, to say they are not real; indeed, his view is that it is this "realm" of being that is finally *most* real.
16. It's important to acknowledge the misleading character of these traditional doxographic terms; "Sautrāntika," especially, seems to have been applied by later Indian commentators (and, following them, by many Tibetans) in ways that better served their own systematic concerns than they serve our understanding of any self-identified Sautrāntikas; cf. Cabezón (1990). Nevertheless, Franco (1997, 73–74) reasonably notes the "quasi unshakable" character of these traditional characterizations, and it will not be out of place for us to use them here.
17. Dunne (2004, 59). For Dunne's complete development of the "sliding-scale of analysis" idea, see 53–79; for a critique, see Kellner (2005).

18. Dunne is not unaware of the sense of the qualifier "epistemic," and his explanation (2004, 59–60n) identifies the same point I'm presently making; his characterization of "epistemic idealism" as the view that "all entities are mental" suggests, however, the stronger, metaphysical point—which, I think, is also suggested by taking "epistemic idealism" to distinguish the "Yogācāra" perspective from "Sautrāntika."
19. My characterizing Dharmakīrti as generally "adopting" an empiricist perspective should not be understood to suggest he ever abandons it; on the view that Dharmakīrti's "Sautrāntika" and "Yogācāra" perspectives are *epistemologically* the same, the point is that even if his claims will be understood differently depending on which perspective we take to be in play, there is little he says from a "Sautrāntika" perspective that he needs to take back when he declares for Yogācāra.
20. On *pratyakṣa*'s use as an adjective (here modifying *arthaḥ*), see Arnold (2005, 177, 277n8).
21. I thus render *anvaya* and *vyatireka* here as, respectively, "presence" and "absence"; I will discuss this further in the fourth section of this chapter.
22. Sanskrit text in Steinkellner (2007, 2, lines 7–11).
23. *Pramāṇavārttika* [3].224 a–b (Shastri 1968, 168).
24. So Manorathanandin, at [3].224c–d: "that being the case, things like the senses, too, because of their also being causes, would be apprehendable" (Shastri 1968, 168).
25. *Pramāṇavārttika* [3].224 c–d (Shastri 1968, 168); cf. the translations of Dunne (2004, 85) and Dreyfus (1997, 383).
26. On the *Ālambanaparīkṣā*, see Tola and Dragonetti (1982), who give, along with a translation, the Tibetan translation and Sanskrit fragments of Dignāga's text, as well as Chu (2006).
27. *Ālambanaparīkṣā* 6, translated from the Sanskrit as preserved in Kamalaśīla's *Tattvasaṃgrahapañjikā* (given by Tola and Dragonetti 1982, 107).
28. See *Ālambanaparīkṣā* 7b (Tola and Dragonetti 1982, 127) for this sense of "cause." Here, the claim is that any "knowable form which is internal" has a "capacity" (*śakti*; Tib., *nus pa*) that creates a further such form.
29. See *Ālambanaparīkṣā* 7a (Tola and Dragonetti 1982, 127). The sense of "cause" in play on this reading is rather like the Ābhidharmikas' *sahabhūhetu*—the kind of "cause" (*hetu*) which simply goes "with [something's] being" (*sahabhū*); see *Abhidharmakośa* 2.50c–d (Pradhan 1975, 83), where Vasubandhu gives the relation between "characteristic" and "characterized" as among the examples of this. See, as well, Meyers (2010, 115–127). I have benefited from conversations on this with Sonam Kachru.
30. Quoting Eltschinger (2010, 430), who has a helpful discussion of Dharmakīrti's qualified divergence from Dignāga in this regard.
31. This expression of the contrast comes in Dharmottara's comments (at Malvania 1971, 69) on Dharmakīrti's consideration of why *yogipratyakṣa*—the "perception"

cultivated by yogic practice—can, despite the subject's agency in its cultivation, reasonably count as an instance of perception. (Cf. Woo 2003; Dunne 2006.) Dharmottara here urges that *yogipratyakṣa* counts as genuinely "perceptual" just insofar as it is distinguished by the same kind of phenomenological vividness that characterizes sensory perception. John Locke advances strikingly similar intuitions about phenomenological vividness as a clue to the distinctively *caused* character of perceptual awareness; see Locke (1689, 632).

32. Translated from Malvania (1971, 74).
33. Dharmottara is here commenting on *Nyāyabindu* 1.14, which says simply that "only that"—*viz.*, the *svalakṣaṇa* indicated in verse 13—"is ultimately existent" (*tad eva paramārthasat*); Malvania (1971, 75).
34. *Pramāṇavārttika* [3].247 (Shastri 1968, 175). This passage's status as a *locus classicus* for Dharmakīrti's view is reflected in its citation by the later Buddhist philosopher Mokṣākaragupta (fl. c. 1100), who adduces it as warranting his own straightforward statement of the account: "A cognition apprehending an object is an effect of the object; for the object, insofar as it is being apprehended, is a cause of the cognition" (translated from Singh 1985, 21). The same passage is also cited (with slight variations) in the *Sarvadarśanasaṃgraha*; see note 36, below.
35. While treating a late invocation of the distinction between *sākāra-* and *nirākāra-vāda* that is itself internal to Yogācāra debates, Kajiyama (1965, 389) reflects the pan-Indic use of the terms in noting that "*nirākāravāda* is held by the Nyāyavaiśeṣika, Mīmāṃsaka, Jaina, and the Vaibhāṣikabauddha" (all of these being "realist" schools), while some form of *sākāravāda* is common to "Sāṃkhya, Vedānta, as well as the Sautrāntikabauddha."
36. So Mādhava (here representing what he takes to be Dharmakīrti's perspective): Reference to mental representations as foundational is not problematic "since, when there is a cognition that [seems to have been] produced by an object in contact with the senses, there is evidence of that object's being inferable by virtue of its being capable of projecting its own appearance, and through the appearance [thus] projected" (translated from Abhyankar 1978, 36). It is following this passage that the last of the foregoing passages from Dharmakīrti (note 34, above) is adduced.
37. *Abhidharmakośa* 4.1a–b (Pradhan 1975, 192). See also Schmithausen (2005, 50, n92); Sanderson (1994, 33); Heim (2003, 531). *Cetanā* is derived from the verbal root √*cint* (to think, be aware, etc.); standard dictionary equivalents include (per Monier-Williams) "consciousness, understanding, sense, intelligence," etc. For further reflections on the category of *cetanā*, see Meyers (2010, esp. chap. 5).
38. I mean by this parenthetical insertion to draw attention to the shift that makes a characteristically Buddhist move toward idealism seem natural. Thus, the intuitively plausible soteriological intuition here is that *how we think* shapes *what we experience*; when that intuition is made the basis of a complete worldview, it can become, as well, an explanation of (what is a logically distinct matter) *what there is to be experienced*. On this point, see Schmithausen (2005, 49–56); Griffiths (1986, 82).

39. So Sanderson (1994, 33), who says of such Ābhidharmika accounts as Dharmakīrti is heir to that "karmic retribution is explained as the culmination of a gradual change in a chain of momentary mind-events initiated by the action [*cittasamtānaparināma*]. The dichotomy between (mental) intention and (material) deed is rejected: there is only intention, latent and active."
40. See note 43, below, for the complete verse that begins this argument.
41. Dharmakīrti's argument here is significant since, insofar as he proposes that only perception and inference have the status of "*pramāṇas*," he wants to avoid allowing that Buddhist scriptures are authoritative in and of themselves; that would be to allow (as some Indian schools of thought held) that the testimony of a tradition could be intrinsically authoritative.
42. This names the supposedly "heterodox" school of materialist skeptics in India. On the likely identity of Dharmakīrti's imagined interlocutor, see Franco (1997, 95–105).
43. This verse well exemplifies the characteristic concision of Dharmakīrti (and the consequent need for commentarial help); in four quarter-verses of eight syllables each, Dharmakīrti thus encapsulates this dialectical progression: "The proof is compassion. This is based on repetition. If it's objected that repetition is unestablished because of thought's dependence upon the body, we deny it based on a refutation of this dependence." (*Pramāṇavārttika* 2.34; text in Shastri 1968, 20, where the verse is numbered 1.36, for reasons explained in note 5, above). Cf. the translations of Franco (1997, 159) and Hayes (2004, 38).
44. *Pramāṇavārttika* 2.35–36a (Shastri 1968, 20–21); cf. Franco (1997, 166); Hayes (2004, 39).
45. Manorathanandin thus glosses Dharmakīrti's *sajātinirapekṣāṇāṃ* ("independent of the same kind"): "independent of a multitude of breaths, etc., which are of the same kind, preceding [the present ones], existing as causes" (*kāraṇabhūtapūrvasajātiprāṇādipuñjanirapekṣāṇāṃ*; Shastri 1968, 20).
46. The status of this last condition as somewhat "up for grabs" is reflected by its later being equated with the *ālayavijñāna* (the nonintentional substratum or "storehouse" consciousness) posited by Yogācāra thinkers.
47. On this idea (and, more generally, on philosophical problems having to do with Buddhist attempts thus to explain continuity), see Griffiths (1986).
48. Among the issues that have occasioned much debate with respect to the category of *mānasapratyakṣa* is how (or even whether) it differs from *svasaṃvitti*; for more on this, see chapter 5. On Dharmottara's reading, however, its status seems not to be of particular consequence; see, on this point, the comment of Stcherbatsky (1958, 28–29, n3).
49. Dennett deploys the "Cartesian theater" metaphor throughout his *Consciousness Explained* (1991).
50. Translated from Malvania (1971, 57).
51. As in *sam-an-antara-pratyaya*, which is thus analyzed as involving a privative affix.
52. Translated from Malvania (1971, 58). Compare Kajiyama (1998, 45), translating a parallel passage from Mokṣākaragupta. Also useful on these issues is the discussion in Mookerjee (1975, 311–318).

53. *Pramāṇavārttika* 2.39 (Shastri 1968, 22, where the verse is numbered 41); cf. the translations of Hayes (2004, 41) and Franco (1997, 186).
54. *Tasmān na tadāśritā buddhiḥ* (Shastri 1968, 22).
55. The asymmetry here is raised as an issue, as well, in the *Nyāyabindu*'s discussion of *manovijñāna*. There, the worry is that *manovijñāna* (which, recall, is the word by which Dharmakīrti refers to *mānasapratyakṣa*, "mental perception") could not count as a *pramāṇa* insofar as it its object seems to be the same as that of the sensory cognition—in which case, it could not be thought to yield any new content, which is among the criteria for any cognition's being a *pramāṇa*. Dharmottara explains (at Malvania 1971, 61), though, that the object of an instance of *manovijñāna* is not, in fact, precisely the same as the object of a sensory cognition; while the latter apprehends only the object itself, the mental sense faculty cognizes that object *as represented by the sense faculty*—which just is to say that it cognizes an instance of sensory "*vijñāna*."
56. See, e.g., Jackson (1993, 230n). Hayes (1993, 120–121) suggests that Dharmakīrti's argument here might also run afoul of some Buddhist views, on which the "heart" (*hṛdaya*) is reckoned as the physical basis of thought.
57. *Pramāṇavārttika* 2.48b–3 (Shastri 1968, 25, where the verse is numbered 50); cf. the translations of Franco (1997, 217) and Hayes (2004, 48).
58. See also Franco (1997, 217ff.), for a lengthy unpacking of this verse.
59. Franco notes, in this regard, that "although the commentaries take the notion of karma to be implied on several occasions, Dharmakīrti himself never uses the word in his proof of rebirth (vv. 34–119)" (1997, 71). He suggests that Dharmakīrti may be "trying to prove rebirth without having recourse to the notion of karma, perhaps because it was unacceptable to the Cārvākas. . . . Yet the role of karma in rebirth is certainly not denied" (72).
60. Translated from Shastri (1968, 25).
61. See note 38, above.
62. Prajñākaragupta's Sanskrit (*karmâiva cetanālakṣaṇam yat param avaśiṣyate*) can be found in Sāṅkṛtyāyana (1953, 57); I have followed Franco's translation (1997, 181), along with his proposed textual emendation (1997, n5).
63. Manorathanandin on *Pramāṇavārttika* 2.36a (translated from Shastri 1968, 21, where the verse is numbered 37); cf. Franco (1997, 105ff.).
64. Translated from Shastri (1968, 21). We will note in concluding that it is significant, given Dharmakīrti's commitments, that the argument thus demonstrates the reality only of *previous* births; given his particular focus on causal explanations, Dharmakīrti may lack the conceptual resources for showing, as well, that this entails the reality of *future* rebirths.
65. *Pramāṇavārttika* 2.51a–b; translated from Shastri (1968, 26), where the verse is numbered 53); cf. the translations of Franco (1997, 234) and Hayes (2004, 50).
66. This is O'Rourke's formulation (2008) of one of the "trenchant objections" to so-called animalist accounts of the person.
67. *Pramāṇavārttika* 2.52 (I here translate from Pandeya 1989, 16, which differs slightly from Shastri 1968, 27); cf. the translations of Franco (1997, 237ff.) and Hayes (2004, 51).

68. This is Franco's translation (Franco 1997, 271) of a passage from Prajñākaragupta's commentary on verses 56–57; Sanskrit at Sāṅkṛtyāyana (1953, 76).
69. Adapted from Franco's translation (1997, 291) from part of Prajñākaragupta's commentary on verse 62; Sanskrit at Sāṅkṛtyāyana (1953, 78).
70. Griffiths (1986) offers an insightful study of the philosophical problems here in play.
71. Adapted from Franco's translation (1997, 291); Sanskrit at Sāṅkṛtyāyana (1953, 78).
72. Adapted from Franco's translation (1997, 292) from Prajñākaragupta's commentary on verse 62; Sanskrit at Sāṅkṛtyāyana (1953, 89).
73. On this point, see Kapstein (2001, 161–177, esp. 169–170).
74. See p. 37.
75. See Franco (1997, 109). Manorathanandin joins other commentators in so reading 36b–d.
76. Verses 36b–37 press the physicalist's own commitments against him, arguing that if a physicalist is willing to credit material factors with the capacity to produce awareness, then he has no grounds for thinking they no longer have that capacity after death. See Shastri (1968, 21), Franco (1997, 173, 180), and Hayes (2004, 40). I do not see that Manorathanandin (whose account is translated by Franco 1997, 110) makes good on his claim that this is said in order to establish the series of future births; it seems clear from the commentarial divergence that this reading of 36b–d is strained.
77. See chapter 4, note 25.
78. See p. 32.
79. Franco (1997, 120); see also Franco (2007). The complete verse says: "That is a cause whose presence (*sattā*) assists [in realizing the effect in question], due to its always being connected to that [effect]; and because of that, it was said [by the Buddha that a cause is identified either by the] seventh, [i.e., locative case, or by saying] 'due to its arising.'" Translated from the Sanskrit at Shastri (1968, 26), where the verse is numbered 51; cf. the translations of Franco (1997, 227) and Hayes (2004, 49).
80. Translated from the Sanskrit at Shastri (1968, 26). It seems a bit strained to suggest, with Manorathanandin, that Dharmakīrti thus means to say that it is particularly the *producer* (*nirvartaka*) of a thing that is really the cause and not only the "auxiliary factors" (*upakārā*), for Dharmakīrti's verse actually makes explicit reference to *upakāriṇī* and none to anything like "*nirvartakatva*." See Franco (1997, 230) on some of the difficulties in this verse and commentaries thereon.
81. Cf. Hayes (1988, 119ff.).
82. For the Sanskrit grammatical tradition, according to Cardona (1967–1968, 345), these terms thus pick out "the constant co-occurrence (*sāhacarya*) of a linguistic item (*śabda*) and a meaning (*artha*). A meaning is not understood unless the item expressing it occurs; if an item occurs a meaning is understood, and when that item is absent the meaning attributed to it is also absent."
83. See pp. 25–26.

84. For more on Dharmakīrti's attempt (in effect) to make causal inferences rather more "deductive" in character, see Hayes and Gillon (2008), Gillon (2009), Inami (1999b), and Lasic (2003).
85. See Schueler (2003, 31–32). I am much indebted to John Taber for having brought this book to my attention.
86. Hence, perhaps, Manorathanandin's straining to say that Dharmakīrti's verse should be understood as picking out a "*nirvartaka*" factor and not merely an "*upakāraka*" one (see note 80, above).

2. THE COGNITIVE-SCIENTIFIC REVOLUTION

1. Boghossian's worry about problematically having to accept the "essential incompleteness of physics" presumably reflects his endorsement of the view that "the realm of the physical is causally complete"; this is among the premises that Harbecke (2008, esp. 18) takes to figure in the "canonical" formulation of the problem of mental causation.
2. See, e.g., Hanna (2010).
3. Cf. Descombes's observation that "an intentional phenomenon is at work whenever a disposition of things can be seen not as the result of the history of each of these things taken separately, but as the result of a thought that embraces an entire set of facts" (2001, 26).
4. He adds: "it is easy to get confused here, because the term 'cause' seems often to be used by philosophers to apply to what are in fact efficient causes. So it is easy to think that in the ordinary, minimal sense 'cause' really *means* 'efficient cause'" (2003, 18).
5. For an essentially similar argument, see Fodor (1985, 77–78), discussed at p. 63, below.
6. See chap. 1, p. 46.
7. So Schueler: "advocates [such as Davidson] of the non-teleological belief-desire explanatory strategy stick firmly" to the view that *the agent's reason* refers to the *mental state* of an agent rather than to "the *contents* of this state, that is to what the agent himself would say or think were his reasons" (2003, 58).
8. Cf. Descombes (2001, 75ff.) on the importance of the decisive shift involved in "getting us to take the attribution to someone of a belief or desire . . . for an attribution of a state."
9. Davidson's position on this is complex, and a thorough characterization of his views would involve elaborating the later position he calls "anomalous monism." Davidson allows that this later view is "*consistent* with the (epiphenomenalist) view that the mental properties of events make no difference to causal relations" but denies that it "*implies* the causal inertness of the mental" (1993, 196).
10. As Fodor puts this at one point, insofar as mental content is "broad," in the sense of being *about* states of affairs out in the world, "behavior is only determined by con-

tent taken *together with modes of presentation*" (Fodor 1994, 50). By instead attending to "narrow" content as explanatorily basic, Fodor means precisely to attend to interior "modes of presentation."

11. Addressing Locke, Leibniz says that insofar as one conceives *similarities* among things, "you are conceiving something in addition [to the things themselves], and that is all that universality is. You will never clearly present any of your arguments without making use of universal truths" (1765, 485).
12. See Rorty (1979, esp. 139–148); see also Bennett (1971, 25). Of his empiricist predecessors, Fodor says to similar effect that since they assumed "the mechanisms of mental causation . . . to be associationistic (and the conditions for association to involve pre-eminently spatio-temporal propinquity) . . . [they] had no good way of connecting the *contents* of a thought with the effects of entertaining it. They therefore never got close to a plausible theory of thinking" (1985, 91). Elaborating his notion of "Thought" (*Gedanke*), Frege particularly opposes Locke's "Ideas": "What is a content of my consciousness, my idea, should be sharply distinguished from what is an object of my thought" (1956, 306). Frege's "thought," then, denotes the intersubjectively available *content* of acts of judging, in contrast to Locke's "Ideas," which denote the particular mental events *bearing* that content.
13. Following Descombes (2001, esp. 164–167).
14. He continues: "Because, to all intents and purposes, syntax reduces to shape, and because the shape of a symbol is a potential determinant of its causal role, it is fairly easy to see how there could be environments in which the causal role of a symbol correlates with its syntax. It's easy, that is to say, to imagine symbol tokens interacting causally in virtue of their syntactic structures." On the senses of "syntax" and "semantics" (and other key ideas also in play) here, see Block and Rey (2008).
15. See chapter 1, pp. 26–28.
16. For illuminating reflections on the issues and perspectives here in play, see Wetzel (2008).
17. For an influential critique of the idea of "narrow content," see Burge (1979).
18. McDowell is here characterizing "the physicalistic modern version of the insistence on autonomy" that he takes to qualify cognitivist accounts as "fully Cartesian."
19. For an avowedly eliminativist account, see Churchland (1981).
20. Thus, on Curtis Brown's presentation of the causal argument for narrow content, the initial premise (denied by eliminativists) is that "mental states causally explain behavior by virtue of the content they have"; the second is that "the causal powers of an entity, its capacity to produce effects, must be intrinsic features of the entity. Thus twins, who share all their intrinsic properties, must share their causal powers." The last premise is just that "broad content does not characterize intrinsic features, at least not essentially; thus twins need not share broad contents." If we are to retain the idea of mental content as explaining anything, it is simply the case "that mental states must have narrow contents, contents that are shared be-

tween twins" (Brown 2007, following Fodor 1987). The argument is easily reversed by proponents of eliminative physicalism, such that any inconsistency among the premises is taken to show the falsity of the first premise.

21. Brown (2007) characterizes this line of argument as one "from introspective access."
22. See also Fodor (1994, 43–48).
23. Bermúdez comments to similar effect: "One question that anyone who seeks to employ the distinction between personal and sub-personal levels must answer is how they are related. If it is thought that explanation at both levels is genuine explanation, then we shall need to know whether what is being explained is the same at both levels, or whether the things explained are distinct" (1995, 365–366).
24. Fodor recognizes the difficulty: "What's harder to argue for (but might, nevertheless, be true) is . . . that the formality condition *can* be honored by a theory which taxonomizes mental states according to their content" (1980, 291). His main answer to this worry, though, is effectively just to invoke the computer metaphor: "That taxonomy in respect of content *is* compatible with the formality condition, plus or minus a bit, is perhaps *the* basic idea of modern cognitive theory" (1980, 292).
25. There is thus, McDowell says, a real question whether we are "entitled to characterize its inner facts in content-involving terms—in terms of its seeming to one that things are thus and so—at all" (1998, 242–243).
26. This is one of the main arguments we will develop in chapter 3. The image of cognitive "suicide" is developed by Baker (1987, chap. 7).
27. For an argument to the effect that Fodor's concession here is not significant, see Aydede (1997).
28. This could be imagined, e.g., along lines suggested by Chomsky.
29. Effectively emphasizing the reference here to particulars, Garfield characterizes Fodor as treating not *propositional* attitudes but *sentential* attitudes; that is, Fodor's is an account according to which the propositional attitudes, "like overt utterances, are biologically instantiated relations *of individuals* to concrete inscriptions of sentence tokens" (1988, 51; my emphasis).
30. Cf. chap. 1, pp. 26–28.
31. Cf. Baker (1987, 93).
32. See also Fodor (1994)—and, for more significant revisions in his thinking, Fodor (2008).
33. Despite Dennett's thus being avowedly "realist" about the propositional attitudes, his eschewing the centrality of the problem of mental causation leads Fodor to characterize him as an *anti*realist, since Fodor's view is that only *being causally efficacious* could make any mental event "real"; see Fodor (1985, 79ff.).
34. The importance for Dennett of a third-person perspective is reflected in his behavioristic commitment to what he calls (with a deliberate attempt to eschew "Cartesian" phenomenology) *heterophenomenology*—the idea that a subject's reports of her own states represent relevant data only insofar as they are regarded as *objective* data on an equal footing with all other such data. See, e.g., Dennett (2003).

35. Schueler: "my explanations of the actions of others in terms of their reasons have as their essential explanatory element that I regard them as doing as I do when I act. That is the central, and essential, explanatory mechanism of such explanations. If this is correct, then clearly it makes sense of the idea that the first person case is prior" (2003, 160). For a similar critique of Dennett, see Bennett and Hacker (2003, 426 [§§ vi–vii]).
36. Of course, Dennett's point in so characterizing his view is to deny what is thus "apparently" the case; I'm suggesting, though, that his account's being finally an *instrumentalist* account of belief is problematic and that his neglect of the constitutively first-personal character of the intelligibility of reason does indeed make his a finally shallow criterion.
37. Compare the dilemma identified by Baker: "On the one hand, if there is something that eludes the physical stance, then Dennett's instrumentalism is imperiled; on the other hand, if nothing eludes the physical stance, then Dennett's intentionalism cannot play its assigned role" (1987, 162).

3. RESPONSIVENESS TO REASONS AS SUCH

1. This line of argument is perhaps most associated with Thomas Nagel, who argues that the subjective character of any conscious organism's experience consists in there being "something that it is like to *be* that organism—something it is like *for* the organism" (1974, 436)—and that *what it's like for the subject* is something essentially different from anything to be said from a third-person perspective. The recently influential work of Chalmers (1995) and Levine (1983, 2001) suggests that there is still a flourishing philosophical project that takes its bearings from this point.
2. On the convergence of some characteristically "continental" and "Anglo-American" concerns in this regard, see Kelly (2001).
3. On the issues raised by the passages here considered (and the whole trajectory of thought initiated by Brentano), see Passmore (1957, 175–202).
4. Cf. Chisholm (1960).
5. John Searle notes in this regard that "intentional states represent objects and states of affairs in exactly the same sense that speech acts represent objects and states of affairs"—but emphasizes that "language is derived from Intentionality, and not conversely. The direction of *pedagogy* is to explain Intentionality in terms of language. The direction of *analysis* is to explain language in terms of Intentionality" (1982, 260). Boghossian (1989, 510) remarks that while in Britain the Sellarsian view generally holds sway, the prevailing view in the United States tends instead to be that (with Searle) "linguistic expressions acquire their semantic properties by virtue of being used with certain intentions."
6. As of December 2010, there were 2,525 items on "Intentionality" in David Chalmers's online bibliography of philosophy of mind (http://consc.net/mindpapers).

For an amusing and illuminating discussion of something of the range of contemporary options, see Haugeland (1998, 127–170).

7. Brentano's approach to intentionality itself reflects some peculiarly "humean" (and more generally British-empiricist) tendencies; indeed, Brentano himself took Locke as one of his principal precursors—see Rollinger (2008, 15n).
8. For these different terms, see *Critique of Pure Reason*, A108, B132, B157. In citing Kant's first *Critique*, I follow the standard convention of referring to the pagination of the first ("A") and second ("B") German editions; the translation I've used (Kant 1781–1787) is Guyer and Wood's.
9. This is the title of McDowell's Woodbridge Lectures (1998b) as well as of a collection of essays (2009a) that includes a revised version of those lectures. The extent to which my reading of Kant is influenced by McDowell will become clear in this chapter.
10. As Kant says, "the same function which gives unity to the various representations in a judgment also gives unity to the mere synthesis of various representations in an intuition, and this unity, in its most general expression, we entitle the pure concept of the understanding" (A79/B105). Cf. Longuenesse (1998, 50): "The two meanings of 'rule,' as rule for sensible synthesis and as discursive rule . . . or major premise of a possible syllogism . . . are indeed linked. Because one has generated a schema, one can obtain a discursive rule by reflection and apply this rule to appearances."
11. McDowell thus refuses that Kant's idea "implies that all of our epistemic life is actively led by us, in the bright light of reason"; that rational capacities are always in play in human experience is reflected, rather, "in the fact that any of it *can* be accompanied by the 'I think' of explicit self-consciousness"—even though "in much of it we unreflectively go with the flow" (2009a, 271).
12. Cf. p. 87, above.
13. See B33–34, defining "intuition" and "sensation." Kant might be taken, at such points, to express just the point Sellars means to attack in critiquing the "myth of the given"—the point that there is a sequence involving, first, *nonconceptual perception* and, subsequently, our understanding engagement therewith. I am persuaded by arguments to the effect that this is not Kant's position, though I will not here defend that as an interpretive point regarding Kant; see, however, McDowell (2009a, 108–126) for an interpretation of Kant such as I here presuppose.
14. See, e.g., B134–35.
15. The reason that normativity will be left out of any dispositional account *regardless* of the number of instances adduced is that the same problem obtains at the level of the social: "The community . . . however exactly specified, is bound to exhibit precisely the same duality of dispositions that I do: it too will be disposed to call both horses and deceptively horsey looking cows on dark nights 'horse.' . . . The communitarian, however, cannot call [these] *mistakes*, for they are the community's dispositions" (Boghossian 1989, 536).
16. For another reading of McDowell as making essentially transcendental arguments, see Baird (2006).

17. See McDowell (2009, 229–232) and Putnam (2002, 177ff.).
18. As Sellars puts this, we are encouraged by such arguments "to notice a new kind of *objective* fact, one which, though a relational fact involving a perceiver, is as logically independent of the beliefs, the conceptual framework of the perceiver, as the fact that the necktie is blue; but a *minimal* fact, one which it is safer to report because one is less likely to be mistaken." (1956:38–39)
19. Compare J. L. Austin's argument that "saying 'I know' is taking a new plunge. But it is *not* saying 'I have performed a specially striking feat of cognition, superior, in the same scale as believing and being sure, even to being merely quite sure': for there *is* nothing in that scale superior to being quite sure." In other words, "knowing" is not simply the consummate or paradigm case of, say, "believing"; rather, to claim to *know* is just to perform a certain *act*, one such that "I *give others my word:* I *give others my authority for saying* that 'S is P.' " (1946, 99).
20. McDowell is here characterizing a "disjunctive conception of perceptual experience" such as "I have found in Sellars."
21. On this reconstruction of it, the argument is much like one that Thomas Reid recurrently pressed against Hume; for Reid, too, it was chief among the contributions of Hume to have shown that representational theories of mind lead inexorably to skeptical problems—which, for Reid as for McDowell, should be taken chiefly to show that such theories cannot be right, insofar as skepticism is finally a performatively incoherent view. See, e.g., Reid (1764, 59–61).
22. An affirmation of this stance often figures in McDowell's replies to critics; see, e.g., note 24, below, as well as McDowell's "responses to critics" in Macdonald and Macdonald (2006).
23. See, e.g., Garfield's sketch (1988, 80–81) of Churchland's "argument from ontogenetic and phylogenetic continuity." See, too, McDowell (1996, 63–65, 69), engaging Gareth Evans's argument from the fact that "we share perception with creatures incapable of active and self-critical thinking." Among the points most recurrently expressed by McDowell's critics (as noted by Macdonald 2006, 223) is that he thus posits an essential discontinuity between human and animal awareness; see, e.g., Collins (1998).
24. Pippin is aware that McDowell would likely charge him here with "asking for exactly what he wants to foreclose, a '*theory* of second nature,' which McDowell writes 'would be a refusal to take the reminder [of second nature] as I intend it'...." (Pippin 2002, 72n6). Cf. note 22, above.
25. See, in this regard, Macdonald (2006).
26. It is, McDowell argues, only insofar as Friedman holds the conception of causation here expressed that he can think McDowell's arguments place him near "the traditional idealist doctrine that the world to which our thought relates is a creature of our own conceptualization" (Friedman 1996, 464; quoted by McDowell 2009, 135).
27. In the discussion to which McDowell refers, Gadamer says "the world of physics cannot seek to be the whole of what exists. For even a world equation that contained everything, so that the observer of the system would also be included in the

equations, would still assume the existence of a physicist who, as the calculator, would not be an object calculated. . . . We cannot see a linguistic world from above in this way, for there is no point of view outside the experience of the world in language from which it could become an object" (Gadamer 1989, 451–452). Thanks to Sonam Kachru for bringing this discussion to my attention.

28. In the slightly revised version of this lecture (2009a, 47n), McDowell—wary, perhaps, of the explicitly ontological overtones of the way he first put it—refers instead to a "claim to exhaust reality." Garfield, in contrast, embraces the conclusion that the issue here "is a matter of ontology, not merely of epistemology" (1988, 120).
29. See chapter 2, pp. 49.
30. A similar point is explicitly made by Macdonald (2006).
31. For a refusal of this characterization by McDowell, see, e.g., McDowell (2006, 238).
32. McDowell (1998b; reprinted in 2009a, with slight revisions, as noted, e.g., at note 28, above). Interestingly, Pippin's above-cited engagement with McDowell (note 24) concludes by encouraging McDowell to go in something more like a Hegelian direction.
33. For example, McDowell characterizes his argument as meant to show that we can have "spontaneity all the way out" (1996, 8n) and that the constitutively normative "obligatedness" of thought to reality "must be in force all the way out to reality" (1996, 42). Again, McDowell takes his project to differ from the kind of empiricism targeted by Sellars just insofar as his own approach "takes capacities of spontaneity to be in play all the way out to the ultimate grounds of empirical judgements" (1996, 67).
34. deVries (2007) notes in this regard that there is a divergence, among readers of Sellars, over how to understand Sellars's scientific realism in relation to the Sellarsian concerns that are particularly advanced by McDowell. See also deVries (2009), an illuminatingly critical review of the two 2009 collections of essays by McDowell.
35. McDowell takes himself to retract aspects of this reading in McDowell (2009a, 122ff.).
36. The same passage occurs (in what is there numbered as note 30) in McDowell (2009a, 42).
37. This passage immediately follows the preceding quotation from McDowell (2009a, 42).
38. Cf. McDowell (2009a, 63), introducing this "sober interpretation" immediately after allowing that "it may seem a dizzying project to embrace relatedness to the real order within the conceptual order."
39. Priest (2002) gives a good treatment of the kind of logical point here developed; see especially 102ff. for his elaboration of Hegel's conceptually parallel critique of Kant. Note that Gadamer makes much the same point in the passage, given above at note 27, that I followed McDowell in adducing.
40. Part 2 of Baker (1987) considers the same question, advancing an argument such as I'm developing here in terms of Kant's second *Critique*. Part 1 of her book ("Will Cognitive Science Save Belief?") argues that notwithstanding the claims of many proponents of cognitive-scientific accounts of intentionality, none of these can

finally be reconciled with semantically evaluable mental content; part 2 ("Is Belief Obsolete?") then represents an argument to the effect that this fact cannot coherently be taken to recommend the conclusion that semantically evaluable mental content is therefore eliminable. Garfield (1988) exemplifies the same dialectic; see especially his chapters 5 ("The Impossibility of Reconciliation") and 6 ("The Impossibility of Elimination").

41. So, for example, Churchland avers that "the relevant network of common-sense concepts does indeed constitute an empirical theory, with all the functions, virtues, *and perils* entailed by that status." (1981, 68; emphasis original)
42. This parallels the fact, she says, that "it is not just that certain appearances of chalk on blackboard are subject to the question 'What does it say?' It is of a word or sentence that we ask 'What does it say?'; and the description of something as a word or a sentence at all could not occur prior to the fact that words or sentences have meaning" (1963, 83).
43. See his development of a comparable point at Kant (1788, 79–81).
44. Cf. chapter 2, note 36. As Kant himself says to similar effect, "It is obvious that if one wants to represent a thinking being, one must put oneself in its place, and thus substitute one's own subject for the object one wants to consider (which is not the case in any other species of investigation)" (A353–354). With this emphasis on the logically basic character of a first-person perspective, the argument from intentionality may come together with arguments from the constitutively phenomenal character of the mental; cf. note 1, above. Citing Nagel (1974), McDowell makes the related point that "we cannot find any use for a distinction between what makes sense and *what could come to make sense to us*" (1998a, 337; emphasis added).
45. Cf. Garfield (1988, 114): "Presumably the theories that will deliver the replacement ontology of mind will do so in virtue of being accepted. But what is acceptance if not belief? Presumably they will provide us with a deeper understanding of the nature of mind. But what is the relevant analysis of understanding?"

4. THE *APOHA* DOCTRINE

1. See chapter 1, pp. 25–26.
2. *Pramāṇavārttika* 1.166; translated from Gnoli (1960, 84).
3. See chapter 1, note 36.
4. See Arnold (2005a, 429n59) for *Abhidharmakośa* references to *viṣayaprativijñapti* as defining cognition; the expression *vijñaptir viṣayasya* is from verse 2ab of Vasubandhu's *Triṃśikā* (Buescher 2007, 50), where this is adduced as one of three basic modes of *vijñānapariṇāma* ("mental transformation"). *Pramāṇavārttika* 2.206 can be found at Shastri (1968, 72), where the verse is numbered 208; cf. Dreyfus (2007, 98–99 [note 6]).
5. *Abhidharmakośabhāṣyam ad.* 5.25: *sati viṣaye vijñānaṃ pravartate, nâsati* (Pradhan 1971, 295). This could also be rendered (giving a slightly different sense) "cogni-

tion functions only with respect to an existent object, not with respect to a nonexistent [object]."

6. See Williams (1981, 229); see also chapter 3, note 3, on a parallel debate in early twentieth-century philosophy.
7. *Ālayavijñāna*, on Griffiths's reading, was posited to account for the continuity of cognition through periods (like the meditative "attainment of cessation") characterized by the absence of *intentional* cognition. Among the questions traditionally raised regarding *ālayavijñāna* was how it could itself be nonintentional and still count as *vijñāna*.
8. For general treatments of the *apoha* doctrine (as elaborated by Dharmakīrti), see Dunne (2004, 116–144), Dreyfus (1997, 205–249), Eltschinger (2010, 401–404), and the various contributions to Siderits, Tillemans, and Chakrabarti, eds. (2011).
9. On candidates for "universals" that traditionally figured in the various realist accounts against which Buddhists argued, see Scharf (1996); see, too, Dravid (1972).
10. Roland Barthes (here defining a function of "myth"), quoted with approval by Bruce Lincoln (1989, 5), whose own analyses owe much to Bourdieu. This kind of analysis has been pursued, with respect to the influence of Mīmāṃsā, by Pollock (e.g., 1985, 1989).
11. Relations among Buddhist arguments for the unreality of these various kinds of things is nicely brought out by Hayes (1988a, 20–24).
12. This is from Dharmakīrti's definition, at *Nyāyabindu* 1.5 (Malvania 1971, 45), of the *kalpanā* ("conception") that perception essentially lacks.
13. Dharmakīrti begins his *Nyāyabindu* with the claim that "the achievement of all human aims is preceded by veridical awareness" (Malvania 1971, 1), taking the facilitation of this "achievement of aims" as integral to any cognition's being a *pramāṇa*.
14. Dreyfus (2007, 107). Though attributing this recognition to Dharmakīrti, Dreyfus allows that he is "using Dharmottara's ideas rather than Dharmakīrti's," thinking it "not unreasonable to argue that Dharmottara said what Dharmakīrti ought to have said, or perhaps said implicitly" (2007, n16). While it surely represents a hermeneutically charitable regarding of Dharmakīrti thus to accept Dharmottara's conventionally commentarial claim to have rightly discerned Dharmakīrti's purport, I take it, rather—and also, I think, not unreasonably—that Dharmottara is significantly revising Dharmakīrti in order to address a real problem in the latter's project. For my elaboration of Dharmottara's revisions (centering on his understanding of the characteristically Buddhist *pramāṇaphala* doctrine), see Arnold (2005, 42–48; 2009; 2010a, 341–343); see, too, Dreyfus (1997, 354–364) and Katsura (1984).
15. See chapter 2, pp. 68–73.
16. Cf. Katsura (1991, 143); Hayes (1988, 254).
17. In this vein, Locke affirms that "faith" consists in "the Assent to any Proposition, not thus made out by the Deductions of Reason; but upon the Credit of the Proposer" (1689, 689)—given which, the epistemic task is just to ascertain that the "proposer" is creditable.

18. Dignāga here alludes to a stock example of a formally valid inference, in which "being made" (*kṛtakatva*) is the reason: "Sound is impermanent, *because of its being made*—just as a pot [is something that we know to be both an artifact, and impermanent]."
19. The Sanskrit of chapter 5 of the *Pramāṇasamuccaya* is presently unavailable, but the Sanskrit of this verse is available as quoted by Kamalaśīla in the *Tattvasaṃgrahapañjikā* (Hattori 1982, 107n1; cf. Shastri 1997, 376), from which I have here translated; see also Hayes (1988, 252) and Hattori (2000, 139) for translations of the same passage.
20. See also Dreyfus (1997, 210), who credits this point to B. K. Matilal.
21. I here follow Katsura (1979) and Hayes (1988, 185–216); see Ganeri (2001, 106–111) for a basically similar interpretation.
22. My translation adapted from Hayes (1988, 298–299); Dignāga's Sanskrit is given in Hattori (1982, 137n32). This verse represents (along with 5.25–28) one of the bases for Katsura's useful tabular presentation (1979, 17).
23. Actually, it seems the math is a little off here, as Dignāga has thus adduced five levels in a categoreal hierarchy and only four degrees of conceptual determinacy corresponding to them; perhaps the overarching category *jñeya* ("knowable") is to be understood as having no conceptual determinacy.
24. The issue of relations is the topic of Dharmakīrti's concise *Saṃbandhaparīkṣā* ("Investigation of Relations"); see Frauwallner (1934).
25. That Dharmakīrti can nevertheless really mean "identity" here relates to the sense in which he offers a finally causal account *even of such conceptual relations*; I will not go into that here, but see, on this point, Dunne (2004, 203–218).
26. See, e.g., Kumārila's *Ślokavārttika*, *apohavāda* 41 (Shastri 1978, 408; Jha 1983, 303).
27. Cf. Hayes (1988, 186). For this line of objection, see, e.g., Kumārila's *Ślokavārttika*, *apohavāda* vv.63–64, 71–72, 83–85; see also Hugon (2009), which presents source material for this critique of *apoha*.
28. I here follow Hayes (1988, 118–130).
29. Note that this locution requires reference only to a particular and to that extent serves Dignāga's goal of explaining this process without presupposing the real existence of universals.
30. It's important to note, though, that Oetke (1994) contests Hayes's strictly epistemic formulation of the relevant criteria, arguing that tradition attests both epistemic and nonepistemic understandings of the *trairūpya* doctrine.
31. It's common to suggest that among the differences between Dignāga and Dharmakīrti is the latter's attempt instead to develop something like a deductive model of inference based on supposedly necessary relations (*svabhāvapratibandha*). Cf. Dunne (2004, 145–222), Ganeri (2001, 121–123).
32. Dharmakīrti, in contrast, would affirm that an inference can go through without reference to both, since on his reading, *vyatireka* amounts basically to contraposition; cf. Dharmottara's commentary on *Nyāyabindu* 2.5 (Malvania 1971, 95–96).
33. Hayes here follows Cardona (1967–1968).

34. The foregoing quotes are from Hayes (1988, 189), here making explicit how Dignāga's account of language maps onto his theory of inference.
35. Translated from Kanakavarman's Tibetan translation, as available in Hattori (1982, 135); cf. the translations of Hayes (1988, 297–298) and Pind (2009, 103).
36. My translation (from the Tibetan in Hattori 1982, 135) is here adapted from that of Hayes (1988, 297–298); cf. Pind (2009, 103–104).
37. Dignāga makes this clear in continuing the above passage, concluding that "the inference is just by way of *vyatireka*" (Tibetan at Hattori 1982, 135); cf. the translations of Hayes (1988, 298) and Pind (2009, 104), as well as Pind (2009, 51–52).
38. See chapter 3, pp. 91–92.
39. This is Hayes's translation (1988, 272) of *Pramāṇasamuccaya* 5.10b (Tibetan at Hattori 1982, 113); cf. Pind (2009, 83). Discussing Dharmakīrti's theorization of the *svabhāvahetu*, Dunne (2004, 221–222) summarizes a similar sort of retreat as possibly available to Dharmakīrti; Dunne explains that this is unsatisfying insofar as the issue "would be reduced to a mere word-game of learning the accepted rules for applying these terms, and it would ignore the question of whether those conventions are based upon the characteristics of ultimately real particulars."
40. See the introduction, p. 7.
41. See, e.g., Tanaka (2009), emphasizing the importance of Dharmakīrti's being able to make a distinction precisely such as Frege's.
42. See p. 126, above.
43. The opening sections of McDowell's *Mind and World* (1996) incisively characterize the problems here identified, with McDowell emphasizing the kind of oscillation this seemingly intractable problem can give rise to.
44. Or "excluded"; variations on the word *vyāvṛtta* frequently describe what has, as it were, been cognitively "done" to whatever is subject to the process of *apoha* ("exclusion").
45. Here translating Manorathanandin's introduction to the passage reckoned in Gnoli's edition (1960, 38) and in Shastri's (1968, 281) as verses 68–70 of the *svārthānumāna* chapter. Recall (here and in all the following references to Dharmakīrti) the issue—noted in chapter 1, note 5—of the order of the *Pramāṇavārttika*'s chapters.
46. Translated from the Sanskrit at Shastri (1978, 281); I follow Manorathanandin in discerning the syntax spread over the verses and in supplying the antecedents of Dharmakīrti's pronouns.
47. Dharmakīrti here exploits a traditional etymological account of *saṃvrtisatya* as involving "obscuration," which is indeed among the principal senses of the verbal root *saṃ-√vṛ*.
48. See chapter 2, p. 50.
49. So, too, Dunne: "Dharmakīrti maintains that a concept, when taken as a mental event, can be considered a particular and thus an object of nonconceptual cognition" (2006, 497).
50. Dreyfus is here glossing *Pramāṇavārttika* 3.166–168; Dreyfus's "reflection" and "aspect" render Dharmakīrti's *pratibimba* and *ākāra*.

51. Commenting on *Pramāṇavārttika* 3.9–10; translated from Shastri (1968, 104).
52. *Pramāṇavārttika* 3.163cd–164ab, translated from Shastri (1968, 150); cf. the translation of Dreyfus (1997, 226).
53. Manorathanandin invokes *saṃketakāla* in commenting on 3.164 (Sanskrit in Shastri 1968, 150).
54. Literally, "ordinary usage involving universals, apposition, and subjects and predicates."
55. Translated from Gnoli (1960, 42); cf. the translation of Dunne (2004, 346–347). This passage is part of Dharmakīrti's lengthy elaboration on *Pramāṇavārttika* I.74–75, discussed below (pp. 138–39, and note 59).
56. Here, I am paraphrasing from Dharmakīrti's autocommentary on *Pramāṇavārttika* 1.68–70 (Sanskrit in Gnoli 1960, 38); cf. Dunne's translation (2004, 339).
57. Commenting on *Pramāṇavārttika* 1.107; Sanskrit in Shastri (1968, 292), where the verse is numbered 108.
58. On this point, see Hugon (2009). Whether Dharmakīrti's appeal to "sameness of effects" successfully addresses the problem is among the chiefly recurrent issues debated by contributors to the volume edited by Siderits, Tillemans, and Chakrabarti (2011). See, e.g., the contribution by Hale, who is not much impressed by Dharmakīrti's move. The contribution by Dreyfus reflects greater sympathy with Dharmakīrti's aim, despite Dreyfus's recognition that, "as many thinkers have argued, such an attempt cannot succeed, for if we accept real similarities, we might as well accept real properties" (Dreyfus 2011, 211). The contribution by Siderits gives a nuanced account of the various intuitions it is possible to have about the issues here in play.
59. So, *Pramāṇavārttika* 1.74: "Some medicinal herbs, even given their plurality, are noticed with regard to soothing fevers, etc., whether singly or together—and others aren't" (translated from Gnoli 1960, 41; cf. the translation of Dunne 2004, 345).
60. "There is just some universal among these kinds of things, and it is just because of this that there is a single effect" (Gnoli 1960, 41; cf. Dunne 2004, 345). Recall, here, Leibniz's similar challenge to Locke (see chapter 2, note 11).
61. *Pramāṇavārttika* 1.75 (translated from Gnoli 1960, 41–42; cf. Dunne 2004, 345–346).
62. Translated from Shastri (1968, 292); cf. Gnoli (1960, 56–57) and Dunne (2004, 121). Manorathanandin explains that Dharmakīrti thus answers the objection that insofar as "thoughts" (*dhī*) are themselves the effects of encounters with particulars, it would seem that reference to thoughts cannot get us any closer to the kind of "sameness" we need: "But thought is the effect of these individuals, and it [therefore] differs for each individual; so how is there the similarity which is *being capable of accomplishing the same goal*?" (from Shastri 1968, 292, *ad* verse 108).
63. Translated from Gnoli (1960, 41); cf. Dunne (2004, 344).
64. See Dunne (2004, 139ff.) for consideration of a related point.
65. That these events are "impersonally" described follows from Dharmakīrti's constitutively Buddhist aim to account for the mental without reference to enduring *persons*.

66. See p. 136, above. Siderits aptly characterizes the problem: "The obvious question to ask at this point is how this second, conception-laden perception comes about. The short answer is that the concept-free perception triggers a trace that then brings about the concept-laden perception. This is a short answer because we are also told that the organism has such a trace due to beginningless ignorance. This seems not to be an answer at all" (2011, 287).
67. Sanskrit quoted by Scharf (1995, 66n), from Helārāja's commentary on the *sambandhasamuddeśa* chapter of Bhartṛhari's *Vākyapadīya*.
68. The verse is *Pramāṇavārttika* 2.4 (available in Shastri 1968, 4), on which Manorathanandin thus elaborates: "Language's being a *pramāṇa*—i.e., its being an inferential reason (*liṅga*)—is with regard to that object (*artha*)—i.e., the aspect (*ākāra*) of a cognition, which aspect has the superimposed form of something external—which is the object (*viṣaya*) of that, i.e. of the speaker's engagement, which is an intention; this [aspect of a cognition] appears in thought, which [thought] consists in an intention. The point is that a conception, which has as its content (*pratibhāsa*) an intended object, is inferred from an uttered word, because of the word's being the effect of that [intention]. But it is not grounded in the reality of the object [referred to], since there is no connection with that."
69. Translated from Gnoli (1960, 107).
70. Cf. chapter 2, p. 71.
71. Characterizing the plausibility of the kind of view (which she is concerned to resist) suggested by Dharmakīrti, Elizabeth Anscombe notes that "it can easily seem that in general the question what a man's intentions are is only authoritatively settled by him"—a fact that "conspires to make us think that if we want to know a man's intentions, it is into the contents of his mind, and only into these, that we must enquire; and hence, that if we wish to understand what intention is, we must be investigating something whose existence is purely in the sphere of the mind" (1963, 42).
72. From Dharmakīrti's autocommentary on *Pramāṇavārttika*1.142; translated from Gnoli (1960, 67). The translation of Dunne (2004, 354–355), I think, even more clearly discloses the problematic move here; the concluding phrases, on his reading, say that "the capacity to refer to things depends on the speaker's wishes (*icchā*) [or needs]. If meaning is not fixed by the wishes (*icchā*) of the person using the expressions, then how could an expression refer to even one thing?"
73. Exemplary of this conflation is Śāntarakṣita's contention that "cows and non-cows are well-established due to different judgments. It is only the word ['cow'] that is not established, and *it is applied according to the wish of the speaker*." This is Hugon's translation (2011, 117; emphasis added) of *Tattvasaṃgraha* 1063; the Sanskrit is at Shastri (1997, 285). For an incisive account (based especially on Śāntarakṣita and Kamalaśīla) of many of the issues we are here considering, see Nance (2012, 86–97).
74. From Dharmakīrti's autocommentary on *Pramāṇavārttika* 1.227; translated from Gnoli (1960, 113–114). Cf. the translation of Dunne (2004, 146n), who comments that "the specific type of inference intended here is an inference from effect . . .

since there is a causal relation between the image in a listener's mind and the utterance of the speaker." I am here emphasizing that there is also held to be a causal relation between the image in the *speaker's* mind and her utterance.

75. Representative of Dharmakīrti's characteristic account of the reducibility of linguistic cognition to inference is the passage from Kamalaśīla that preserves the Sanskrit of Dignāga's *Pramāṇasamuccaya* 5.1 (see note 19, above). Regarding, then, Śāntarakṣita's *Tattvasaṃgraha* 1514 (which says what is inferred from an utterance is just a speaker's intention), Kamalaśīla explains: "And that intention is understood from the utterance because of [the utterance's] being the effect of that, but not as being [directly] expressible" (Shastri 1997, 376). Consider, too, the argument of Dharmakīrti's *Santānāntarasiddhi* ("Establishment of other [mental] continua"; see Katsura 2007). Here, Dharmakīrti considers whether Yogācāra thinkers have the conceptual resources necessary to explain our knowledge of other minds—something thought by "Sautrāntikas" to be more easily explained on their view. Arguing that everything the Sautrāntikas say can also be said with reference simply to "appearances," Dharmakīrti here, too, argues that the basis for our knowledge of other minds is inference based on a *kāryahetu* (cf. Inami 2001, 466)—an inference to the effect that just as our own actions are preceded by our intentions, so, too, the observable actions of others must similarly be the effects of "intentions" occurrent for them. This kind of argument might be contrasted, e.g., with a transcendental argument to the effect that our having the concept of other minds is itself a condition of the possibility of our attributing mental states even to ourselves.
76. Consider, too, Anscombe's follow-up to the above-cited passage (see note 71) on the plausibility of claims to the effect that questions of an agent's *intentions* are best settled, introspectively, by the agent; against this, Anscombe argues (1963, 42–43) that the constitutively normative character of the *answers* to "Why?" questions entails that the agent cannot, after all, be thought uniquely to provide the definitive word. Her point, I take it, is that it is not entirely *up to the agent* what she means by what she says nor whether what she means involves something *true*; to that extent, the significance of "Why?" questions is not decisively settled with reference to anything inside the agent's head.
77. See p. 136, above.
78. Cf. chapter 2, p. 71, above.
79. This verse occurs as *Pramāṇaviniścaya* 1.8 (Steinkellner 2007, 10) and as *Pramāṇavārttika* 3.174 (Shastri 1968, 153). I follow Manorathanandin's commentary on the latter occurrence of the verse in taking *śabdakalpanam* ("verbal conception") as the subject term for which the two long compounds in the first half of the verse are adjectival (i.e., *bahuvrīhis*). So Manorathanandin: "For a verbal conception is familiar as that of which the mode is recollection of a previously apprehended convention—that whose nature is association, in this way, of a word [previously] experienced as being expressive." See Taber (2005, 97) for a translation of this verse, considered in the context of his characterizing the differences between Dharmakīrti and the Mīmāṃsakas on the issues here in play.

80. For Dharmakīrti (as for Dignāga), being *conceptual* is virtually coextensive with being *linguistic*—see Taber (2005, 207–210, n14) on the closeness of these. See also note 86, below.
81. Translated from Steinkellner (2007, 8).
82. Translated from Steinkellner (2007, 8).
83. Translated from Steinkellner (2007, 9).
84. See chapter 2, p. 71.
85. See chapter 2, p. 70.
86. *Nyāyabindu* 1.5 (Malvania 1971, 47): *abhilāpasaṃsargayogyapratibhāsā pratītiḥ kalpanā*. This verse figures in some Tibetan interpretations of Dharmakīrti's *apoha* doctrine, which take the verse as Dharmakīrti's statement of an "alternative" definition of *kalpanā*—one that is meant to clear the way for his positing of (what his epistemology so clearly needs) an intermediate link between perceptions and concepts. The characteristically Tibetan reading of the verse is exploited by Dreyfus (1997, 220–222); on the nature of (and problems with) this reading, see Tillemans (1999, 238–39n22). Malvania's edition confirms Tillemans's suggestion (following Dharmottara's reading) that the initial compound is a *bahuvrīhi* modifying *pratītiḥ*.
87. Dignāga had defined *kalpanā* simply as "association with name and genus and so forth" (at *Pramāṇasamuccaya* 1.3d and *vṛtti*; Sanskrit at Steinkellner 2005, 2); cf. Hattori (1968, 25) and note 80, above. Some of the examples that Dharmottara takes to show the possibility of thought's being merely *suitable* for association with discourse (without actually *being* so associated)—and, hence, the possibility that pre- or nonlinguistic beings can evince *kalpanā*, even though that is defined vis-à-vis discourse—are taken by the grammarian Bhartṛhari to show that *there is no nonlinguistic cognition*; cf. Matilal (1990, 124–128).
88. Translated from Malvania (1971, 48).
89. I find Dharmottara's use of the pair *vācya* and *vācaka* counterintuitive here, since, in fact, *both* of these would seem to denote abstractions (precisely parallel to Saussure's "signified" and "signifier," respectively); since it is clear that what is needed here is a dichotomy in which one term is a *particular*, I render *vācya* here as "referent" rather than as "signified."
90. Translated from Malvania (1971, 52).
91. Dharmottara's task here would be further complicated by phenomenological considerations, since we do not experience ourselves as *moving* from one level of description to the other but simply as *understanding the sentence*. Discussing an observation from Husserl (1970, 282–284), Dummett thus emphasizes that "we hear or read the words *as* saying whatever it is that they say; only by a heroic effort can we hear them as mere sounds or see them as mere shapes" (2004, 11).
92. Translated from Malvania (1971, 52–53).
93. The insight, in particular, that "we do not, *qua* expressing it, live in the acts constituting the expression as a physical object—we are not interested in this object—but we live in the acts which give it sense" (Husserl 1970, 584).

94. Also to the point in this regard are characteristic comments from one of Husserl's contemporaneous crusaders against psychologism, Gottlob Frege, who pressed a precisely similar insight particularly against the typically Lockean understanding of "Ideas" as particular mental representations; cf. chapter 2, note 12.
95. *Pramāṇavārttika* 1.137–138; translated from Gnoli (1960, 66).
96. See p. 143, above.
97. *Pramāṇavārtika* 1.72; translated from (Gnoli 1960, 40).
98. See Dunne (2004, 344n14). Cf. Karṇakagomin (in Sāṅkṛtyāyana 1943, 176): *saṃjñā saṃketakriyā yadarthikā*. To similar effect, Manorathanandin uses the denominative form *saṃketayati* ("to fix by convention"), commenting: "'Signification has that as its purpose' means that language, too, is devised (*saṃketyate*) with respect to exclusion of what is different, and has that as its scope" (Sanskrit at Shastri 1968, 282).
99. The Sanskrit is at Gnoli (1960, 40), and the point is no less problematic if we render it to reflect the passive voice used therein: "Linguistic conventions are made (*saṃketaḥ kriyate*) in order . . . "
100. Dharmakīrti here again suggests that the relevantly similar "effects" produced by distinct particulars consist in subjectively experienced cognitions.
101. *Pramāṇavārttika* 1.141–142 (from Dharmakīrti's autocommentary on which I adduced the passage given at note 72, above); translated (with emphasis added) from Gnoli (1960, 66); cf. the translation of Dunne (2004, 353).
102. Translated from the Sanskrit at Shastri (1968, 301). See, as well, Dharmakīrti's autocommentary at Gnoli (1960, 68); particularly in Dunne's translation of the latter, the question-begging is stark: "in order to facilitate practical action . . . someone applies a convention-establishing . . . statement: 'The causes are such-and-such and so-and-so.' One uses these expressions such that *the listener somehow knows all of the causes*" (2004, 356; emphasis added).
103. *Pramāṇavārttika* 3.171; Shastri (1968, 152).
104. Translated from Shastri (1968, 152).
105. Translated from Shastri (1953, 137).
106. Cf. Dunne (2004, 114–115), where there are a couple of occurrences of the word *vidhi* translated as "affirmation." Pind comments that "the question of affirmation traditionally was linked up with the assumption of real universals" (2011, 70). See also Pind (2009, 133–134n) and Abhyankar (1977, 328–329, s.v. *vidhi*).
107. See also Weiss (2010, 37–44), where Weiss's analysis closely parallels ours.
108. Cf. chapter 2, p. 72.

5. THE *SVASAṂVITTI* DOCTRINE

1. Tillemans is here explicating *Pramāṇavārttika* 4.109.
2. On some of the interpretive options regarding *svasaṃvitti*, see Matilal (1986, 148–160), Williams (1998), Ganeri (1999), and MacKenzie (2007).

3. See chapter 3, p. 99.
4. Among the burdens of this chapter will be to clarify the meaning of the foregoing paragraph. For his part, Bilgrami takes Kant's transcendental idealism to be compatible with his own view, but allows that the kind of idealism exemplified by Berkeley "would raise questions for the contrast" (2006, 29).
5. Cf. page 248, note 16, above.
6. Dharmakīrti explicitly adopts a Yogācāra perspective only "at the end of the third chapter, starting with the prologue at vv. 194ff" (Dunne 2004, 60n). This comprises all of the *Pramāṇavārttika* passages considered in the present chapter. On the order of chapters in the *Pramāṇavārttika*, recall chapter 1, note 5.
7. See chapter 1, pp. 24–25.
8. The famous argument of Vasubandhu's *Viṃśatikā*, verses 11–15 (cf. Kapstein 2001, 181–204)—an argument to the effect that realism about external objects is inconceivable, insofar as realists both *must* and *cannot* give an account of atoms—represents the Buddhist tradition's principal *metaphysical* argument for Yogācāra idealism. For more on this point, see Arnold 2008, 15–18.
9. *Tattvasaṃgraha* 1999 (Sanskrit in Shastri 1997, 478); see, too, Williams (1998, 1–35). I have interpreted Śāntarakṣita's as a basically transcendental understanding of *svasaṃvitti*; see Arnold (2005b).
10. See chapter 3, pp. 96–98.
11. On *yogipratyakṣa*, see Woo (2003) and Dunne (2006).
12. The scholarly consensus is that Dignāga proposed *three* kinds of *pratyakṣa*, while Dharmakīrti instead takes there to be four; see, e.g., Franco (1993, 2004). On the recent availability of a reliable Sanskrit text of Dignāga, see Franco (2006), reviewing Steinkellner et al. (2005). On the basis of the now-available text of Jinendrabuddhi's commentary, Steinkellner (2005) has ventured a "hypothetical reconstruction of the Sanskrit text" of the *Pramāṇasamuccaya*, from which I have translated the passages from Dignāga cited in this chapter; for verse 6, the Sanskrit is at Steinkellner (2005, 3).
13. Translated from Steinkellner (2005, 3); cf. Hattori (1968, 31).
14. On *mānasapratyakṣa* vis-à-vis *manovijñāna*, see not only pp. 33–35, above, but also Arnold (2010a, 336–340) for further discussion and textual citations. See, too, Mookerjee (1975, 311–318).
15. The same idea may be suggested by Dignāga's claim (in his autocommentary on *Pramāṇasamuccaya* 1.6ab) that *mānasapratyakṣa* "has as its content objects like form and so forth" (*rūpādiviṣayālambanam*)—where "form" (*rūpa*) refers to the object particularly of the *ocular* sense faculty—and at the same time that it "engages *aspects* of experience" (*anubhavākārapravṛttaṃ*; cf. note 13, above).
16. Translated from Steinkellner (2005, 2); cf. Hattori (1968, 26).
17. See Arnold (2005a, 459–460).
18. Adducing the same quotation in commenting on Vasubandhu's treatment (in the *Abhidharmakośa*) of the cognitive outputs of the five material senses, the commentator Yaśomitra takes the passage to make just the point Candrakīrti sees; see Shastri (1998, 72).

19. Such an understanding of *mānasapratyakṣa* is in fact suggested by Dharmakīrti's commentator Prajñākaragupta, who holds (according to Hisayasu Kobayashi) that "mental perception is a cognition which grasps its object as 'this' (*idam iti jñānam*)" (2010, 240)—a view that brings to mind just the view of *manovijñāna* that Candrakīrti presses against Dignāga.
20. The whole exchange reads: "If the self-awareness of things like passion [counts as] *pratyakṣa*, conceptual cognition (*kalpanājñānam*), too, [should be] so called. [Response:] That's true; even conceptual thought is admitted [as being *pratyakṣa*] in terms of self-awareness—[but] not with respect to [its] object, because of the conceptual construction [of that]." Translated from Steinkellner (2005, 3); cf. Hattori (1968, 27). See also Taber (2005, 103–105), sketching a Mīmāṃsaka critique that engages the point.
21. For my earlier characterization of Dignāga's arguments here, see Arnold (2005, 34–36); the present engagement with *Pramāṇasamuccaya* 1.8cd–10 can be understood as revising that treatment. See, too, Kellner (2010) for a close reading of the arguments.
22. The issues are thus framed in terms of the Sanskritic *kāraka* analysis of the forms of words required to characterize any action; cf. Dunne (2004, 15–22).
23. Translated from Steinkellner (2005, 3); cf. Hattori (1968, 28). I here follow Kellner (2010, 219n46) in taking *jñāna* as the implied subject of the clause. While I'm persuaded by Kellner that there is thus a correction to be made to my translation of this elsewhere, I do not see that the change makes a difference for the interpretive aims I'm here pursuing.
24. See Arnold (2009) for an annotated translation of the passages I here have in mind; see also p. 121, along with p. 262n14.
25. Translated from Steinkellner (2005, 3–4); cf. Hattori (1968, 28).
26. Jinendrabuddhi thus postdates Dharmakīrti, whom he quotes throughout his commentary on Dignāga's *Pramāṇasamuccaya*. This tendency of later commentators to read Dignāga in light of Dharmakīrti is one basis for the widely held sense of these thinkers as exemplifying a monolithic project.
27. Translated from Steinkellner, Krasser, and Lasic (2005, 66). Reading the complex relative clause here without recourse to variables, we could translate: "that action which is completed (*prasiddhim upayāti*) has as instrument that instrument because of which it is immediately (*avyavadhānena*) [completed]." Thanks to Horst Lasic and Whitney Cox for comments helpful to my understanding of this passage.
28. *Karmaṇi*, here meant in the grammatical sense.
29. On the sense of *-bhūta* as "being like, similar," see Apte (1992, 1204, s.v. "*bhūta*").
30. Translated from Steinkellner, Krasser, and Lasic (2005, 66).
31. Translated from Steinkellner, Krasser, and Lasic (2005, 66–67).
32. Jinendrabuddhi (at Steinkellner, Krasser, and Lasic 2005, 69) glosses Dignāga's *atra* as "with regard to perception, as that has been previously described."
33. Translated from Steinkellner (2005, 4); cf. Hattori (1968, 28): "or [it can be maintained that] the self-cognition or the cognition cognizing itself . . . is here the result [of the act of cognizing]—."

34. Kellner (2010, 270) worries that this characterization of his argument unwarrantedly takes Dignāga's discussion here to be about "normative aspects of epistemology, about a hierarchy among means of valid cognition." Whether or not it's right to deny that such concerns are immediately in play for Dignāga, that it's reasonable to think he may nevertheless be committed to such a view is evidenced, I think, by the prevalence of this reading of him in the later Indian tradition.
35. This view is recommended by Jinendrabuddhi: "Earlier, awareness of an object was said [to be] the result; hence, the word '*vā*' has the sense of [expressing] an option" (Steinkellner, Krasser, and Lasic 2005, 69). Hattori (1968, 101n.1.60) similarly comments: "In *k. 8cd* and the *Vṛtti* thereon, the cognition possessing the form of an object, i.e., the apprehension of an object (*viṣayâdhigati*), has been regarded as *phala*. . . . an alternative view recognizing *sva-saṁvitti* as *phala* is put forward here." While Kellner concurs with this, she is finally concerned to argue much as I am arguing here—that, in particular, Dignāga's disjunctive syntax "does not indicate a shift from externalism to internalism, but rather a change in perspective from external objects in PS(V) 1.8cd to validly cognised objects in general, *regardless of whether they are conceived as internal or external to the mind*" (2010, 223; emphasis added).
36. Translated from Steinkellner (2005, 4); cf. Hattori (1968, 28).
37. Translated from Steinkellner (2005, 4); cf. Hattori (1968, 28): "Every cognition is produced with a twofold appearance, namely, that of itself [as subject] (*svābhāsa*) and that of the object (*viṣayābhāsa*). The cognizing of itself as [possessing] these two appearances or the self-cognition (*svasaṁvitti*) is the result [of the cognitive act]."
38. I thus read the subjective-genitival *tasya* as *jñānasya* and Dignāga's *ubhayābhāsasya* as a *bahuvrīhi* modifying that; this is warranted by Jinendrabuddhi (note 41, below), who clearly reads *ubhayābhāsa* thus as a *bahuvrīhi*. See Kellner (2010, 220n54), who notes that I have previously read this passage differently (and, I now think, incorrectly). Compare Chu, who renders the passage with an objective genitive: "Cognition arises with two appearances: the appearance of the cognition itself and the appearance of the object-field. *A self-awareness of these two appearances* is the result" (2006, 239; emphasis added).
39. Translated from Steinkellner, Krasser, and Lasic (2005, 68, line 11).
40. Translated from Steinkellner, Krasser, and Lasic (2005, 68, lines 12–14).
41. Translated (with emphasis added) from Steinkellner, Krasser, and Lasic (2005, 69, lines 13–15). I take the *bahuvrīhi* compound (*ubhayābhāsam*) in Jinendrabuddhi's first sentence to support my provision of the antecedent of the pronominal "its," as well as my reading of Dignāga's commentary on 1.9 (note 38, above).
42. See pp. 168–69, above.
43. On Dignāga's *saviṣayam* here as an indeclinable, adverbial compound, see Kellner (2010, 222n58).
44. The insertion is supported by Jinendrabuddhi, who thus specifies the antecedent of the pronoun: *viṣayābhāsatâiva jñānasya pramāṇam iṣyate*; See Steinkellner, Krasser, and Lasic (2005, 72).

45. Translated from Steinkellner (2005, 4); cf. Hattori (1968, 28–29).
46. Translated from Steinkellner (2005, 4). Note that *yadābhāsaṃ*'s being a *bahuvrīhi* for *jñāna* is recommended by much of what precedes this, corresponding to (what we saw earlier) *svābhāsam* and *viṣayābhāsam*, etc. (in addition to which, grammatically, it can only be a *bahuvrīhi*). Thus, I read *yadābhāsam* as "*yadābhāsaṃ jñānam*," "that cognition of which the phenomenal content is x." Hattori comments (1968, 105n1.67): "In this verse the Yogācāra view is clearly expounded."
47. Note that as modifying *jñānam* (note 46, above), the *bahuvrīhi* compound *yadābhāsam* is effectively equivalent to *jñānasya viṣayābhāsatā*; that is, to characterize cognition as "having some content" (*yadābhāsam*) just is to adduce the state of affairs of "cognition's being contentful."
48. See note 46, above.
49. On this argument, see Iwata (1991), Chakrabarti (1990), and Eltschinger (2010, 430–432).
50. See chapter 3, pp. 96–98, above. Thanks to Rick Nance for suggesting to me this way of characterizing Dharmakīrti's main argument for *svasaṃvitti*.
51. See pp. 161–62, above.
52. I noted above (note 4) that Bilgrami allows that Berkeleyan idealism undermines his "governing disjunction."
53. See the first section of chapter 1.
54. Translated from Shastri (1968, 197).
55. See chapter 1, pp. 33–36, above.
56. Commenting on [3].324a–c; translated from Shastri (1968, 197).
57. See chapter 1, pp. 26–28, above.
58. This is Manorathanandin's prose restatement of Dharmakīrti's verse 3.334, translated from Shastri (1968, 199–200); cf. Dunne's translation (2004, 277n).
59. See chapter 4, pp. 136–37; and chapter 1, p. 27.
60. Translated from Shastri (1968, 200).
61. See p. 171, as well as note 33.
62. See p. 169, above.
63. Translated from Shastri (1968, 200). On this passage, see Taber (2010, 290–294).
64. Translated from Shastri (1968, 200).
65. *Pramāṇaviniścaya* 1.54a–b; translated from Steinkellner (2007, 39). Watson (2010, 305n26) gives relevant sources for the widely quoted verse that begins thus. On possible analyses of the compound *sahopalambhaniyama*, see Iwata (1991, 66–109).
66. Translated from Steinkellner (2007, 40).
67. This can be taken to recommend Taber's characterization (2010, 292–293) of the *sahopalambhaniyama* argument in terms of the Identity of Indiscernibles.
68. Translated from Steinkellner (2007, 40).
69. Translated from Steinkellner (2007, 40).
70. Translated from Steinkellner (2007, 41); cf. Dreyfus and Lindtner (1989, 47): "The fact that an object (*viṣaya*) exists does not mean that it is perceived. On the contrary, it is [perceived] by its perception!"

71. I thus read the feminine pronoun *sā* (see note 72, below, for the complete passage) as having *tadupalambhasattā* as its antecedent; Dreyfus and Lindtner differently read: "So [the existence of an object] does not [provide us] with valid cognition . . ." (1989, 47).
72. So Dharmakīrti: "And this [i.e., awareness itself], which is without warrant (*sā câprāmāṇika*), does not block transactions based on the [supposed] existence [of external objects]; [indeed,] given the non-establishment of that [i.e., of awareness itself], there is non-establishment of the object, too; hence, everything would be destroyed, because of the impossibility of transactions regarding existence when there is non-establishment even of the existent. Therefore, insofar as one is non-apprehending"—that is, insofar as the conceptually basic fact of *being aware* does not obtain—"no awareness of anything is known at all." Translated from Steinkellner (2007, 41).
73. See p. 181, above.
74. Translated from Steinkellner (2007, 41–42).
75. Moriyama (2010, 267–273) adduces some passages that can be taken to support this characterization—passages, in particular, figuring in Dharmakīrti's case for *yogi-pratyakṣa* (the kind of "perceptual" awareness cultivated by yogins), which is thought to include yogic awareness *of others' minds*. In this context, *svasaṃvitti* is invoked (at *Pramāṇavārttika* 3.456) to distinguish first-personal awareness of mental states from a yogin's third-personal awareness *of someone else's* such states. Dharmakīrti argues, then, that *if* one accepts yogic awareness of others' minds but *not svasaṃvitti*, then, absurdly, there can be no distinguishing these.
76. Translated (with emphasis added) from Steinkellner (2007, 42).Dreyfus and Lindtner (1989, 47) translate: "Cognition manifests itself as such, simply because it is its nature to do so. There is not the slightest [thing] apart from it, as in the case of self-cognition. This also means that such a [cognition] is not a cognition apart from (*anyathā*) an 'object.' There is no ['blue object'] apart from the experience of blue, etc. So, [we] experience blue, etc., because [blue, etc.] appears that way; this being the blue nature of such [self-cognition]."
77. Cf. chapter 3, p. 97.
78. See p. 179.
79. See chapter 3, p. 98.
80. See chapter 1, pp. 21–22.
81. I here follow Dunne (2004, 256–260), who distinguishes these as (respectively) the "telic meaning" and the "causal meaning"; see also Nagatomi (1967–1968), whom Dunne himself follows.
82. See Arnold (2005, 50–51) on this point.
83. There is a useful summary of Dunne's reconstruction here in Duerlinger (2008, 612).
84. See chapter 4, p. 142.
85. Translated from Ono (2000, 63); see also Inami (1999, 3, together with his notes 14–15).
86. See chapter 1, p. 29.

87. Translated from Ono (2000, 65); cf. Dunne (2004, 317, 406–408) for similar comments from Śākyabuddhi.
88. On the relationship between *causal efficacy* and *momentariness*, see chapter 1, p. 22.
89. My engagement with Rāmakaṇṭha follows Watson (2006, 2010).
90. See chapter 3, p. 86.
91. Cf. chapter 4, note 16.
92. Watson's translation (2006, 223); Watson's edition of the Sanskrit is at Watson (2006, 396).
93. Watson's translation (2006, 250); Rāmakaṇṭha's Sanskrit is cited at Watson (2006, 249).
94. For phenomenological reflections in the same vein, see especially Husserl (1991).
95. For Rāmakaṇṭha's elaboration of what he thus takes to be the Buddhist account, see Watson (2006, 230–231); on Hume's account of personal identity, see p. 85, above.
96. Watson's translation (2006, 244); Rāmakaṇṭha's Sanskrit is given on the same page. I have substituted "Dharmakīrti" for Watson's "you" in the bracketed insertion.
97. A101–102; see p. 86, above.
98. On this point, see Watson (2010, 311–312).
99. See Watson (2010, 310n44) for Rāmakaṇṭha's Sanskrit.

6. INDIAN ARGUMENTS FROM PRACTICAL REASON

1. See chapter 5, pp. 187–88, above.
2. For these passages from Kant, see chapter 3, pp. 49–50, above.
3. On this tradition of thought, see Arnold (2005, part II; 2010), Bhatt (1962), Clooney (1990), Jha (1964), Taber (2005), and Verpoorten (1987).
4. The traditions of *Pūrva* ("prior") and *Uttara* ("subsequent") Mīmāṃsā differ chiefly over which portion of the "Vedic" corpus should be thought definitive. While Pūrva Mīmāṃsā centers on the part of that corpus epitomized by the *Brāhmaṇas*, *Uttara Mīmāṃsā* instead takes its bearings from the part, comprising the *Upaniṣads*, traditionally styled "Vedānta" ("culmination of the Veda"), which is how Uttara Mīmāṃsā is familiarly denominated.
5. This is said in Śabara's introduction to *Mīmāṃsā Sūtra* 1.1.2; see Frauwallner (1968, 16) and Jha (1973–1974, 4).
6. Frauwallner (1968, 22–24); Jha (1973–1974, 8–9).
7. On the train of argument here, see Taber (forthcoming).
8. Saussure: "In separating language [*langue*] from speaking [*parole*] we are at the same time separating: (1) what is social from what is individual; and (2) what is essential from what is accessory and more or less accidental. Language [*langue*] is not a function of the speaker; it is a product that is passively assimilated by the individual. . . . Speaking on the contrary, is an individual act. It is wilful and intellectual" (1959, 14).

9. Which, note well, denote *abstractions*; a "signifier" is not just "a word" but what it is in virtue of which innumerable acoustic events can be understood as *utterances of the same word*.
10. See Scharf (1996).
11. The argument considered here was also advanced by proponents of the tradition of Sanskrit grammarians; cf. Matilal (1990, 26–30) and Taber (forthcoming).
12. Translated from Frauwallner (1968, 46); cf. the translation of Jha (1973–1974, 24–25).
13. Cf. chapter 4, pp. 122–23, above.
14. The same argument was ventured by Johann Herder; see Gode and Moran (1966, 99–100). See, too, Megill (1975) and Hacking (2002); thanks to Sonam Kachru for having brought the latter sources to my attention.
15. Recall Śākyabuddhi's "*saṃketakriyā*" (see chapter 4, p. 154, above).
16. Cf. chapter 2, pp. 68–69, above.
17. That Durkheim's arguments in this regard should converge with the broadly Kantian sort of argument I've been venturing throughout is hardly coincidental; indeed, as is clear from the introduction to his *Elementary Forms of Religious Life* (see esp. Durkheim 1995, 12–18), Durkheim aimed precisely for something like a "naturalized" version of Kant—one that accepts the Kantian intuition that the categories integral to conceptual thought essentially transcend individuals, but that also tried to give a historical account of the emergence and development of these categories.
18. *Saṃbandhākṣepaparihāra*, verse 12; translated from Shastri (1978, 455); cf. Jha (1983, 349).
19. Verse 13 (Shastri 1978, 455; Jha 1983, 349–350).
20. So verse 21, which concludes: "And because of the difference between the ideas of the speaker and the auditor, ordinary usage is destroyed" (translated from Shastri 1978, 457; cf. Jha 1983, 351).
21. Verses 22cd–23 (translated from Shastri 1978, 457; cf. Jha 1983, 351).
22. Verse 24a–b: "If there is at all to be availability to the auditor, the interlocutor could not speak [words that are] unavailable" (translated from Shastri 1978, 457; cf. Jha 1983, 351–352).
23. From Pārthasārathi's comment on verse 24b; translated from Shastri (1978, 457).
24. Verses 137cd–138ab (translated from Shastri 1978, 481; cf. Jha 1983, 373).
25. From Pārthasārathi's commentary on verse 138ab; translated from Shastri 1978:482.
26. Verses 138cd–139ab (translated from Shastri 1978, 482; cf. Jha 1983, 373).
27. On Mīmāṃsaka epistemology and its plausible claim to represent an elaboration of common-sense intuitions, see Arnold (2005, part II).
28. Which is expressed in Pārthasārathi's introduction to verse 139cd, which thus attempts to salvage convention theories of linguistic origins: "But utterance (*vākyam*) isn't the only way of creating even linguistic relations, since there is the possibility of a way such as indication by gesture (*hastanirdeśa*), etc." Translated from Shastri (1978, 482).

29. Verses 139cd–140a (translated from Shastri 1978, 482; cf. Jha 1983, 374).
30. See chapter 2, pp. 72–73.
31. See Krasser (1999).
32. Cf. chapter 4, pp. 136–37, above.
33. It's interesting to note, in this regard, McDowell's concession that "the good questions we can raise in the evolutionary context come as close as good questions can to the philosophical questions I want to exorcize" (1996, 124n).
34. Cf. note 17, above, on the context of Durkheim's arguing thus.
35. George Steiner remarks that "language and death may be conceived of as the two areas of meaning or cognitive constants in which grammar and ontology are mutually determinant" (1998, 129) See also Valberg (2007) on the unimaginable character of our own deaths.
36. This is a question that gets at the heart of what is reasonably taken as the task of metaphysics, on some understandings thereof; cf. Gendler and Hawthorne (2002).
37. See Baker (1987, 123ff.) and Garfield (1988, 109ff.).
38. Ganeri (2007, 106, and *passim*) particularly reflects on *hermeneutic* versions of this problem, considering Indian discussions of textual "vehicles" whose content "implies that the vehicle itself is empty or unreal or merely illusory."
39. For Candrakīrti's critique of *svasaṃvitti*, see *Madhyamakāvatāra* 6.72–78 (Huntington 1989, 166; La Vallée Poussin 1970a, 166–174)—an argument summarized by Candrakīrti in the first chapter of the *Prasannapadā* (see Arnold 2005a, 434–435). For Kumārila's critique, see *Ślokavārttika, pratyakṣa* 79 (Taber 2005, 81) and, especially, *śūnyavāda* 64ff. (Jha 1983, 154ff.; Shastri 1978, 205ff.). Mīmāṃsakas' animus toward *svasaṃvitti* was owing to their uncompromising realism and their particular wariness of epistemic arguments for idealism.
40. Arguing as much, the nineteenth-century Tibetan thinker Mi-pham exploited the fact that Candrakīrti's critique of *svasaṃvitti* does not hit its mark given a constitutive understanding of *svasaṃvitti*. Interested in both affirming the preeminence of Candrakīrti's thought *and* in retaining the *svasaṃvitti* doctrine despite Candrakīrti's unqualified critique thereof, Mi-pham took Śāntarakṣita's constitutive understanding of *svasaṃvitti* as normative; Mi-pham then takes the fact that Candrakīrti's critique doesn't obviously touch Śāntarakṣita's view as evidence for the (exegetically dubious) claim that Candrakīrti meant to show only the *ultimately* unreal character of *svasaṃvitti*, which is left in play conventionally just insofar as *Śāntarakṣita*'s understanding remains in play. (Williams 1998 is framed by this conversation; see, too, chapter 5, p. 163, above, for Śāntarakṣita's understanding of *svasaṃvitti*.)
41. On the "Humean" point about causation that I have recurrently invoked, see especially chapter 1, p. 46, above. On Hume's *appeal* to causal explanation, see chapter 3, p. 85.
42. See chapter 1, pp. 21–22, above.
43. Here, I am paraphrasing from *Pramāṇavārttika* 3.4, as explained by Manorathanandin; see Shastri (1968, 100). My account is also informed by Inami's (1999) work on this passage and on Prajñākaragupta's explication thereof; see, too, Inami (1999b).

44. Translated from Shastri (1968, 100).
45. *Pramāṇavārttika* 3.4 (Shastri 1968, 100–101).
46. Shastri (1968, 101; emphasis added).
47. Siderits (2009) frames this problem in terms of the question of whether reductionism is coherently *expressible*.
48. On possible senses of *svabhāva*, see Westerhoff (2009, 19–52). I concur with Oetke that insofar as the Mādhyamika point is that there is "nothing which meets the necessary requirements for the status of a *paramārthasat*-entity," it's reasonable to understand "the phrase '*x* has a *svabhāva*' . . . as an idiomatic variant for the concept of something's being constituted by or founded in entities of the *paramārtha*-level"; it's clear that in saying "there is no *dharma* of which it can be said that it possesses a *svabhāva*," Mādhyamikas just mean to deny that there is anything "constituted by or founded in" ultimate existents (Oetke 1991, 323n).
49. For Nāgārjuna's emphasis of the equivalence of emptiness with dependent origination, see *Vigrahavyāvartanī* 22 (Bhattacharya 1990, 55–56, 107–108), and *Mūlamadhyamakakārikā* 24.18 (La Vallée Poussin 1970b, 503; cf. Garfield 1995, 69). For a formal account of the sense it makes to think things are dependently originated "all the way down" (and of that's not necessarily involving a regress), see Priest (2009).
50. See Arnold (2005, 143–204); an annotated translation of Candrakīrti's engagement with Dignāga is available in Arnold (2005a), which can be consulted for the textual specifics of the argument I'm reframing here.
51. Thanks to Sonam Kachru for much discussion of these issues and for the "coming into view" locution that figures prominently henceforth.
52. See Westerhoff's discussion (2009, 26–27) of the significantly different kinds of "dependence" relations that proponents of Madhyamaka have in view—chiefly, "existential" and "notional" dependence relations.
53. See pp. 213–14, above.
54. Nāgārjuna, *Mūlamadhyamakakārikā* 10.15; translated from La Vallée Poussin (1970b, 212).
55. Among the countless examples that might be given of Buddhist discussions involving the terms Nāgārjuna here deploys, see Kapstein (2001, 351–353), translating from chapter 9 of Vasubandhu's *Abhidharmakośabhāṣyam*.
56. So Apte (1992, 471; s.v. *upādānam*).
57. Candrakīrti says as much in introducing 10.15d (La Vallée Poussin 1970b, 213).
58. See Arnold (2005, 162–174).
59. In fact, the gerund *upādāya* effectively becomes an indeclinable particle meaning "with reference to" or "dependent on"; I suggest, though, that Nāgārjuna and Candrakīrti invite attention to the underlying verbal sense insofar as their talk of *upādāya prajñapti* often comes in their ringing of the changes on the verbal root *upā-√dā*.
60. *Mūlamadhyamakakārikā* 27.8; translated from La Vallée Poussin (1970b, 577–578).

61. From Candrakīrti's commentary on *Mūlamadhyamakakārikā* 27.8; text at La Vallée Poussin (1970b, 578).
62. See p. 216, above.
63. The phenomenon of "infant amnesia"—the fact of an adult person's generally having no memories from prior to the age of three or so, notwithstanding that developing infants are clearly "remembering" a great deal—surely has something to do with the emergence into linguisticality.
64. The issues here, of course, are more complex than this; see Siderits (2003, 157–195) for a full elaboration of the "semantic antirealist" account briefly engaged here.
65. See p. 231, above. More precisely, "A statement is ultimately true iff it corresponds to mind-independent reality and neither asserts nor presupposes the existence of anything not in the final ontology" (Siderits 2009, 60).
66. See, too, Johnston (2009, 46–47) on *intelligibility* as what goes missing on "scientistic" accounts of what there is.

CONCLUDING REFLECTIONS

1. For a critique of physicalism that takes its bearings from a basic rethinking of causation, see Rosenberg (2004)—and, to similar effect, Strawson (2006) and Chalmers (1996, 151–155).
2. See, e.g., Dreyfus (1997, 451–460).
3. In the latter vein, see, e.g., Masuzawa (2005) and Fitzgerald (2007).
4. E.g., "concepts that 'excite' more inference systems, fit more easily into their expectations, and trigger richer inferences (or all of these) are more likely to be acquired and transmitted than material that less easily corresponds to expectation formats or does not generate inferences" (Boyer 2001, 164).
5. So, e.g., Pyysiäinen: "Extremely complicated ideas (or instead their material tokens) can be stored in books and on computers, but they are part of culture only insofar as they are part of cognitive causal chains connecting material causal processes such as visual perception with semantic contents" (2009, 5).
6. Barrett (2010) gives a nuanced critique (along lines similar to those exemplified here) particularly of the *computational* view of thought that figures in much cognitive-scientific research in religious studies—but urges that jettisoning this view doesn't entail the abandonment of the whole cognitive-scientific project in this regard. See, too, Smith (2009), whose critique of scientistic studies of religion has affinities with mine, but who has reservations about some lines of argument I have used, as well as about the antiscientific uses sometimes made of such arguments.

References

Abhyankar, K. V. 1977. *A Dictionary of Sanskrit Grammar*. 2nd ed. Baroda: Oriental Institute.

Abhyankar, K. V., ed. 1978. *Sarva-darśana-saṁgraha of Sāyaṇa-Mādhava*. 3rd ed. Poona: Bhandarkar Oriental Research Institute.

Anscombe, G. E. M. 1963. *Intention*. 2nd ed. Cambridge, Mass.: Harvard University Press, 2000.

Apte, V. S. 1992. *The Practical Sanskrit-English Dictionary*. Rev. and enlarged ed. Kyoto: Rinsen.

Arnold, Dan. 2005. *Buddhists, Brahmins, and Belief: Epistemology in South Asian Philosophy of Religion*. New York: Columbia University Press.

—. 2005a. "Materials for a Mādhyamika Critique of Foundationalism: An Annotated Translation of *Prasannapadā* 55.11 to 75.13." *Journal of the International Association of Buddhist Studies* 28, no. 2: 411–467.

—. 2005b. "Is *Svasaṃvitti* Transcendental? A Tentative Reconstruction Following Śāntarakṣita." *Asian Philosophy* 15, no. 1: 77–111.

—. 2006. "On Semantics and *Saṃketa*: Thoughts on a Neglected Problem with Buddhist *Apoha* Doctrine." *Journal of Indian Philosophy* 34: 425–427.

—. 2008. "Buddhist Idealism, Epistemic and Otherwise: Thoughts on the Alternating Perspectives of Dharmakīrti." *Sophia* 47, no. 1 (April): 3–28.

—. 2009. "Dharmakīrti and Dharmottara on the Intentionality of Perception: Selections from *Nyāyabindu* (*An Epitome of Philosophy*)." In *Buddhist Philosophy: Essential Readings*, ed. William Edelglass and Jay L. Garfield, 186–196. Oxford: Oxford University Press.

—. 2010. "Kumārila." In *Stanford encyclopedia of philosophy*. http://plato.stanford.edu/entries/kumaarila.

——. 2010a. "Self-Awareness (*Svasaṃvitti*) and Related Doctrines of Buddhists Following Dignāga: Philosophical Characterizations of Some of the Main Issues." *Journal of Indian Philosophy* 38: 323–378.

Asad, Talal. 1993. *Genealogies of Religion: Discipline and Reasons of Power in Christianity and Islam*. Baltimore, Md.: Johns Hopkins University Press.

Austin, J. L. 1946. "Other Minds." In *Philosophical Papers*, 3rd ed., ed. J. O. Urmson and G. J. Warnock, 76–116. Oxford: Clarendon Press, 1979.

Aydede, Murat. 1997. "Has Fodor Really Changed His Mind on Narrow Content?" *Mind and Language* 12, nos. 3–4: 422–458.

Baird, Bryan. 2006. "The Transcendental Nature of *Mind and World*." *Southern Journal of Philosophy* 44: 381–398.

Baker, Lynne Rudder. 1987. *Saving Belief: A Critique of Physicalism*. Princeton, N.J.: Princeton University Press.

Barrett, Nathaniel. 2010. "Toward an Alternative Evolutionary Theory of Religion." *Journal of the American Academy of Religion* 78, no. 3: 583–621.

Bennett, Jonathan. 1971. *Locke, Berkeley, Hume: Central Themes*. Oxford: Clarendon Press.

Bennett, M. R., and P. M. S. Hacker. 2003. *Philosophical Foundations of Neuroscience*. Oxford: Blackwell.

Bermúdez, Jose Luis. 1995. "Syntax, Semantics, and Levels of Explanation." *Philosophical Quarterly* 45, no. 180: 361–367.

Bhatt, G. P. 1962. *Epistemology of the Bhāṭṭa School of Pūrva Mīmāṃsā*. Varanasi: Chowkhamba Sanskrit Series Office.

Bhattacharya, Kamaleswar. 1990. *The Dialectical Method of Nāgārjuna: Vigrahavyāvartanī*. 3rd ed. Delhi: Motilal Banarsidass.

Bilgrami, Akeel. 2006. *Self-Knowledge and Resentment*. Cambridge, Mass.: Harvard University Press.

Block, Ned, and Georges Rey. 2008. "Mind, Computational Theories of." In *Routledge Encyclopedia of Philosophy*, ed. E. Craig. http://www.rep.routledge.com/article/W007SECT3.

Boghossian, Paul. 1989. "The Rule-Following Considerations." *Mind*, n.s., 98, no. 392: 507–549.

——. 2003. "The Normativity of Content." *Philosophical Issues* 13, no. 1: 31–45.

Boucher, Daniel. 1991. "The *Pratītyasamutpādagāthā* and Its Role in the Medieval Cult of the Relics." *Journal of the International Association of Buddhist Studies* 14, no. 1: 1–27.

Bourdieu, Pierre. 1977. *Outline of a Theory of Practice*. Cambridge: Cambridge University Press.

Boyer, Pascal. 2001. *Religion Explained: The Evolutionary Origins of Religious Thought*. New York: Basic Books.

Brandom, Robert. 2000. *Articulating Reasons: An Introduction to Inferentialism*. Cambridge, Mass.: Harvard University Press.

Brentano, Franz. 1973. *Psychology from an Empirical Standpoint*. Ed. Oskar Kraus, trans. Antos C. Rancurello et al. London: Routledge and Kegan Paul.

Brooks, David. 2008. "The Neural Buddhists." *New York Times* (May 13).

Brown, Curtis. 2007. "Narrow Mental Content." In *Stanford Encyclopedia of Philosophy*. http://plato.stanford.edu/entries/content-narrow/.

Buescher, Hartmut, ed. 2007. *Sthiramati's Triṃśikāvijñaptibhāṣya: Critical Editions of the Sanskrit Text and Its Tibetan Translation*. Vienna: Verlag der Österrichischen Akademie der Wissenschaften.

Burge, Tyler. 1979. "Individualism and the Mental." Reprinted in *Foundations of Mind: Philosophical Essays*, 2:100–150. Oxford: Oxford University Press, 2007.

Cabezón, José. 1990. "The Canonization of Philosophy and the Rhetoric of Siddhānta in Indo-Tibetan Buddhism." In *Buddha Nature: A Festschrift in Honor of Minoru Kiyota*, ed. Paul Griffiths and John Keenan, 7–26. Reno, Nevada: Buddhist Books International.

Cardona, George. 1967–1968. "*Anvaya* and *Vyatireka* in Indian Grammar." *Adyar Library Bulletin* 31–32: 313–352.

Carey, Benedict. 2005. "Scientists Bridle at Lecture Plan for Dalai Lama." *New York Times* (October 19).

Chakrabarti, Arindam. 1990. "On the Purported Inseparability of Blue and the Awareness of Blue: An Examination of Sahopalambhaniyama." In *Mind Only School and Buddhist Logic*, ed. Doboom Tulku, 17–36. New Delhi: Tibet House/Aditya Prakashan.

Chalmers, David J. 1995. "Facing Up to the Problem of Consciousness." *Journal of Consciousness Studies* 2, no. 3: 200–219.

——. 1996. *The Conscious Mind: In Search of a Fundamental Theory*. Oxford: Oxford University Press.

Chisholm, Roderick M. 1960. *Realism and the Background of Phenomenology*. Glencoe, Ill.: Free Press.

Chisholm, Roderick M., and Wilfrid Sellars. 1957. "The Chisholm-Sellars Correspondence on Intentionality." Reprinted in *Intentionality, Mind, and Language*, ed. Ausonio Marras, 214–248. Urbana: University of Illinois Press, 1972.

Cho, Francisca. 2008. "The Aesthetics of Neural Buddhism." *Immanent Frame* (July). http://www.ssrc.org/blogs/immanent_frame/2008/07/08/the-aesthetics-of-neural-buddhism.

Chu, Junjie. 2006. "On Dignāga's Theory of the Object of Cognition as Presented in *PS(V)* 1." *Journal of the International Association of Buddhist Studies* 29, no. 2: 211–253.

Churchland, Paul. 1981. "Eliminative Materialism and the Propositional Attitudes." *Journal of Philosophy* 78, no. 2: 67–90.

Clooney, Francis X. 1990. *Thinking Ritually: Rediscovering the Pūrva Mīmāṃsā of Jaimini*. Vienna: Institut für Indologie der Universität Wien.

Collins, Arthur W. 1998. "Beastly Experience." *Philosophy and Phenomenological Research* 58, no. 2: 375–380.

Davidson, Donald. 1963. "Actions, Reasons, and Causes." Reprinted in *Essays on Actions and Events*, 3–20. Oxford: Oxford University Press, 1980.

——. 1988. "The Myth of the Subjective." Reprinted in *Subjective, Intersubjective, Objective*, 39–52. Oxford: Oxford University Press, 2001.

——. 1993. "Thinking Causes." Reprinted in *Truth, Language, and History*, 185–200. Oxford: Oxford University Press, 2005.

Davidson, Richard J., and Anne Harrington, eds. 2002. *Visions of Compassion: Western Scientists and Tibetan Buddhists Examine Human Nature*. Oxford: Oxford University Press.

Dawkins, Richard. 2006. *The God Delusion*. Boston: Houghton Mifflin.

deCharms, Christopher. 1998. *Two Views of Mind: Abhidharma and Brain Science*. Ithaca, N.Y.: Snow Lion.

Dennett, Daniel. 1981. *Brainstorms: Philosophical Essays on Mind and Psychology*. Cambridge, Mass.: The MIT Press.

—. 1987. *The Intentional Stance*. Cambridge, Mass.: The MIT Press.

—. 1991. *Consciousness Explained*. Boston: LittleBrown.

—. 2003. "Who's on First? Heterophenomenology Explained." *Journal of Consciousness Studies* 10, nos. 9–10: 19–30.

—. 2006. *Breaking the Spell: Religion as a Natural Phenomenon*. New York: Viking.

Descombes, Vincent. 2001. *The Mind's Provisions: A Critique of Cognitivism*. Princeton, N.J.: Princeton University Press.

deVries, Willem A. 2007. Review of Jay F. Rosenberg, *Wilfrid Sellars: Fusing the Images* (Oxford University Press, 2007). *Notre Dame Philosophical Reviews*. http://ndpr.nd.edu/review.cfm?id=13307.

—. 2009. Review of John McDowell, *The Engaged Intellect* and *Having the World in View* (both Harvard University Press, 2009). *Notre Dame Philosophical Reviews*. http://ndpr.nd.edu/review.cfm?id=17105.

Dravid, Raja Ram. 1972. *The Problem of Universals in Indian Philosophy*. Delhi: Motilal Banarsidass.

Dreyfus, Georges. 1996. "Can the Fool Lead the Blind? Perception and the Given in Dharmakīrti's Thought." *Journal of Indian Philosophy* 24: 209–229.

—. 1997. *Recognizing Reality: Dharmakīrti's Philosophy and Its Tibetan Interpreters*. Albany, N.Y.: SUNY Press.

—. 2007. "Is Perception Intentional? A Preliminary Exploration of Intentionality in Dharmakīrti." In *Pramāṇakīrtiḥ: Papers Dedicated to Ernst Steinkellner on the Occasion of His Seventieth Birthday*, ed. Birgit Kellner et al., part 1, 95–113. Vienna: Arbeitskreis für tibetische und buddhistische Studien, Universität Wien.

—. 2011. "Apoha as a Naturalized Account of Concept Formation." In *Apoha: Buddhist Nominalism and Human Cognition*, ed. Mark Siderits et al., 207–227. New York: Columbia University Press.

Dreyfus, Georges, and Christian Lindtner. 1989. "The Yogācāra Philosophy of Dignāga and Dharmakīrti." *Studies in Central and East Asian Religions (Journal of the Seminar for Buddhist Studies, Copenhagen and Aarhus)* 2: 27–52.

Duerlinger, James. 2008. [Review of Dunne, *Foundations of Dharmakīrti's Philosophy*]. *Philosophy East & West* 58, no. 4: 608–614.

Dummett, Michael. 2004. *Truth and the Past*. New York: Columbia University Press.

Dunne, John. 2004. *Foundations of Dharmakīrti's Philosophy*. Boston: Wisdom Publications.

—. 2006. "Realizing the Unreal: Dharmakīrti's Theory of Yogic Perception." *Journal of Indian Philosophy* 34: 497–519.

Durkheim, Émile. 1995. *Elementary Forms of Religious Life*. Trans. Karen Fields. New York: The Free Press.

Eltschinger, Vincent. 2010. "Dharmakīrti." *Revue internationale de philosophie* 64, no. 253: 397–440.

Field, Brent. 2008. "Is This Anything or Is This Nothing?" *Immanent Frame*. http://www.ssrc.org/blogs/immanent_frame/2008/08/22/is-this-anything-or-is-this-nothing/.

Fitzgerald, Timothy. 2007. *Discourse on Civility and Barbarity: A Critical History of Religion and Related Categories*. Oxford: Oxford University Press.

Flanagan, Owen. 2007. *The Really Hard Problem: Meaning in a Material World*. Cambridge, Mass.: The MIT Press.

Fodor, Jerry. 1975. *The Language of Thought*. Cambridge, Mass.: Harvard University Press.

——. 1980. "Methodological Solipsism Considered as a Research Strategy in Cognitive Psychology." Reprinted in *Husserl, Intentionality, and Cognitive Science*, ed. Hubert L. Dreyfus, 277–303. Cambridge, Mass.: The MIT Press, 1982.

——. 1985. "Fodor's Guide to Mental Representation: The Intelligent Auntie's Vade-Mecum." *Mind*, n.s., 94, no. 373: 76–100.

——. 1987. *Psychosemantics*. Cambridge, Mass.: The MIT Press.

——. 1990. *A Theory of Content and Other Essays*. Cambridge, Mass.: The MIT Press.

——. 1994. *The Elm and the Expert: Mentalese and its Semantics*. Cambridge, Mass.: The MIT Press.

——. 2006. *Hume Variations*. Oxford: Oxford University Press.

——. 2008. *LOT 2: The Language of Thought Revisited*. Oxford: Oxford University Press.

Franco, Eli. 1993. "Did Dignāga Accept Four Types of Perception?" *Journal of Indian Philosophy* 21: 295–299.

——. 1997. *Dharmakīrti on Compassion and Rebirth*. Vienna: Arbeitskreis für tibetische und buddhistische Studien Universität Wien.

——. 2004. "On *Pramāṇasamuccayavṛtti* 6ab Again." *Journal of Indian Philosophy* 32: 57–79.

——. 2006. "A New Era in the Study of Buddhist Philosophy." *Journal of Indian Philosophy* 34: 221–227.

——. 2007. "Prajñākaragupta on *Pratītyasamutpāda* and Reverse Causation." In *Pramāṇakīrtiḥ: Papers Dedicated to Ernst Steinkellner on the Occasion of His Seventieth Birthday*, ed. Birgit Kellner et al., part 1, 163–185. Vienna: Arbeitskreis für tibetische und buddhistische Studien, Universität Wien.

Frauwallner, Erich. 1934. "Dharmakīrtis Saṃbandhaparīkṣā: Text und Übersetzung." *Wiener Zeitschrift für die Kunde des Morgenlandes* 41: 261–300.

——. 1968. *Materialien zur ältesten Erkenntnislehre der Karmamīmāṃsā*. Vienna: Hermann Böhlaus Nachf.

Frege, Gottlob. 1956. "The Thought: A Logical Inquiry." *Mind* 65, no. 259: 289–311.

Friedman, Michael. 1996. "Exorcising the Philosophical Tradition: Comments on John McDowell's *Mind and World*." *Philosophical Review* 105: 427–467.

Gadamer, Hans-Georg. 1989. *Truth and Method*. 2nd ed. New York: Continuum.

Ganeri, Jonardon. 1999. "Self-Intimation, Memory and Personal Identity." *Journal of Indian Philosophy* 27: 469–483.

——. 1999b. *Semantic Powers: Meaning and the Means of Knowing in Classical Indian Philosophy*. Oxford: Oxford University Press.

——. 2001. *Philosophy in Classical India: The Proper Work of Reason*. New York: Routledge.

——. 2007. *The Concealed Art of the Soul: Theories of Self and Practices of Truth in Indian Ethics and Epistemology*. Oxford: Oxford University Press.

Garfield, Jay L. 1988. *Belief in Psychology: A Study in the Ontology of Mind*. Cambridge, Mass.: The MIT Press.

——. 1995. *The Fundamental Wisdom of the Middle Way: Nāgārjuna's* Mūlamadhyamakakārikā. Oxford: Oxford University Press.

Gasser, Georg, ed. 2007. *How Successful Is Naturalism?* Frankfurt: Ontos.

Geertz, Clifford. 1973. "The Growth of Culture and the Evolution of Mind." In *The Interpretation of Cultures*, 55–83. New York: Basic Books.

Gendler, Tamar Szabó, and John Hawthorne. 2002. "Introduction: Conceivability and Possibility." In *Conceivability and Possibility*, ed. T. S. Gendler and J. Hawthorne, 1–70. Oxford: Clarendon Press.

Gillon, Brendan S. 2009. "The Role of Knowledge of Causation in Dharmakīrti's Theory of Inference." In *Buddhist Philosophy: Essential Readings*, ed. William Edelglass and Jay L. Garfield, 197–204. Oxford: Oxford University Press.

Gnoli, Raniero, ed. 1960. *The Pramāṇavārttikam of Dharmakīrti: The First Chapter with the Autocommentary: Text and Critical Notes*. Rome: Istituto Italiano Per Il Medio ed Estremo Oriente.

Gode, Alexander, and John H. Moran, trans. 1966. *On the Origin of Language*. Chicago: University of Chicago Press.

Godlove, Terry. 2002. "Saving Belief: On the New Materialism in Religious Studies." In *Radical Interpretation in Religion*, ed. Nancy Frankenberry, 10–24. Cambridge: Cambridge University Press.

Griffiths, Paul. 1986. *On Being Mindless: Buddhist Meditation and the Mind-Body Problem*. La-Salle, Ill.: Open Court Press.

Hacking, Ian. 2002. "How, Why, When, and Where Did Language Go Public." In *Historical Ontology*, 121–39. Cambridge, Mass.: Harvard University Press.

Halbfass, Wilhelm. 1992. *On Being and What There Is: Classical Vaiśeṣika and the History of Indian Ontology*. Albany, N.Y.: SUNY Press.

Hanna, Robert. 2010. [Review of Ralph Ellis and Natika Newton, *How the Mind Uses the Brain (to Move the Body and Image the Universe)*]. *Notre Dame Philosophical Reviews*. http://ndpr.nd.edu/review.cfm?id=21692.

Harbecke, Jens. 2008. *Mental Causation: Investigating the Mind's Powers in a Natural World*. Frankfurt: Ontos.

Hattori Masaaki. 1968. *Dignāga, On Perception, Being the Pratyakṣapariccheda of Dignāga's* Pramāṇasamuccaya *from the Sanskrit Fragments and the Tibetan Versions*. Cambridge, Mass.: Harvard University Press.

——. 1982. "*Pramāṇasamuccaya* Chapter 5: *Anyāpohaparīkṣā*, with Jinendrabuddhi's Commentary, Edited Tibetan with Sanskrit Fragments." *Memoirs of the Faculty of Letters, Kyoto University* 21: 103–224.

—. 2000. "Dignāga's Theory of Meaning: An Annotated Translation of the *Pramāṇa-samuccayavṛtti*, Chapter V: *Anyāpohaparīkṣā*." In *Wisdom, Compassion, and the Search for Understanding*, ed. Jonathan Silk, 137–146. Honolulu: University of Hawai'i Press.

Haugeland, John. 1993. "Pattern and Being." In *Dennett and His Critics: Demystifying Mind*, ed. Bo Dahlbom, 53–69. Cambridge, Mass.: Blackwell.

—. 1998. *Having Thought: Essays in the Metaphysics of Mind*. Cambridge, Mass.: Harvard University Press.

Hayes, Richard. 1988. *Dignāga on the Interpretation of Signs*. Dordrecht: Kluwer.

—. 1988a. "Principled Atheism in the Buddhist Scholastic Tradition." *Journal of Indian Philosophy* 16: 5–28.

—. 1993. "Dharmakīrti on Rebirth." In *Studies in Original Buddhism and Mahāyāna Buddhism*, ed. Egaku Mayeda, 1:111–129. Kyoto: Nagata Bunshodo.

—. 2004. "On the Buddha's Authority: A Translation of the Pramāṇasiddhi Chapter of Dharmakīrti's *Pramāṇavārttika* [first 59 verses only]." Unpublished ms. http://www.unm.edu/~rhayes/download.html.

Hayes, Richard, and Brendan Gillon. 2008. "Dharmakīrti on the Role of Causation in Inference as Presented in *Pramāṇavārttika Svopajñavṛtti* 11–38." *Journal of Indian Philosophy* 36: 335–404.

Heim, Maria. 2003. "The Aesthetics of Excess." *Journal of the American Academy of Religion* 71, no. 3: 531–554.

Houben, Jan E. M. 1995. *The Saṃbandha-samuddeśa (Chapter on Relation) and Bhartṛhari's Philosophy of Language*. Groningen: Egbert Forsten.

Hugon, Pascale. 2009. "Breaking the Circle: Dharmakīrti's Response to the Charge of Circularity Against the *Apoha* Theory and Its Tibetan Adaptation." *Journal of Indian Philosophy* 37: 533–557.

—. 2011. "Dharmakīrti's Discussion of Circularity." In *Apoha: Buddhist Nominalism and Human Cognition*, ed. Mark Siderits et al., 109–124. New York: Columbia University Press.

Hume, David. 1739. *A Treatise of Human Nature*. Ed. L. A. Selby-Bigge; 2nd ed. revised by P. H. Nidditch. Oxford: Clarendon Press, 1978.

—. 1757. *The Natural History of Religion*. In *Principal Writings on Religion*, ed. J. C. A. Gaskin. Oxford: Oxford University Press, 1998.

Huntington, C. W., with Geshe Namgyal Wangchen. 1989. *The Emptiness of Emptiness: An Introduction to Early Indian Mādhyamika*. Honolulu: University of Hawaii Press.

Husserl, Edmund. 1970. *Logical Investigations*. 2 vols., continuous pagination. Trans. J. N. Findlay. Amherst, N.Y.: Humanity Books.

—. 1991. *On the Phenomenology of the Consciousness of Internal Time (1893–1917)*. Trans. John Barnett Brough. Dordrecht: Kluwer.

Inami Masahiro. 1999. "Can Causality be Truly Determined?" Paper presented at the 12th conference of the International Association of Buddhist Studies, Lausanne, Switzerland.

—. 1999b. "On the Determination of Causality." In *Dharmakīrti's Thought and Its Impact on Indian and Tibetan Philosophy*, ed. Shoryu Katsura, 131–154. Vienna: Verlag der Österreichischen Akademie der Wissenschaften.

——. 2001. "The Problem of Other Minds in the Buddhist Epistemological Tradition." *Journal of Indian Philosophy* 29: 465–483.

Iwata Takashi. 1991. *Sahopalambhaniyama: Struktur und Entwicklung des Schlusses von der Tatsache, daß Erkenntnis und Gegenstand ausschließlich zusammen wahrgenommen werden, auf deren Nichtverschiedenheit.* Stuttgart: Franz Steiner Verlag.

Jackson, Roger. 1985. "Dharmakīrti's Refutation of Theism." *Philosophy East and West* 36, no. 4: 315–348.

——. 1993. *Is Enlightenment Possible? Dharmakīrti and rGyal tshab rje on Knowledge, Rebirth, No-Self, and Liberation.* Ithaca, N.Y.: Snow Lion.

Jha, Ganganath. 1964. *Pūrva-Mīmāṃsā in Its Sources.* 2nd ed. Varanasi: Banaras Hindu University Press.

Jha, Ganganath, trans. 1973–1974. *Śābara-bhāṣya.* 2nd ed. Baroda: Gaekwad's Oriental Series (vols. 66, 70, 73).

——, trans. 1983. *Ślokavārtika: Translated from the Original Sanskrit with Extracts from the Commentaries "Kāśikā" of Sucarita Miśra and "Nyāyaratnākara" of Pārtha Sārathi Miśra.* Delhi: Sri Satguru.

Johnston, Mark. 2009. *Saving God: Religion After Idolatry.* Princeton, N.J.: Princeton University Press.

Kajiyama Yuichi. 1998. *An Introduction to Buddhist Philosophy: An Annotated Translation of the* Tarkabhāṣa *of Mokṣākaragupta.* Vienna: Arbeitskreis für tibetische und buddhistische Studien Universität Wien.

——. 1965. "Controversy Between the Sākāra- and Nirākāra-vādins of the Yogācāra School—Some Materials." Reprinted in *Studies in Buddhist Philosophy: Selected Papers,* ed. Katsumi Mimaki et al., 389–400. Kyoto: Rinsen, 2005.

Kant, Immanuel. 1781–1787. *Critique of Pure Reason.* Trans. Paul Guyer and Allen W. Wood. Cambridge: Cambridge University Press, 1999.

——. 1788. *Critique of Practical Reason.* Trans. Mary Gregor. Cambridge: Cambridge University Press, 1997.

——. 1783. *Prolegomena to Any Future Metaphysics That Will Be Able to Come Forward as Science.* Rev. ed. Trans. Gary Hatfield. Cambridge: Cambridge University Press, 2004.

Kapstein, Matthew. 2001. *Reason's Traces: Identity and Interpretation in Indian and Tibetan Buddhist Thought.* Boston: Wisdom Publications.

Katsura Shoryu. 1979. "The *Apoha* Theory of Dignāga." *Indogaku Bukkyogaku Kenkyu* 28, no. 1: 16–20.

——. 1984. "Dharmakīrti's Theory of Truth." *Journal of Indian Philosophy* 12: 215–235.

——. 1991. "Dignāga and Dharmakīrti on *Apoha.*" In *Studies in the Buddhist Epistemological Tradition,* ed. Ernst Steinkellner, 129–146. Vienna: Verlag der Österreichischen Akademie der Wissenschaften.

——. 2007. "Dharmakīrti's Proof of the Existence of Other Minds." In *Pramāṇakīrtiḥ: Papers Dedicated to Ernst Steinkellner on the Occasion of His Seventieth Birthday,* ed. Birgit Kellner et al., part 1, 407–421. Vienna: Arbeitskreis für tibetische und buddhistische Studien, Universität Wien.

Kellner, Birgit. 2005. "Dharmakīrti's Exposition of *Pramāṇa* and *Pramāṇaphala* and the Sliding Scale of Analysis." Paper presented at the Fourth International

Dharmakīrti Conference, Vienna, August 2005. http://www.birgitkellner.org/index.php?id=132.

—. 2010. "Self-Awareness (*Svasaṃvedana*) in Dignāga's *Pramāṇasamuccaya* and *-vṛtti*—A Close Reading." *Journal of Indian Philosophy* 38: 203–231.

Kelly, Sean D. 2001. *The Relevance of Phenomenology to the Philosophy of Language and Mind*. New York: Garland.

Kenner, Hugh. 1968. *The Counterfeiters: An Historical Comedy*. Baltimore, Md.: Johns Hopkins University Press.

Kobayashi, Hisayasu. 2010. "Self-Awareness and Mental Perception." *Journal of Indian Philosophy* 38: 233–245.

Krasser, Helmut. 1999. "Dharmakīrti's and Kumārila's Refutations of the Existence of God: A Consideration of their Chronological Order." In *Dharmakīrti's Thought and Its Impact on Indian and Tibetan Philosophy*, ed. Shoryu Katsura, 215–223. Vienna: Verlag der Österreichischen Akademie der Wissenschaften.

Kripke, Saul. 1982. *Wittgenstein on Rules and Private Language*. Cambridge, Mass.: Harvard University Press.

La Vallée Poussin, Louis de, ed. 1970a. *Madhyamakāvatāra par Candrakīrti: Traduction tibétaine*. Bibliotheca Buddhica 9. Osnabrück: Biblio Verlag.

—. 1970b. *Mūlamadhyamakakārikās (Mādhyamikasūtras) de Nāgārjuna, avec la Prasannapadā Commentaire de Candrakīrti*. Bibliotheca Buddhica 4. Osnabrück: Biblio Verlag.

Lasic, Horst. 2003. "On the Utilisation of Causality as a Basis of Inference: Dharmakīrti's Statements and Their Interpretation." *Journal of Indian Philosophy* 31: 185–197.

Leibniz, G. W. 1765. *New Essays on Human Understanding*. Trans. Peter Remnant and Jonathan Bennett. Cambridge: Cambridge University Press, 1996.

Levine, Joseph. 1983. "Materialism and Qualia: The Explanatory Gap." *Pacific Philosophical Quarterly* 64: 354–361.

—. 2001. *Purple Haze: The Puzzle of Consciousness*. New York: Oxford University Press.

Lincoln, Bruce. 1989. *Discourse and the Construction of Society*. Oxford: Oxford University Press.

Locke, John. 1689. *An Essay Concerning Human Understanding*. Ed. Peter H. Nidditch. Oxford: Clarendon Press, 1975.

Longuenesse, Béatrice. 1998. *Kant and the Capacity to Judge: Sensibility and Discursivity in the Transcendental Analytic of the* Critique of Pure Reason. Princeton, N.J.: Princeton University Press.

Lopez, Donald. 2002. "Introduction." In *A Modern Buddhist Bible: Essential Readings from East and West*, vii–xli. Boston: Beacon Press.

—. 2008a. "The Buddha According to Brooks." *Immanent Frame*. http://www.ssrc.org/blogs/immanent_frame/2008/06/12/the-buddha-according-to-brooks/.

—. 2008b. *Buddhism and Science: A Guide for the Perplexed*. Chicago: University of Chicago Press.

Lutz, Antoine, John D. Dunne, and Richard J. Davidson. 2007. "Meditation and the Neuroscience of Consciousness: An Introduction." In *The Cambridge Handbook of Consciousness*, ed. Philip David Zelazo et al., 499–551. Cambridge: Cambridge University Press.

Macdonald, Cynthia, and Graham Macdonald, eds. 2006. *McDowell and His Critics*. Malden, Mass.: Blackwell.

Macdonald, Graham. 2006. "The Two Natures: Another Dogma?" In *McDowell and His Critics*, ed. Cynthia Macdonald and Graham Macdonald, 222–235. Malden, Mass.: Blackwell.

McDowell, John. 1996. *Mind and World: With a New Introduction*. Cambridge, Mass.: Harvard University Press.

—. 1998. *Meaning, Knowledge, & Reality*. Cambridge, Mass.: Harvard University Press.

—. 1998a. *Mind, Value, and Reality*. Cambridge, Mass.: Harvard University Press.

—. 1998b. "Having the World in View: Sellars, Kant, and Intentionality," *Journal of Philosophy* 95, no. 9: 431–491.

—. 1998c. "Précis of *Mind and World*." *Philosophy and Phenomenological Research* 58, no. 2: 365–368.

—. 2006. "Response to Graham Macdonald." In *McDowell and His Critics*, ed. Cynthia Macdonald and Graham Macdonald, 235–239. Malden, Mass.: Blackwell.

—. 2009. *The Engaged Intellect: Philosophical Essays*. Cambridge, Mass.: Harvard University Press.

—. 2009a. *Having the World in View: Essays on Kant, Hegel, and Sellars*, Cambridge, Mass.: Harvard University Press.

MacKenzie, Matthew D. 2007. "The Illumination of Consciousness: Approaches to Self-Awareness in the Indian and Western Traditions." *Philosophy East & West* 57, no. 1: 40–62.

McMahan, David L. 2004. "Modernity and the Early Discourse of Scientific Buddhism." *Journal of the American Academy of Religion* 72, no. 4:897–933.

—. 2008. *The Making of Buddhist Modernism*. Oxford: Oxford University Press.

Malvania, Paṇḍita Dalsukhbhai, ed. 1971. *Paṇḍita Durveka Miśra's* Dharmottarapradīpa. 2nd ed. Patna: Kashiprasad Jayaswal Research Institute.

Mansfield, Vic. 2008. *Tibetan Buddhism and Modern Physics*. Philadelphia: Templeton Foundation Press.

Masuzawa, Tomoko. 2005. *The Invention of Religions: Or, How European Universalism Was Preserved in the Language of Pluralism*. Chicago: University of Chicago Press.

Matilal, B. K. 1986. *Perception: An Essay on Classical Indian Theories of Knowledge*. Oxford: Clarendon Press.

—. 1990. *The Word and the World: India's Contribution to the Study of Language*. Delhi: Oxford University Press.

Megill, Allan. 1975. "The Enlightenment Debate on the Origin of Language and its Historical Background." Ph.D. dissertation, Columbia University.

Meyers, Karin. 2010. "Freedom and Self-Control: Free Will in South Asian Buddhism." Ph.D. dissertation, University of Chicago.

Miyasaka Yūsho, ed. 1971–1972. "Pramāṇavārttika-kārikā (Sanskrit and Tibetan)." *Acta Indologica* 2: 1–206.

Mookerjee, Satkari. 1975. *The Buddhist Philosophy of Universal Flux: An Exposition of the Philosophy of Critical Realism as Expounded by the School of Dignāga*. Delhi: Motilal Banarsidass (reprint).

Moriyama Shinya. 2010. "On Self-Awareness in the Sautrāntika Epistemology." *Journal of Indian Philosophy* 38: 261–277.

Nagatomi Masatoshi. 1967–1968. "*Arthakriyā*." *Adyar Library Bulletin* 31–32: 52–72.

——. 1980. "*Mānasa-Pratyakṣa:* A Conundrum in the Buddhist *Pramāṇa* System." In *Sanskrit and Indian Studies: Essays in Honour of Daniel H. H. Ingalls*, ed. Nagatomi Masatoshi, 243–260. Dordrecht: Reidel.

Nagel, Thomas. 1974. "What Is It Like to Be a Bat?" *Philosophical Review* 83, no. 4: 435–450.

Nance, Richard F. 2012. *Speaking for Buddhas: Scriptural Commentary in Indian Buddhism*. New York: Columbia University Press.

Newberg, Andrew, Eugene d'Aquili, and Vince Rause. 2001. *Why God Won't Go Away: Brain Science and the Biology of Belief*. New York: Ballantine.

Oetke, Claus. 1991. "Remarks on the Interpretation of Nāgārjuna's Philosophy." *Journal of Indian Philosophy* 19: 315–323.

——. 1994. *Studies on the Doctrine of Trairūpya*. Vienna: Arbeitskreis für Tibetische und Buddhistische Studien, Universität Wien.

Ono, Motoi. 2000. *Prajñākaraguptas Erklärung der Definition gültiger Erkenntnis (Pramāṇavārttikālaṃkāra zu Pramāṇavārttika II 1-7), Teil I: Sanskrit-Text und Materialien*. Vienna: Österreichische Akademie der Wissenschaften.

O'Rourke, Michael. 2008. [Review of Eric T. Olson, *What Are We? A Study in Personal Ontology* (Oxford University Press, 2007)]. *Notre Dame Philosophical Reviews*. http://ndpr.nd.edu/review.cfm?id=12724.

Pandeya, Ram Chandra, ed. 1989. *The* Pramāṇavārttikam *of Ācārya Dharmakīrti, with the Commentaries* Svopajñavṛtti *of the Author and* Pramāṇavārttikavṛtti *of Manorathanandin*. Delhi: Motilal Banarsidass.

Passmore, John. 1957. *A Hundred Years of Philosophy*. London: Duckworth.

Peirce, Charles Sanders. 1976. *The New Elements of Mathematics by Charles S. Peirce*. Vol. 3. Ed. Carolyn Eisele. Atlantic Highlands, N.J.: Humanities Press.

Pessin, Andrew, and Sanford Goldberg, eds. 1996. *The Twin Earth Chronicles: Twenty Years of Reflection on Hilary Putnam's "The Meaning of 'Meaning.'"* London: M. E. Sharpe.

Pind, Ole. 2009. "Dignāga's Philosophy of Language: Dignāga on Anyāpoha: Pramāṇasamuccaya V: Texts, Translation, and Annotation." Ph.D. dissertation, University of Vienna.

——. 2011. "Dignāga's *Apoha* Theory: Its Presuppositions and Main Theoretical Implications." In *Apoha: Buddhist Nominalism and Human Cognition*, ed. Mark Siderits et al., 64–83. New York: Columbia University Press.

Pippin, Robert B. 1987. "Kant on the Spontaneity of Mind." *Canadian Journal of Philosophy* 17, no. 2: 449–476.

——. 2002. "Leaving Nature Behind: Or Two Cheers for 'Subjectivism.'" In *Reading McDowell: On* Mind and World, ed. Nicholas H. Smith, 58–75. New York: Routledge.

Pollock, Sheldon. 1985. "The Theory of Practice and the Practice of Theory in Indian Intellectual History." *Journal of the American Oriental Society* 105, no. 3: 499–519.

——. 1989. "Mīmāṃsā and the Problem of History in Traditional India." *Journal of the American Oriental Society* 109, no. 4: 603–610.

——. 2006. *The Language of the Gods in the World of Men: Sanskrit, Culture, and Power in Premodern India*. Berkeley: University of California Press.

Pradhan, Prahlad, ed. 1975. *Abhidharmakośabhāṣyam of Vasubandhu*. Patna: K. P. Jayaswal Research Institute.

Priest, Graham. 2002. *Beyond the Limits of Thought*. Oxford: Clarendon Press.

——. 2009. "The Structure of Emptiness." *Philosophy East & West* 59, no. 4: 467–480.

Putnam, Hilary. 1981. "Two Conceptions of Rationality." In *Reason, Truth, and History*, 103–126. Cambridge: Cambridge University Press.

——. 2002. "McDowell's Mind and McDowell's World." In *Reading McDowell: On* Mind and World, ed. Nicholas H. Smith, 174–190. New York: Routledge.

Pyysiäinen, Ilkka. 2009. *Supernatural Agents: Why We Believe in Souls, Gods, and Buddhas*. Oxford: Oxford University Press.

Reid, Thomas. 1764. *Thomas Reid's Inquiry and Essays*. Ed. Ronald Beanblossom and Keith Lehrer. Indianapolis: Hackett, 1983.

Rollinger, Robin D. 2008. *Austrian Phenomenology: Brentano, Husserl, Meinong, and Others on Mind and Object*. Frankfurt: Ontos Verlag.

Rorty, Richard. 1979. *Philosophy and the Mirror of Nature*. Princeton, N.J.: Princeton University Press.

Rosenberg, Gregg. 2004. *A Place for Consciousness: Probing the Deep Structure of the Natural World*. Oxford: Oxford University Press.

Sacks, Mark. 2005. "The Nature of Transcendental Arguments." *International Journal of Philosophical Studies* 13, no. 4: 439–460.

Sāṅkṛtyāyana, Rāhula, ed. 1938–1940. "Dharmakīrti's *Pramāṇavārttika* with a Commentary by Manorathanandin," *Journal of the Bihar and Orissa Research Society* 24/3–26/3.

——. 1943. *Karṇakagomin's Commentary on the Pramāṇavārttikavṛtti of Dharmakīrti*. Kyoto: Rinsen, 1982 (reprint).

——. 1953. *Pramāṇavārttikālaṃkāra (Prajñākaragupta)*. Patna: Kashi Prasad Jayaswal Research Institute.

Sanderson, Alexis. 1994. "The Sarvāstivāda and Its Critics: Anātmavāda and the Theory of Karma." In *Buddhism into the Year 2000*, 33–48. Bangkok: Dhammakaya Foundation.

Saussure, Ferdinand de. 1959. *Course in General Linguistics*. New York: McGraw-Hill.

Scharf, Peter M. 1995. "Early Indian Grammarians on a Speaker's Intention." *Journal of the American Oriental Society* 115, no. 1: 66–76.

——. 1996. *The Denotation of Generic Terms in Ancient Indian Philosophy: Grammar, Nyāya, and Mīmāṃsā*. Philadelphia: American Philosophical Society.

Schmithausen, Lambert. 2005. *On the Problem of the External World in the* Ch'eng wei shih lun. Tokyo: The International Institute for Buddhist Studies.

Schueler, G. F. 2003. *Reasons and Purposes: Human Rationality and the Teleological Explanation of Action*. Oxford: Clarendon Press.

Searle, John. 1982. "What Is an Intentional State?" In *Husserl, Intentionality, and Cognitive Science*, ed. Hubert L. Dreyfus, 259–276. Cambridge, Mass.: The MIT Press.

Sellars, Wilfrid. 1956. *Empiricism and the Philosophy of Mind: With an Introduction by Richard Rorty and a Study Guide by Robert Brandom*. Cambridge, Mass.: Harvard University Press, 1997.

—. 1967. *Science and Metaphysics: Variations on Kantian Themes*. Atascadero, Calif.: Ridgeview.

—. 1991. *Science, Perception, and Reality*. Atascadero, Calif.: Ridgeview.

Shastri, Swami Dwarikadas. 1998. *Ācāryayaśomitrakṛtasphuṭārthavyākhyopetam Ācāryavasubandhuviracitam svopajñabhāṣyasahitañ ca Abhidharmakośam*. Bauddha Bharati Series 5–8 (printed in two volumes). Varanasi: Bauddha Bharati.

Shastri, Swami Dwarikadas, ed. 1968. *Pramāṇavārttika, Ācāryamanorathanandivṛttiyuktam*. Varanasi: Bauddha Bharati.

—. 1978. *Ślokavārttika of Śrī Kumārila Bhaṭṭa, with the Commentary Nyāyaratnākara of Śrī Pārthasārathi Miśra*. Varanasi: Tara Publications.

—. 1997. *Tattvasaṅgraha of Ācārya Shāntarakṣita with the Commentary "Pañjikā" of Shri Kamalashīla*. 2 vols., continuous pagination. Varanasi: Bauddha Bharati.

Siderits, Mark. 2001. "Buddhism and Techno-Physicalism: Is the Eightfold Path a Program?" *Philosophy East & West* 51, no. 3: 307–314.

—. 2003. *Personal Identity and Buddhist Philosophy: Empty Persons*. Burlington, Vt.: Ashgate.

—. 2007. *Buddhism as Philosophy: An Introduction*. Indianapolis, Ind.: Hackett.

—. 2009. "Is Reductionism Expressible?" In *Pointing at the Moon: Buddhism, Logic, Analytic Philosophy*, ed. Mario D'Amato, 57–69. Oxford: Oxford University Press.

—. 2011. "Śrughna by Dusk." In *Apoha: Buddhist Nominalism and Human Cognition*, ed. Mark Siderits et al., 283–304. New York: Columbia University Press.

Siderits, Mark, Tom Tillemans, and Arindam Chakrabarti, eds. 2011. *Apoha: Buddhist Nominalism and Human Cognition*. New York: Columbia University Press.

Singh, B. N., ed. 1985. *Bauddha-Tarkabhāṣā of Mokṣākaragupta*. Varanasi: Asha Prakashan.

Smith, Barbara Herrnstein. 2008. "Cognitive Machinery and Explanatory Ambitions." *Immanent Frame*. http://www.ssrc.org/blogs/immanent_frame/2008/06/16/cognitive-machinery-explanatory-ambitions/.

—. 2009. *Natural Reflections: Human Cognition at the Nexus of Science and Religion*. New Haven, Conn.: Yale University Press.

Stcherbatsky, Th. 1958. *Buddhist Logic*. Vol. 2. 'S-Gravenhage: Mouton.

Steiner, George. 1998. *After Babel: Aspects of Language and Translation*. 3rd ed. Oxford: Oxford University Press.

Steinkellner, Ernst. 2005. "Dignāga's Pramāṇasamuccaya, Chapter 1: A Hypothetical Reconstruction of the Sanskrit Text." http://www.oeaw.ac.at/ias/Mat/dignaga_PS_1.pdf.

Steinkellner, Ernst, ed. 1967. *Dharmakīrti's Hetubinduḥ*. 2 vols. Vienna: Hermann Böhlaus Nachf.

—. 2007. *Dharmakīrti's Pramāṇaviniścaya, Chapters 1 and 2*. Beijing and Vienna: China Tibetology Publishing House, Austrian Academy of Sciences Press.

Steinkellner, Ernst, Helmut Krasser, and Horst Lasic, eds. 2005. *Jinendrabuddhi's Viśālāmalavatī Pramāṇasamuccayaṭīkā: Chapter 1, Part I: Critical Edition*. Beijing and Vienna: China Tibetology Publishing House, Austrian Academy of Sciences Press.

Stich, Stephen P. 1983. *From Folk Psychology to Cognitive Science: The Case Against Belief*. Cambridge, Mass.: The MIT Press.

Strawson, Galen. 2006. "Realistic Monism: Why Physicalism Entails Panpsychism." In *Consciousness and Its Place in Nature: Does Physicalism Entail Panpsychism?*, ed. Anthony Freeman, 3–31. Exeter: Imprint Academic.

Strawson, P. F. 1966. *The Bounds of Sense: An Essay on Kant's* Critique of Pure Reason. London: Routledge.

Taber, John. 2003. "Dharmakīrti Against Physicalism." *Journal of Indian Philosophy* 31: 479–502.

——. 2005. *A Hindu Critique of Buddhist Epistemology: Kumārila on Perception: The "Determination of Perception" Chapter of Kumārila Bhaṭṭa's* Ślokavārttika. New York: Routledge Curzon.

——. 2010. "Kumārila's Buddhist." *Journal of Indian Philosophy* 38: 279–296.

——. Forthcoming. "Mīmāṃsā and the Eternality of Language." In *The Columbia Guide to Classical Indian Philosophy*, ed. Matthew Kapstein. New York: Columbia University Press.

Tanaka, Koji. 2009. "A Dharmakīrtian Critique of Nāgārjunians." In *Pointing at the Moon: Buddhism, Logic, Analytic Philosophy*, ed. Mario D'Amato et al., 101–113. Oxford: Oxford University Press.

Taylor, Mark C., ed. 1998. *Critical Terms for Religious Studies*. Chicago: University of Chicago Press.

Tillemans, Tom J. F. 1999. "On the So-called Difficult Point of the *Apoha* Theory." In *Scripture, Logic, Language: Essays on Dharmakīrti and His Tibetan Successors*, 209–246. Boston: Wisdom Publications.

——. 2000. *Dharmakīrti's Pramāṇavārttika: An Annotated Translation of the Fourth Chapter (Parārthānumāna), Volume 1 (k.1–148)*. Vienna: Verlag der Österreichischen Akademie der Wissenschaften.

——. 2003. "Metaphysics for Mādhyamikas." In *The Svātantrika-Prāsaṅgika Distinction: What Difference Does a Difference Make?*, ed. Georges Dreyfus and Sara McClintock, 93–123. Boston: Wisdom.

Tola, Fernando, and Carmen Dragonetti. 1982. "Dignāga's Ālambanaparīkṣāvṛtti." *Journal of Indian Philosophy* 10: 105–134.

Valberg, J. J. 2007. *Dream, Death, and the Self*. Princeton, N.J.: Princeton University Press.

Varela, Francisco J., Evan Thompson, and Eleanor Rosch. 1991. *The Embodied Mind: Cognitive Science and Human Experience*. Cambridge, Mass.: The MIT Press.

Verpoorten, Jean-Marie. 1987. *Mīmāṃsā Literature* (*A History of Indian Literature*, ed. Jan Gonda, vol. VI, fasc. 5). Wiesbaden: Otto Harrassowitz.

Wallace, B. Alan. 2007. *Contemplative Science: Where Buddhism and Neuroscience Converge*. New York: Columbia University Press.

Watson, Alex. 2006. *The Self's Awareness of Itself: Bhaṭṭa Rāmakaṇṭha's Arguments Against the Buddhist Doctrine of No-Self*. Vienna: Sammlung de Nobili Institut für Südasien-, Tibet- und Buddhismuskunde der Universität Wien.

——. 2010. "Bhaṭṭa Rāmakaṇṭha's Elaboration of Self-Awareness (*Svasaṃvedana*), and How It Differs from Dharmakīrti's Exposition of the Concept." *Journal of Indian Philosophy* 38: 297–321.

Weiss, Bernhard. 2010. *How to Understand Language: A Philosophical Inquiry*. Montreal: McGill-Queen's University Press.

Westerhoff, Jan. 2009. *Nāgārjuna's Madhyamaka: A Philosophical Introduction*. Oxford: Oxford University Press.

Wetzel, James. 2008. "Wittgenstein's Augustine: The Inauguration of the Later Philosophy." *Polygraph: An International Journal of Culture and Politics* 19–20: 129–147.

Williams, Paul. 1981. "On the Abhidharma Ontology." *Journal of Indian Philosophy* 9: 227–257.

——. 1998. *The Reflexive Nature of Awareness: A Tibetan Madhyamaka Defence*. London: Curzon.

Wittgenstein, Ludwig. 1958. *Philosophical Investigations*. Trans. G. E. M. Anscombe. New York: Macmillan.

Woo, Jeson. 2003. "Dharmakīrti and His Commentators on Yogipratyakṣa." *Journal of Indian Philosophy* 31: 439–448.

Index

MLBD

SACRED BOOKS OF THE BUDDHISTS SERIES

Reprinted Under License from **Pali Text Society**

- **A Buddhist Manual of Psychological Ethics** : Translation of the First Book in Abhidhamma Piṭaka entitled Dhammasaṅgaṇī—With Introductory Essay and Notes by *C.A.F. Rhys Davids.*
- **The Book of the Gradual Sayings** : Translation of Anguttara Nikāya, the Fourth Collection of Sutta Piṭaka **(5 Vols.)**—Tr. by *F.L. Woodward* and *E.M. Hare.*
- **The Book of the Kindred Sayings** : Translation of Saṁyutta-Nikāya **(5 Vols.)**—Tr. ,Ed. & Introduction by *C.A.F. Rhys Davids,* Tr. by *F.L. Woodward.*
- **The Collection of the Middle Length Sayings** : Translation of Majjhima Nikāya, the Second Collection of the Sutta Piṭaka containing 152 suttas. **(3 Vols.)**—Tr. from the Pali by *I.B. Horner.*
- **Compendium of Philosophy** : Translation of Abhidhammattha-Saṅgaha)—With Tr., Introductory Essay and Notes by *Shwe Zan-Aung,* Rev. & Ed. by *C.A.F. Rhys Davids.*
- **Culavaṁśa** : Translation from German Translation by Wilhelm Geiger. A Continuation of *Great Chronicle of Ceylon* (Mahāvaṃśa) : **(2 Pts. in One)**—by *C. Mabel Rickmers.*
- **Dialogues of the Buddha** : Dīgha Nikāya, the First Collection of Sutta Piṭaka **(3 Vols.)**—Translation from the Pali by *T.W. Rhys Davids* and *C.A.F. Rhys Davids.*
- **Dictionary of Pali Proper Names (2 Vols.)**—*G.P. Malalasekera.*
- **English-Pali Dictionary** —*Venerable A.P. Buddhadata.*
- **The Expositor** : Translation of Atthaśālinī, Buddhaghoṣa's Commentary on Dhammasaṅgaṇī, the First Book of Abhidhamma Piṭaka—Tr. by *Pe Maung Tin,* Rev. & Ed. by *C.A.F. Rhys Davids.*
- **Conditional Relations [Paṭṭhāna] (2 Pts.)** Part I : Guide, Part II : Translation of Caṭṭasaṅgāyana Text of the Seventh Book of Abhidhamma Piṭaka—Tr. by *U. Narada Mula Patt Thana Sayadow,* Assisted by *U. Thein Nyun.*
- **The Jātaka or Stories of the Buddha's Former Births (6 Vols. in 3 Pts.)**: Translation from the Tenth Book of Khuddaka Nikāya of Sutta Piṭaka—Ed. by *E.B. Cowell,* Tr. by *Robert Chalmers, W.H.D. Rouse, H.T. Francis* and *R.A. Neil.*
- **Pali-English Dictionary**—*T.W. Rhys Davids* and *William Stede.*
- **Pali Metre** : A Contribution to the History of Indian Literature—*A.K. Warder.*
- **Points of Controversy** (Subjects of Discourse) : A Translation of the Kathāvathu from the Fifth Book of Abhidhamma Piṭaka—Tr. by *S.Z. Aung* and *C.A.F. Rhys Davids.*
- **The Sutra of Golden Light** : Translation of Suvarnabhasottamasūtra—*R.E. Emmerick.*

BUDDHIST TRADITION SERIES

Gen. Ed. E. STEINKELLNER and Jt. Gen. Ed. A. V. ROSPATT, Founder Ed. Late *ALEX WAYMAN*

1 **Indian Buddhism**—*Hajime Nakamura*
2 **Nagarjuniana**—*Chr. Lindtner*
3 **Chinese Monks in India**—*Latika Lahiri*
4 **Buddhism in Central Asia**—*B.N. Puri*
5 **Dharmakīrti's Theory of Hetu-Centricity of Anumāna**—*Mangala R. Chinchore*
6 **The Legend of King Aśoka**—*John S. Strong*
7 **Buddhist Insight**—*George R. Elder*
8 **Buddhism Transformed**—*Richard Gombrich* and *Gananath Obeyesekere*
9 **The Buddhist Tantras**—*Alex Wayman*
10 **The Lion's Roar of Queen Śrīmālā**—*Alex Wayman* and *Hideko Wayman*
11 **The Buddha Nature**—*Brian E. Brown*
12 **Evolution of Stupas in Burma**—*Sujata Soni*
13 **Buddhist Parables**—*Eugene Watson Burlingame*
14 **The Debate of King Milinda**—*Bhikku Pesala*
15 **The Chinese Madhyama Āgama and the Pāli Majjhima Nikāya**—*Bhiksu Thich Minh Chau*
16 **Sudden and Gradual**—*Peter N. Gregory*
17 **Yoga of the Guhyasamājatantra**—*Alex Wayman*
18 **The Enlightenment of Vairocana**—*Alex Wayman* and *R. Tajima*
19 **A History of Indian Buddhism**—Tr. *Hirakawa Akira*, Ed. *Paul Groner*
20 **Introduction to the Buddhist Tantric Systems**—*F.D. Lessing* and *Alex Wayman*
21 **Anāgatavaṃsa Desanā**—Tr. *Udaya Meddegama*, Ed. *John C. Holt*
22 **Chinnamasta**—*Elisabeth Anne Benard*
23 **On Voidness** —*Fernando Tola* and *Carmen Dragonetti*
24 **Nāgārjuna's Refutation of Logic (Nyāya) Vaidalyaprakaraṇa**—*Fernando Tola* and *Carmen Dragonetti*
25 **The Buddhist Art of Nagarjunakonda**—*Elizabeth Rosen Stone*
26 **Discipline**—*J.C. Holt*
27 **Philosophy and its Development in the Nikāyas and Abhidhamma**—*Fumimaro Watanabe*
28 **Untying the Knots in Buddhism**—*Alex Wayman*
29 **Early Buddhist Theory of Knowledge**—*K.N. Jayatilleke*
30 **Calming the Mind and Discerning the Real**—Tr. *Alex Wayman*
31 **A Comparative Study of the Pratimoksha**—*W. Pachow*
32 **Rise of the Esoteric Buddhism in the Tibet**—*Eva M. Dargyay*
33-35 **Saṃyuktābhidharmahṛdaya (3 Parts)** *Bart Dessein*
36 **A Millennium of Buddhist Logic (Pt. I)**—*Alex Wayman*
37 **The Buddhist Pilgrimage**—*Duncan Forbes*
38 **Chanting the Name of Mañjuśrī**—*Alex Wayman*
39 **The Literature of the Personalists of Early Buddhism**—*Bhikshu Thich Thien Chau*
40 **The Laṅkāvatāra Sūtra** —*D.T. Suzuki*
41 **Studies in the Laṅkāvatāra Sūtra**—*D.T Suzuki*
42 **The Vimalakīrti Sūtra**—*Burton Watson*
43 **The Gāndhārī Dharmapada**—*John Brough*
44 **Imaging Wisdom**—*Jacob N. Kinnard*
45 **Pain and Its Ending**—*Carol S. Anderson*
46 **Apparitions of the Self**—*Janet Gyatso*
47-49 **Rules for Nuns according to the Dharmaguptakavinya (3 Parts)**—*Ann Heirmann*
50 **The Chinese Hevajraṛantra**—*Ch. Willemen*
51 **The Historical Buddha**—*H.W. Schumann*, Tr. from the German *M.O'c Walshe*
52 **Dana:** Giving and Getting in Pali Buddhism—*Ellison Banks Findly*
53 **Hermeneutics and Tradition in the Samadhinirmocana Sutra**—*John Powers*
54 **Skillful Means**—*John W. Wchroeder*
55 **The Two Truths in Chinese Buddhism**—*Chang-Qing Shih*
56 **The Bodhisattva Path**—*Jan Nattier*
57 **Becoming the Buddha**—*Donald K. Swearer*
58 **Approaching the Land of Bliss**— Eds. *Richard K.Payne & Kenneth K. Tanaka*
59 **Indian Monastic Buddhism**—*Gregory Schopen*
60 **Caste and Buddhist Philosophy**—*Vincent Eltschinger*

The Collected Works of
LOUIS DE LA VALLEE POUSSIN (In Five Volumes)

Advisory Board: **E. STEINKELLNER, D.S. RUEGG, L. SCHMITHAUSEN, K.L. DHAMMAJOTI, LOKESH CHANDRA**

Edited by: **GELONG LODRO SANGPO**

Vol. I : *Abhidharmakoshbhasya of Vasubandhu* (Printed in Four Parts). Translator: GELONG LODRO SANGPO. **Part 1:** Introduction by K L DHAMMAJOTI, Preface by ETIENNE LAMMOTE, Bibliographical Addendum by HUBERT DUTT, Introduction by LVP, Remarks by GELONG LODRO SANGPO, Translations: *Ch. 1*— Expositions of the Elements (*Dhatunirdesa*), and *Ch. 2*— Exposition of the Faculties (*Indriyanirdesa*); **Part 2:** Translations: *Ch. 3*— Expositions of the World (*Loknirdesa*); *Ch. 4*—Exposition of Action (*Karmanirdesa*), *Ch. 5*— Expositions of the Proclivities (*Anusayanirdesa*); **Part 3:** A Summary of the Path by LVP; Translation: *Ch. 6*— Exposition of the Path and the Persons (*Margapudgalanirdesa*); *Ch. 7*— Exposition of the Cognitions (*Jnananirdesa*); *Ch. 8*— Exposition of the Meditative Attainments (*Samapattinirdesa*); **Part 4:** Translation: *Ch. 9*—Treatise of the Refutation of the Person (*Pudgalapratisedha-prakarana*); Bibliography; Indices.

Published in 2012; ISBN: 978-81-208-3607-5

Vol. II : *Vijnaptimatratasiddhi of Xuan Zang* (To be printed in Two Parts). Translators: GELONG LODRO SANGPO and GELONGMA MIGME CHODRON, with the assistance of ALEXANDER MAYER. **Part 1:** Preface by DAVID SEYFORT RUEGG; Bibliographical Note on LVP by ETIENNE LAMOTTE; Summary and discussion on the *Vijnaptimatratasiddhi* by BHIKKHU K L DHAMMAJOTI; Translations: *Ch. 1-7;* **Part 2:** Translations: *Ch. 8-15*— Appendix (by LVP); Indices.

Vol. III: *Studies on Abhidharma, Yogacara, and Madhyamaka.* Translators: GELONG LODRO SANGPO and GELONGMA MIGME CHODRON; Preface by DAVID SEYFORT RUEGG. **Part 1:** Abhidharma, *Section 1:* The Truths and Dependent Origination, *Section 2:* The Path, Nirvana and the Body of the Buddha, *Section 3:* Time and Existence and other Abhidharma Writings, *Section 4:* Other Abhidharma related writings; **Part 2:** Yogachara; **Part 3:** Madhyamaka.

Vol. IV: *Studies on Tantra, Vinaya, Hastings Articles, Buddhist Notes.* Translators: GELONG LODRO SANGPO and GELONGMA MIGME CHODRON; Preface by DAVID SEYFORT RUEGG. **Part 1:** Vinaya; **Part 2:** Tantra; **Part 3:** The Thirty six Hastings Articles; **Part 4:** The Nineteen *Notes Bouddhiques* (1922-30).

Vol. V: *Miscellaneous Works.* Translators: G L SANGPO and G M CHODRON; Preface by D S RUEGG. **Part 1:** Various Book Publications; **Part 2:** Miscellaneous Notes and Articles.

SACRED BOOKS OF THE EAST

(50 VOLUMES)

Series Editor : F. Max-Müller

These volumes of the Sacred Books of the East series include translations of all the most important works of the seven non-Christian religions that have exercised a profound influence on the civilisations of the continent of Asia. The Vedic Brahmanic system claims 21 volumes, Buddhism 10, and Jainism 2; 8 volumes comprise Sacred Books of the Parsis; 2 volumes represent Islam; and 6 the two main indigenous systems of China. Translated by twenty leading authorities in their respective fields, the volumes have been edited by the late F. Max Müller. The inception, publication and the compilation of these books cover almost 34 years.

I. BUDDHISM

Vol. 49: Buddhist Mahayana Texts (2 Parts)
Vol. 11: Buddhist Suttas
Vol. 10: The Dhammapada and Sutta Nipata
Vols. 35 & 36: The Questions of King Milinda (2 Parts)
Vol. 21: The Saddharma Pundarika or the Lotus of the True Law
Vols. 13, 17 & 20: Vinaya Texts (3 Parts)

II. CHINESE

Vol. 19: The Fo-Sho-Hing-Tsan-King
Vols. 3, 16, 27, 28, 39 & 40: The Sacred Books of China (6 Parts)

III. A GENERAL INDEX

Vol. 50: A General Index to the Names and Subject-matter of the Sacred Books of the East

IV. ISLAM

Vols. 6 & 9: The Qur'an (2 Parts)

V. JAINISM

Vols. 22 & 45: The Jaina Sutras (2 Parts)

VI. PARSIS

Vols. 5, 18, 24, 37 & 47: Pahlavi Texts (5 Parts)
Vols. 4, 23 & 31: The Zend-Avesta (3 Parts)

VII. VEDIC-BRAHMANIC SYSTEM

Vol. 8: The Bhagavadgita with the Sanatsujatiya and the Anugita
Vols. 29 & 30: The Grihya-Sutras: Rules of Vedic Domestic Ceremonies (2 Parts)
Vol. 42: Hymns of the Atharva Veda together with Extracts from the Ritual Books and the Commentaries
Vol. 7: The Institutes of Vishnu
Vol. 25: The Laws of Manu
Vol. 33: The Minor Law Books
Vols. 2 & 14: The Sacred Laws of the Aryas as Taught in the Schools of Apastamba, Gautama, Vasishtha and Baudhayana (2 Parts)
Vols. 12, 26, 41, 43 & 44: The Satapatha Brahmana According to the Text of the Madhyandina School (5 Parts)
Vols. 1 & 15: The Upanishads (2 Parts)
Vols. 34 & 38: The Vedanta Sutras (2 Parts)
Vol. 48: The Vedanta-Sutras (with the commentary by Ramanuja)
Vols. 32 & 46: Vedic Hymns (2 Parts)

ENCYCLOPEDIA OF INDIAN PHILOSOPHIES

General Editor: KARL H. POTTER

- I. **Bibliography [Sections I and II] (1995)**—Ed. *Karl H. Potter*
- II. **Indian Metaphysics and Epistemology :** The Tradition of Nyāya Vaiśeṣika up to Gaṅgeśa (1977)—Ed. *Karl H. Potter*
- III. **Advaita Vedānta up to Śaṁkara and His Pupils (1981)** —Ed. *Karl H. Potter*
- IV. **Sāṁkhya:** A Dualist Tradition in Indian Philosophy (1987) —Eds. *Gerald James Larson & Ram Shankar Bhattacharyya*
- V. **The Philosophy of the Grammarians (1990)**—Eds. *H.G. Coward & K. Kunjunni Raja*
- VI. **Indian Philosophical Analysis:** Nyāya-Vaiśeṣika from Gaṅgeśa to Raghunātha Śiromaṇi (1993)—Eds. *Karl H. Potter & Sibjiban Bhattacharyya*
- VII. **Abhidharma Buddhism with to 150 A.D. (1996)**—Eds. *Karl H. Potter,* with *Robert E.Buswell Jr., Padmanabh S. Jaini & Noble Ross Reat*
- VIII. **Buddhist Philosophy from 100 to 350 A.D. (1999)** —Ed. *Karl H. Potter*
- IX. **Buddhist Philosophy from 350 to 600 A.D. (2003)** —Ed. *Karl H. Potter*
- X. **Jain Philosophy [Part I] (2007)**—Eds. *Dalsukh Malvania & Jayendra Soni*
- XI. **Advaita Vedānta from 800 to 1200 A.D. (2006)**—Ed. *Karl H. Potter*
- XII. **Yoga: India's Philosophy of Meditation (2008)**—Eds. *Gerald J. Larson & Rama Shankar Bhattacharyya*
- XIII. **Nyāya-Vaiśeṣika Philosophy from 1515 to 1660 A.D. (2010)** —Eds. *Sibjiban Bhattacharyya & Karl H. Potter*
- XIV. **Jain Philosophy [Part II] (2012)**—Eds. *Karl H. Potter & Piotr Batcerowicz*
- XV. **Bhedābheda and Dvaitādvaita Systems (2013)**—Eds. *M.M. Agrawal & Karl H. Potter*
- XVI. **Pūrvamīmāṁsā Philosophy (2014)**—Eds. *K.T. Pandurangi & Karl H. Potter*
- XVII. **Jain Philosophy [Part III]**—Eds. *Karl H. Potter & Piotr Batcerowicz*
- XVIII. **Dvaita Vedānta Philosophy**—Ed. *Karl H. Potter*
- XIX. **Acintyabhedābheda Philosophy**—Ed. *Karl H. Potter*
- XX. **Viśiṣṭādvaita Vedānta Philosophy**–Eds. *Stephen A. Phillips & Karl H. Potter*
- XXI. **Buddhist Philosophy from 600 to 750 A.D.**—Ed. *Karl H. Potter* with an introduction by *Eli Franco* and *Karen Lang*
- XXII. **Buddhist Philosophy from 750 onword**—Ed. *Karl H. Potter*
- XXIII. **Śuddhādvaita Vedānta Philosophy**—Ed. *Karl H. Potter*